Nature's Entrepôt

History of the Urban Environment | Martin V. Melosi and Joel A. Tarr, Editors

Nature's Entrepôt

Philadelphia's Urban Sphere
and Its Environmental Thresholds

Edited by Brian C. Black
and Michael J. Chiarappa

University of Pittsburgh Press

Published by the University of Pittsburgh Press, Pittsburgh, Pa., 15260
Copyright © 2012, University of Pittsburgh Press
This paperback edition, 2020
All rights reserved
Printed on acid-free paper

Chapter 10 © 2005, 2012, Anne Whiston Spirn

Cataloging-in-Publication data is available from the Library of Congress

ISBN 13: 978-0-8229-6650-0
ISBN 10: 0-8229-6650-6

Cover art: Tim Conte, *Last View, GIlbert Building*, 2006–2007. Oil on Linen.
Cover design: Ann Walston

Contents

Nature's Entrepôt

FIGURE I.1. Charles Willson Peale, *Self-Portrait of the Artist in His Museum* (1822). Courtesy of Pennsylvania Academy of the Fine Arts.

Brian C. Black

Introduction

IT IS ONE OF THE most memorable images of the early republic. The principal figure, a slightly portly man wearing knickers and a long jacket, pulls back the red velvet curtain to reveal a grand hall lined with seemingly endless shelves, each holding stuffed and mounted animals. The image is an invitation, a welcoming. In this 1822 self-portrait, Charles Willson Peale invites us to view his grand collection, a celebration of all that is natural in North America at the close of the 1700s. Passing Peale, one gains access to a real physical locale, full of knowledge about the natural wonders of North America; when we view the image and recall this collector and artist's role in American history, though, his invitation also functions on a symbolic level.

An artist and a naturalist, Peale grounded the fledgling American nation in a sense of its natural history. As the nation reinterpreted human society in profoundly new ways, fought for its freedom and definition a few times, and emphasized resource and economic development to establish long-term national growth, Peale made sure that these national ideals also included the context of the natural surroundings. His perspective fed many of the intellectual developments that followed, for many of his contemporaries shared his outlook. Over time, this conception of nature shaped a consistent paradigm in American thought. Particularly during the nineteenth century, this intellectual paradigm provided an alternative to the region's predominant effort to expand capitalism and economic development, forming what the cultural theorists Leo Marx and Perry Miller have called a "counterforce." Indeed, a volume on the environmental history of Philadelphia might well be inconceivable had Peale and his scientific colleagues not helped lay the intellectual underpinnings of natural history in the young nation.

In addition to recognizing this unique intellectual foundation, which is partly rooted in Philadelphia, Pennsylvania, the present volume provides an opportunity to inform the approach of environmental historians as they study urban spaces throughout human history. In recent scholarship, environmental historians including Ari Kelman, Matthew Klingle, and others have recast the stories of specific cities, seeking to revise both the accounts of local stories and the field of environmental history in general. In *Common Fields*, for instance, Andrew Hurley suggests that environmental history, which traces its origins to only the 1970s, established "a false dichotomy between the urban and the natural" that led many of its practitioners to resist telling stories of urban America. Although this may have been initially true, the reluctance to confront urban America has been shattered by superb environmental histories of New Orleans, Seattle, Los Angeles, Phoenix, Tucson, Houston, Boston, and Pittsburgh. Many of these grew from the realization expressed by Hurley when he wrote: "If city planners, policy makers, and property holders have not always appreciated the complex natural processes that support urban life, they have nonetheless constructed their cities and organized urban space in the context of a physical world not entirely of their own making." Tracing these stories, even if they appear "unnatural," empowers environmental historians to put "the environment back into the city, or at least into the history of the city."[1]

In *Nature's Entrepôt*, we use a broad definition of environmental history that goes beyond the nature/culture relationship to admit that, particularly in an urban environment, humans take a considerable toll on the natural environment. Continuing in the tradition of Joel Tarr, Martin Melosi, and others, our interest in exploring Philadelphia's environmental history begins with this admission, and this book thus includes chapters that emphasize efforts to mitigate human impact, the push and pull to create a sustainable urban environment in the City of Brotherly Love. Throughout different technological eras, the city has endured as a system in which humans live, albeit with variations in impact and control, rigidity and sprawl. Thanks to contributions by these earlier scholars, as well as Andrew Isenberg in *The Nature of Cities,* the chapters in *Nature's Entrepôt* need not be concerned with "proving the relevance of urban places."[2]

Therefore, while exploring a foundation in the more utilitarian portions of the city's development, *Nature's Entrepôt* emphasizes Philadelphia's growth and the innumerable variables of location and economic development that contributed to it. Beyond all boosterism, writes the historian William Cronon in *Nature's Metropolis,* his study of Chicago's development, "cities had their roots in natural phenomena but ultimately grew because, for whatever reason, people chose to migrate to them. The demographic pull of cities suggested yet another theoretical basis for predicting urban growth. Cities were like stars or planets, with gravitational fields that attracted people and trade like miniature solar systems."[3] Although Philadelphia's spatial development differs significantly from Chicago's, the city clearly did evolve through an interplay with a "service area," or hinterland. Early on colonists had clustered into settlements along the water for reasons of safety and trade. The early port settlements were lifelines connected back to Europe. Boston was founded in 1631, and Manhattan Island, around 1625. Philadelphia followed in 1681. These early ports combined with southern ports on the Atlantic, including Savannah, Georgia, and Charleston, South Carolina, to provide the connection for trade to Europe. In each case, the developing ports centered cities on rows of wharves that grew out of tightly packed streets full of storefronts and warehouses.

The streets in these seaports often differed markedly from those of later inland urban centers. Then as now, ships must maintain balance or risk foundering in stiff winds and high seas. In the seventeenth and eighteenth centuries, most vessels carried stacks of stones, which were usually larger than bricks. Called "ballast rock," this material could be shifted around as a ship's holds grew full or empty. When ships called on foreign ports, they would on- or offload this rock as needed. Most ports wound up with a superfluous supply of ballast rock that could then be used as cobblestones for streets. The collections of stone from around the world can make streets unlike any others in the United States. In addition to the ballast-rock streets, products of the sea itself, such as seafood, oils, and bone, dominated port cities. More important for national development, though, ports fueled the development of specific hinterlands.

"Commerce, not shipbuilding or fishing," writes the historian Benjamin Labaree, "is what distinguishes significant seaports from other seacoast communities."[4] He describes seaports as entrepôts for culture and goods. As such, they also served broad swaths of interior land, with goods from both interior and exterior flowing through the port city. Relying on ports for trade in either direction, these hinterlands grew around the idea of access—normally defined as a wagon ride of no more than a few hours—and had a symbiotic relationship to seaports thanks to the economic possibilities the ports embodied.

Of North America's coastal towns, New York was the most favored by nature to become a major seaport. Early on, however, New York lost its initial lead to Philadelphia, which by 1760 was the nation's leading port. Even in 1815, all of America's population centers bordered some body of water. Indeed, the rapidly growing port of Cincinnati, on the Ohio River, was the only population center not located on the Atlantic Ocean. Of the nation's 8.5 million inhabitants, roughly 85 percent lived along the Atlantic coast, with about half the nation's population residing in New England and the Mid-Atlantic states. With roads largely undeveloped, Americans depended on the waters for food, transportation, and trade. In 1830 the French observer Alexis de Tocqueville wrote, "No other nation in the world possesses vaster, deeper, or more secure ports for commerce than the Americans. . . . Consequently Europe is the market for America, as America is the market for Europe. And sea trade is as necessary to the inhabitants of the United States to bring their raw materials to our harbors as to bring our manufactures to them. . . . I cannot express my thoughts better than by saying that the Americans put something heroic into their way of trading."[5] These patterns of growth will be a primary subject of some of the chapters to follow; we start with Peale, however, because there is a larger story emanating from Philadelphia's relationship with its natural surroundings.

Just as Philadelphia has served as the "first city" of the American republic, so too can it be viewed as initiating Americans' unique relationship with nature in a larger sense. Beneath establishing the nation's lofty relationship with nature, however, Philadelphia's environmental history has a hard-packed, organic core. The chapters in this volume explore the city as a changing environment, a meeting place between human ideas and living patterns—culture—on the one hand and natural constraints or details on the other. Pouring the foundation for these stories is the other priority of this introduction: setting the context of European settlement in the swampy, diverse locale that became Philadelphia.

SETTLEMENT

Situated between the Delaware and Schuylkill rivers, the Philadelphia region comprises parts of Bucks, Montgomery, Delaware, and Chester counties as well as Philadelphia County.[6] Although elevation in the Inner Coastal Plain stays below 100 feet above sea level, the hills of the piedmont lead inland to rise above 300 feet. In addition to the two major rivers, navigable streams defined the area for early inhabitants. This complex watershed provided prehistoric peoples with many attractive resources, including minerals, water life, and good soil for agriculture.

For early inhabitants, though, forests constituted one of the region's most reliable resources. Although lost to blight later, the chestnut defined much of these forests, which also included oak, hickory, white pine, beech, walnut, and sycamore, with an undergrowth of dogwood, chestnut sprouts, ironwood, and many other species. White-tailed deer, wild turkeys, beavers, otters, muskrats, and many other small mammals prospered in such an environment, supporting significant populations of wolves, black bears, mountain lions, and panthers. The fruits and wildlife maintained by this understory made the region bountiful for the first recorded human inhabitants, the Lenape.

Scholars have used radiocarbon dating to piece together a snapshot of the region's vegetation prior to European settlement, but one of the most fascinating finds came in a much less scientific manner: while digging for a subway in 1931, workers uncovered upright cypress stumps thirty-eight feet below street level (ten feet below sea level). Such trees are now relegated to the warm, moist climate of the southern United States and demonstrated that approximately 40,000 years ago, the Philadelphia region had been significantly warmer. Paleoindian humans moved through the area and established a settlement in approximately 8,600 BCE at the Shawnee Minisink site, which lay in the floodplain of the Delaware River and Brodhead Creek. Approximately 2,800 years ago, climatic conditions stabilized and allowed humans to establish permanent settlements in the area and to live a more sedentary lifestyle. These new modes of living led to the development of horticulture, ceramics, and village life.[7] These patterns developed through the early 1500s, when European traders and trappers recorded interactions in the Delaware Valley with diverse inhabitants now referred to as the Lenape.

Scientists have established that the Lenape organized their regional existence around productive resource collection. Summer fishing stations allowed significant food collection to take place. Land clearing enhanced hunting grounds and allowed Lenape villages to develop community agricultural fields. By 1500 a dozen Lenape bands existed in the Philadelphia region, where they occupied the west banks of the Delaware River, from Old Duck Creek in northern Delaware up to Tohickon Creek. The word *Lenape,* or *Renappi,* their name for themselves, means "the people" in their language.[8]

Contact with Europeans began after 1524, when Verrazano sailed his caravel *La Dauphine* up the Mid-Atlantic region, observing and recording the residents. A century and a half later, William Penn made his first written description of the Lenape, characterizing them as "swarthy": "Boys . . . go a-fishing till ripe for the woods, which is about fifteen; then they hunt; and after having given some proofs of their manhood by a good return of skins, they may marry, else it is a shame to think of a wife. The girls . . . hoe the ground, plant corn, and carry burdens. . . . The wives are the true servants of their husbands."[9]

By the late 1600s, Dutch and Swedish settlers had purchased tracts of land from the Lenape on the western shore of the Delaware. After English settlement overpowered the others, the Lenape began negotiations with Penn, who wished to acquire property for a new city of his own design. Unlike many other indigenous groups, the Lenape had a tradition of property exchange. John L. Cotter writes: "Not only did each band, or extended family, collectively inherit its rights to a specific drainage along the Delaware or the Schuylkill from the previous generation, it also had the right to sell this land independently of other bands."[10] In one of the first perfectly legal transactions between indigenous leaders and European settlers, Penn paid Lenape generous quantities of goods.

Following this transaction, by the 1730s the Lenape had begun a westward migration. Recording their migration has proven difficult for scholars, but the few rock shelters littered with ceramics and other materials that they left behind have allowed archaeologists to piece together their habits and living patterns. Most famous, the Montgomery site in Chester County has allowed scholars to study a Lenape burial ground. Although residents in the twentieth century came to have significant interest in and appreciation of these early humans, the primary focus of the next century and half was regional development.

During the 1600s the same attributes that brought the Lenape to the confluence of these rivers attracted the Dutch and then the English and Finns as well. By 1655 Dutch soldiers were sweeping through Swedish settlements to create New Netherland, and by 1664 English soldiers under the direction of Charles II's brother James, the duke of York, had begun taking New Netherland. Within months English dominion had been established over what would become the colonies of New York and New Jersey, as well as areas on the western shore of the Delaware River. When James lost interest in his New World colonies shortly thereafter, trustees were assigned to oversee them. In a series of subsequent land deals, the thirty-year-old William Penn grew in prominence, in 1681 being named lord proprietor of the 45,000 square miles of land.[11]

With an emphasis on creating a religious refuge for his fellow Quakers, Penn established Pennsylvania, the twelfth of the thirteen American colonies. As proprietor, Penn had powers of government as well as hereditary ownership of the land; in recompense, he paid the king two beaver skins per year and one-fifth of all the gold and silver found in the province. At this time, the population along both shores of the Delaware comprised approximately 2,000 Europeans of various descent with a similar number of Lenape. Penn's true quest, though, was to create a town that would contrast with the division and decay that marked many English towns. After considering various plots, Penn settled on 1,200 acres stretching between the Schuylkill and the Delaware rivers to realize his dream of Philadelphia.

In the decades that followed, residents used many methods to put these natural resources to work, many of which inform the topics of the chapters that follow; however, Philadelphia also played a significant role in creating the intellectual framework for other, nonutilitarian ways of viewing natural resources.

ESTABLISHING A NATURAL HISTORY

In the early 1800s many Americans believed that their nation was turning a corner, changing from a settler society into a more civilized nation to rival those of Europe. In trying to stimulate such a society, many Americans made extensive comparisons between the United States and the long-standing European civilizations. The young American nation compared unfavorably in many categories, especially the arts and other aspects of culture. In its natural wonders, however, the United States enjoyed an indisputable majesty. For this reason, some Americans sought new ways to highlight the natural splendor that distinguished their land from Europe. They came to believe that even though the United States had little history when compared to European nations, it could offer a measurable natural history, something with which Europeans had lost touch. The work of these early naturalists helped to construct an alternative to development, a fashion for valuing nature that eventually evolved into the conservation of resources and the environmental thought of the twentieth century.

As did most cities, Philadelphia enacted policies and practices reflecting the environmental ethic that developed in the twentieth century, but it had already played a critical role in the formative era of naturalist thought, the late 1700s. During this era, a few largely self-taught patriot scientists sought to chronicle North America's everyday nature and natural history as a matter of both science and nationalism. The leader at this moment was Charles Wilson Peale, who established the United States' first natural history museum in Philadelphia in 1784.[12] The 1822 self-portrait might seem to embellish the role of Peale's guidance, but he truly did play a critical role, as is evidenced by his written invitation to the opening of his museum:

> Mr. Peale respectfully informs the Public, that having formed a design to establish a MUSEUM, for a collection, arrangement and preservation of the objects of natural history and things useful and curious, in June 1785 . . . he began to collect subjects, and to preserve and arrange them in Linnaean method. . . . The museum having advanced to be an object of attention to some individuals, . . . he is there for the more earnestly set on enlarging the collection with a greater variety of birds, beasts, fishes, insects, reptiles, vegetables, minerals, shells, fossils, medals, [and] old coins. . . . With sentiments of gratitude, Mr. Peale thanks the friends of the Museum, who have beneficially added to his collection a number of precious curiosities, from many parts of the world, . . . from Africa, from Indies, from China, from the Islands of the great Pacific Ocean, and from different parts of America.[13]

Referred to as "natural history," this effort to know the continent through the creatures living on it spurred at least one of the young nation's first unified, federal undertakings: Peale's effort to excavate a mastodon skeleton from New York State starting in the late 1700s.

Excavated by Peale from a Hudson River valley farm in 1801, the mastodon quickly became a national spectacle when brought to Philadelphia for study. The ability to excavate and reassemble the skeleton also became an important symbol for the stability of the young republic. For many Americans, the animal's symbolic meaning far outweighed its scientific significance as evidence of extinct species or a prehuman past. "Indeed," writes the historian Paul Semonin, "while Lewis and Clark were exploring the western wilderness, Peale had remounted his skeleton with its tusks pointing downward to magnify its ferocity." Most historians view this as a representative moment of scientific naïveté, yet Semonin suggests that this understandable lapse instead demonstrates that the mastodon was "the nation's first prehistoric monster," used by the nation's founders as "a symbol of dominance in the first decades of the new republic."[14]

Beyond spectacle, though, what should this discovery's role have been? In January 1802, shortly after having become president in the previous year, Thomas Jefferson, a vigorous advocate for efforts to establish the nation's natural history, wrote a letter to Peale in which he weighed the degree to which federal dollars should be used to support the Philadelphian's preservation efforts:

> No person on earth can entertain a higher idea than I do of the value of your collection nor give you more credit for the unwearied perseverance and skill with which you have prosecuted it, . . . but as to the question whether I think that the U.S. would encourage or provide for the establishment of your Museum here? I must not suffer my partiality to it to excite false expectations in you, which might eventually be disappointed. You know that one of the great questions which has decided political opinion in this country is whether Congress is authorized by the constitution to apply the public money to any but the purposes specially enumerated in the constitution? Those who hold them to enumeration have always denied that Congress has any power to establish a National Academy. . . . If there were an union of opinion that Congress already possessed the right, I am persuaded the purchase of your Museum would be the first object on which it would be exercised.[15]

Unsuccessful in this funding effort, Jefferson's passion found an outlet in the 1803 Lewis and Clark Expedition, which Jefferson almost single-handedly funded with federal dollars. As part of their preparation for the journey, Jefferson had Meriwether Lewis travel to Philadelphia to receive advice from Peale, the nation's leading naturalist.

Even without federal support after its founding in 1784, the privately financed museum became a mainstay for Philadelphia science and culture. To establish his museum, Peale relied heavily on the help of his sons: Rubens, Franklin, Titian II, Rembrandt, and Raphaelle. To provide context for the American beasts, the Peales accepted donations of trophy animals shot all over the world from many Americans, including George Washington. Other American collectors donated insects, shells, and plants collected internationally. The primary goal of the collection, however, remained to collect knowledge of North America. To this end, following their journey, Lewis and Clark presented Peale with many specimens taken during their exploration of the North American continent. At the turn of the century, Peale listed his holdings as including over 100 quadrupeds; 700 birds; 150 amphibians; and thousands of insects, fish, minerals, and fossils. Peale also began to collect and catalog various specimens of hitherto unknown creatures and biological oddities.

The commitment to this record of the nation's natural history represented an important watershed to the United States. In the intellectual incubator of Philadelphia, Peale's work inspired and grew from that of others, in particular the work of the American Philosophical Society, founded by Benjamin Franklin, Peale, and others in 1743. Many esteemed Americans moved in and out of this society; of particular importance to Peale's work, though, were John James Audubon, Alexander Wilson, and the Bartrams. Raised on the family's 284-acre farm in Mill Grove, near Valley Forge, Audubon grew up hunting and fishing while also studying the arts. To locate specific species, Audubon learned to study the "nature of the place," which he described as involving the determination of various geological, climatological, and botanical characteristics of the land: "whether high or low, moist or dry, whether sloping north or south, or bearing tall trees or low shrubs"; doing so, he said, "generally gives hint as to its inhabitants."[16] Similarly, Wilson was serving as a Philadelphia-area schoolteacher at the turn of the nineteenth century when he met William Bartram, who inspired his interest in ornithology. Much as Audubon did for his own project, Wilson traveled widely to create his nine-volume collection *American Ornithology*, which was published by 1814, prior to Audubon's publication. Wilson's work illustrated 268 species of birds, 26 of which had not previously been described. Finally, John Bartram and his son William used their training in botany and horticulture to create some of the best-known naturalist writing in American history. Although they traveled throughout the American South, their home was along the Schuylkill River, approximately three miles from Philadelphia.

The combined efforts of these writers and painters functioned with the collections of Peale to shape a foundation for the study of natural history in the United States that would be supplemented with the passions of romanticism and transcendentalism in the mid-1800s. Peale, along with the rest of his naturalist cohort, looked both backward and forward. This group's collective intellect shaped the crucial threshold or portal through which Philadelphia's environmental imagination was unleashed in various tangible forms over more than three centuries. Their combined thought became emblematic of the exchanges—social, cultural, technological, and biological—that lay at the heart of Philadelphia's continuous transformation into the twenty-first century. Short strands of this environmental ethic have proven remarkably resilient and adaptive, forming the essence of this city's standing as a place or metropolitan sphere and also as a symbolic leader we call nature's entrepôt.

ORGANIZING *NATURE'S ENTREPÔT*

Peale and Philadelphia's other naturalist thinkers in the late 1700s and early 1800s knew that natural history provides context to human existence. Although these individuals may have experienced professional or business success in other fields, their passions focused on the indisputable fact that human culture is connected to and affected by the natural environment. In the following pages, we have tried to remain faithful to this basic precept as we trace the city's general patterns of development from its founding to the present. These insightful and pathbreaking chapters are written by scholars young and old, many of whom would not refer to themselves as environmental historians; nonetheless, they discuss the city in ways that share common approaches and concerns, ones we can most effectively subsume under the heading of "environmental history."

The chapters in part one primarily focus on Philadelphia before 1800. Craig Zabel and Elizabeth Milroy each explore the physical construction of Philadelphia. Zabel looks particularly at Penn's influence, while Milroy emphasizes the aesthetic romanticism that fueled the development of urban parks. The challenges of the young metropolis inform Thomas Apel's exploration of disease and pandemic in the early city.

Part two picks up with specific episodes of growth and development in the late eighteenth- and early nineteenth-century city. Donna J. Rilling considers the environmental consequences of early industry in the urban core. Michal McMahon explores Dock Creek and the prioritizing of Philadelphia's waterfront and ocean-borne trade; Carolyn T. Adams looks for patterns within the city's expansion before 1900, as the urban core moved into the hinterland in the form of diverse small industrial pursuits.

These developments necessitate the discussions in part three. Adam Levine's chapter traces infrastructural development, particularly sewers and water systems, while Michael J. Chiarappa examines the use of the Delaware Estuary's marine resources by those residing within the Philadelphia metropolitan area from the eighteenth through early twentieth centuries, tracing some of the cultural, environmental, and economic patterns resulting from these extractive practices. These developments resulted in the modernization of the city's form, which is the topic of Robert J. Mason's chapter on suburbanization and sprawl.

Finally, the scholars whose work appears in part four demonstrate the contemporary implications of these earlier patterns. Although not exhaustive, the chapters in this part are written by a host of prominent scholars who have used their specialties to help us better understand the nuances of the modernizing city: Anne Whitson Spirn on landscape and urban planning as a stimulus for community renewal; Diane Sicotte on environmental justice; Domenic Vitiello on sustainability, particularly that of food; and Ann N. Greene on animal management and coexistence. We hope that this overview of contemporary issues in Philadelphia will spur others to think critically about the city, including its present and future.

As we take a more contemporary view of the patterns in Philadelphia's past, however, it remains crucial to acknowledge significant earlier efforts to catalog the city's unique accomplishments. In *First City* the historian Gary B. Nash scratched the surface of Philadelphia's historical importance when he wrote: "The two most important documents in the history of the United States, the Declaration of Independence and the Constitution of 1787, were drafted and signed at the State House in Philadelphia, not Independence Hall. The city was also the site of the first American paper mill, hospital, medical college, subscription library, street lighting, scientific and intellectual society, bank, and government mint. The city served on and off as the official capital of the country until 1800."[17]

A bit more recently, Russell Weigley's *Philadelphia: A 300-Year History* demonstrated the city as it stood at time of the nation's bicentennial, in 1976, a symbol of the entire nation's past and future. Given its role in U.S. history, such national significance is impossible to avoid. Throughout its history, however, Philadelphia has been more than a symbol; it has also been a place to live and to call home.

In his seminal study *Private City* the historian Sam Bass Warner argued that during the city's early days, its structure helped to dictate and reinforce its culture. "It was the unity of everyday life, from tavern, to street, to workplace, to housing," he writes, "which held the town and its leaders together in the eighteenth century. This unity made it possible for the minority of Revolutionary merchants, artisans, and shopkeepers to hold together, run the town, and manage a share of the war against England, even in the face of Quaker neutrality and Tory opposition."[18]

By 1860, Warner observes, "the flood of change had so far run that Philadelphia had become something new to the world and new to America—a modern big city."[19] He argues that the structure of the municipality that took shape in the nineteenth century determined many of the successes and failures of the twentieth century. In the following pages, we hope that a glance backward at lessons from earlier times will launch greater scrutiny of the Philadelphia metropolitan area's environmental history and help Philadelphia achieve successes in the present century, with the issues covered in part four perhaps showing the way.

PART I | Ideal and Reality in the Early City

Craig Zabel

1 | William Penn's Philadelphia

The Land and the Plan

PHILADELPHIA STANDS ON A SITE well-suited for founding a city. In 1683 William Penn wrote: "The situation is a neck of land, and lies between two navigable rivers, Delaware and Schuylkill, whereby it has two fronts upon the water, each a mile, and two from river to river. Delaware is a glorious river, but the Schuylkill being a hundred miles boatable above the falls."[1] The wide and deep Delaware River, on the east edge of Philadelphia, gave ready access to the Atlantic Ocean, while the Schuylkill River, on the west, provided a gateway to the interior of Pennsylvania.[2] Penn's surveyor general, Thomas Holme, boasted that the "land of the city" between the two rivers was "level, dry, and wholesome"; "such a situation," he added, was "scarce to be paralleled."[3] Upon this plot of two square miles, Penn and Holme would grid off their city, which was to be both a "holy experiment" and a shrewd strategy to generate economic wealth.[4] This urban plan provided an ordered matrix for the future growth of the city, but would the vagaries of human activity on the irregularities of the land itself match Penn's ideals for early Philadelphia?

The founding of Philadelphia resulted from the confluence of a spreading English empire, religious tensions, and the need to pay off a royal debt. Sir William Penn Sr. (1621–1670), an admiral in the British navy, had been a loyal royalist during the restoration of the Stuart monarchy under King Charles II and had loaned considerable money to the Crown. Admiral Penn's eldest son, William Penn Jr. (1644–1718), grew up in a privileged world of landed estates in England and Ireland, but he was expelled from Oxford and converted to the religion of the Society of Friends (Quakerism), serving as an outspoken leader for the persecuted group and often being imprisoned for his beliefs (including a stay at the Tower of London).[5] In their denial of class distinctions, refusal to take oaths, lack of hierarchy, and unorthodox religious practices, Quakers were considered a threat to the status quo of English society and the Church of England.[6] The 1681 chartering of a new American colony named in honor of Admiral Penn, "Pennsylvania" (roughly, Penn's Woods), would pay off a lingering debt to the Penn family and charge the admiral's son with removing a significant group of Quakers from England to experiment with their religion far away, at the edge of the British empire. The British colonies along North America's Atlantic seaboard were proving to be a success, but Dutch and Swedish settlements in the Middle Atlantic region were encroaching on the early centers of English settlement in Virginia and Massachusetts. Nonetheless, having fallen to the Dutch in 1655, New Sweden, located along the Delaware River, was seized by England in 1664, as was New Amsterdam (renamed New York); the newly chartered colony of Pennsylvania would thus solidify a keystone at the heart of England's North American possessions.

In his "Charter of Pennsylvania," issued March 4, 1681, Charles II established this colony in honor of the deceased Admiral Penn's "diverse services" and naval victories and stipulated that William Penn Jr. and his heirs would be the "true and absolute" proprietors of Pennsylvania.[7] The royal motivations for this new colony are clarified as being the search for imperial expansion and economic gain and a Christian obligation to "civilize" the local Native Americans: "out of commendable desire to enlarge our English empire, and promote such useful commodities as may be of benefit to us and our dominions, as also to reduce the savage natives by gentle and just manners, to the love of civil society and Christian religion."[8] Although the charter acknowledges a preexisting Native American population, the document treats the land for this "ample colony" as there for the taking, since it was "not yet cultivated and planted."[9]

The charter established a perception of Pennsylvania as a land of undeveloped natural resources just waiting for the arrival of Europeans to be made useful and productive. This is seen in its all-inclusive environmental inventory:

We do also give and grant unto the said William Penn, his heirs and assigns, the free and undisturbed use, and continuance in, and passage unto
and out of all singular ports, harbors, bays, waters, rivers, isles, and inlets,
belonging unto, or leading to and from the country and islands aforesaid,
and all the soils, lands, fields, woods, underwoods, mountains, hills, fenns,
isles, lakes, rivers, waters, rivulets, bays, and inlets, situated, or being
within, or belonging to the limits or bounds aforesaid, together with the
fishing of all sorts of fish, whales, sturgeon and all royal and other fishes,
in the seas, bays, inlets, waters or rivers within the premises, and all the
fish therein taken; and also all veins, mines, minerals and quarries, as well
discovered as not discovered of gold silver, gems, and precious stones, and
all other whatsoever, be it stones, metals, or any other thing or matter
whatsoever found, or to be found within the country, isles, or limits aforesaid.[10]

William Penn's task was to parcel out the land and establish a working community: "[We] give and grant unto the said William Penn, his
heirs and assigns, free and absolute power to divide the said country
and islands into towns, hundreds, and counties and to erect and incorporate towns into boroughs, and boroughs into cities, and to make and
constitute fairs and markets therein." Penn and his heirs were furthermore required to deliver two beaver skins to Windsor Castle each New
Year's Day and one-fifth of any gold or silver ore found in the area.[11] Penn
saw this as an opportunity to leave behind the injustices of his native
England and create afresh a true Christian model for all. In 1681 he op-
timistically wrote that the colony could provide "an example . . . to the
nations"; "There may be room there," he said, "for such a holy experiment."[12]

Penn's colonists, however, would be moving not to an untouched
wilderness but to a land already occupied by European immigrants
and Native Americans. For several decades small groups of Europeans had sought to trade and farm in the Delaware River valley. In 1680
one gentleman observed of New Castle County (now Delaware) that it
was "planted promiscuously by Swedes, Finlanders, Dutch and English."[13] The local Leni-Lenape (or Delaware) Indians and the more inland
Susquehannocks, who lived along the Susquehanna River, were already
being displaced by the late seventeenth century.[14] William Penn would
have an uncommon respect for Native Americans (he even attempted
learning the language of the Leni-Lenape), and through his treaties he
strove to deal with them fairly and honorably. The land that early Pennsylvania would occupy, however, had a relatively sparse Native American population, making the founding of a colony that much easier. Even

in pre-Columbian times, the Delaware and Susquehanna watersheds had been peripheral to the main habitation patterns of Native American populations.[15] Moreover, most Indians first encountered Europe not in face-to-face meetings with immigrants but rather with the microbes they brought with them. Devastating diseases new to the Americas proved to be the unwitting biological advance guard of European settlement. Smallpox, measles, typhus, and pneumonia quickly became epidemics spreading from Native Americans trading with Europeans on the coast and rivers to those living inland, who had never seen a European. By the time significant Western settlement was established, the Native American population had already undergone a devastating reduction.[16] Francis Daniel Pastorius, a prominent leader in Germantown (just north of Philadelphia), noted this phenomenon in 1684: "The Indians . . . grow less numerous here daily, . . . since for the most part they wish to quit this land and to withdraw some hundred miles farther into the woods." Pastorius morosely observed the rationale: "For they have a superstition, that as many Indians must die each year as the number of Europeans that newly arrive."[17]

The Native Americans differed from the European settlers dramatically in the way they used and conceived the land. William Penn observed that the Indians possessed and sought little: "They care for little because they want but little; and the reason is, a little contents them. . . . We sweat and toil to live; their pleasure feeds them. I mean, their hunting, fishing, and fowling, and this table is spread everywhere."[18] The semisedentary Native Americans stepped lightly on the land but enjoyed a diet that was far more varied and healthy than that of the average European. The food that Native American men brought in through hunting, trapping, and fishing was supplemented by the crops raised by the women. The indigenous groups grew corn, beans, and squash, typically sown together, providing a rich mix of vegetables from an ecologically advanced approach to agriculture that differed markedly from the monoculture of European fields.[19] The Native American wigwams seemed small and insubstantial to European eyes; Penn noted: "Their *houses* are mats, or barks of trees set on poles, in the fashion of an England barn, but out of the power of the winds, for they are hardly higher than a man."[20] The circular arrangement of their villages was informal and organic, in strong contrast to the rigid rectilinear plan that would organize Philadelphia.[21] In sum, the colonist-occupied landscape was illegible, silent, and foreign to the Native Americans and vice versa.[22]

Early commerce with the Europeans centered on the lucrative fur trade, which decimated animal populations far inland and also introduced substantial quantities of European metal to the material culture of the Native Americans, technologically influencing their work and combat while eroding their self-sufficiency as they became dependent on European goods and alcohol.[23] Penn observed: "Since the Europeans came into these parts, they [the Native Americans] are grown great lovers of strong liquors, rum especially, and for it exchange the richest of their skins and furs. . . . But when drunk, one of the most wretchedest spectacles in the world."[24]

The temperate climate of Pennsylvania would prove to be pleasing to Europeans, since it lacked both New England's harshly cold winters and the southern colonies' suffocatingly hot summers.[25] William Penn wrote: "The air, heat, and cold resemble the heart of France." Moreover, he praised the weather and skies of Pennsylvania as brighter and more invigorating than those of Europe: "From December to the beginning of the month of March, we had sharp frosty weather; not foul, thick black weather as our northeast winds bring with them in England, but a sky as clear as in summer and the air dry, cold, piercing, and hungry; yet I remember not that I wore more clothes than in England. . . . We enjoyed a sweet spring, no gusts, but gentle showers and a fine sky. . . . The summer . . . we have had extraordinary heats, yet mitigated sometimes by cool breezes."[26]

A common fear of European colonists entering this "New World" was the threatening expanse of a land that seemed to be totally wild. Such an image was countered by the Latin roots of the colony's name, Penn's Woods, which evoked a gentleman's park rather than an endless, untamed forest.[27] William Penn vigorously promoted his new colony by describing Pennsylvania not as a frightening wilderness but as a land of rich natural abundance, a paradise found, almost a Garden of Eden. In one letter, he extolled the region's rich botanical diversity: "The soil good, the springs many and delightful, the fruits, roots, corn, and flesh as good as I have commonly eaten in Europe. I may say of most of them better. Strawberries ripen in the woods in Spring, and the last month, peas, beans, cherries, and mulberries. Much black walnut, chestnut, cypress, or white cedar, and mulberry are here. . . . Vines are here in abundance everywhere; some may be as big in the body as a man's thigh."[28] Elsewhere, Penn enumerated the animal life:

> Of living creatures, *fish, fowl,* and the beasts of the woods, here are divers sorts, some for food and profit, and some for profit only. For food as well as profit, the elk, as big as a small ox, deer bigger than ours, beaver, raccoon, rabbits [and] squirrels, some eat young bear, and commend it. Of

fowl of the land, there is the turkey (forty and fifty pound weight), which is very great, pheasants, heath-birds, pigeons, and partridges in abundance. Of the water, the swan, goose, white and gray, brants, ducks, teal, also snipe and curlew, and that in great numbers; but the duck and teal excel.... Of fish, there is the sturgeon, herring, rock, shad, catshead, sheepshead, eel, smelt, perch, roach; and in land rivers, trout, some say salmon, above the Falls. Of shellfish, we have oysters, crabs, cockles, conches and mussels.... The creatures for profit only by skin or fur ... are the wildcat, panther, otter, wolf, fox, fisher, mink muskrat and of the water the whale for oil.[29]

Into this rich ecosystem of Pennsylvania, Penn and his colonists would import many European crops and animals. William Penn himself cultivated English grass for forage.[30] The concept of domesticated farm animals was completely alien to the Native Americans.[31] For the colonists, using livestock to farm reflected their Christian right of dominion over animals, one they exercised while subduing, civilizing, and transforming the wilderness into improved fields of agriculture.[32] Penn boasted, "We have no want of *horses*.... Two ships have been freighted to Barbados, with horses ... since my arrival. Here is also plenty of cow-cattle and some sheep; the people plow mostly with oxen."[33] In addition to importing European agricultural staples and livestock, the trans-Atlantic ships incidentally brought harmful weeds, insects, and vermin that would have a permanent impact on the land's ecology, just as diseases had devastatingly reduced Native American populations.[34]

The local Native Americans viewed the land as something that sustained them, that gave them life and was animated by spirits. It was not necessarily something that was *possessed* in an abstract sense of ownership, particularly if one was not present and making use of it.[35] Yet the Europeans had a strong tradition of personal possessions and land ownership; in Genesis 1:28, God commands humankind to "subdue the earth" and gives people "dominion . . . over every living thing that moves on earth."[36] The first act of settlement in Pennsylvania was to buy the land, presumably forever, from the Indians. In the terms of such treaties, the Native Americans received consumable material goods that would be gone in less than a generation. In the Quaker interest in peace and fairness, Penn and his agents were diligent in acquiring all the land through such treaties, which they deemed to be fair. One such treaty consummated in the summer before Penn's arrival demonstrates this sort of exchange. The Delaware Indians (Leni-Lenape) would "fully, clearly, and absolutely grant, bargain, sell, and deliver unto the said William Penn, his heirs and assigns, forever, all that or those tract or tracts lying and being in the province of Pennsylvania aforesaid, beginning at a certain white oak"; conversely, the Indians would receive from the English

> three hundred and fifty fathoms of wampum, twenty white blankets, twenty fathoms of stroudwaters [a woolen cloth], sixty fathoms of duffels, twenty kettles (four whereof large), twenty guns, twenty coats, forty shirts, forty pair of stockings, forty hoes, forty axes, two barrels of powder, two hundred bars of lead, two hundred knives, two hundred small glasses, twelve pair of shoes, forty copper boxes, forty tobacco tongs, two small barrels of pipes, forty pair of scissors, forty combs, twenty-four pounds of red lead, one hundred awls, two handfuls of fishhooks, two handfuls of needles, forty pounds of shot, two bundles of beads, ten small saws, twelve drawing knives, four ankers of tobacco, two ankers of rum, two ankers of beer, and three hundred guilders.[37]

William Penn's agents and colonists began to arrive in nascent Pennsylvania in the fall of 1681. To ensure a successful colony, Penn's recruiting efforts had targeted yeomen, artisans, shopkeepers, and well-to-do merchants.[38] Penn himself would arrive about a year later, in October 1682. Penn's promotions of his colony proved successful, for dozens of ships made the voyage, and he drew Quakers and other colonists from several nations, particularly England, Wales, Holland, and Germany. Many initially lived in makeshift shelters designed for mere survival, sometimes rough caves along the river or simple log cabins following the Swedish example.[39] Such rustic lodgings were temporary, for early Philadelphia would emerge as a city of brick (made from the abundant river clay).[40] Although life was certainly challenging in this new world, early Pennsylvania did not suffer any severe "starving times" like those that had hampered certain earlier colonial efforts.[41] Before his arrival, Penn had initially envisioned Philadelphia as a sprawling development of country estates along some fifteen miles of Delaware River's west bank, with his own house in the center, where the main wharf would be.[42] The ease of connection between ocean-going vessels and the land was a priority in Penn's instructions: "Be sure to make your choice where it is most navigable, high, dry, and healthy; that is, where most ships may best ride, of deepest draft of water, if possible to load or unload at the bank or quayside without boating and lightering of it."[43] In 1681 Penn described the object of this early scheme as his "green country town": "Let every house be placed, if the person pleases, in the middle of its plot as to the breadth way of it, that so there may be ground on each side for gardens to orchards or fields, that it may be a green country town, which will never be burnt and always be wholesome."[44] The holdings of earlier English, Dutch, and Scandinavian settlers thwarted this expansive scheme, however, and Penn's agents initially purchased just a mile of frontage along the Delaware to found Philadelphia.[45] Eventually, a city far more ordered than the one Penn first envisioned would be designed on a two-square-mile plot spreading across a neck of land between the Delaware and Schuylkill rivers.

In 1682 William Penn worked with Thomas Holme (1624–1695), his surveyor general and a fellow Quaker, in developing the definitive plan, or "plat-form," for Philadelphia (see figure 1.1), which was published in 1683 in London as part of a promotional document entitled "Letter to the Free Society of Traders."[46] A regular grid is the driving force behind this plan. Irregular woodlands laced by streams between two rivers were transformed into a repeating succession of squared lots to define an ordered, efficient, and rational city. Le Corbusier, a twentieth-century promoter of the gridded modern city, observed: "Man walks in a straight line because he has a goal and knows where he is going."[47] The gridiron as an urban plan goes back to antiquity and has flourished many times in the Western world, showing up as ancient Roman new towns for military veterans, ideal Renaissance plans, and colonial settlements throughout New Spain following the promulgation of the Laws of the Indies (1573).[48] In the English colonies of North America, the regular order of Philadelphia's grid contrasted sharply with the informal, organic, medieval plan (begun in 1630) of Boston's twisted and wandering streets. Penn likely thought of Philadelphia's ordered grid principally in contrast to London's medieval web of streets, whose congestion and poor sanitation had made a crucible for plagues and eventually the Great Fire of 1666. Although conditions improved in the rebuilding after the fire, London was not dramatically redesigned according to the ideal plans proposed by the likes of Sir Christopher Wren. The 1666 plan for London by Richard Newcourt is often suggested as a possible source for Philadelphia, although there are significant differences. Another possible source may have been the plan of Londonderry, in northern Ireland, which Thomas Holme may have known. The 1638 nine-square grid of New Haven, Connecticut, provides a small-scale precursor in the English colonies.[49]

Whatever the sources for their scheme, Penn and Holme created a large-scale plan for a major new city that would guide its development for centuries to come. The simplicity of a grid has several advantages, especially for a new city.[50] Straight lines and right angles are the easiest to survey, plot, and build upon. Purchasers of land both locally and back in England knew exactly where their lots were. Circulation across a gridiron of streets maximizes clarity, convenience, and efficiency, and such an approach allows the greatest ease in finding locations. A grid-

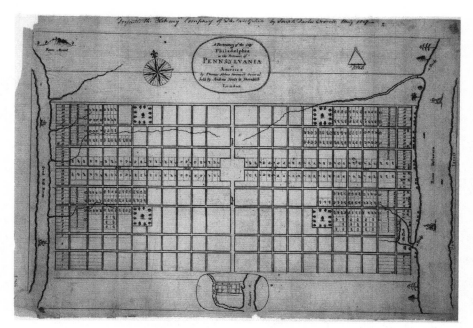

FIGURE 1.1. Thomas Holme (with instructions from William Penn), *A Portraiture of the City of Philadelphia in the Province of Pennsylvania in America* (ca. 1812), reproduction of 1683 map. Courtesy of the Library Company of Philadelphia.

iron can also have negative consequences in its inflexibility, its total disregard for the preexisting natural topography, and its numbing redundancy.[51] As the city was being laid out, subtle changes were made to the 1682–1683 plan to accommodate the natural realities of ravines, streams, swamps, and so on.[52] Nonetheless, the grid would remain ever present. When the London-dwelling Charles Dickens visited Philadelphia in 1842, he found it "distractingly regular" and quipped that he "would have given the world for a crooked street."[53]

Dividing Philadelphia into quadrants, two principal central streets crossing at right angles were planned to be wider than the rest (100 feet wide rather than 50): High Street (now Market), running east–west, and Broad Street, running north–south, met at the city's center square. In the geometric spirit of this arrangement, the other north–south streets were numbered, but Penn would eventually name the other east–west streets after the trees local to Philadelphia, such as Chestnut, Walnut, and Pine, once more glorifying the region's natural abundance rather than individuals.[54] Such an ordered plan would be the matrix on which the city could thrive in future days. One can also surmise that this city of repeating squares reflects the Quaker values of social equality, universal toleration and acceptance (within certain religious and racial limits), and aesthetic plainness. After all, Penn had named his city Philadelphia, indicating it to be the "City of Brotherly Love." This was not to be a city of grand-manner gestures creating a hierarchy of spaces and boulevards leading to major monuments through baroque radiating avenues, as one sees in the plans of Maryland's capital, Annapolis (drafted in 1694 by Governor Francis Nicholson), and the later national capital of Washington, D.C. (drawn up in 1791 by Pierre-Charles L'Enfant).[55]

A large green square was planned for the heart of Philadelphia. Holme explained: "In the center of the city is a square of ten acres; at each angle are to be houses for public affairs, as a meetinghouse, assembly or state house, market house, school house, and several other buildings of public concerns."[56] Viewing the matter abstractly, Penn thought that the main public buildings should gather at the geographic heart of his plan, but this ideal ignored the natural and pragmatic human proclivity to settle first along the two rivers that bracketed the plan and were the major arteries of commerce, particularly the Delaware River. Even though one of the earliest Quaker meetinghouses was built on Centre Square in 1695, it was soon dismantled (1702), and this square would not be fully developed until after the Civil War, when its green was traded for the Second Empire baroque grandiosity of Philadelphia's city hall (1871–1901), which filled the entire square.[57] This vacuum at the center of Philadelphia's plan during the late seventeenth century in some ways reflects the nonhierarchical ways of the Quakers, who establish no clergy. In a pattern that continues to this day, religious gatherings in a Quaker meetinghouse did not center on an altar, pulpit, or minister; rather, the Quakers sat in benches facing one another, filling the seats by order of arrival, not rank or wealth (except for a special "stand" for elders), and the congregation would sit in silence until any member was moved to stand by the "Inner Spirit" (which they held all to possess) and preach or pray.[58] Philadelphia's initially empty central square, then, is completely opposite to the Puritan model of New England, where the meetinghouse, with its central pulpit and required Sunday services, were the centerpiece and authoritarian hub of every Puritan village. For the Quakers, a meetinghouse was not even needed; early Quaker settlers often gathered in private homes.[59]

Along with Centre Square, another distinguishing feature of Penn and Holme's plan were four smaller greens: "There are also in each quarter of the city, a square of eight acres, to be for the like uses, as the Moorfield's in London."[60] Perhaps Penn and Holme envisioned that these more neighborhood-specific greens might be developed along the lines of London's residential squares, such as Lincoln's Inn Fields, with which Penn was familiar, or Moorfields, which Holme mentions.[61] The growth of residential squares in seventeenth-century London provided select neighborhoods with uncommon greenery, airy breadth, and regularity as a respite to the congestion prevalent elsewhere in the city. The placement of the four squares within Philadelphia's grid is ingenious in that the streets generally approach the squares at the corners, making them more discrete and contained, rather than formally opening them up to long perspectives by having streets abut the centers of the squares.[62]

By the 1680s the Delaware Valley had entered an era of relative peace in its European settlers' relations with local Native Americans and other European powers. Although he was an admiral's son, William Penn was a Quaker and thus a pacifist, and his new city would have none of the military installations that characterized most colonial settlements. In fact, many of the earliest colonial efforts began with the erection of a fort and palisades, as one sees in Jamestown (1607), Plymouth (1620), and New Amsterdam (1625), a clear acknowledgment that one's first step into the wilderness would probably be one of conflict. William Penn sought peace, and his city of brotherly love would not be walled or militarized. In this respect, the city contrasted with the remnants of New Sweden. For example, the Old Swedes' Church (also known as Gloria Dei, built in 1698–1700), which stands in southeastern Philadelphia, replaced a former log blockhouse that the Swedes had built along the Delaware for defense.[63]

Holme's 1683 plan for the city shows an interesting detail: many of the individual lots are defined and numbered for sale or rent. These lots cluster toward the two rivers and are linked by a continuous string of lots on both sides of High Street. The "First Purchasers" who came to America were allotted land near the Delaware, while absentee buyers were typically given lots near the Schuylkill.[64] Holme and Penn were planning for twin river cities linked by a market street and its unifying institutions at the central square, with future growth (on the undivided blocks) filling in the rest of Philadelphia. The actual growth of the city in many ways defied the balance of this plan. The center would remain empty, very few were drawn to build along the Schuylkill, and almost all the early development occurred along the Delaware, with settlers even building beyond the north and south ends of the grid just to be on that river.[65] The city was not growing east to west, as the plan implied it would; the realities of the land were trumping an abstract plan in the early settlement of Philadelphia. However, High Street (now Market) did start to define an early and limited east-west development into the interior, resulting in a T-shaped or bell-shaped settlement pattern along the river that is typical of early colonial ports.[66] Moreover, the true heart of early Philadelphia lay in the east end of High Street, not Centre Square, with the city's primary open-air market developing down the spine of this wide thoroughfare. A belfry-topped brick head house (built in 1707–1710 by Samuel Powell), with an open market below and a town hall/courthouse on its second floor, in the English manner, was built at the intersection of High and Second streets, terminating the wooden market sheds.[67] This long simple structure became the nexus of local government and the commercial distribution point for the fresh food raised, fished, or hunted in the surrounding countryside. The intersection of High and Second streets also became the religious center of early Philadelphia when Quakers built the brick Great Meetinghouse in 1695 just south of the previously mentioned head house and Anglicans built Christ Church (1696–98) to the north.[68] The diminutive wooden structure of the first Christ Church was replaced by the grand and richly embellished current structure (built in 1727–1744 and 1751–1754 under the direction of Dr. John Kearsley and Thomas Smith) in the latest manner of Christopher Wren's City churches in London.[69] The high-style Georgian fashion of this Anglican church culminating with a spire contrasted sharply with the plain Quaker meetinghouse across the street, which appeared to be a large but modest residence rather than a major public structure.[70]

The eastern edge of the Penn-Holme plan was Front Street, which ran along the top of a bluff about two stories above the Delaware River. Eventually Water Street would be added below the bluff, and tall warehouses and houses would be built between the two streets to accommodate the change in elevation.[71] Shipyards built vessels from the abundant local lumber, while docks and wharves jutted out into the river to facilitate the loading and unloading of goods. These fingerlike extensions into the river were Philadelphia's connection to the world.[72] William Penn was not able to monopolize trade through a lone wharf that he alone controlled, as he had intended in his initial plans.[73]

Penn had first envisioned a "green country town" of generous lots and widely spaced building (thus avoiding the disease and fire that had plagued London), but the average resident of a port and merchant city wants to live and work in convenient and accessible locations within the community, not in widely separated and distant blocks in a partially claimed wilderness. Private owners began to introduce cross streets and alleys that bisected Penn's large blocks to facilitate better circulation and to build more densely. An excellent remnant of this trend is the lovingly preserved Elfreth's Alley (begun in 1703) with its narrow breadth and its cramped, shoulder-to-shoulder diminutive townhouses, which were mostly rented by the families of craftsmen who probably could not afford the more generous houses on the large lots that Penn had envisioned.[74] Lewis Mumford remarked that Elfreth's Alley "reduced the living quarters to doll's-house size."[75] Nevertheless, in 1698 an early Quaker settler of Philadelphia boasted, "The Industrious (nay Indefatigable) Inhabitants have built a Noble and Beautiful City, and called it Philadelphia, which contains about two thousand Houses, all Inhabited; and most of them Stately, and of Brick, generally three Stories high, after the Mode of London, and as many as several Families in each. . . . All these Alleys and Lanes extend from the Front Street to the Second Street. . . . There are also beside these Alleys and lanes, several fine Squares and Courts with this Magnificent City."[76]

Despite being so strongly associated with the founding of Philadelphia, William Penn traveled to Pennsylvania only twice, and then for relatively brief stays: 1682–1684 and 1699–1701. He felt that his main work in founding the colony required his presence back in London to fight such battles as a Maryland border dispute with Lord Baltimore. With the fall of the Stuart monarchy, he temporarily lost his charter to Pennsylvania and spent more time in jail. Nonetheless, he would work until the end of this life to bring success to this colonial effort, even though his approach was usually that of an absentee landlord.

During his second trip to Philadelphia, Penn rented and lived in the "Slate Roof House" (see fig. 1.2). Built for a well-to-do merchant, this brick house reflected older English manor traditions with its wings and clustered chimneys, while it sported a few modest Renaissance refinements with its symmetry, belt course, cornice, hipped roof, and pedimented entrance.[77] For a fairly substantial house, it is an essay in restraint and understatement.

Early Philadelphia architecture in general tended to be practical, ordered, and well built and was characterized by a prevalence of brick and sensible pent-eave roofs.[78] During this most Quaker period in the city's history, however, the proclivity for plainness is quite evident, though Georgian exuberance began to diversify Philadelphia's architecture in the eighteenth century (as seen in the second Christ Church). William Penn's attitudes toward architectural style can possibly be discerned from his comments about proper Quaker dress in his book *Some Fruits of Solitude: Wise Sayings on the Conduct of Human Life* (1693); the following sartorial guidelines could just as easily be applied to one's home:

FIGURE 1.2. Depiction of the "Slate Roof House," designed by James Porteus, Philadelphia, ca. 1684. Illustration is an 1836 watercolor by William L. Breton; the house was demolished 1867. Courtesy of the Library Company of Philadelphia.

74. Choose your clothes by your own eyes, not by someone else's. The plainer and simpler, the better. Don't choose clothes that are either unattractive or showy; make your choices based on usefulness, or modesty, and appropriateness—not on pride.

75. If you are clean and warm, it is enough; more than this robs the poor and pleases the extravagant. . . .

77. We are told truly that meekness and modesty are the rich and charming garments of the soul. The less showy our outward attire is, the more distinctly and brilliantly does the beauty of the inner garments shine.[79]

Penn expected to make a good income from the sale and rent of land since he and his heirs were the "true and absolute" proprietors of Pennsylvania. "Though I desire to extend religious freedom, yet I want some recompense for my trouble," Penn acknowledged in 1681.[80] First Purchasers were lured by the fertile agricultural lands surrounding Philadelphia plus much smaller lots distributed within the city of Philadelphia.[81] The city lots were not as generous as intended in Penn's first scheme, so purchasers were compensated with "liberty lands" just outside the city's grid to the north and west, presumably to encourage suburban estates.[82] A portion of the city's grid was left unsold, thus providing a reserve of real estate to generate funds (through sale or rents) for William Penn's family in the future. Yet after the first flush of land sales, Penn's less than stellar management of his finances led to money problems for the rest of his life.[83]

For many, the true lure of Pennsylvania was not the city of Philadelphia but the surrounding country and the opportunity to develop one's own prosperous farm, an opportunity that rarely presented itself back in England.[84] One colonist observed in 1698: "Two Men may clear between Twenty and Thirty Acres of Land in one Year, fit for the Plough, In which Oxen are chiefly us'd."[85] Fields were cleared and water power was harnessed as stone gristmills were built along streams.[86] About 1687 *A Map of ye Improved Part of Pennsylvania*, drawn by Thomas Holme, was published showing the division of land beyond the city proper (see fig. 12.1). The plan of rural growth beyond the city's grid shows a patchwork of townships and land holdings. Straight lines and right angles skew and twist to accommodate the irregular topography. Rivers and streams are the wandering frames that unite these holdings. Many individual plots are long narrow strips with a short end along the river, a setup that maximized the number of rural farms with access to rivers. At the outer fringe of the settled land, the straight lines end and random trees indicate an endless "wilderness" and invitation for future generations.[87]

Philadelphia was the hub for this agrarian kingdom, the gathering point for the agricultural and other natural riches of the countryside and an entrepôt that economically, politically and culturally connected his city to the British Empire and the rest of the world. The colony proved to be perhaps too much of a financial success, which may have tainted several of the original religious ideals behind the colony. With his long absences, William Penn never managed to exploit what should have been a lucrative charter. Few wanted to pay what he felt he was owed, leaving Penn with serious financial woes.[88] His "holy experiment" also suffered in that once the Quakers were removed from the persecution of England and other regions, they were no longer unified in their oppression.[89] Benefiting from a profitable new city and colony, they found fixating on the simple life to be less attractive when they were prospering. Disputes and arguments occasionally created serious fissures among the Friends. One notorious example occurred in 1693 when two factions of Quakers brought axes into a meetinghouse and proceeded to chop their rivals' galleries into splinters.[90] The religious tolerance of Penn's colony also attracted other religious groups and nationalities.[91] Some shared Penn's ideals, as did the German Pietists who founded Germantown north of Philadelphia. In promoting this German settlement, which he described as lying "on black rich soil" and being "half surrounded with pleasant streams," their leader, Francis Daniel Pastorius, encouraged those still back in the homeland to "depart the sooner the better" from what he called "the European Sodom."[92] Other immigrants brought other religions, including the Quakers' former oppressors, the Anglican Church. This religious tolerance eventually diluted the Quakers' unity within the city. Toleration of diverse groups preempted a single "holy experiment" of Friends. But acceptance was far from universal. Slavery of Africans and their descendents was an accepted (although occasionally debated) practice in early Philadelphia; William Penn himself owned slaves.[93] In 1682 a Quaker merchant who was moving to Pennsylvania wrote his brother in Barbados, asking that he buy and send him black slaves: "I desire thee to provide me 2 good stout Negro men such as are like to be pliable and good-natured and ingenious."[94] Philadelphia found itself linked in a lucrative trans-Atlantic circle of trade encompassing African slavery, Caribbean plantations, raw materials and produce from the North American colonies, and manufactured goods from England.

Although William Penn rented Philadelphia's Slate Roof House during his second visit to Pennsylvania, his true home was not even within the city's grid. During his first visit, Penn had begun building Pennsbury Manor (erected in 1683–1684), a country estate twenty-six miles up the Delaware River from Philadelphia. Like an English dandy being rowed along the Thames, Penn traveled from Pennsbury to Philadelphia by a personal barge that was possibly oared by his black slaves, a trip of roughly five hours.[95] After Penn's death, the manor house fell into ruin and eventually was demolished. It was reconstructed using scant historical evidence in 1937–1939.[96] A visitor in 1698 described it as a "Great and Stately Pile" with a slate roof, and a surviving gateleg table hints that it was richly furnished.[97] The manor included several outbuildings, including a bake/brew house, as well as gardens, agricultural fields, meadows, and livestock, all tended first by black slaves and later by indentured servants.[98] Pennsbury provided Penn an escape from Philadelphia, which by 1699 was more crowded, contentious, and immoral than the city he had first envisioned.[99] Moreover, he preferred the life of the English country house, such as his estate back in England, Warm-

FIGURE 1.3. Edward Hicks, *The Peaceable Kingdom* (ca. 1833), oil on canvas, 17 7/8 × 23 15/16 in. (45.4 × 60.8 cm), 1985.17. Courtesy of the Pennsylvania Academy of the Fine Arts, Philadelphia, John S. Phillips bequest, by exchange (acquired from the Philadelphia Museum of Art, originally the 1950 bequest of Lisa Norris Elkins).

inghurst Place, in Sussex.[100] A major commercial success, Philadelphia was now one of the largest cities in America's English colonies, yet Penn no longer called it his "holy experiment" but instead characterized it as a "licentious wilderness."[101] Penn, the city planner, had ironically been too successful in being the catalyst for a thriving mercantile city, for his own sympathies were always more rural than urban. For example, he told his followers, "A country life is preferable: there we see the works of God. But in cities we see little other than the works of humanity. The one provides a better subject for our contemplation than the other.... God's works [nature] declare his power, wisdom, and goodness. Ours, for the most part, declare our pride, folly and excess, God's works are more useful; ours, chiefly, are for showiness and lust."[102]

After his death, the image of William Penn would take on a mythic guise, one particularly fostered by Benjamin West's painting *William Penn's Treaty with the Indians* (1771–1772) and its subsequent engravings.[103] Although this specific event may not have occurred, it depicts

Penn standing as the eternal peacemaker as he consummates a treaty with the Leni-Lenape under nature's embrace in the form of the legendary "Treaty Elm" along the Delaware River, while robust brick buildings in the background make the colonists' claim to the land permanent. West explained: "The great object I had in forming that composition was to express savages brought into harmony and peace by justice and benevolence."[104] This theme is reprised by the early nineteenth-century folk artist and Quaker Edward Hicks in his numerous depictions of the iconic image of Penn's Treaty (co-opted from West's painting), which is now conflated with a biblical prophecy (Isaiah 11:16). In his paintings titled *The Peaceable Kingdom,* various incongruous beasts "lie down" with one another and innocent children in peaceful harmony: a utopian dream of early Pennsylvania (see fig. 1.3).[105] By the second half of the eighteenth century, however, Penn's vision of peaceful coexistence with Native Americans had degenerated into bloody conflict and displacement.[106]

By the end of the nineteenth century, Philadelphia's founder received an oxymoronic monumental tribute: the thirty-six-foot bronze statue of William Penn (by Alexander Milne Calder) placed atop Philadelphia's city hall in 1894.[107] Cast on a scale worthy of Caesar, this is probably the last kind of memorial that any humble Quaker would want. Nonetheless, Penn stands like the Colossus of Rhodes at the heart of his grid plan for Philadelphia. His hat crests at 548 feet in the air as he looks northeast to the legendary site of the Treaty Elm and ironically beyond to Pennsbury, representing the country life that he preferred to the city he founded.

Elizabeth Milroy

2 | "Pro Bono Publico"

Ecology, History, and the Creation of Philadelphia's Fairmount Park System

IN NOVEMBER 2008 PHILADELPHIANS VOTED overwhelmingly to eliminate the sixteen-member Fairmount Park Commission and to con-
solidate the management of the Fairmount Park system with the city's
recreation department.[1] The new "Philadelphia Parks and Recreation"
is headed by a commissioner who is appointed by the mayor. The commissioner works with an advisory body called the Commission on Parks
and Recreation (PaRC), which is composed of fifteen members, nine of
whom are appointed by the mayor from nominations made by the City
Council and six of whom serve ex officio.[2] Philadelphia Parks and Recreation is responsible for protecting the city's largest ecological and
cultural resource. In voting as they did, residents authorized an administrative structure that has been standard in other American cities for
decades, though this was not the first attempt to disband the Fairmount
Park Commission, which had been formed in 1867. Indeed, the commission's long life reflects both the deep history and the idiosyncrasy of
park making in Philadelphia. This chapter chronicles the history of the
commission's creation and the circumstances that gave rise to its unique

combined approach to natural lands conservation and historic preservation, circumstances that also may have contributed to its abolition.

On the eve of its demise, the Fairmount Park Commission comprised
six officials or their delegates from city government and ten private citizens appointed by the Court of Common Pleas. It governed sixty-three
neighborhood parks covering roughly 9,200 acres, or 10 percent of the
city's area. It also worked with more than sixty volunteer organizations and advocacy groups that supported the improvement and maintenance of parklands and recreational facilities. The Fairmount Park
system incorporated the largest collection of historic properties in the
state of Pennsylvania, including the Philadelphia Zoo (the oldest zoo in
the United States) and the Philadelphia Museum of Art, as well as incomparable eighteenth- and nineteenth-century houses and early industrial
landmarks, most notably the Fairmount Water Works, images of which
are a mainstay of the city's promotional literature.[3]

Yet Fairmount Park receives scant attention in histories of park
design and city planning, even in some modern social and political
histories of the city.[4] Some confusion is caused by terminology: what
Philadelphians call "Fairmount Park" is more accurately the East and
West parks on the banks of the Schuylkill, the oldest sections of the Fairmount Park *system* under its modern administrative structure. Historians also have assumed that Philadelphia's modern park system was established wholly in response to the creation of New York's Central Park.[5]
This misunderstanding has obscured the system's singularity and its
true genealogy. It is true that, as in New York and other American cities, Philadelphia's nineteenth-century park advocates were principally
members of the local elite who wanted to improve the quality of public
works and regulate public recreation. But the parks laid out by Frederick Law Olmsted and his contemporaries were newly invented spaces,
inserted into cities as sections of the urban space considered in need of
"improvement" were excavated and replanted according to a designer's
preconceived plan. Philadelphians, by contrast, built Fairmount Park
opportunistically from existing landscapes and historic properties, in
the process reviving but also modifying a long neglected part of William
Penn's founding vision.

Penn envisioned green public squares distributed throughout a
measured street grid. The Fairmount Park system evolved to counter
the rigidity of this grid. It was a massive conservation and preservation
effort carried out along major waterways that formed a kind of circulatory system leading from East and West parks—dubbed "a heart of nature" by the founding commissioners—to nourish a sense of collective

identity among the city's disparate neighborhoods.[6] The need to protect the public water supply, chiefly the Schuylkill River, played a crucial role in the park system's creation, a protracted process begun early in the nineteenth century and affirmed by the Park Act of 1867, which created the Fairmount Park Commission. By the mid-1880s, tracts along Wissahickon Creek as well as the Schuylkill had been expropriated. The conservation of major watersheds continued into the twentieth century; by the 1970s the Fairmount Park system had expanded to incorporate land along Cobbs, Pennypack, Tacony, and Poquessing creeks.

THE TEMPERATE CITY

The most innovative features of William Penn's 1683 plan for Philadelphia were not the streets set out on a grid but the four landscaped public squares laid out around the central public square as a system of interrelated parks.[7] The implementation of Penn's plan was long delayed, however, because the immediate needs of the colony precluded methodical planning and building. Economic reliance on shipping thwarted consistent settlement across the grid as settlers clustered along the Delaware. Most important, Penn never legally confirmed the city government's jurisdiction over the squares. For more than a century after the city's founding, even as streets were laid out according to the grid plan, Penn's innovative squares languished: the northeastern and southeastern squares were used as burying grounds; the western squares lay vacant or were used as trash dumps (see fig. 1.1 in the previous chapter).[8]

At the start of the nineteenth century, the history of Philadelphia's public water supply and its public green spaces merged, and Penn's squares were rescued from years of neglect. In 1799 theories that devastating epidemics arose from polluted springs and wells in the area led to the establishment of a municipally administered water supply system that pumped water from the Schuylkill to a reservoir at Centre Square designed by Benjamin H. Latrobe (see fig. 2.1). An early petition stressed the link between public health and well-maintained green space, urging city government to provide more opportunities for "innocent relaxation from laborious occupations" and to create spaces that would "invigorate the constitution and improve the health" of its citizens by purifying the atmosphere and mitigating the effects of extreme heat in the summer season. Accordingly, the square was landscaped with tidy lawns and Lombardy poplars; in 1809 a fountain was erected at its center.[9]

But Latrobe's Centre Square pump house soon proved inadequate,

FIGURE 2.1. William Birch, *The Water Works in Centre Square* (1800), engraving, from *The City of Philadelphia as It Was... in 1800*. Courtesy the Library Company of Philadelphia.

and in 1812 construction began on a larger and more efficient facility located at Fairmount, a hill on the east bank of the Schuylkill just north of the city limits. Here technology and the scenic landscape worked symbiotically. The waterworks complex was one in a cluster of engineering landmarks dramatically sited at the river. Just to the south was the Upper Ferry Bridge, the world's longest single-span bridge when it opened in 1813. In 1822 the world's longest dam was erected across the river to power the waterworks. And along the west bank, the canals and locks of the Schuylkill Navigation Company went into operation in 1827. Second only to Niagara Falls in popularity, Fairmount drew flocks of tourists, who came to view the achievements of modern engineering, stroll through the adjacent gardens, and climb to the top of the reservoir to survey the still picturesque estates that lined the river banks to the north (see fig. 2.2).[10]

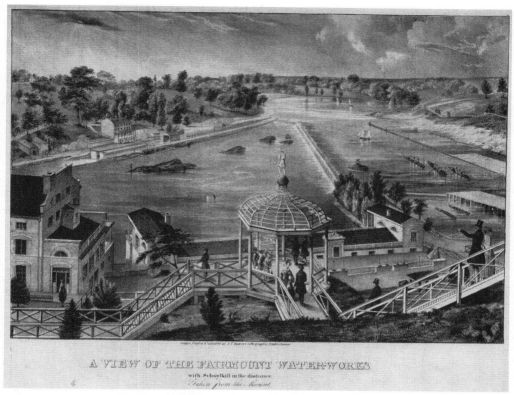

FIGURE 2.2. John T. Bowen, *A View of the Fairmount Waterworks with Schuylkill in the Distance. Taken from the Mount* (1838), color lithograph. The Historical Society of Pennsylvania.

Paintings, prints, and later photographs of the Fairmount waterworks advertised that Philadelphia encouraged and facilitated temperance among its citizens. But pollution caused by increasing industrialization in and around the city undermined this vision of health and compounded threats of social disorder. Damming of the Schuylkill had created a slack-water lake north of Fairmount that bred disease.[11] By the late 1840s, factories, railroads, breweries, warehouses, and icehouses along the river disfigured the landscape and posed serious health dangers by dumping industrial effluents into the river. Rapid and unregulated industrialization and unprecedented growth fueled by increased immigration heightened concerns about living conditions. Recurring epidemics exposed the threats created by overcrowding and inadequate sanitation. Strikes and race riots that erupted in the city during the 1840s heightened concerns about adequate policing.[12]

ASSEMBLING FAIRMOUNT PARK

Calls for stricter policing of the river district coincided with shifts in landscape aesthetics that inspired Philadelphia's park advocates, like their counterparts in other U.S. cities, to envision the development of larger, picturesque green spaces that would mitigate the rigidity of the gridiron.[13] The Schuylkill River had long been a popular recreational site. During the eighteenth century, members of the city's elite escaped the city, spending summers in elegant villas with extensive lawns and formal gardens built atop the bluffs to catch cooling breezes. At the turn of the nineteenth century, the Schuylkill "villa district" was one of the most celebrated scenic areas in the country. As the elite families departed, however, the villas were put to use as taverns and breweries. Residents of the new middle- and working-class neighborhoods of Fairmount and Spring Garden to the east and Powelton, Hestonville, and Mantua on the west bank swam in the river in summer and skated on it in winter. Rowing clubs built boathouses above the dam. Erstwhile lawns and ornamental gardens became ad-hoc picnic grounds and playing fields.

The former estates offered sizable open spaces for development. In 1844 the city purchased the Lemon Hill estate, then being operated as a tavern, to hinder development and increased pollution and to provide the working classes with pure air as well as pure water in a retreat from "the heat and bustle of the town." Because Lemon Hill lay outside the city limits, however, no consistent form of administrative oversight could be implemented. This was corrected in 1854 when the Consolidation Act joined the city to the county, and Philadelphia grew to encompass more than 140 square miles, making it the largest U.S. city in terms of area; it would soon be one of the most densely industrialized as well.[14] Provision for public park areas was stipulated in the Consolidation Act, and in 1855 Lemon Hill was duly rededicated as "Fairmount Park."[15] But obstacles still lay in the path of its development. Many residents and politicians questioned the purchase of suburban land when important public works projects were stalled by the city's limited budget. And how, asked one city council member, could the acquisition of selected riverside properties ensure a clean water supply when factories continued to operate upriver?[16]

Local park advocates were piqued by the successful progress of New York's Central Park, though they took heart that the Manhattan park could not compete with the Schuylkill riverscape. "For inherent pastoral beauty, and sublime surrounding scenery, Fairmount Park is a gem," declared the horticulturist William Saunders, "compared to which the Central Park, of New York, is as a granite boulder." Indeed, the river lent considerable symbolic resonance not available in artificially created spaces. "[The] Schuylkill River presents all the serenity and calm seclusion of a lake, [and] its river existence induces to further and deeper reflection," Saunders asserted, adding, "The poetical mind will trace it to its brooklet source—an infant river—now coursing along smoothly in the open light, refreshing itself by an occasional dip under a shady bank . . . or as it frets and foams down the rocky cataract indistinctly visible through the canopy, until, as it nears the haunts of busy man it expands its proportions and assumes the appearance of placid maturity—a fitting emblem of human progress. So much are the beauties of nature dependent upon association of ideas."[17]

Agitation for the Schuylkill park was fueled by the writings of the landscape architect and theorist Andrew Jackson Downing, who envisioned parks as spaces where nature and culture would combine to "soften and humanize" America's city dwellers, "educate and enlighten the ignorant, and give continual enjoyment to the educated." Statues, monuments, and buildings "commemorative at once of the great men of the nation, of the history of the age and country, and the genius of our highest artists" would embellish forests and greenswards. Zoos and horticultural societies could be housed within the park's precincts, as could museums that, placed in such a setting, would showcase "great expositions of the arts . . . far more fittingly than in the noise and din of the crowded streets of the city."[18] Downing especially admired Lemon Hill, and Philadelphians in turn embraced his idea that "beautiful cottages and country houses" could provide models "to the cause of morality, good order, and the improvement of society." Lemon Hill and the other river villas transformed the park into a significant place of memory.[19] The preservationist dimension of park development was affirmed in 1857 when dozens of citizens jointly raised money to purchase the Sedgeley estate, which adjoined Lemon Hill to the north, in order to enlarge the park. In 1859 the city ran a competition to solicit landscaping designs and selected the plan devised by James C. Sidney and Andrew Adams to unite the two estates.[20]

Citizens' groups lobbied the city to acquire even more land on the west bank of the river, including the former Penn family estates of Lansdowne and the Solitude. Pamphleteers called for a park that would rival the greatest parks of Europe, territories such as London's Hyde Park or the Bois de Boulogne in Paris, which covered hundreds of acres.[21] Fears that the city's budget was inadequate were stilled when Union victory in the Civil War ushered in a period of prosperity. Yet Philadelphians also were reminded that while fresh water from local rivers and streams fueled the postwar economy, these waterways were increasingly polluted. In particular, the Schuylkill, which supplied the city's drinking water, had deteriorated as industrial production increased. Calls for the city to enforce stricter regulations along the river multiplied. As one critic observed, "one of the guiltiest parties to the work of willfully corrupting the stream is the City itself which drinks it."[22]

The Pennsylvania state legislature then passed the Fairmount Park Act of 1867, officially reconfirming the dedication of land on both sides of the Schuylkill to public use. "Purchase of the contemplated tract of ground on the west bank of the river will stimulate and encourage private enterprise in that quarter of the city," noted one newspaper; it added, "Capitalists will commence operations so soon as work is begun upon the Park, and the increased taxation consequent upon the enhanced price of property will make up the amount paid for the property."[23] In an effort to insulate the park from the vagaries of municipal partisan politics, legislators removed its administration from the direct control of city councils by creating the Fairmount Park Commission, to be composed principally of private citizens appointed by the courts.

OPPORTUNISTIC EXPANSION

The founding commissioners were lawyers and businesspeople who regarded public service as a good business strategy. They also assumed that a single large and "central" park would preserve the natural landscape more effectively and be cheaper and safer than many dispersed smaller parks because it would be more easily supervised. Within weeks of their first meeting, the commissioners had ascertained that still more land was needed. Yet again, a private donor appeared, with Jesse George bequeathing the city his substantial farm just west of Lansdowne. Expansion was affirmed in the Supplementary Park Act of 1868, which also incorporated suggestions made by the landscape architects Frederick Law Olmsted and Calvert Vaux, who had recommended adding more land on the west bank. In particular, they had urged the acquisition of Wissahickon Creek, both to provide "unparalleled attractions for pleasure driving" on the shoreline road planned for the east side of the Schuylkill and to broaden the range of landscape types in the park (see fig. 2.3).[24]

As early as 1790, Benjamin Franklin had proposed that Philadelphia draw water from the Wissahickon. In 1854 John Cook, a "gentleman re-

FIGURE 2.3. E. and H. T. Anthony, *Wissahickon Creek: Germantown Bend* (ca. 1870), albumen print (stereoview). Author's collection.

siding near the Wissahickon," and Charles Megarge, who owned a paper mill on the creek, commemorated Franklin's plan within the newly consolidated city by building a public water fountain, ornamented with the inscription "Pro Bono Publico . . . Esto Perpetua" (for the public good . . . may it forever endure) at a spring near the Indian Rock Hotel. Like the Schuylkill, the Wissahickon was an industrial waterway long celebrated for its picturesque scenery. By this date, however, more than fifty mills and tanneries lined its banks, pumping chemicals and detritus into the creek and thence to the Schuylkill.[25] By expropriating the Wissahickon, closing down the mills, and enclosing the Schuylkill watershed for almost six miles, the commissioners revived Franklin's project and expanded the buffer against ongoing pollution.

The 1867 and 1868 park acts granted the commissioners jurisdiction over a rich and diverse territory, ranging from the manicured gardens of the waterworks and Lemon Hill to the rolling meadows of East and West parks and the forested ravines along the Wissahickon. The commissioners hired all park staff (including an independent police force); wrote and enforced rules and regulations; controlled the designation and construction of roads and streets in the park, as well as the licensing of public transit there; supervised all construction; and managed expenditures for improvement and maintenance. By 1870 purchase negotiations with property owners were well underway. New surveys confirmed boundaries and furnished data for maps. Unneeded buildings were demolished or renovated. Recreational activities in park areas were most dramatically affected as fields and riverbanks once relatively unsupervised were now regulated. Swimming in the Schuylkill was prohibited. Rowing clubs, now organized as the "Schuylkill Navy," were permitted to remain, but only if they built permanent boathouses. Croquet was permitted, while baseball and football were discouraged, and park users frequently complained to the commissioners about ballplayers interrupting more sedate activities.[26]

Unlike their counterparts in other cities, who typically followed a landscape architect's design to develop and maintain a specific territory, the Fairmount Park commissioners had no single plan or strategy for managing an ever-expanding collection of roughly contiguous properties in various stages of "improvement." Indeed, many park areas lacked clear boundaries, especially along the Wissahickon, where the forested ravines often obscured boundaries between private and newly public property. In their first annual report, the commissioners identified two approaches to park management. The first preserved the status quo, seeking "to find rather than make pleasing contours" in forests, lawns, and pathways within the existing terrain. The second reconfigured the landscape according to a plan "prescribed according to the well-considered rules of art, without much regard to the original shape of the surface," which had to "be modified so as to conform to the requirements of the ideal creation." The first approach respected established landscapes and was economical; the second might produce a "work of surpassing and rare excellence" but was expensive. The Fairmount Park commissioners embraced the first option. "The diversified character of the grounds, and the abundance of noble trees and groves give us, at many points, a Park made to our hands, replete with objects which form nature's share of its adornment" they reported, noting that most important planned improvements were carriage roads and walking paths "skillfully designed . . . to facilitate the enjoyment of fine views of the Park and the surrounding scenery."[27] And many Philadelphians agreed with this, assuming that the preservationist purpose of Fairmount Park would minimize the need for intrusive landscape management. "It is the amazement of every visitor who is taken there," the author of a city guidebook wrote of the Devil's Pool, in the Wissahickon. "Though but a morning's walk from the city, this barbaric scene is a taste of the primitive wilderness in its rudest expression. A Park containing such a bit of Nature is already full-furnished, and hardly needs the hand of 'improvement.'"[28]

There was lingering resistance. Some residents thought the park system too large and inaccessible for poorer residents who could not afford the new trolley service. Calling the park "a rich man's playground," critics challenged the legality of the commission and derided the park as an impractical and expensive conspiracy of land developers and idle dilettantes to make profits from useless property at the taxpayer's expense.[29] Supporters praised the park's accessibility and orderly informality. The associated regulations benefited park users, avowed one writer, for the commissioners had "thoughtfully sought to furnish to the masses of the people, every facility of access to their property" and had imposed only "such restraints to their enjoyment of it as were necessary to prevent unwarranted license." There were no "Keep Off the Grass" signs, noted another. All classes were welcome. And whereas no respectable woman would enter a European park without a chaperone, female visitors to Fairmount Park were assured that they would not encounter "nuisances" or harassment.[30]

As expropriations proceeded, the process of managing and regulating the park became increasingly complex. In particular, the commissioners had to formulate effective collaborations with new independent organizations and institutions that claimed access to the park, in keeping with Downing's model. These included the Fairmount Park Art Association, a private citizens' group chartered in 1872 to commission public sculptures throughout the city and the park, and the Zoological Society of Philadelphia, granted land for the country's first zoo, which opened in West Park in 1874. At the same time, land purchases ate up appropriations, leaving little money for improvements. In 1873 the commissioners sued the city to approve a million-dollar appropriation for purchases and permanent improvements on the grounds that the 1867 park act "required" the city to "raise by loans, from time to time, such moneys as [would] be necessary" to improve the park. But the suit failed when the presiding judge determined that the language of the legislation gave city councils full authority to determine park appropriations. Rather than devise an alternative revenue mechanism, as in Baltimore, where a percentage of public transportation fares was earmarked for that city's new Druid Hill Park, the commissioners acquiesced. Thenceforth, the optimism of earlier annual reports would diminish as their pleas for increased funding went unanswered.[31]

One reason for the commissioners' failure to challenge the 1873 decision may date back to 1871, when the U.S. Congress had selected Philadelphia to host a world's fair marking the centenary of American independence. It was the logical site: the Declaration of Independence was read at Philadelphia in 1776, the city had hosted the Constitutional Convention in the 1780s, and Philadelphia had served as the federal capital during the 1790s. Reinforcing Philadelphia's suitability were the ample open space in West Park and the historical significance of the many eighteenth-century houses that still stood along the Schuylkill. "Every foot of ground in the park teems with association," announced a guidebook to the event, commonly known as the Centennial Exhibition, adding, "It is no raw creation, laid down in an inert and sleeping suburb, far in advance of a city's march of improvement, and ignorant of a history. Long before we were a nation, this garden was trodden by footsteps that are now historic; its very sods are sensitive; they vibrate to the memories of two hundred years."[32]

The commissioners enthusiastically supported the exhibition— and several raised money for the event as members of the Centennial Board of Finance—because they recognized that it would fund physical infrastructure improvements as well as promote Philadelphia as a world-class city. With money from the city, state, and private sources, as well as the somewhat grudging federal government, the commissioners built sewers, roads, and paths, along with fountains and gardens, to serve an innovative "city" of exhibition pavilions that covered 236 acres in West Park. Here the nation commemorated its history and celebrated its technological progress as American designers and manufacturers tested their products against foreign rivals. Two of the buildings were permanent. Horticultural Hall was a public conservatory, and Memorial Hall housed the art and design collections of the new Pennsylvania Museum and School of Industrial Art. When the exhibition closed, in November 1876, more than ten million people had viewed exhibits ranging from livestock to Japanese porcelain, from Alexander Graham Bell's new telephone to George Washington's uniform.[33]

Once the Centennial Exhibition was over, the commissioners had to return to making do with inadequate appropriations. Their 1878 annual report compared the funding of Philadelphia's parks to that for New York's: from 1872 to 1877 annual appropriations for Fairmount Park (by this date 2,648 acres and growing) averaged $222,000; annual appropriations for Central Park (roughly one-third the size at 862 acres) averaged $790,000.[34] Fatigued by the world's fair, the commissioners would let twenty years pass before they again published a separate report: throughout the 1880s and 1890s, accounts of work on the park were short enough to be incorporated into the city engineer's report.

THE CITY PARKS ASSOCIATION

Financial difficulties and a moribund commission did not discourage park expansion. Indeed, Fairmount Park's incremental origins inspired new strategies for park development in the city. In 1884 lingering concerns that Fairmount Park was "as inaccessible as the forests of the Alleghenies" for many poor Philadelphians prompted city councils to pass an ordinance directing the municipal survey department to prepare plans for new small parks and squares throughout the metropolis. In 1888 local supporters formed the City Parks Association to lobby for the ordinances and appropriations needed to realize this plan and to solicit gifts of money or land. Familiar rhetoric was revived: association members cited the physical and moral benefits of open spaces as well as the need to identify viable areas for development.[35] By 1898 the city had, through gifts and expropriations, acquired twenty-nine of the thirty-nine areas identified for acquisition, ranging from sizable tracts at Bartram's Garden, Stenton, and League Island to smaller areas developed as playgrounds, such as Starr Garden at Lombard and Sixth streets. Among the benefactors inspired by this campaign was Wistar Morris, who in 1891 bequeathed the city a twenty-acre tract on Indian Run that would later be incorporated into Cobbs Creek Park, and Robert Ryerss, who in 1896 similarly bequeathed the city Burholme, his sixty-five-acre estate within the Pennypack watershed, stipulating that it be used as a public park.[36]

The association advocated for a network of outlying watershed parks linked by parkways similar to Boston's Metropolitan Park System that would extend through suburbs and towns within twelve miles of Philadelphia, encompassing "Cobb's Creek, Pennypack Creek, Tacony Creek, [and] Mill Creek in Montgomery County," as well as other locations that would "offer great opportunities" (see fig. 2.4). The authors of a 1901 report expressed confidence that legal barriers could easily be removed in order to create "a superb parkway [that] would . . . follow the Schuylkill [north] to Mill Creek, the latter [northwest] to its headwaters near Rosemont, cross to the headwaters of Cobb's Creek, follow

FIGURE 2.4. F. Von Rapp, *Cobb's Creek* (1901), from *Thirteenth Annual Report of the City Parks Association* (Philadelphia, 1901). Courtesy Van Pelt Library, University of Pennsylvania.

it [south] to the Schuylkill . . . [and] then to Bartram Garden." Another parkway that would link the Valley Forge battlefield to Fairmount Park was, the authors insisted, "no more visionary a scheme than the idea of the Wissahickon Creek Drive must have seemed when the project was first suggested."[37]

Some past and current Fairmount Park commissioners or their relatives sat on the board of the City Parks Association, and during the first decade of the twentieth century, as city government slowed the acquisition of neighborhood parks and playgrounds, the two groups formed an alliance to improve the integrated management of green space throughout the municipality and in particular to acquire acreage along the previously mentioned watersheds. Indeed, it was quite apparent that land acquisitions along the Schuylkill and the Wissahickon had failed to protect the city's water supply. Philadelphia became notorious for the poor quality of its water as typhoid rates mounted alarmingly and citizens campaigned to replace the obsolete Fairmount Water Works.[38] By 1900 more than four hundred acres had been added along the Wissahickon north to Andorra. Beginning in 1904, a series of ordinances condemned what would amount to just under eight hundred acres along Cobbs

Creek, a tributary of the Schuylkill in West Philadelphia, as parkland and the site of a new parkway. Ordinances condemning tracts along the Pennypack (1,254 acres) and Tacony creeks (227 acres), both tributaries of the Delaware in the northeast, were passed beginning in 1905 and 1908, respectively. Once again private individuals primed the pump with land donations, the benefactors including William Sellers, a park commissioner whose family owned the Milbourne mills, which stood on sections of Cobbs Creek acquired for the park after 1900.[39]

The systematic expropriation of such vast areas occurred in large part because by the turn of the twentieth century, men associated with the Republican "machine" that controlled much of Philadelphia's municipal politics dominated the park commission. These powerful individuals included the utility monopolist P. A. B. Widener, the banker Edwin Stotesbury, and the lawyer John Johnson. As Domenic Vitiello has recounted, having supplanting the elite engineer-industrialists who had built Philadelphia's post–Civil War economy, these men used the power of the park commission to target certain industrial sections of the city for redevelopment. Inspired by new approaches to integrated urban planning promoted by the City Beautiful movement and aided by the City Parks Association lobby and other civic associations, the commissioners pushed through major urban renewal projects, most notably a parkway (later named after Benjamin Franklin) modeled after Paris's Champs Élysées that led from the new city hall at Centre Square northwest through Logan Square to East Park. When completed in 1918, this avenue inserted a dramatic diagonal into the repetitive grid of streets, linking the public and private institutions of culture and governance in the center city to the park and ultimately to the new suburban developments in Chestnut Hill and the city's far northeast.[40]

At the same time, by removing hundreds of workers' houses, the parkway project destabilized the industrial area called Bush Hill, the site of factories and ancillary workshops, prompting the Baldwin Locomotive Works, the largest of these, to move out of the city. When the Fairmount Water Works was decommissioned in 1911, the commissioners renewed a plan, first proposed by the founding commissioner Joseph Harrison in 1871, for a public art museum at Fairmount. Long-standing plans to transfer the Pennsylvania Museum collections from Memorial Hall to a larger edifice were revived, and a temple of art was built atop the Fairmount reservoir at the end of the parkway. When opened in 1928, the parkway and relocated Pennsylvania Museum of Art became the new main entrance to the oldest sections of the Fairmount Park system.[41]

THE DEMISE OF THE FAIRMOUNT PARK COMMISSION

In theory, the Fairmount Park Commission was a nonpartisan organization. In fact, it operated as a kind of shadow government, with its
own territories, budget, and police force. Though officially appointed
to five-year terms, many of the financiers, attorneys, and industrialists
who dominated the commission served for life. And like many members
of the governing boards of Philadelphia's philanthropic and cultural
institutions, commissioners often were related by blood or marriage:
it was not unusual for the sons and even grandsons of previous commissioners to win appointment.[42] For many years controversy dogged
ambitious projects, such as the parkway and the museum, both of which
took years to complete, yet the commissioners seemed immune to ac-
cusations of graft and patronage. In particular, no one questioned the
steady rate of sizable land purchases. This situation continued until
the mid-1930s, when the significant cost overruns incurred by the art
museum's construction were made public, at which point the reform
mayor S. Davis Wilson recommended eliminating the commission on
the grounds of malfeasance.[43]

In a 1937 report, a state-level investigative committee determined
that the commissioners focused too much on land acquisition and city
beautification. The committee noted that because many commissioners
failed to attend meetings, important decisions often were made without a quorum. Such practices exacerbated patterns of lax fiscal oversight, which had led the commission to overpay for unnecessary land
purchases, tolerate incompetent staff performance, and accept ques-
tionable policy decisions, some of which ignored or contravened city
ordinances. But the most damning sign of what the committee called
the commissioners' "czaristic" disregard for public welfare was their
failure to develop recreational facilities on a par with those of other
American cities. "With due justice to the Commissioners," the committee noted, "it may be pointed out that they have looked upon the park
very much as a wealthy gentleman might look upon his own vast and
beautiful estate thrown open to certain limited public interests and
enjoyment." Concluding that the part-time voluntary service of the appointed and ex-officio commissioners, none of whom were trained in
parks management, was neither satisfactory nor efficient, the committee recommended that the commission be abolished.[44]

In response, the park commission created a committee on recreation and added some recreational facilities. But there was little more
follow-up. Mayor Wilson died suddenly in 1939, and the outbreak of war

derailed further efforts at reform. While the commissioners may have overpaid for many of the acquisitions questioned by Wilson and other critics, their policies could be viewed as a good-faith effort to assemble the system of outlying parks first envisioned by earlier city ordinances. Indeed, demands for improved recreational facilities could as easily have been directed to the city's Bureau of Recreation, housed within the Philadelphia Department of Public Welfare since 1919, which had jurisdiction over many of the small parks developed during the City Parks Association campaigns.[45] The resiliency (and power) of the park commission, which at this point controlled roughly 10 percent of the city's land, was reflected in Philadelphia's Home Rule Charter of 1951. Under the charter, the Bureau of Recreation was elevated to departmental status, charged with providing "comprehensive and coordinated programs of cultural and physical recreational activities." The charter also stipulated that the Fairmount Park Commission be "placed" in the new recreation department. Nonetheless, it did not promulgate any reporting structure or make any explicit changes to the commission's mandate or authority. According to Robert Crawford, the first commissioner of recreation under the new system, the department would work "jointly" with the park commission to determine recreational sites within parks managed by the commission. In truth, Philadelphia's parks and recreational areas now were governed by two parallel organizations.[46] And as Philadelphia's industrial economy declined, the adversarial relationship between city government and the Fairmount Park Commission intensified.

Even as park appropriations waned, the commission held fast to its mandate of protecting existing parks from private development and conserving watersheds through a system of linked parks. During the early 1960s, it managed to defeat both the Philadelphia Industrial Development Corporation's attempt to build an industrial facility in Fernhill Park and a plan to convert East River Drive (now Kelly Drive) to a limited-access highway. In the early 1970s, the commission finally acquired sections of the Poquessing (122.76 acres) to protect this Delaware tributary. More recently, the cancellation of long-standing proposals to build the Pulaski Expressway (to be designated PA 90) prevented incursions into the Tacony and Pennypack watersheds.[47]

But threats to the territories and waterways that constitute Philadelphia's incomparable "circulatory system" have mounted. As early as the late 1940s, the commissioners were unable to prevent construction of the Schuylkill Expressway through West Park. The most effective threat was fiscal. By the 1970s the departure of many industries had diminished the city's tax base, and maintenance of the park system strained already parsimonious appropriations. In 1960 appropriations directed to the Fairmount Park Commission made up 2.26 percent of city's general fund operating budget. Early in the 1970s the Park Guard was abolished and absorbed into the municipal police force. By 1980 appropriations had declined to 0.71 percent, forcing the commissioners to make deep cuts in staffing and park operations. In the fiscal year 2009, the appropriation amounted to only 0.32 percent of the city's operating budget.[48] Now severely understaffed and underfunded, the commissioners were increasingly unable to mount a united front against pressures from city councils. Strategic plans were commissioned and then shelved. The park system's greatest strength—its size and diversity— became a weakness as the many individual parks and their advocates competed for dwindling resources. The criticisms of the commission first enumerated in the 1930s resurfaced, including the perceived lack transparency in commission appointments and policy-making decisions, the insufficient expertise among the commissioners in park management, and the ambiguous administrative relationship with the (also chronically underfunded) Department of Recreation. In 2006 Robert N. C. Nix III, president of the commission, came out in favor of abolishing the body to give the city government a greater sense of ownership of Philadelphia's unique park system.[49]

The diminishing effectiveness of the commission as the steward of Philadelphia's parks was most clearly demonstrated in 2007 when the city council approved an Institutional Development District (IDD) granting the Fox Chase Cancer Center a long-term lease on just over nineteen acres to expand its campus into Burholme Park, the sixty-five-acre estate donated by Robert Ryerss and his heirs. A minority of commissioners opposed the lease as finally negotiated.[50] The incursion was prevented when, in the fall of 2008, Judge John W. Herron of the Orphans' Court determined that any lease of parkland to a private, commercial entity for nonrecreational use abrogated the terms of the public trust doctrine. In his decision, Herron emphasized that financial duress could not justify the proposal: "One hundred years of decisional law simply does not recognize such pressures as a raison d'être for eviscerating our heritage to future generations and our need for recreational space for our inner city youth and adult population, many of whom have chosen to live, work and invest in the City, in part, because of the rich environment offered by our public park lands and open spaces." Significantly, however, the judge did not address environmental issues, despite testimony that the development would harm the Pennypack watershed.[51]

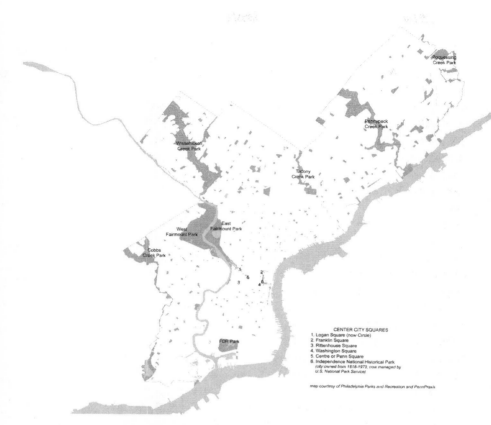

FIGURE 2.5. Philadelphia's Fairmount Park System, with major watershed parks identified (2011). Courtesy of Philadelphia Parks and Recreation and PennPraxis.

The Fox Chase Cancer Center immediately appealed, but in December 2009 the Commonwealth Court upheld the lower court's decision, reiterating that the municipal government has a duty to hold the property "in trust for its originally intended use as parkland." The court further noted that the park was still being actively used by the public, calling it "popular and important," and cautioned that donated parks in the commonwealth should not be leased or sold by municipalities trying to balance budgets.[52]

Throughout the Fairmount Park Commission's existence, most of its members endeavored to fulfill the founding mandate to provide adequate green space and to protect Philadelphia's water supply. The commission's systematic acquisition of major watersheds has ensured the preservation and protection of these fragile ecosystems. But the commission also fostered a climate of passive indifference among many citizens who assumed the city's parks were adequately maintained and protected by well-intentioned yet insulated stewards who were unaccountable to voters. Notwithstanding the commission's efforts over many decades, a map of the current Fairmount Park system reveals that Philadelphia is *less* green than are many other U.S. cities (see fig. 2.5). Today, more than two hundred thousand Philadelphians live farther than a ten-minute walk from any public green space.[53]

Philadelphians voted to abolish the Fairmount Park Commission in the hope that the city's incomparable green spaces and historic sites could be administered with greater transparency and accountability. But structural weaknesses still nag Philadelphia's parks administration. It remains to be seen whether the commissioner of parks and recreation, who is a mayoral appointee, or the Commission on Parks and Recreation, an advisory body whose members are recruited by the city council, will be willing or able to protect public parks from the kinds of economic and political pressures that were exerted during the Burholme controversy. The mandate of the new parks commission is to draft and implement policies and standards governing the use of Philadelphia's park and recreational land and facilities. It is also tasked with "making recommendations to enhance revenue opportunities" with a view toward reestablishing Philadelphia as a leader in parks and recreational administration so as to "sustain the legacy of William Penn's 'greene, countrie town.'"[54] Yet city government has seemed unwilling or unable to devise a dedicated funding stream that could alleviate the park's reliance on the politically charged appropriations process. Politicians enthuse about greening Philadelphia by planting more trees and preserving more open land, yet funding for maintenance, for cleaning and repairs of existing landscapes and structures, has remained woefully inadequate. In their efforts to sustain William Penn's legacy, the present and future members of PaRC must remember that they also have inherited the perplexing legacy of the Fairmount Park Commission.

Thomas Apel

3 | The Rise and Fall of Yellow Fever in Philadelphia, 1793–1805

FROM 1793 TO 1805, PHILADELPHIA hosted six epidemics of yellow fever, killing about 10,000 people in all. As the fever ravaged the city, the
question of its origins dominated informed medical inquiry. Where did
Philadelphia's yellow fever outbreaks originate, and why did the disease suddenly begin to afflict the coastal city? Two centuries later, and
still no one has yet offered precise answers to these questions. Hap-
pily, the modern scholar has something that late eighteenth- and early
nineteenth-century physicians and researchers lacked: an accurate
knowledge of the malady's etiology. Yellow fever is a mosquito-borne
disease, so it requires a certain combination of specific environmental
conditions to appear, the most important of them in this context being
a fresh supply of *Aedes aegypti* mosquitoes each epidemic year, for this
vector species cannot survive Philadelphia's winters. To determine the
causes of the yellow fever epidemics, then, we must view Philadelphia
both as an environment that satisfied the biological necessities of the
vector and as an important commercial and cultural center whose inhabitants maintained extensive contacts with areas where yellow fever

has been endemic. This method of investigation promises not only to reveal the origins of yellow fever in Philadelphia during the 1790s but also to answer a far more interesting question: why did yellow fever suddenly disappear after the epidemic of 1805?

Historians have devoted much attention to social and cultural consequences of the yellow fever epidemics, especially the great epidemic of 1793, but have not focused on the environmental aspects.[1] A few works have considered the urban conditions of Philadelphia that allowed various diseases, including yellow fever, to prosper, but no one has provided a comprehensive explanation for the rise and fall of yellow fever in the city from 1793 to 1805.[2] Scholars who have attempted to explain the advent of yellow fever have generally blamed the Domingan refugees who arrived in Philadelphia in the summer of 1793 fleeing the Haitian Revolution. While this influx of refugees may explain yellow fever's appearance in 1793, it fails to explain later epidemics in years when such refugees did not enter Philadelphia in significant numbers.[3] Nevertheless, Saint-Domingue did contribute to the outbreak of yellow fever, but in a more indirect way. According to David Geggus, who has studied Britain's role in the Haitian Revolution, the introduction of thousands of nonimmune British soldiers into Saint-Domingue in late 1792 and 1793 produced a violent upsurge in yellow fever, which had lain dormant for the preceding two decades. This "pandemic" spread throughout the West Indies and even up to Philadelphia via thousands of refugees.[4] Although Geggus does not pursue the connection between the introduction of British troops and the rise of yellow fever in Philadelphia later in the 1790s, he does illuminate the essential pattern that would repeat itself during the yellow fever years; without exception, yellow fever appeared in Philadelphia only when it was present in epidemic form in the West Indies. Furthermore, the appearance of epidemic yellow fever in the West Indies usually corresponded to the infusion of new troops into the region.

In this chapter I explain the rise and fall of yellow fever in early national Philadelphia. To do so, I reconstruct the urban environmental conditions in Philadelphia in the late eighteenth and early nineteenth centuries, noting why yellow fever struck so severely in 1793 and 1798. Building on works by scholars of the Caribbean, I synchronize the yellow fever epidemics in Philadelphia with the events in Saint-Domingue and elsewhere in the West Indies, highlighting the true source of each occurrence. I also address the most vexing problem in the historiography of the subject by explaining why the disease disappeared from Philadelphia. Unlike the rise of yellow fever, its fall had little to do with the West Indies. Indeed, in the years following 1805, yellow fever epidemics continued to rage in regions where Philadelphian merchants traded. Despite the presence of the necessary epidemiological ingredients, however, outbreaks failed to occur in their own city. In fact, even before yellow fever completely disappeared from Philadelphia, the severity of the epidemics there had declined markedly. Something important had changed. For one, growing numbers of Philadelphians had acquired immunity to the disease by contracting it and surviving. More important, public health developments in the city interfered with the vector's ability to transfer the virus. Quarantine measures isolated victims, making it more difficult for the *Aedes aegypti* mosquitoes to travel between an infected person and a healthy one, and various sanitation projects had the unanticipated effects of destroying the species' breeding grounds.

ETIOLOGY OF YELLOW FEVER

Yellow fever is caused by a virus that originated in Central Africa about 3,000 years ago.[5] It is known as an arbovirus, meaning that it is transmitted to humans via arthropods, usually mosquitoes but also ticks. In its jungle, or sylvan cycle, the yellow fever virus is exchanged between monkeys and mosquitoes. In this process, an infected mosquito feeds on a monkey, transferring the virus. If another mosquito should happen to feed on that same monkey, the virus can enter the second mosquito, which can then spread it further. Often, however, humans interfere in this cycle and contract yellow fever. When this happens, the infected human can start a new process, the urban cycle, in which the yellow fever virus sustains itself between a susceptible human population and female *Aedes aegypti* mosquitoes.[6] This is what happened in Philadelphia from 1793 to 1805.

Once it has entered a human host, the yellow fever virus affects its victims in two distinct stages. In the first, victims run high fevers and experience generalized pain throughout their bodies, as well as headaches, chills, nausea, and vomiting. After three or four days, these symptoms will disappear. For the lucky ones, about 75–85 percent of yellow fever victims, the symptoms will never return. For the other 15–25 percent, the symptoms will reappear after a day's remission. In this second stage, the fever takes on its lethal form. Victims begin to exhibit the telltale signs of yellow fever: a deep jaundice, fever, and delirium. Internal hemorrhage often occurs, and the victims are frequently observed to vomit up partially digested blood, the infamous "black vomit." Some patients have been known to bleed from their ears, noses, and eyes as well. Some 20–50 percent of victims in this second stage will die. Death usually results from hemorrhaging in the stomach and intestinal tract or failure of the kidneys or liver.[7]

The yellow fever vector, the *Aedes aegypti* mosquito, undoubtedly originated in Africa, whence it was accidentally exported by slave traders sometime in the sixteenth or seventeenth century. The species would never have been able to settle permanently in most regions of North America, including Philadelphia, where winter temperatures frequently drop below its minimum threshold of 6°C (42.8°F).[8] It could have found a home in the West Indies, however, where seasonal temperatures remain sufficiently high throughout the year. It may have been sugar merchants who carried *A. aegypti*, along with the yellow fever virus, to the United States during some summers. This would have been easy for a species as well adapted to urban environments as *A. aegypti* is. This particular species prefers to breed in small pools of water, such as those found in the bilges of ships or on the quays of most port cities. The creature especially thrives in artificial containers, such as rain barrels, pots, horse troughs, and just about anything else that collects water.[9] One theory holds that it found a niche in the West Indies partly as a result of the sugar industry, which supplied all the mosquito's necessities: copious amounts of artificial containers for breeding, sugary water, and susceptible Europeans.[10] *Aedes aegypti* also possesses the advantage of having hardy eggs. Though they require water to hatch, its eggs can live in dry environments for many weeks without adverse effects.[11]

YELLOW FEVER IN NORTH AMERICA

Yellow fever had struck North America's British colonies several times prior to the great epidemic of 1793, but never before with such devastating effect. The first reported appearance of the disease in the colonies dates back to 1693, when it simultaneously affected Boston, Philadelphia, and Charleston. In 1702 yellow fever caused its first major panic when it hit New York, killing as many as 570 people. The epidemic grew so frightening, in fact, that members of the colony's General Assembly decided to leave the city and convene in Jamaica, Queen's County.[12] Charleston bore the brunt of the malady's impact in the mid-eighteenth century, experiencing noteworthy visitations in 1732, 1739, 1745, and 1748.[13] These were rare occurrences, however. During most of the eighteenth century, its appearances were sporadic and comparatively mild in North America.

When yellow fever began to afflict Philadelphia in the summer of 1793, it came as quite a shock. The first signs appeared in the middle of

August on Water Street, where a number of victims began to display its dreadful symptoms. By the end of the month, the virus had spread both rapidly and widely, sending the entire city into a panic. In response, most of the citizens who were able to do so left the city. In all, about 20,000 people, roughly 40 percent of Philadelphia's population, fled.[14] By August 25 the situation had deteriorated to the point that Dr. Benjamin Rush—the most respected physician in the United States at that time— could mournfully write that yellow fever "mocks in most instances the power of medicine."[15] The fever would continue to rage into November, by which time it had killed well over 4,000 people, and possibly as many as 5,000.[16]

After the 1793 epidemic, yellow fever failed to strike Philadelphia for three consecutive years. By late July and early August of 1797, however, it once again began to creep its way into the city, and even though thousands of citizens again fled the city, 988 Philadelphians had died by the outbreak's end.[17] Yellow fever came back to Philadelphia in the summer of 1798, an event that became the nation's second most deadly epidemic to that point, killing an estimated 3,645 people.[18] After another occurrence, in 1799, which resulted in the deaths of 720 people, yellow fever epidemics in Philadelphia never again reached similar levels of mortality.[19] In 1802 and 1805 yellow fever killed about 300 people each year, but after that it did not return again until 1820, which marked its last appearance in the city.[20]

THE RISE OF YELLOW FEVER: POPULATION, CLIMATE, AND IMMUNITY

From an epidemiological standpoint, invading pathogens require a concurrence of circumstances to render them epidemic. Since yellow fever is spread by a mosquito, one of the essential factors is a large population of mosquitoes, especially ones carrying the virus. Yellow fever epidemics also require a large population of nonimmune human hosts and a high population density. Ultimately, the virus cannot survive unless spread from mosquito to mosquito. Humans are merely brief intermediaries in this cycle; they are infectious for only about three to six days, during which time a mosquito must bite them to acquire the virus.[21] A larger population thus increases the chances that a mosquito will contract the virus by biting an infected human and then spread the disease by biting an uninfected one. To be epidemic, the yellow fever virus must proliferate in this precarious cycle of transmission.

By the 1790s Philadelphia, then the nation's largest and most prominent city, possessed both a large population and high population densi-

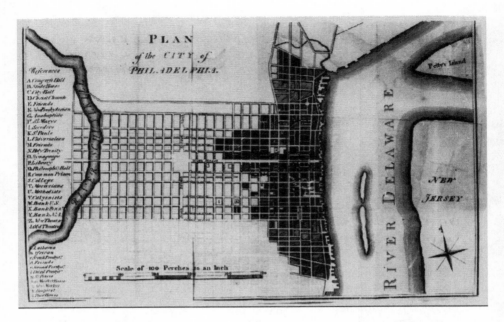

FIGURE 3.1. Map of Philadelphia in 1794, from James Hardie, *A Short Account of the City of Philadelphia* (Philadelphia: Jacob Johnson, 1794), 1.

ty. According to the U.S. census, Philadelphia had a population of 44,096 in 1790. Despite the thousands of deaths that had occurred as a result of yellow fever, by 1800 this number had grown to 67,811.[22] Given that hundreds, if not thousands, of people were visiting Philadelphia during its summers, it could have had a population well over 50,000 before each of its major epidemics. Moreover, the city's residents lived in densely settled areas. In a sense, late eighteenth-century Philadelphia was outgrowing itself. Rapid population growth in the preceding decades—from 26,789 in 1770 to 44,096 in 1790—had not been matched by an expanding city center. As a result, Philadelphia's inhabitants lived in crowded conditions, stuffed into the houses that clustered in the east side of the city along Water Street, near the Delaware River (see fig. 3.1).[23] This arrangement guaranteed that most Philadelphians were easily within the 1,000-meter maximum flying range of the *Aedes aegypti* mosquitoes, which would have lodged along the quays when they arrived.[24]

The demographic situation certainly meant that Philadelphia was susceptible to yellow fever epidemics, but the virus killed more people during the 1790s, especially 1793, than modern statistics on the illness's mortality would have projected. The previously provided numbers, which reflect the most up-to-date information on yellow fever, indicate that on average only 25 percent of people who contract yellow fever progress to the second stage and that only 50 percent of that group die.[25] If these generous estimates hold true, the 4,000 to 5,000 deaths that occurred would have required between 32,000 and 40,000 infected persons.[26] We know that upward of 20,000 people left the city during the early stages of the epidemic, leaving roughly 35,000 people behind, meaning that nearly all of them would have had to contract yellow fever. Clearly, this was not the case.

There are at least four separate possibilities that can explain the heightened mortality rates in Philadelphia in 1793 and perhaps 1798 as well. First, the particular strain of yellow fever that struck Philadelphia could have been more virulent than are many of the strains that modern observers study, just as influenza varies in infectiousness and severity from year to year. Second, Philadelphians had poor dietary habits: they ate a lot of meat, they drank a lot of alcohol, and they did not eat many vegetables. Thus, while they probably had enough proteins, sugars, and starches, they did not consume enough vitamins to build healthy immune systems.[27] Third, medical treatments for yellow fever may have harmed patients more than they helped. Many physicians, for example, practiced bloodletting. Benjamin Rush, an inveterate supporter of this type of treatment, would drain his patients two or three times a day, taking as much as a pint in each evacuation.[28]

Finally, modern studies may have introduced sampling bias into the calculations because they reveal only the standard mortality rates for populations in Africa and South America, where yellow fever has long been endemic. It is likely, for example, that some Africans have attained partial genetic immunity to yellow fever through centuries or even millennia of exposure to it.[29] According to this view, yellow fever would not affect Africans as severely as it would some others. Europeans, however, never had the chance to gain either genetic or acquired immunity, rendering their immune systems less capable of recognizing and coping with the disease. Therefore, their mortality rates would be much higher. This hypothesis runs into some problems, however, when we consider that yellow fever has affected South America for only about three hundred years. South Americans could have attained genetic immunity, though only if yellow fever had exerted a tremendous selective pressure on the populations (perhaps on par with that of bubonic plague in Europe). But genetic change may have occurred in other ways. Yellow fever affected certain South American regions where lots of slaves lived, so that African genes and their immunities may have moved into the larger gene pools there.

Evidence from Philadelphia's yellow fever years strengthens the thesis of black immunity. Contemporary Philadelphians almost universally noticed that yellow fever affected blacks less severely than whites. During the early stages of the 1793 epidemic, Benjamin Rush even encouraged the members of the black community to volunteer at the city hospital, believing that they were completely resistant to yellow fever. He later backed away from this claim when he noticed that many black people did in fact die, but he nevertheless always maintained that blacks were more resistant than whites.[30] Likewise, in his study of the 1793 epidemic, the physician Isaac Cathrall remarked, "Blacks of every description . . . were less liable to it [yellow fever] than the white inhabitants; and the negroes originally from the coast of Africa were scarcely ever affected."[31]

This superior resistance of blacks, however, does not necessarily indicate that they possessed genetic immunity, for they may have acquired immunity by contracting yellow fever and surviving. The blacks from the coast of Africa to whom Cathrall alluded may have resisted it better because they had caught the illness in Africa, but if they had been born in the United States rather than in Africa or any other region where the virus was endemic, then only genetic immunity can explain their higher resistance. In this case, the fact that Cathrall described them as "negroes *originally* from the coast of Africa," not simply as the "negroes from the coast of Africa," contains additional significance. His use of the word *originally* may imply that they were at least second-generation African Americans. William Currie gives further evidence on this point. In his treatise on the 1793 epidemic, Currie wrote, "The negroes that were native to America were also liable to it, though not in the same proportion as the whites."[32] If true, this statement lends credence to the notion that some Africans possess genetic immunity, because even the Africans born in the United States seemed able to resist yellow fever better than whites could.

This discussion of immunity sheds valuable light on the severity of the yellow fever epidemics in Philadelphia in the 1790s. Without genetic or acquired resistance, the European inhabitants of Philadelphia, who composed the vast majority of the population, were bound to suffer heavily. Indeed, only about two thousand black people lived in Philadelphia at the beginning of the 1790s. By the end of the decade, this number had grown to about 6,500, as slaves and free blacks flocked to the city known for its abolitionism and tolerance.[33] The rest of the 50,000-plus population possessed no innate or acquired immunity to yellow fever during the first epidemic. The number of immune Philadelphians would have grown by the time that the second, third, and fourth epidemics came around, because many people acquired immunity to the virus by contracting it and surviving. The influx of newcomers, however, partially compensated for the growing number of Philadelphians who possessed immunity.

While the population of Philadelphia sustained the yellow fever virus, the city's geographic position enabled the yellow fever vector, the *Aedes aegypti* mosquito, to thrive. Philadelphia's summers are usually hot and humid, making it the perfect environment for this species, which prefers to feed in hot weather. In fact, the yellow fever mosquito is an incredibly finicky animal. It is reluctant to feed when the temperature is between 16°C and 25°C (61–77°F) and will not feed at all if the temperature is below 16°C. It prefers to feed when the temperature is between 26°C and 35°C (77–95°F). Observers have further noticed that the mosquito is most active when the temperature is 28°C with humidity. Temperatures over 40°C (105°F) can kill the mosquito.[34] During the 1790s, the daily temperatures in the summer and early fall in Philadelphia tended to hover between the low 70s and the low 90s Fahrenheit.[35] These temperatures, combined with humidity, made Philadelphia a perfect home for *A. aegypti,* at least during the summer and early fall. This partly explains why the yellow fever epidemics occupied the months of August, September, and October.[36]

Contemporary Philadelphians always noticed that mosquitoes were unusually active in epidemic years, though they never connected the two causally. In the summer of 1793, an anonymous contributor to *Dunlap's American Daily Advertiser,* a Philadelphia newspaper, wrote, "Whoever will take the trouble to examine their rain-water tubs, will find millions of mosquitoes fishing about the water with great agility, in a state not quite prepared to emerge and fly off." The same author then proceeded to explain how to kill these "troublesome" insects.[37] During the 1793 epidemic, Benjamin Rush remarked that some of his patients had itchy red spots on their skin that "resembled moscheto bumps."[38] In an 1804 essay, the physician Phineas Jenks noted that "musquitoes, cockroaches, ants were observed to be uncommonly numerous previous to the appearance of yellow fever in 1797."[39] Thomas Condie also noticed that "many tribes of insects," including mosquitoes, prevailed before the 1798 epidemic.[40] These were isolated observations, however. Medical practitioners in the eighteenth century had not yet begun to consider the notion that insects spread disease.[41]

THE WEST INDIAN ORIGIN OF YELLOW FEVER

Of course, it is not enough that Philadelphia's environment was capable of hosting *A. aegypti*. For yellow fever to break out, Philadelphians had to import both the virus and the mosquito each epidemic year. Where, then, did the virus and the vector originate? Only by carefully considering Philadelphia's connections to, and involvements with, the places and events in the Atlantic world, particularly those areas where yellow fever existed in endemic form, can we accurately locate the sources of its yellow fever epidemics. The appearance of yellow fever in any given year depended on two factors: a supply of people who could carry the virus and the insect vector to Philadelphia and, more important, their interactions with regions that were already experiencing yellow fever epidemics. This latter point proved crucial, for the presence of yellow fever epidemics elsewhere made it much easier for potential carriers to contract the virus and then unwittingly transport *A. aegypti* to Philadelphia. During Philadelphia's epidemic years, events in Saint-Domingue provided both necessities.

Scholars have long implicated the refugees from Saint-Domingue in the rise of yellow fever in Philadelphia. Even contemporary Philadelphians blamed the hundreds of French-speaking people who entered the city in the summer of 1793.[42] They were probably correct. As the violence escalated in Saint-Domingue, the first wave of about four hundred refugees fled the colony, trickling into Philadelphia in May and June 1793. The numbers grew throughout the summer and into fall, as 502 whites and 204 blacks entered in July and another 682 whites and 193 blacks debarked in August and September. In all, more than two thousand black and white Domingans arrived in Philadelphia in 1793.[43] The steady flow of refugees ensured a constant supply of virus carriers, and this, more than any other single factor, probably accounts for the high mortality totals during that year.

Nevertheless, while the arrival of refugees satisfactorily explains the appearance of yellow fever in 1793, it fails to account for the epidemics in 1797, 1798, 1799, 1802, and 1805. With the exception of 1798, when eight vessels carrying 343 British evacuees from Saint-Domingue docked in city's harbor, the other epidemic years saw no large group of people entering Philadelphia directly from that colony.[44] Without a yearly supply of Domingan refugees, the virus and mosquito must have come from another source—the merchants who maintained extensive commercial contacts in the West Indian Islands, whose sultry conditions sustained many tropical diseases, including yellow fever. The short transit time between the West Indies and Philadelphia—about three weeks—allowed sailors and mosquitoes to share the yellow fever virus until both arrived in the city.

The 1780s and 1790s witnessed a marked expansion of American trade with the West Indies in general and Saint-Domingue in particular. In the years before the American Revolution, Philadelphia sent an average of 262 ships to the West Indies, and it received an average of 244.[45] After the Revolution, when the United States had shed burdensome British restrictions on trade with French, Spanish, and Dutch colonies, the West Indies trade prospered even more.[46] In this period, the merchants from Philadelphia increasingly opted to do their business with the planters and traders in Saint-Domingue, the most populous colony in the West Indies and the leading producer of sugar and coffee. From 1793 to 1798 the number of vessels arriving in Philadelphia from that colony made up anywhere from one-quarter to one-third of all foreign-port arrivals. In 1795, 1796, and 1797, more than two hundred ships entered Philadelphia's harbor from Saint-Domingue each year. Though the amounts declined after 1797, impressive numbers of vessels continued to arrive. In the epidemic years of 1798, 1802, and 1805, 119, 99, and 26 ships arrived in Philadelphia from Saint-Domingue, respectively.[47]

The existence of potential virus carriers alone was meaningless, however; for merchants or sailors to contract yellow fever, they had to enter an area, usually a city, that was already experiencing an epidemic. In the two decades preceding the 1793 epidemic, the conditions in the West Indies were not right for yellow fever epidemics. After more than a century in the region, the virus had settled into the mostly black populations in endemic form. The slave revolt in the French colony of Saint-Domingue and the subsequent introduction of European troops shattered this stasis. The sudden appearance of tens of thousands of nonimmune soldiers, combined with their movements from port to port, created disastrous epidemiological conditions. The hungry *A. aegypti* mosquitoes found a bounty of sources for their blood meals and in the process of feeding transferred the yellow fever virus from person to person. Once created, the epidemiological cycle proved nearly impossible to break, for soldiers lived, slept, marched, and fought in close quarters, making it easy for the mosquitoes to sustain the virus in their midst. Without the respite of the winter frosts, only time could sever yellow fever's hold on the European armies—enough people had to die or acquire immunity for an epidemic to end. As hundreds of Philadelphian merchants traded in these epidemic zones, potential virus carriers inevitably became actual carriers.

From 1793 to 1802 the incidences of yellow fever in Philadelphia reflected its activities in Saint-Domingue. The arrival of six thousand nonimmune French soldiers in Saint-Domingue in late 1792 sparked an epidemic in the colony that persisted through the next year, spreading to neighboring islands and to Philadelphia through the movements of troops, merchants, and refugees.[48] In addition to feasting on this infusion of nonimmune soldiers, *A. aegypti* undoubtedly benefited from the hotter, wetter conditions created by the major El Niño of 1793.[49] Yellow fever persisted in Saint-Domingue over the next three years, but without the major infusion of new troops, as in 1793, it failed to spread elsewhere. The summer of 1796 brought some twelve thousand fresh British soldiers to the West Indies. The resulting epidemic reached Philadelphia the following summer and then reappeared in 1798, when the British hastily abandoned the war with the rebel slaves, sending many infected soldiers to ports all over the Atlantic. Though some fighting continued elsewhere in the Caribbean, especially on Guadeloupe, the activity of yellow fever waned in 1799 because of a lack of new nonimmunes and a decline in trade. The sudden invasion of thousands of French soldiers under Charles Leclerc in the early months of 1802 offered virus-carrying *A. aegypti* mosquitoes plenty of vulnerable targets.[50] Not surprisingly, yellow fever erupted in Philadelphia in 1802.

By 1805 Europeans had abandoned the hope of successfully reasserting control over Saint-Domingue, leaving the Haitians in control of their own nation. Trade between the United States and the newly named Haiti suffered as a result of disruptions to the plantation complex combined with the federal government's unwillingness to recognize the legitimacy of an independent black state. Under the administration of the Francophile and slaveholder Thomas Jefferson, the United States gradually moved away from official relations with Haiti. Fearing that the example of a black revolution might promote slave revolts in the South, as it did for Gabriel's Rebellion in 1800, Jefferson pressured Congress to pass laws that interfered with the Haitian trade. Congress went so far as to pass a law that banned all trade with Haiti in 1805. Despite the relegalization of trade in 1810, commerce between the United States and Haiti never recovered.[51]

Unable to get their sugar and coffee from Haiti, the merchants of Philadelphia turned increasingly to the Spanish West Indies, especially Cuba. From 1792 to 1817, the population of Cuba doubled as planters and slaves poured into the island to fuel its nascent sugar industry.[52] Cubans began exporting sugar to the United States in unprecedented amounts. In 1806, the year after the American embargo on the Haitian trade, Cuba easily surpassed Haiti as the leading supplier of sugar to the United States.[53] The sources of yellow fever outbreaks similarly shifted to Cuba, where thousands of nonimmune newcomers created the appropriate epidemiological circumstances. Cuba hosted major epidemics in 1805, 1807, and 1811, and yellow fever continued to affect other islands in the West Indies and the United States.[54] With the city's extensive commercial connections to Cuba and other places with yellow fever, Philadelphians should have imported the virus and its mosquito vector after 1805, just as they had done previously. Why, then, did yellow fever fail to impact Philadelphia after 1805? Furthermore, why had the epidemics precipitously decreased in severity after 1799?

PUBLIC HEALTH AND THE FALL OF YELLOW FEVER

While the end of the Haitian Revolution may have reduced the likelihood of importing yellow fever, public health developments in Philadelphia played the decisive role. When the disease first struck in 1793, Philadelphia's public health apparatus was small and inadequate. The city's entire public health schema consisted of two positions: the health officer of the port, then Nathaniel Falconer, and the port physician, then James Hutchinson. The Commonwealth of Pennsylvania had enacted a series of health laws that, among other things, detailed the process by which the health officer should detain ships in quarantine. The laws also called for the creation of a quarantine station on Province Island, in the Delaware River. By 1793, however, these public health institutions were in poor shape; the quarantine station suffered from a lack of funding, and the health laws actually constrained the health officer's authority to detain suspicious incoming vessels.[55]

The Pennsylvania legislature responded to the 1793 epidemic immediately, creating a comprehensive quarantine law that went into effect on September 9. The new quarantine law, entitled "An Act to prevent infectious Diseases being brought into this Province," granted sweeping authority to the health officer and rectified the chronic budget deficiency on Province Island. Under the terms of the new law, the health officer exercised the power "to prevent all such vessels, as he may, for the preservation of the public health, judge necessary, from being brought nearer to the city than Little Mud-Island." The health officer could also board, inspect, and if necessary quarantine any vessel entering the Port of Philadelphia. The new quarantine law also gave the governor of Phila-, delphia, then Thomas Mifflin, the power to "draw a warrant or warrants on the state-treasurer . . . for any sum not exceeding three thousand dollars."[56]

After 1793 the state legislature consistently expanded the powers of the health officer and the scope of Philadelphia's public health laws. New health laws appropriated funds to hire more health officials and to outfit the quarantine hospital with adequate, up-to-date supplies. They empowered the city to employ "pilots" who would monitor the port, making sure that no ship escaped the detection of the public health officials. Laws prescribed harsh penalties for transgressors, and they specified the exact procedures for handling a crisis, such as a ship carrying sick passengers.[57] By the end of the decade, Philadelphia had erected a rigorous quarantine system capable of examining almost every ship that entered its port.

Nonetheless, one may wonder how successfully health officials intercepted sick passengers. The very fact that yellow fever struck Philadelphia in 1797 and 1798, after the quarantine apparatus had developed, seems to suggest that it was not especially effective. In some instances, however, the health inspectors did catch ships infested with yellow fever before they reached Philadelphia. On July 8, 1798, for example, the pilots intercepted a merchant ship, the *Deborah,* most recently from Jérémie in Saint-Domingue. The *Deborah* carried not only a cargo of sugar, cocoa, and coffee but also five sick passengers who had contracted yellow fever. Three of the sailors had already died at sea.[58] After visiting the ship, the health officer ordered that all the sick passengers be transferred to the quarantine hospital, while the remaining passengers, ninety-five in all, were to be left on the ship, at anchor in the Delaware. On July 16 the health officer deemed that the remaining ninety-five passengers were no longer threats, and so he allowed them to enter the city.[59] Even by modern standards, this was a relatively sound reaction. The eight days that elapsed between the arrival of the *Deborah* and the release of the quarantined passengers should have been long enough for the virus to have produced symptoms in one of the ninety-five passengers if any of them were carrying it. Furthermore, by isolating the potential carriers of the yellow fever virus, the health officials would have reduced the ability of any nearby *A. aegypti* mosquitoes to contract and transfer the virus.

Not everyone agreed that quarantine was the most effective means to prevent yellow fever. In fact, a number of physicians—including Benjamin Rush—thought that quarantine was absolutely powerless against it. These physicians supported the medical theory that held disease to result from environmental conditions, such as the composition of the air, noxious effluvia, or putrefying vegetable matter. Adherents to this model of disease transmission (localists) thought that improved sanitation, proper ventilation, and general cleanliness—including the removal of garbage from city streets and the management of the water supplies—were the best ways to prevent yellow fever and disease more generally.[60] This differed sharply from the view of the quarantine supporters (contagionists), who thought that disease results from human-to-human contagion, the "transmission of some morbid material from one individual to another."[61] These theoretical differences bred discord in the American medical community. Contagionists, who thought that Philadelphia imported yellow fever, were inclined to view localist measures as ridiculous, while the localists, who thought that yellow fever was neither contagious nor imported, believed that quarantine was pointless; in their conceptions, the very conditions of the city produced it.

From the beginning, localist physicians actively vied for the recognition of their doctrine. During the 1793 epidemic, for example, Rush urged city officials to remove a pile of "damaged coffee" from one of the wharves because he thought that it was emitting a putrid exhalation that gave rise to the disease.[62] Jean Devèze, a localist physician from Cap François, in Saint-Domingue, made similar recommendations. To prevent the spread of the disease through miasma, he counseled the police to "attend to the cleanliness of the quays and the streets," to prevent water from stagnating, to dispose of putrid fruit and vegetables, and to rid the city of "tan yards and starch manufactories." Interestingly, Devèze also urged the appropriate city officials to erect an aqueduct of sorts to pump water from the Delaware and Schuylkill rivers into the city. Devèze believed that this water system would ensure clean water for the city's inhabitants and consequently reduce the risk of epidemic yellow fever.[63] Subsequent authors would similarly identify the water in Philadelphia as a possible source of yellow fever. In their account of the 1798 epidemic, Condie and Folwell complained about the "noxious effluvia" emanating from a number of pits that had been dug around the city "to receive the water from the gutters, in those parts of the city, where there [was] no natural declivity to carry it off." Though they did not specifically claim that the noxious effluvia from these catchments produced yellow fever, they noted anxiously that the first victims lived in the vicinity.[64]

Unfortunately for the inhabitants of Philadelphia, city and state officials were slow to enact localist measures. They preferred the time-tested methods of quarantine, which had been in place since the founding of the colonies.[65] Had they listened to the localists, public health authorities might have been able to prevent, or at least mitigate, the outbreaks in 1797 and 1798, because clearing stagnant bodies of water would have destroyed A. aegypti's prime breeding grounds. The yellow fever virus can survive only by being transmitted from mosquito to mosquito, so the most effective way to eliminate the virus is to go after the mosquito or the mosquito's habitat. Without the least understanding of vectors or viruses, the localists had found an effective means of preventing yellow fever.

After consecutive epidemics in 1797 and 1798, city leaders realized that the public health system needed change. As a result, the Common Council of Philadelphia formed a committee of political and business elites charged with improving sanitation. The committee members agreed that polluted water was the main problem, and so they focused on creating a water system that would serve the entire city.[66] The committee apparently considered a number of plans before accepting the design of the English architect Benjamin Henry Latrobe, who happened to be in Philadelphia designing the Bank of Pennsylvania building. Latrobe planned on constructing two steam engines that would pump water from the Schuylkill River, delivering it first into a large culvert and then into a series of wooden pipes and street hydrants strategically placed throughout the city. The city would finance the construction and maintenance of the waterworks by charging rent to those whose homes and businesses were connected to the network of pipes. The poor, however, could get their water for free at any of the hydrants in the city.[67] Latrobe began construction in 1799, and by 1801 the Centre Square Water Works was delivering piped water.[68]

Before the completion of the Centre Square Water Works, Philadelphians had obtained water using a variety of traditional means. Some simply took buckets of water from wells and cisterns, while others used the dirty river water. The majority of Philadelphians, however, collected water in rain barrels or else dug holes or trenches in which rainwater would gather.[69] These practices inadvertently created hundreds of breeding spots for A. aegypti. By eliminating the necessity of keeping standing water in people's yards, then, the waterworks also eliminated a potential breeding ground for the mosquito.

In an 1805 diary entry, Elizabeth Drinker specifically correlated the introduction of the waterworks to a decline in the number of mosquitoes: "The Musquitoes are more numerous and troublesome than for some years past, the reason for their absence lately I have imputed to the introduction of the Schuylkill water, which prevents the necessity of keeping rain water standing in the yards as formerly."[70] Drinker was writing during a yellow fever epidemic, which makes sense in the light of her complaint about the number of mosquitoes. In 1805, however, only about three hundred people died.[71] After the completion of the water-works, even an unusually large population of mosquitoes, such as the one that Drinker reported, was not big enough to produce a widespread epidemic on the scale of those in 1793, 1797, 1798, and 1799. The water-works marked an enormous step for Philadelphia's public health system; indeed, it was the most crucial factor in the fall of yellow fever in Philadelphia.[72]

In 1793 Philadelphia possessed all the conditions necessary to host a yellow fever epidemic: it had the largest population of any U.S. city, it had a high population density, and its hot and humid summers allowed the *Aedes aegypti* mosquito to thrive. Furthermore, Philadelphians inadvertently supplied *A. aegypti* with hundreds of breeding grounds by collecting water in rain barrels and other containers. Extensive commercial contact with the rebellious colony of Saint-Domingue, where yellow fever prospered as a result of the influx of nonimmune troops, guaranteed the importation of the virus and vector. In the aftermath of the Haitian Revolution, yellow fever moved to Cuba with the massive influx of people who were hoping to profit from the island's rapidly expanding sugar industry. Despite its constant presence in Cuba, however, the disease never struck Philadelphia after 1805. The fall of yellow fever therefore had much less to do with the events in the Caribbean than it did with reforms in the city; advances in public health hindered *A. aegypti* by inhibiting its ability to transfer the virus from the infected to the healthy and by destroying its breeding grounds, thereby drastically reducing its population.

Before the microbiological breakthroughs of Louis Pasteur and Robert Koch in the 1870s and 1880s, physicians struggled in vain to detect the causes of disease. With logic and intuition as their only weapons, they fought mostly losing battles against crafty microorganisms that had evolved survival strategies through millennia of natural selection. Handicapped as they were, physicians could be both irremediably harmful and remarkably effective. Bleeding, for example, had no therapeutic value and in fact only worsened patients' conditions. The ultimate success of Philadelphia's public health measures, however, suggests that some doctors were on the right track. Though historians usually treat them as quacks and imbeciles, American physicians of the eighteenth and early nineteenth centuries possessed surprisingly sophisticated conceptions of disease. This is not to suggest that they were correct; rather, they had detected plausible ways in which disease can operate. We know, for instance, that miasmas and noxious effluvia do not produce yellow fever, or any other disease, for that matter. But localists were intuitively right to implicate stagnant pools of water in the production of yellow fever. Likewise, humans do not communicate yellow fever directly to one another, as the contagionists believed, but they do communicate it to a mosquito, which in turn communicates it to another human. So in a transitive sense, it does spread from human to human. Contagionists simply left out the insect intermediary.

Ironically, as physicians investigated the origins of the contagion that afflicted their nation's capital city, a far different kind of contagion occupied the minds of slaveholding Americans—the "contagion" of black liberty, which threatened to infect the slaves in the South and inspire a massive insurrection. Conversely, antislavery advocates condemned the slave trade as a "plague" or "contagion" infecting the body politic.[73] Both proslavery and antislavery ideologues used the language of disease to convey their anxieties about slavery. Their metaphors proved more accurate than they could have known, because slavery, freedom, and yellow fever were all intimately related. After all, the yellow fever virus and A. aegypti originated in Africa and then spread to the Americas in the ships of slave traders; the Haitian Revolution—a resounding call for the freedom of the enslaved—prompted the introduction of thousands of nonimmune soldiers into Saint-Domingue, sparking the epidemics of the 1790s and early nineteenth century; and merchants transported the disease to Philadelphia in vessels filled with goods that slaves had produced. Though slavery and freedom were not real contagions, the actions that people took either to preserve or attain these opposing states of being created the disease environment of 1793–1805. Philadelphians not only paid dearly for their precious commodities of sugar, coffee, and cocoa but in a larger sense suffered for their involvement, however indirect, in a system of labor that exploited millions.

PART II | Locating Patterns of Industry and Commerce in the Expanding City

Donna J. Rilling

4 | Bone Boilers

Nineteenth-Century Green Businessmen?

IN 1834 CHARLES CUMMING GRASPED the promise of a nascent industry. By midcentury, his firm had an extensive regional network of suppliers and customers. The Philadelphia city government, too, relied on his services, especially in times of crisis. As profits and markets grew, Cumming invested in additional facilities and expanded production. To shorten the time from raw materials to finished products, he keenly scrutinized the efficiency of communication with his suppliers. Cumming experimented with manufacturing processes, diversified his product line, and found emerging markets for new wares. His operations made money, and he gained a reputation for character, ability, and economy. The success of his Philadelphia enterprise funded expansion into the New York City market, where his son Edward took charge of a branch business.

Charles Cumming was a bone boiler. His manufactories turned dead animals (horses, dogs, and cats) and remnants of slaughtered livestock (beeves, calves, sheep, and pigs) into usable materials. Cumming depicted himself as a recycler of waste and redeemer of materials vital to the nineteenth-century industrial and agricultural economy. His genius kept Philadelphia free of disease caused by the odors of decomposing body parts, he proclaimed, by commanding a network of waste haulers that operated with speed, regularity, and rationality. Constant innovation led Cumming to adopt and rework mechanical and chemical processes to transform refuse. His enterprise converted materials that were "hitherto lost or wasted" into "indispensable articles of Commerce." Such public spiritedness, he asserted, saved municipalities and taxpayers enormous expense in collection and disposal. Moreover, Cumming maintained that he and his fellow renderers were not the only ones to profit from this extraction of value from waste: his enterprise lifted the financial boats of butchers, who thus received bucks for bones; farmers, who bought manure; manufacturers, who procured a steady supply of materials for industrial production; laborers, who held jobs; and city governments, whose tax bases prospered. The bone boiler Cumming cast himself as a forward-looking manufacturer and virtuous public servant at the vanguard of America's new industrial age.[1]

Not all contemporaries viewed Cumming and his peers in this light. Some insisted that these "dealer[s] in grease and garbage" lacked merit as entrepreneurs who seized opportunities created by rapid urban growth and industrial demand.[2] Others denied them to be virtuous public servants, deeming them instead spewers of noisome smells, collectors of putrefying carcasses, magnets of maggots, and tormenters of neighborhoods. They never willingly moved far beyond the slaughter yards, public markets, and city streets where they collected bones, offal, and carcasses. Viewed from this perspective, their very presence in outlying neighborhoods impeded the geographical and social progress of upper-class Philadelphians who hoped to create a romanticized suburban landscape. Board of Health inspections, nuisance charges, and private lawsuits did not always evoke their sense of the commonweal or their ready assent to relocate their foul-smelling reminders of death.

In the following pages I examine the rendering industry in Philadelphia through the experiences of Cumming, one of Philadelphia's largest bone boilers at midcentury and the sole industry voice to emerge from this period, audible thanks to legal complaints against him. In a protracted suit that began in 1851 and ended (or fizzled out) inconclusively around 1854, Cumming defended himself against charges brought by nearby residents who complained that his manufactory was a nuisance. On the defensive, Cumming promoted himself as a modern, progressive, and public-spirited Philadelphian. No doubt his assertions were strategic, but we should not dismiss them. Furthermore, while his motivations and attitudes cannot be ascribed to all renderers, Cumming's fellow tradesmen faced similar challenges and opportunities.

Cumming's story sheds light on three themes in urban environmental history. First, it addresses the topic of solid waste in crowded cities and the imperfect solutions that municipalities implemented. As cities grew in population and area, the challenges of horse manure, human privy soil, slaughterhouse offal, and tannery refuse occupied municipal authorities and residents. Collection often proved inadequate, whether owing to the ambivalence of cities in assuming responsibility, the incompetence or dishonesty of contractors, or simply the monumentality of ever-increasing waste piles. Nonetheless, municipalities persisted in searching for ways to turn waste into profit—for example, by selling manure to farmers and considering a similar use for human privy waste. In the face of mounting volume, expanding populations, fewer convenient (and inexpensive) places for manure yards and poudrette pits, and the relentless mounds of animal carcasses and remnants, officials must have welcomed the prospect that Cumming and other bone boilers could rid Philadelphia of refuse at little or no direct cost to the city government.[3]

Animal rendering contributed to another realm of nuisance, however—namely, foul odors understood to impinge on public health, private comfort, and property values (as Cumming's neighbors protested). Nineteenth-century Philadelphians (as well as Britons and other Europeans) adhered to a long-standing belief that odors signaled disease-carrying "miasmas." Decomposition of bodies and vegetable matter caused these miasmas.[4] Household privies and standing water thus drew the attention of Philadelphia's Board of Health commissioners. Soap boileries, candleworks, slaughterhouses, distilleries, sugar refineries, and other enterprises also operated under threat that they could be indicted for producing "noxious" or "noisome" smells that endangered the public health. Proprietors could see their businesses shut down and their properties and improvements sacrificed if they were forced to relocate. A second theme Cumming's enterprise raises, then, highlights the ongoing struggle to define nuisance in the context of evolving manufacturing processes and new industries. Ideas about disease, shifting municipal regulatory powers, and inconsistent judicial decisions contributed to this challenge. Christine Meisner Rosen suggests that in nuisance cases, nineteenth-century courts treated "traditional" businesses (among them bone boileries) more strictly than new industries (for example, gas and chemical manufactories).[5] While people had been boiling animal parts to harvest fat and bones for centuries, I argue that the rendering business in Cumming's time took on many of the attributes of new manufacturing enterprises. The scope of Cumming's activities in several spheres—harnessing by-products for other manufacturing, developing markets, organizing his business, using chemicals and new mechanical methods, and working with arms of the state to achieve his goals—complicates the static characteristics implied in the term *traditional*. Contemporaries, too, began to distinguish the rendering business as it emerged in the 1840s from the earlier trade of "bone boiling."[6] The Philadelphia court was from the outset clearly sympathetic to the complaints from Cumming's neighbors, supporting Rosen's thesis that such "traditional" activities as rendering were held to a legal standard more stringent than the established dictum against nuisance, "use your own so as not to injure others." But after the initial decision, the court worked with restraint over several years to find compromises and levels of odors and pollution from Cumming's manufactory that might be acceptable to the community, suggesting that the treatment of "traditional" industries is not so easily distinguished from that of new ones.[7]

The archival record in *Smith v. Cumming*, the Philadelphia civil court case against Cumming, also highlights the perspectives gained by examining manuscript court materials. The case record includes the Smiths' complaint; Cumming's responses; testimony from householders, business owners, and workers; and the results of an investigation by an appointed commissioner. Thus the manuscript materials give voice to a far greater range of persons than the published decision of the judges (and, in this instance, continue the case beyond the court's initial proclamation). The rich background of such cases tells a complicated story of motivation, beliefs, compromise, accommodation, and deception.

Cumming's voice, finally, contributes to recent discussions examining "loop-closing" actions on the part of manufacturers, that is, altering production methods to capture residuals (e.g., solid waste, chemicals, and heat) that otherwise would be discarded into the urban waste stream. What motivated manufacturers to adopt techniques to maximize the use or sale of their by-products? Were nineteenth-century animal renderers innovative businessmen who purposely sought manufacturing efficiency and strove to harness by-products to increase profitability? Or were they hopeless pot-boilers who resisted change and instead continued to throw vast quantities into the waste stream until forced to account for pollution by protesting neighbors, health reformers, and government regulators?[8]

Neither extreme fairly characterizes Cumming's actions. When Cumming established his business in 1834, developments that would later support animal rendering on a large scale remained in their early stages. Cumming needed to build organizational networks and find markets for every element—bones, hides, manes, marrow, and so on—that could be extracted from carcasses. His rationale of waste conversion, moreover, highlighted ingenuity, efficiency, and order, all of which were tenets of nineteenth-century American industrial progress. A lawsuit beginning more than fifteen years after the founding of his business later pushed Cumming to even further innovation, but even before community protests and legal complaints surfaced, he was far from a greasy man wedded to sloppy methods and crude processes.

I first describe the animal-rendering trade and explain why it both grew in scale and developed in scope during the second quarter of the 1800s. I then turn to the nuisance case brought by Mary Ann Smith and Virginia Smith and their attempts to stop what they deemed an offensive business. Cumming's responses to the charges and how he articulated his role in waste recovery make up the final section. I highlight Cumming's self-fashioning as a leader in a rationally organized enterprise, a progressive manufacturer espousing up-to-date chemical and mechanical innovations, and finally, a virtuous public servant in the industrial metropolis.

THE CARCASS AND MEAT REFUSE BUSINESS IN PHILADELPHIA

Animal renderers did not broadcast their work skinning and boiling carcasses or collecting, boiling, and grinding bones, though they did advertise the products they sold. Indirect or euphemistic references, while they might have mitigated neighbors' concerns over rotting flesh, mask the techniques and strategies that businesses and municipalities used to discard animal bodies and body parts and how (and why) those methods evolved. Manufactures that utilized some portion of an animal carcass were closely interrelated, moreover, making it difficult to discern specifically which products (e.g., hide whips, glue, fertilizer, neat's-foot oil, or curled hair) tradesmen made. Activities also changed over the lifetime of a business. As a bone boiler, Cumming sometimes processed solely bones; at other times he added whole carcasses and the products he could make from them to his repertoire. He also used gelatinous stock produced in rendering tubs at one location to shape bars of glue in molds at another facility and, depending on the context, answered concurrently to "bone boiler" and "glue manufacturer."

For these reasons, the evolution of urban animal rendering can be only approximated, gleaned from the sparse record of tradesmen, unhappy neighbors, and officials. In eighteenth-century America, many soap makers and tallow chandlers, requiring animal fat to make soap and candles, boiled animal parts (particularly the fat procured from butchers) in cauldrons. Dead cows, dogs, and cats nonetheless ended up in Philadelphia's creeks and contributed to unsightly and smelly waterways. Dead horses similarly showed up in public thoroughfares, though the strain on cities seems to have been eased by the tendency to retire aged or lame horses to farm work.[9] Before carcass rendering, cities also rid themselves of bodies by cutting them up and sending them to farms to be worked into the soil for fertilizer. By the second quarter of the nineteenth century, however, increasingly specialized trades found value in many parts of dead animals and slaughterhouse remnants.[10] When Cumming began glue manufacturing in 1834, he transformed animal sinews, parts of carcasses, and hides and skins from tanners' remnants. By the late 1840s, he was heavily engaged in rendering horse carcasses as well.[11]

The number of horses employed in transportation, hauling, machine operation, and leisure riding rose dramatically in cities in the nineteenth century and was a primary factor in Cumming's success. By 1819 seventy stagecoach lines, offering over one thousand arrivals and departures weekly, linked Philadelphia to nearby towns and distant cities. A dozen years later, omnibuses (horse-drawn coaches that operated on fixed routes and schedules) served neighborhoods within the county. Omnibuses were a boon to affluent Philadelphians, many of whom settled in suburban residential enclaves now within easy reach of the city's commercial district. By 1848 Philadelphia's companies were operating 138 omnibuses on eighteen routes, each omnibus requiring four or more horses. A few years later, the number of omnibuses had increased to 300; the population of horses also rose, even while the breeding of bigger and stronger horses and changes in the design of coaches to reduce weight and drag led to more efficient use of animal power.[12]

Between 1840 and 1850, the national horse population increased by 12 percent, most of which, according to the historian Ann Norton Greene, concentrated in the northern region of the United States. In addition to playing a role in urban transportation, horses hauled loads and cart wagons, powered machines, pulled leisure carriages, and carried leisure and sport riders. Philadelphians, fearing explosions of steam boilers, kept horses to pull railroad cars (decoupled from locomotives) from the outskirts of the city into its urban terminals. Growth in Philadelphia's equine population created opportunities for Cumming, though

TABLE 4.1. Cattle brought into the Philadelphia market

YEAR	BEEVES	COWS	SWINE	SHEEP	TOTAL
1845	51,289	18,805	26,455	56,948	153,506
1846	47,500	14,480	18,670	55,810	136,460
1847	50,270	16,700	22,450	57,800	147,220
1848	67,211	14,108	47,690	76,820	205,829
1849	68,120	14,320	46,700	77,110	206,250
1850	68,750	15,120	46,900	82,500	213,270
1851	69,100	15,400	46,700	83,000	214,200
1852	71,200	14,420	49,200	81,200	216,020
1853	71,900	15,100	53,300	72,300	212,600
1854	73,400	15,350	78,000	61,000	227,750
1855	55,200	11,530	65,300	132,500	264,530
1856	61,978	12,900	103,350	240,700	418,928
1857	62,400	14,700	95,700	342,000	514,800

Source: *Hunt's Merchants' Magazine and Commercial Review* 34 (1856): 380.

dead horses, not ambulatory ones, made his livelihood. Fortunately for him, the stress of hauling, stopping, starting, and clopping on stone or macadam roads, as well as the rapid spread of diseases in crowded stables and careless regimens of feeding and work, produced a rich supply of moribund horses.[13]

Between 1830 and 1850, the number of human residents in urban Philadelphia doubled to more than 360,000.[14] The volume of refuse (residuals) from the meat that the burgeoning population consumed was a second factor in creating opportunity for Cumming. In Cumming's day, Philadelphia's meat trade was a decentralized business with autonomous dealers, among them independent drovers, ad-hoc partners, and commission merchants.[15] Though most of the cattle (beeves, cows, sheep, and pigs) that Philadelphians consumed came from midwestern and southwestern states, traveling to the city by rail or on the hoof, local farmers produced a sizable portion of it.[16] Parties who brought cattle into the city availed themselves of the public drove yards to make small sales to butchers and slaughterhouses, as well as somewhat larger lot sales to speculators and intermediaries. Likely typical of butchers was Jacob Knorr, who purchased animals a few at a time; in an average month, Knorr killed twenty cattle.[17] In 1851 small slaughterhouses still operated throughout Philadelphia's most populous neighborhoods, though some sections of town were known for their concentrations of butchers. Slaughterhouses could not legally retail directly to consumers, who continued to visit Philadelphia's regulated public markets held at locations in urbanized parts of the county.

Data for the cattle trade in Philadelphia show a steady though not continuous rise in animals for sale at the city drove yards (see table 4.1; economic downturns and epizootics contributed to sporadic declines in the trade). These figures only approximate meat consumption in Philadelphia and, by extrapolation, the volume of refuse from slaughtered animals. Cattle not bought in Philadelphia (though, it seems, included in these figures) were transported to New York City and other markets. The figures also do not reflect the "large number brought in by butchers," as well as the meat that was brought in on market wagons from surrounding areas.[18]

The decentralized nature of the meat trade, combined with its small-scale character but rising volume, had ramifications for waste collection and processing in Philadelphia. In collecting bones and offal from slaughterhouses and markets, Cumming needed to send his carters throughout diverse parts of the commercial and industrial sections of Philadelphia. He also circulated them less frequently among the farms on the outskirts of the built city and throughout the county to pick up carcasses of dead horses and cattle.

How did the meat trade relate to refuse problems, and to what extent did Cumming's business ameliorate them? According to a contemporary Philadelphia drover, the average bull weighed around 1,200 pounds in those days and could yield about 720 pounds of beef. It also yielded 10 pounds of tongue; 50 pounds of "green blood"; 95 pounds of "green hide"; 80 pounds of "rough fat"; 50 pounds of head and feet; 100 pounds of entrails, lungs, liver, and heart; and 95 pounds of water, manure, and "waste."[19] Some of the butcher's by-products found ready uses, such as blood for sugar refining, hide for leather, and fat for soap and candle manufacture. But at least a third of a bullock was destined for the bone boiler's kettle. In 1851 beeves brought into the city's cattle market would produce over 13,820 tons of waste; cows, sheep, and pigs would add to the pile. Cumming estimated his daily collection of waste and animal carcasses at ten tons (as did the Smiths, who complained about his business); over the course of the year, his carters would have collected around 3,000 tons of animal parts. That tonnage, however, included the 1,500 horses that he collected, on average five per day.[20] Alone, then, Cumming could not have processed more than a fourth of the waste from the beeves portion of the cattle market, with plenty of bones, fat, and offal left over for others.

Although the national manufacturing census did not capture Cumming's rendering plant, an approximation of the scale of his business can be gleaned from the production at his glue works, which received glutinous stock from the rendering establishment. Cumming was perhaps the third largest among Philadelphia glue manufacturers. In 1850 he claimed to have $60,000 invested in the glue operation, and he employed fifty men. Cumming's manufactory produced items valued at $75,000. Two other firms recorded gross sales twice that amount. If Cumming's glue production is a good indication, he was perhaps third largest among Philadelphia bone boilers, too.[21]

While Cumming enjoyed the benefits of the rise in the horse population and in overall meat consumption, he and fellow renderers also gained from the emergence of industrial processes that needed the materials that bone boilers distilled and from the broadening of a consumer market demanding goods that used materials bone boilers supplied to manufacturers. Lampblack factories, for example, further processed bones from the boilery into a substance used in writing and printing inks (also in shoe blacking), products critical to a nation newly awash in newspapers, novels, and penny press features. Curled hair was another material supplied by boileries (as well as by piggeries and slaughterhouses). Made from the tails and manes of horses, the switches of cattle, and the hair of pigs, which was picked, boiled, baked, and processed to give it twists like coils of springs, curled hair was a "comparatively modern" industry, a commentator wrote in 1871. Animal hair curled in Philadelphia, the center of the industry, stuffed upholstered furnishings in the homes of the nation's new middle class. Carriages, omnibuses, and railroad cars used curled hair in their seat cushions.[22] Hide whip manufacturers, too, converted small strips of hide ("substances that would [otherwise] be worthless") into "products of commercial value." In the opinion of a contemporary, "without consumption in this way," such wastes would have been "troublesome to remove or . . . nuisances to the community." Whip makers also used bone for the stocks (handles) of the whips.[23] Philadelphia captured the industry in the early nineteenth century and remained for some decades "the only place in the world where [raw-hide] whips were made."[24] Likewise, Philadelphia was a leader in the manufacture of umbrellas and parasols, which used turned bones for handles. Bones from the boilery were used alongside ivory and whalebone for surgical and dental instruments, which benefited patients because a shift in women's fashions and the use of whalebone corsets and hoops made whalebone increasingly scarce and expensive.[25]

The rising demand for fertilizers, especially by farms that marketed garden crops to urban consumers, was another critical factor in the growth of the animal-rendering business. Cumming claimed that his fertilizer, made from remnants left at the bottoms of his tubs, was highly revered by market gardeners who grew food for Philadelphia consumers. By 1851 such "artificial manures" were gaining popularity. (Peruvian guano, the fad fertilizer of the 1840s, waned in the face of its expense and questions about its efficacy.) Agricultural periodicals debated the advantages of ground versus calcined (burnt) bone, the best methods for speeding bone's decomposition, and the virtues of super-phosphate fertilizer. "Super-phosphate of Lime" (ground bones, broken down using sulfuric acid mixed with manure or rendering slurry and other ingredients) and "bone-dust" quickly became major industries in Philadelphia.[26]

THE LAWSUIT

In March 1851 two sisters, Mary Ann and Virginia Smith, filed a complaint against Cumming in the Philadelphia Court of Common Pleas. The Smiths were genteel spinsters and major landowners; Kenderton Smith, their father, was aggressively selling building lots to the "better sort" before his death a few months prior to the initiation of the suit.[27] By 1851 the Kenderton area was a growing mecca for upper-class Philadelphians in search of salubrious country air. The sisters and the well-heeled men and women who bought lots and built suburban villas in Kenderton embraced a romanticized ideal of rural living popularized by Andrew Jackson Downing. Downing even designed landscaping for some of the houses in adjacent Germantown, which had grown thanks to recently expanded railroad service connecting it to more urban parts of Philadelphia.[28] Enter Charles Cumming, whose bone boiling and glue making had gained him a reputation as a rich "money making man" able to "buy all he want[ed]."[29] Cumming had just moved to a nine-acre site about a quarter-mile from the Smith mansion, where he began erecting buildings and installing apparatus for a rendering operation. His glue factory remained at Sixth and Master streets, in an increasingly populous section of town, but Cumming had decided to move the carcass- and bone-boiling processes elsewhere. Real estate was scarce and expensive near Sixth and Master, and though he had already defended himself successfully in 1846 against charges that his glue-production facility endangered the public with its foul odors, he likely did not want to chance his luck again. He acquired the lot near Kenderton to expand and diversify his business.[30]

The Smiths, meanwhile, fearing disease, a precipitous drop in property values, and an unpleasant accumulation of putrid flesh and noxious smells, charged that Cumming's establishment would be a nuisance if allowed to operate in their neighborhood. A few months later, seeing that Cumming had readied his facility and smelling odors that implied it to be in operation, the Smiths asked that the court order Cumming to cease production immediately, without its hearing evidence. The difference between the initial complaint (anticipating a nuisance) and the motion for an injunction (which did not establish the facts of manufacturing activity) led the court to deny the Smiths' request on technical grounds. Judge Parsons, speaking for the court, however, was clearly eager to side with the Smiths, and rather than dismiss the case, he instructed them to amend their complaint and resubmit their motion.[31] Parsons granted the amended request for an injunction to halt Cumming's operations in August 1851. Parsons seemed particularly piqued when Cumming claimed that no "putrid matter [had] . . . been kept or deposited on the premises" even as he continued to carry on the "'business of boiling and stewing the flesh and bones of dead animals.'"[32] (Cumming apparently did not deem the flesh to be "putrid," or partially decomposed and forming miasmatic gases, because, he said, he collected only "fresh" meat and carcasses.) But Parsons also noted precedents in Philadelphia finding that bone boiling "in a thickly populated part of the city or districts, was a nuisance *per se*" and thus entitled nearby residents to special relief (i.e., "special injunction") while the case to consider shutting down a facility proceeded.[33]

By the following summer, Cumming had modified the boiling process, and the court lifted the injunction while the case progressed. Summer's activity gave a court-appointed examiner occasion to investigate Cumming's factory in full swing. The examiner found the odors barely perceptible, and the injunction remained suspended. Hot weather the following summer (July 1853), however, led to further complaints. The Kenderton resident William Warner protested that "swarms of MAGGOT FLIES, . . . their stinking bodies gorged and their feet filled with the foul and putrid food on which they feed at [Cumming's] Factory, . . . infested his house" and crawled over his "victuals." The court reimposed the injunction, but Cumming continued rendering and in December 1853 was finally cited for violating it. The court ordered more testimony, but the docket entries and filed papers stop there, with no physical remnants of the depositions or clarification as to the ultimate outcome of the case. By the time of its inconclusive and puzzling end, the lawsuit had spanned three years.[34]

SELF-FASHIONING

A Leader in a Rationally Organized Industrial Enterprise

Throughout the suit, Cumming invoked the language of American manufacturing prowess to defend his animal rendering operation. He exuded the optimism of vigor and abundance: "employed without intermission," his men were "constantly engaged daily and hourly in collecting" the "incalculable quantities of bones and animal matter" from "many and innumerable places." And he emphasized his operation's alacrity, throughput, rhythm, thoroughness, and organization. His factory, he maintained, was a "sure, speedy and efficient means" by which animal matter could be "converted and disposed of without detriment to health and without injury and expense to the public." Communications about dead horses and cows on city streets seemed to reach the factory on wings; Cumming dispatched carts to fetch carcasses without delay. Once in the plant, Cumming's workers immediately set to processing offal and bones. Speed—a cliché of American manufacturing genius—was crucial in treating animal waste, lest it putrefy and incite fears of contagion. Only "fresh" offal (and carcasses), Cumming insisted, was accepted by his employees, and the efficiency with which they collected it and brought it under cover ensured safety for Philadelphians. (Speed also protected the carcasses' value, which diminished once rigor set in.) The court examiner, who in other ways was critical of Cumming's operation, underscored the rapid reception and processing of wagon-loads of remains.[35]

A Technologically Progressive Manufacturer

In defending his business, Cumming projected the image of a technologically progressive cutting-edge manufacturer. "Mechanical and chemical means" that had "but recently been discovered" and that allegedly eliminated odors won Cumming a suspension of the first injunction.[36] The descriptions of these mechanical means suggest something akin to the steam tanks patented by Ebenezer Wilson in Cincinnati in 1844. The tanks revolutionized Cincinnati's trade. Wilson subsequently traveled to Philadelphia looking for manufacturers interested in buying a right to use his patented apparatus (at least one soap boiler adopted it then), so it is possible that Cumming knew of and installed Wilson's invention. Imagine a giant pressure cooker with valves for draining stock at various levels in the pot. The critical element in Wilson's system is that the boiling takes place in a closed system rather than in large stock-pots without lids, as had apparently been the method that bone boil-eries and soap factories commonly used before the innovation. Wilson's tank also made it much easier to drain fat from the stock without inter-rupting the boiling process.[37]

Chemicals were also critical to the changes Cumming made to elimi-nate (or at least reduce) smells. Testimony suggests further innovation in the specific chemicals and combinations of chemicals used, as well as in the point at which they were applied in the process. During the initial boiling of bones and offal, Cumming added muriatic (i.e., hydrochloric) acid to the tubs to eliminate the stench. Subsequently, plaster of paris (hydrated calcium sulfate) was added to the boiled solution to bind with the remnants of flesh, which then fell to the bottom of the solution. Pul-verized charcoal (long recognized as a deodorizer and filter), gypsum, and sawdust were mixed with the flesh to reduce the smell. By these methods and a "liberal use of antiseptic and deodorizing agents"—not otherwise described but possibly including sulfuric acid—the stench was, according to the court investigator, "in a great measure . . . de-stroyed."

The processing water (or "Thin Broth"), while stripped of some of its smell, remained glutinous. Cumming initially discharged it into a rivu-let that flowed through his property and joined Three Mile Run (also known as Gunner's Run). But the effluent gave the creek "an inky hue, of a disagreeable, sickening smell, and covered [it] with a viscid scum."[38] Downstream, the nursery owner William Maupay had no choice but to continue to use the creek water, however foul, to irrigate his plants, even though his hydraulic ram clogged daily with the glutinous material. In July 1852 the examiner found the creek "unfit for the use of [dairy] cattle, as well as for domestic [and] other purposes." Cumming responded by denying that any "particle of any matter" came from his establishment, but he also appeased the court by constructing reservoirs. He added lime, charcoal, and another secret "ingredient" (perhaps again muriatic acid) to the water and allowed the basins to sit for several weeks before discharging them. Maupay insisted that the water remained foul, but Cumming's actions were further evidence of greeting complaints with innovation. As crude as they appear now, Cumming's mechanical and chemical methods were then state of the art, and they convinced the court to allow him to resume business until further complaints arose a year later. Thus through his innovations, Cumming fashioned himself a pioneer in a creative industry.[39]

A Virtuous Public Servant in the New Industrial Age

Cumming was quick to point to the economic contributions and ripple effects of his business. He tapped into contemporary liberal economic ideas endorsing the accumulation of wealth by manufacturers, whose profitable businesses, it was alleged, would spread their benefits. Some sixty to eighty employees owed their livelihood to his operation. Their cumulative weekly wages totaled $400, thus annually injecting close to $21,000 into the mid-nineteenth-century economy. He further argued that stopping business would injure butchers. Cumming had contracts with butchers for their refuse; he reckoned he paid them in total as much as $30,000 yearly.[40]

In elaborating on the benefits of his rendering concern, Cumming tapped into a Protestant bourgeois ethic of frugality as well as a fascination with American technological prowess and ingenuity. He made useful items out of material others discarded as waste: "fat from the bones of bullocks horses and cows" produced extracts used to make soap and "neats foot oil," the latter substance useful to machinists and tanners; bones were used to make various implements, including buttons, brushes, and umbrellas; hooves, to make combs; refuse of hooves, to make "prusiate [sic] of pot ash" (i.e., bone meal for fertilizer); and the gelatinous "glue stock" he produced, to make glue for use in the cabinet-making and construction trades. These items were vital in an age when consumer goods (e.g., umbrellas and parasols for the urban middle class) and mechanization (necessitating oil for machines) were ubiquitous and central components of industry. Moreover, each year Cumming produced some forty to fifty thousand bushels of manure for fifteen area farmers. To stop rendering would not only harm himself and his employees, he insisted, but also hinder a multitude of industrious producers and threaten to halt the region's well-oiled economy.

And what else did Philadelphia propose to do with its animal refuse? Cumming played to the fear of contagion in his argument. Did the authorities need to be reminded of the summer of 1849, when cholera endangered the city? Persuaded by the Board of Health messengers, Cumming did agree to "[desist] from the use of dead horses . . . in his factory," thereby curtailing odors associated with deadly miasmas. The Board of Health then had to remove the carcasses from the public streets and bury them in a mass grave located in a spot about which few could complain: the field behind the state penitentiary. But the horses "died in such large numbers, that they could not be buried rapidly enough for the purposes of the general health, [and] when buried they emitted an

[un]wholesome and offensive effluvia which spread to a great distance, and became and was a public nuisance of the worst imaginable character." Overwhelmed, the Board of Health sheepishly asked Cumming to again "take dead horses into his factory and use them for the purposes of his . . . business." Virtuous public citizen that he was, Cumming complied.[41]

At several strategic points, Cumming accommodated to some of the complaints of his neighbors, but he also reminded his critics of the services he provided for the commonweal. At the Kenderton area facility, for example, he quickly stopped boiling animal carcasses. (This was the most visible and perhaps the smelliest part of the operation.) He thereafter specialized in bones and offal. Lest his accommodation be deemed insufficient, he warned the court about the consequences of closing him down entirely. Without his services in converting offal to "beneficial and desirable ends," Cumming argued, "no means [would] exist to relieve the City and County . . . of . . . animal matter." It would then become pernicious. It would collect in many dispersed places in large quantities and "at all times." One senses the appeal to unstoppable and unpredictable agents of contagion, assisted in their work by the decentralized character of Philadelphia's trades. Cumming spelled out the threat: "Every slaughter house and market will become a nuisance, of an alarming and dangerous character, universally throughout" Philadelphia. Animal matter would become a "speedily decomposing" plague "of the worst kind spread over every part of our city." Only Cumming and his fellow renderers could save the city from such a fate.[42]

Regard for the public weal went hand-in-hand with profit in manufacturing; for Cumming, it produced affluence. Exactly how long he persisted as the Smiths' neighbor, however, is unclear. Evidence hints that he continued at the site for another few years after the inconclusive last entry in the court docket. He then sold the rendering part of the business to a major competitor. He maintained the glue factory at Sixth and Master until about 1859 and as late as 1866 continued to deal in glue (though likely not to manufacture it). When choice land on the Wissahickon Creek (within Philadelphia County) became available in 1869, despite his age (he was then in his late sixties) and his affluence, Cumming tried unsuccessfully to purchase it for another glue factory.[43]

Cumming's ethic of conversion was grounded in the ideology of nineteenth-century business. This virtuous citizen saw himself enlarging the economic pie, advancing industrial and urban progress, and keeping Philadelphia salubrious in the process. He projected himself to be at the forefront of a new trade—and carcass rendering in the 1840s was new in the sense that the producers of umbrellas, hide whips, and cabinet ware for a widened consumer market, as well as the builders and fixers of machines, barely existed a generation or two earlier. It was a business that required efficiency, speed, systems of transportation and communication, and mechanical and chemical innovations. Its processes were dynamic, and its entrepreneurs, creative. Not unlike other enterprises in the antebellum economy, it made value where few had initially seen it. Incentives for using "residuals" from the boiling process—starting, in fact, with "waste" carcasses, offal, and bones—were great, as each extracted material could be sold.

Bone boiling, of course, was an imperfect solution to the disposal of horse and livestock remains, especially in the face of the mounting horse population and the growing meat trade. It rid Philadelphia's citizens of the direct costs of disposing of animal carcasses, and it contributed tax revenue to the city, but it produced other pollutants, including obnoxious odors and glutinous liquid waste. Such pollutants, however, might well be deemed private nuisances, not public cases, and thus municipal authorities could deflect responsibility onto individual litigants to take up their causes at personal expense and in county courts. Even if litigants encountered judges who deemed bone boileries to be nuisances in "crowded" neighborhoods, it could take years to shut down or remove an offensive establishment. Compromises, productive innovations, economic contributions, legal arguments, and dissembling—plus the paucity of disposal alternatives to the city—meant that Kenderton residents would need to tolerate maggot flies on their dinner plates for years after Judge Parson's sympathetic hearing.

Michal McMahon

5 | "Publick Service" versus "Mans Properties"

Dock Creek and the Origins of Urban Technology in
Eighteenth-Century Philadelphia

DOCK CREEK WAS A COMPLEX entity even before its civil history began. By the time of Philadelphia's founding in 1682, the cove and streams of the watercourse in its natural state had already been used by the native peoples and European settlers who moved along the lower Delaware River. What the Delawares called the Coocanocon provided a safe harbor when rough weather caught small boats nearby on the broad river. The tidal cove presented an ideal site to set fish traps and collect shellfish, gather seaweed to be used for fertilizer, and cut hay from the abundant *Spartina*, the grass that filled the salt marsh bordering parts of the cove. So apparent were the cove's utilities that, before William Penn and his party arrived, Swedish settlers had built a tavern and a log cabin near the marshy area north of it.[1]

Along the mile-long eastern border of the townsite for Philadelphia, only the cove cut through the high banks of the river. It lay just above the extensive marshes that covered the bottom of the wedge formed by the convergence of the Delaware and its main tributary, the Schuylkill. Small hills around the cove nonetheless marked the site as the high, dry land Penn had sought. Because the cove was located on the lower, tidal

Delaware, the river fed its waters as much as did the small watershed that extended to the ridge dividing the two rivers. Water entered from the land mostly by subterranean paths, yet surface waters flowed in from the watershed's three streams. The smallest, from the south, later called the Little Dock, entered where the cove cut through the river-bank; two larger streams flowed from the west, above the cove. What residents called the Dock, the swamp, or (sometimes) the creek was thus a hybrid body of water, part tidal cove and salt marsh and part running stream.[2]

The Dock's importance to Philadelphia began the day in October 1682 when Penn stepped onto the landing at Blue Anchor Tavern. Gary B. Nash has shown how Penn and the early settlers made the area "around the cove the commercial center of town" and "the focal point of the import and export trade." Citizens reminded the Pennsylvania Provincial Council in 1700 that the cove was "the Inducing reason . . . to Settle the Town" in that spot.[3] The decision rested not only on the cove's usefulness to commerce but also on amenities it offered, for it served as a parklike setting for fine residences and quasi-public gardens.

Although largely unrecognized by modern scholars, the cove and creeks served chiefly as a manufacturing and materials-processing center for the growing city. These activities strengthened Philadelphia's role as the vital center of a regional marketing system. Yet to cove and city, the area's service as a manufacturing center held a more concrete meaning that contemporaries early recognized. As parts of the cove were walled and lined with docks, the same citizens who instructed the Provincial Council on the creek's centrality protested its treatment as a sump for domestic and manufacturing wastes. All this, of course, stemmed from a single geological fact: that, in the words of a 1784 legislative act, the small watercourse was the conduit through which the city's "most populous and central parts" drained.[4]

The very hydrological and geological features that drew settlers to the banks of the watercourse would prove to be of the utmost importance for Philadelphia's inhabitants as they built over the land. Although founded more than half a century after Boston and New York, Philadelphia had passed New York in size by 1700 and by 1760 had drawn abreast of Boston. Mixing the natural properties of the watershed with this rapid growth created an environment of great complexity.[5] The relationships of these elements, the needs of settlement and the givens of ecology, would shape the city.

Settlement and ecology did not peacefully converge. By 1730 both the land and city had entered a conflict that would determine the fate of each. As the Dock became so dangerously polluted as to be linked with deadly disease, it moved from being the useful and pleasant center of a town to being a center of civic dispute. For half a century, Philadelphia's leaders debated fundamental issues of urban form, environment, technical choice, and the politics of land use and development. In an emerging social order framed essentially by commercial and large-scale manufacturing interests, ecological questions formed at the edges of a conflict between competing social values, personal desires, and political and economic interests. The debate faded during the 1760s, when community leaders devised a comprehensive infrastructural solution to the city's urban problems and the onset of the American Revolution diverted attention to other concerns.

Urban scholars have long acknowledged the national influence of Philadelphia's experience in city building, particularly through the grid design chosen by Penn and his associates in 1681. In his pioneer study of urban growth during the half-century following the Revolution, Richard C. Wade extended Philadelphia's influence beyond street plans to urban technologies and the design of infrastructures. In accounting for urbanization in the trans-Appalachian West, Wade found specific instances in which Philadelphia's choices led western cities to adopt specific urban technologies ranging from street lighting and central watering systems to market-house design and the construction of river landings. By 1818 a Pittsburgh editorial writer could declare Philadelphia to be "the great seat of American influence."[6]

Although watering systems were being adopted or considered by other towns and cities during this period, Philadelphia's reputation was in large part launched when the city's leaders built the nation's first large-scale water system, doing so between 1799 and 1801. At a time when the water supplies of Boston and New York were equally polluted, Philadelphia's initiative justly earned the city a reputation as an influential pioneer in urban development.[7] Yet viewing Philadelphia's waterworks as marking the origins of urban technology in the United States misses the path that led to that event, a path that ran through the 1700s. To follow that route is to encounter not only Dock Creek but also an evolving drainage system that was finally to include the creek itself. This earlier story confirms Philadelphia's role as a model for much of the nation's development, but in a far more complex way than Wade's post-Revolution model suggests. The series of choices made by Philadelphia's leaders reveals a pattern of economic responses to settlement that would be repeated as the nation expanded across the continent.[8]

Dense settlement patterns and concentrated industrial activity early marked a colony that virtually began its existence as a booming regional center. Long before the nineteenth century, when urban historians and historians of technology generally begin their studies, urban growth induced the need to establish technical means to support it. Environmental historians have long recognized the major role technology plays in environmental change, but they have tended to study rural environments rather than urban ones.[9]

Approaching city building by uncovering the matrix of this earlier city expands the ways in which not only the history of technology and urbanization but also environmental history can broaden our perspective. For such an investigation, moreover, no other colonial city can compare with Philadelphia as a model for urban and, by extension, regional development in the nation. Not only does Philadelphia's rapid rise to urban hegemony in the English colonies recommend it for study, but the role of the Middle Colonies themselves reinforces the city's significance. Entrepreneurial energy and pragmatic self-interest make the civil history of Philadelphia and the Dock an exemplary tale for understanding city building and national expansion.[10]

At its narrative core, the Dock's story depicts an eighteenth-century city responding to the challenge of accommodating growth to natural utilities and amenities. Competing visions of the creek as advantage or problem, private property or public place, forced Philadelphia's leaders to grapple with demands for a healthy city environment. This interplay required devising organizational structures and technical procedures for paving and cleaning streets, establishing drainage and water retrieval systems, and handling and disposing of solid and liquid wastes generated by households and materials-processing industries. Ultimately, it meant making the city livable.

The story of the Dock extends beyond its importance in demonstrating the intersection of ecology and the technological underpinnings of the American city. Whether the Dock was perceived as a docking facility, a swamp, a cove and salt marsh, or a creek, its treatment during the middle decades of the eighteenth century raised fundamental social and political questions concerning both the relative weight of public and private values in the shaping of the city environment and the value of a community's store of scientific and technical knowledge. The adjudication of these values and the uses made of the knowledge can be seen in the decisions made about such matters as public works engineering proposals and the siting and regulation of industrial activities. And so, seen from the angle of the Dock, the story of building early Philadelphia resides in a social arena in which competing economic and political interests juggled questions of public rights and private purposes.

POLLUTION AND THE "LIBERTIES OF TRADESMEN": THE POLITICAL RESPONSE

In the middle of concerns about private interests and public order sat the graphic problem of pollution and the large-scale processing operations that clustered around Dock Creek. These facilities included a brewery, tanyards, distilleries, and a slaughterhouse, all with vital links to the watercourse. Environmental problems had long existed alongside the positive attributes of Penn's green country town: in 1705, as in 1711, 1720, 1726, and 1750, grand juries recorded complaints about impassable roads, jammed sewers, and standing pools of water.[11]

The idea that filth and pollution led to disease appeared frequently in formal complaints from citizens. In 1699 inhabitants had blamed the periodic visitations of epidemic disease on the two tanyards located on the cove. Seven years later, a group of residents charged the brewery above the drawbridge at Front Street with being "injurious to people." In 1712 citizens complained simply of "standing water" in the area. By the 1730s the problems stemming from unregulated manufacturing and dense settlement were coalescing into poor drainage and inadequate waste removal procedures. At Third and Market streets, for example, "a deep, dirty place" existed "where the public water" gathered "for want of a passage." Wastewater from residences and manufactories flowed overland into the Dock and the Delaware. Except for a few sewers covered by the municipal government, most remained open culverts until after 1750.[12]

By midcentury, environmental problems presented the city's central domestic challenge, and the Dock and its environs had become the center of pollution and controversy. Critics increasingly focused their complaints on the tanyards, which by 1730 numbered at least eight (counting separately the small yards scattered around the intersection of the creek's branches above Third Street). Tanneries not only covered much of the land around the Dock but were scattered throughout the length of the stream. One set below the drawbridge at Front Street and two sat just above Front on the western bank. Two were located at the top of the Dock, just below Third, and three surrounded the banks of the stream system between Third and Fourth streets.

Since the tannery pits and yards dominated the area, residents pointed to the tanneries as the primary source of the polluted waters of the stream and the foul air in the neighborhood. Most seriously, it seemed to residents that the stench of the tanyards must somehow be related to the nearly annual epidemics and to the endemic disease residing permanently in the urban core. Given the persistence of pollution, some epidemic diseases—tuberculosis, smallpox, and, with the aging settlement, waterborne contagions such as typhoid fever—might well have seemed endemic. Yet the citizens' complaints were problematic. If the illnesses of which they complained were yellow fever or smallpox, then Philadelphia's busy seaport was likely responsible for introducing the vectors carrying these epidemic diseases. As contributors to the accumulating filth in the city, however, the tanneries might truly have been linked to epidemic diseases, such as tuberculosis, as well as to endemic diseases such as the common cold and pneumonia.[13]

Not only the number of tanneries but the nature of the tanning process itself made the physical state of the watercourse a central and persistent issue throughout the century.[14] A tannery was generally a large operation, containing a number of structures necessary for transforming hides into leather. Although hides sometimes came from farmers, city tanneries more often relied on nearby slaughterhouses because they were more reliable sources of hides.

Slaughterhouses were traditionally located near streams, along with cattle pens, as was the one on the south side of the Dock. Around them, horn works, chandlers, and soap- and glue-boiling yards made use of the slaughterhouses' by-products. But the largest users of slaughterhouse leavings were the tanneries. A tannery included mills for grinding the bark used in tanning and vats and pits for soaking the hides so that workers could remove the hair, tan the hide, and give texture to the leather. The method of curing varied according to the intended use, whether for saddles or for women's gloves. Beyond the yard, then, the tanneries also supported a cluster of linked manufacturing activities, including shoemaking, saddle making, leather processing, and glove making.

Water was needed throughout the processing of the hides. Initial treatment consisted of soaking the hides in lime pits. The vats measured thirty-six square feet on average, but some were twice that size. Vats were usually wooden structures made to function like "a small water meadow slightly sunk."[15] A retaining dike wall was built around the vat, and in rural settings, water was flooded in from the adjacent stream. Whether serving a country tanyard or an urban yard with wells and a nearby tidal cove, the water always returned to its source along with the various substances that had been added, including acidic liquids resulting from the refuse of cider presses, sour milk, and fermented rye and alkaline solutions made up of buttermilk and some forms of dung. The process signified as well the strong connections between the industrial activities around the Dock and the countryside. Breweries, tanneries, slaughterhouses, and distilleries gathered the products of the countryside (primarily animals and grain), processed them, and discarded the unused by-products on the Dock's watershed.

Although tanning involved a series of chemical processes, tanners during the 1700s used traditional techniques without understanding the underlying chemistry. Nonetheless, even before a chemical revolution began to transform the trade near the end of the century, this ancient and critical materials-processing industry rested on a complex body of skills and lore that tanners shared.

If the situation in Philadelphia had involved only craft lore and chemical knowledge, the issue of pollution might have been approached more dispassionately. But this perceived villain was in fact a large, sprawling processing industry responsive to growing export and domestic markets and already in conflict with shoemakers who complained about shoddy materials and with curriers who objected when some tanners added currying to their yards' activities, thus threatening the curriers' livelihoods. The precipitating factor turned out to be the long-standing suspicion that the odors and standing wastes around the cove caused pestilence, a comprehensive term for any virulent and contagious disease. A series of severe epidemics during the 1730s led the inhabitants once again to home in on the tanyards. Individual citizens, organized groups of petitioners, and Dock Creek craft manufacturers became involved; they in turn drew in the chief governing institutions of the province: the proprietor, the Provincial Assembly, and the Philadelphia municipal corporation, a self-perpetuating body of freemen created by Penn that included the mayor, a recorder, an assessor, and a council of aldermen and common councilmen. The complaints became detailed attacks on pollution and the location of industrial operations. Finally, the debate broadened to include the polluted state of the city and intensified as the degraded environment appeared ever more dangerous.

As the central arena of debate in the province, the assembly was the site for the first of a series of dramatic confrontations over the condition of the Dock and its environs. It began during the spring of 1739 when a "great number" of inhabitants petitioned the legislators to correct conditions pervading the Dock's neighborhood. The residents specified "the great annoyance arising from Slaughter-Houses, Tan-Yards, Skinner Lime Pits, etc. erected on the publick Dock, and Streets, adjacent."

Besides seeking a ban on the construction of new tanneries, the petitioners wanted existing yards "removed within such Term of Years" as would "be judged reasonable."[16]

No one saw the issue as an abstract question of rights, as the petitioners made clear. They wanted not only to relocate the tanyards from the city to the Delaware but also to regulate the use of the land on and around the Dock.[17] After noting that the watercourse had recently been navigable as far as Third Street, the petitioners charged the tanyards with diminishing the value of other properties in the area by destroying the amenities that formerly graced the watercourse and its banks, including hanging gardens, grassy slopes, and clear waters.

Within a few days, the tanners countered with their own petition in which they asked for a copy of the original petition and time to respond. In their petition, the tanners admitted that the pits could give off offensive smells but charged the residents in the area of the Dock with going to unreasonable lengths to remove the tanyards when only a regulation would be necessary.[18] Apparently impressed with their arguments, the assembly gave the tanners until the next session, to be held at the end of the summer, to provide a plan.

In August, when the assembly turned again to the dispute, the tanners welcomed the petitioners' willingness to accept the tanyards if they were "so regulated as to become inoffensive." In a detailed scheme to clean up their yards, the tanners proposed that "the Tan-yards be well paved between all the Pitts, and wash'd once every Day." They added: "Let the Watering-Pools and Masterings (which are the only Parts that afford offensive Smells) be inclosed on every Side, and roofed over, within which Inclosure may be a subterranean Passage to receive the Washings and Filth of the Yard into the Dock or River at High-Water: Let the whole Yard be likewise inclosed on all Sides with some strong close Fence, at least seven or eight Foot high, and every Tanner be obliged every Week to cart off his Tan, Horns, and such offensive Offalls."[19] The assembly accepted the tanners' regulations and left the yards on the Dock; at the same time, it charged the municipal corporation with enforcement but withheld authority adequate to the task.

As if to acknowledge the inadequacy of its decision, the provincial legislators promised to consider a request for the power to force compliance should it become necessary.[20] The legislative decision underscored the substantial and long-standing power of the tanners. The large number of names on their counterpetition attested to their social influence as well. All six tanners who defended their rights before the assembly and in the pages of Philadelphia's *American Weekly Mercury* stood among the town's elite. Though perhaps lowest on the social scale, John Snowden, John Ogden, John Howell, and William Smith were nonetheless influential citizens, and two signers of the letter in the *Mercury,* William Hudson Jr. and Samuel Morris, stood securely in the ranks of Philadelphia's Quaker elite. Hudson and Morris also brought extensive political connections to the tanners' cause. The twenty-eight-year-old Morris had married into the prominent Cadwallader family.[21] His tanyard lay on the western bank of the Dock, near the bottom of the curve extending from the stem to Second Street. Nearby was John Snowden's yard, at the base of Society Hill near Front Street. John Ogden's yard was set north of the Dock below Third, bordering the first of several tanneries owned by William Hudson Sr.

The main yard of Hudson's operation lay on the north bank, below Third and between Dock and Chestnut streets, near the headwaters of the Dock. Besides the tannery, the elder Hudson's mansion and carriage house sat on the lot. Hudson Sr., who retained possession of the Hudson properties until his death, in 1742, had arrived in 1685 and soon added to his standing in the community by marrying a daughter of a leading Quaker family. After acquiring one of the two yards located on the Dock in 1700, he established several additional yards during the early decades of the century, all of them operated by his son William and his son-in-law John Howell in 1739. Howell's yard bordered on Fourth, sitting at the highest point of the industrial area that followed the creek.[22]

The sheer physical presence of the tanners in the town must have contributed to their bold act of celebrating the assembly's decision with a parade. At that point, the town's leading newspapers joined the debate. Taking opposing sides, the *Pennsylvania Gazette* and the *American Weekly Mercury* ran articles that reinforced the picture of the Dock presented by the original petitioners and the tanners. Accompanying the rich description were ideas that clarified the political and economic issues being debated. The passionate exchange described a cluster of processing industries on the banks of the watercourse. It documented the city's many uses of the cove and creek and added to the ecological understanding already present in fifty years of complaints from the community. Such concentrated attention from the newspapers to the physical state of the city, unusual in the presses of the day, responded to the critical level of pollution and the arrival of "autumnal fever" during the months of August and September.[23]

The involvement of the *Gazette* and the *Mercury* testified to the power of the contending interests, each of which drew a newspaper to its side. The petitioners had the power of numbers and of their residence

in the area. Their supporters included rising members of the community, such as the *Gazette's* editor, Benjamin Franklin, who had long used
his weekly to defend and advance public property ideas like those expressed in the initial petition. In this instance, however, the letter addressed to "Mr. Franklin" that appeared during the last week of August
1739 and covered the entire front page of the weekly argued for alternative uses of the town center and for more controls over land use.[24]

The assembly's failure to provide a means of enforcement left the
tanners free to claim victory. As they pointed out in a joint letter to the
Mercury, the assembly had "upon the whole" rejected the petitioners'
request and upheld the tanners' "right to follow their Trades within the
City." Further, they insisted that the municipal corporation's right to approach the assembly belonged no less to them.[25]

Through August and into September, even while admitting that their
yards were "a nusance" and "voided many unwholesome smells," the
tanners continued to argue their rights. In their defense, they sketched
a picture of a city in which sources of pollution were pervasive. A great
amount of waste converged on the Dock, they pointed out, which served
as "a Receptacle for all kinds of filth from a very great part of the Town."
Water no longer entered at a volume sufficient to carry off waste deposited at the head of the cove. Nor was the cleansing force of the tide adequate before the "abundance of Necessary-houses" that lined the Dock
and drained directly into the watercourse.[26]

The industrial sources of pollution were comparably diverse, as the
tanners strenuously argued. According to the tanners, their critics failed
to censure butchers, whose trade they deemed "much more offensive
than Tanning," because it was convenient to have the slaughterhouse
near the center of town. And why charge the tanners alone with the responsibility for "Tann, Horns, Dead Dogs, Country People losing their
Dogs, Tanners Dogs biting People, a Dog mangled, [and] an other rescu'd
from a Slaughter-House"? When the protesting citizens had put these
complaints before the assembly, the tanners pointed out, that body had
found them so "impertinent to the point" it had not even replied.[27]

The Dock Creek tanners insisted that they were not alone responsible; "a gentleman . . . of some note" had cited the tanyards in Southwark,
a settled area on the Delaware directly south of Philadelphia, as "truly
offensive." To their critics' point that New York City had banned tanyards, the tanners countered that tanyards were allowed throughout
the "Towns and thick settled Parts of Great-Britain" and existed in the
wards of London with the approval of the lord mayor's government.[28]

"The Affair of the tanners had made a great deal of Noise" in the city,

Mercury's editor, Andrew Bradford, wrote in mid-August. Yet the 1739 dispute revealed more than an understanding of the problems of the congested core. Questions of public rights and private land use were bared as well. To Franklin, the Dock and its utilities provided a "publick service" to the city; to Bradford, it was "mans property." The one account that appeared in the *Gazette* responding to the tanners' initial letter included detailed answers to the arguments put forth by Bradford and the tanners. Public rights to the Dock and the land around it, the article maintained, rested on traditions beginning before 1700. Even Dock Street had been given "with the Dock for publick Service."[29]

Removing the tanyards from the area around the Dock promised to enlarge public spaces within the city and thus allow smoother passage through the town center and make it easier to fight fires. Of course, nearby property owners would especially benefit; Franklin admitted that improvements resulting from the relocation of tanneries would make the land more valuable to the residents. As for the tanners' right to property, Franklin and the protesters suggested that the city could move the tanyards to a similarly "convenient" place.[30]

In a postscript to the *Mercury* piece published two weeks later, Bradford insisted that no place near the city was as convenient as the Dock. The tanners would have to bear the costs of tearing down and rebuilding any structures that could not be moved, and the increased distance would raise the costs of carrying goods to market. Besides, the poor would be deprived of an annual 400 to 500 cartloads of tanbark for fuel, "a material article to the City." Against the force of such arguments, the author of the *Gazette* article had already argued that the final issue went beyond agreeing on "the damage done" to actually assessing the relative weight of damage done to tanners and damage done "to the city."[31]

Everyone agreed on the sources of pollution and its impact on the Dock Creek area. Resolving claims of competing values called for balancing public costs and benefits against the costs and needs of private business. Those who viewed the Dock as a public good and stressed public rights faced tremendous obstacles in a society that had gone far to privatize the possessions and purposes of civil society.[32] Franklin assumed the tanners would bear the expense of relocation yet suggested that the municipal corporation might recommend a "convenient" location. This captured the spirit of Penn's charter promise that the corporation would recognize the rights and property of "persons."

But what of the tanners' charge that the petitioners acted more out of self-interest than out of concern for the city? The *Gazette* author had admitted self-interest in arguing that the removal of the tanyards would increase the value of the area around the Dock. Although Franklin would later move to within a block of the Hudson and Howell complex of tanneries, in 1739 he lived north of High Street. While he was located on the Dock's watershed, with his buildings set close to Front, Franklin suffered more from the market buildings on High that fronted his property and from the closeness of Bradford's printing shop than from the sluggish waters of the Dock. Beyond the market shambles, a small alley opened into Letitia's Court, named for Penn's daughter, who had owned the lot earlier in the century.

It would be easy to see a politically courageous act in a thirty-three-year-old newspaper publisher's willingness to cover his entire front page with a letter criticizing one of the most powerful groups in the city. A young printer still rising in the community, Franklin could not lightly squander the goodwill of wealthy Quaker tanners. Yet however much Franklin's concerns went beyond the value of his property, that value, was nonetheless a factor, even though his shops and home stood more than two blocks from the yards. The Dock's condition was seen as injurious to property values and the quality of daily life throughout the settled watershed.[33]

Nor did Bradford let the obvious personal investment pass: "Here is the Rabit! Good people observe what a concern they have for the promotion of lots!" The tanners' aims were no different, Bradford insisted. They wanted the opposition to show signs of "some tenderness to mans properties."[34]

The 1739 dispute had linked the issue of public rights and land-use policy to the problem of pollution. It also demonstrated the community's emerging awareness of the connections between hydrological systems and settlement patterns. In Franklin's *Proposal for Promoting Useful Knowledge,* written in 1743 to launch the American Philosophical Society, his list of areas of knowledge needed by the colonials included land drainage techniques and methods of building pumps for retrieving and distributing water.[35] Franklin's growing understanding of technical design and scientific experimentation was manifest in the stove he designed and through his electrical investigations, all achievements of the 1740s. The same understanding could be seen in his approach to public works technology and his broad awareness of the city's infrastructural needs. The conjunction of these interests with his growing financial stake in his adopted city led to Franklin's involvement in the affairs of the Dock for more than thirty years.

The other parties in the dispute over the Dock were similarly aware of links between technology and nature. The original protesters connected the pollution of the cove with the state of the streams and watershed above it. The tanners asserted a meaning of the cove's location when they described the upper parts of the Dock as being "without sufficient water to carry" off the filth that flowed into the cove "from a very great part of the town." They demonstrated their grasp of hydrological matters and the significance of the fact that pollution from throughout the city flowed into the Dock.[36] Their claims implied a sense of the relationship between dense settlement and cleared land and the amount of sediment that joined the garbage in the cove.

Arguments offered on all sides of the debate pointed to drainage and waste removal as the central urban challenges at midcentury. Bradford recognized this when he linked the state of the tanneries to the condition of the Dock and the town: "And truly, as the Dock is now circumstanced, they must be fine Nos'd that can distinguish the smell of Tannyards from that of the Common sink of near half Philadelphia, that for want of Passage stands putrified, Carrion too frequently thrown there, and the Excrement from nearly Thirty Houses of Office communicating with the Dock, and lodged on the sides every Fresh."[37] Domestic and manufacturing wastes were often indiscriminately dumped or placed in pits, and many streets remained unpaved and covered with standing water after rains. Waste liquids from processing operations came from the oil and color shops of distillers and from soap boilers and chandlers to mix with rainwater runoff before filtering into an aquifer from which, through public and private wells, the city drew its water. In one way or another, nearly all wastes entered the Dock, the major exit point in the colonial city's natural drainage system.

With the decision of the Provincial Assembly in 1739, official consideration of the dispute had effectively ended. But the issue did not disappear as a matter of public concern. After all, the legislative action and the newspaper debate of 1739 had amplified complaints that had been simmering since before 1700. And so, less than a decade later, the state of the Dock once more led to public consideration, this time in the form of a major study by a committee of the municipal corporation.

The immediate result of the study was a report offering general policy recommendations and an engineering proposal for a public works project to revitalize the Dock. Its reception by the assembly and the proprietor, two potential sources of external revenue, and the response of the Common Council of Philadelphia itself reveal even more about the leaderships' commitments to the ordering of space in the city.

THE 1748 AND 1763 PROPOSALS TO RESTORE THE DOCK: THE ENGINEERING RESPONSE

The municipal corporation's initiative came in the fall of 1747, following the decade's second harsh attack of epidemic disease. The descriptions of the Dock's condition that emerged from the 1739 dispute alone suggest that the Common Council's aim of reviving the Dock as a multi-purpose wharving facility and an urban amenity presented a daunting task. Yet some still saw the Dock as, in the words of the city recorder and councilman Tench Francist, a potential "ornament to the city." As late as the 1740s, a large home was begun on the south bank of the lower Dock, recalling the days in which the wealthiest settlers built houses along its banks.[38]

Yet the issues relevant to the Dock stretched beyond a stately new house, as might have been read into the building's destruction by fire before being completed. The presence of "mansions," a label given to William Hudson's home at Third and Chestnut, with only his and Ogden's tanyards between him and the Dock and creek, failed to alter the prevailing belief that the cove increasingly resembled "a foul, uncovered sewer." Most of the watercourse, from the mostly walled portion that ran from the Delaware to the bridge at Third Street all the way to the twin streams that dissected the block above Third, between Chestnut and Walnut, was a major blight that literally split the southeastern quadrant of the town. Nor could the situation be expected to improve when a new market house had to be built in 1745 on Second, below Pine, in response to the dense residential expansion south of the Dock, where short rows of two- and three-story "tenements" were replacing rural estates and cleared land.[39]

The slaughterhouses and the skinning troughs, lime pits, and large piles of dry and soaking bark of the tanyards lay on both sides of the Dock. Within the watercourse itself, industrial waste joined silt eroding from bare land and unpaved streets. Inhabitants regularly used the Dock as a receptacle for the city's domestic refuse, human and animal sewage, and dead animals.[40] Residents and visitors more and more referred to the town's once-prized watercourse as a common "sink" or sewer.

Epidemics were common. They had come in the form of smallpox three times during the 1730s, and in 1741 some five hundred people died of yellow fever thought to have been brought in on a ship. The next year, the pesthouse was moved from Tenth and South streets to an island in the mouth of the Schuylkill. After yellow fever again came in 1747, arriving during the first hot days of July and lasting into September, the municipal corporation named a committee to assess the continuing problem of the polluted Dock and to propose means for cleaning up the environs. The committee was to consider especially the remaining marsh and to recommend "the best method of improving the sd swamp for the general use and benefit of the city."[41]

As constituted by the Common Council, the committee comprised both council members and other citizens. The half-dozen leading citizens who formed the ad-hoc committee demonstrated the growing potential for a systematic engineering response to Philadelphia's growth. Among them, only Franklin revealed a strong interest in science per se, yet all but one were technically knowledgeable and experienced in public and industrial undertakings. The only nontechnologist, William Logan, shared Franklin's receptivity to new ideas about agriculture and, as had Franklin, experimented in that area. The committee represented, in short, an emerging community of men involved in industrial entrepreneurship and the mechanical arts.

Two members, John Stamper and Logan, were distinguished chiefly as successful merchants. By working on the committee, Stamper, a rising merchant, apparently gained a new reputation in the building arts as well. In December 1751 the council contracted with him to perform work on the south end of the drawbridge at Front Street and along the south side of the Dock extending east to the Delaware side of Water Street. Stamper agreed to do all "according to the plan of the city, in the best and workmanlike manner." When he became mayor in 1760, Stamper built a fine Georgian house on Pine Street south of the Dock.[42]

Logan derived his distinction in the city in large part from his father, James, a former governor who had served Penn in several capacities. William, who had followed his father in trade, joined the Common Council in 1743 and in 1747 replaced his father on the governor's council. He held both positions until the councils were suspended in 1776. When his father died, in 1751, William quit the mercantile business and moved to the family farm, where he gained a reputation as a progressive agriculturalist and wrote an essay entitled "Memoranda in Husbandry."[43]

Unlike Stamper, Edward Warner brought extensive experience in construction to the committee's deliberations. He described himself as a merchant and "of the city of Philadelphia, [a] house-carpenter." A man of means and position, Warner had obtained his wealth from his former master, a carpenter and builder who died childless in 1737 and left his fortune to Warner and a fellow apprentice. Warner's master had been a founder of the Carpenter's Company, a trade association of builders and artisans that Warner later joined.[44]

Three committee members—Samuel Rhoads, Samuel Powel, and Benjamin Franklin—formed a core engineering group on the committee. All were born between 1704 and 1711 and spent most of their lives in Philadelphia. In their work, personal pursuits, and public service activities, they demonstrated an interest in manufacturing and infrastructural development and a knowledge of machines. Rhoads's activities documented a knowledge of construction and pumping machinery. In 1744 he served the council by inspecting the Schuylkill ferry at Market Street; his investigation led him to recommend removing the existing buildings and putting up new ones. A year earlier, he had sat with Powel on a committee to inspect and recommend repairs to the city's fire engines.[45]

Although chiefly a merchant, Powel's father had won a reputation as a prominent builder and architect and a "carpenter of high ability." When the son was fourteen, the elder Powell erected a bridge over Dock Creek at Walnut Street, and in 1734 father and son constructed a "public wharf and regulated the streets" on the south side of the Dock near Front Street. As they explained a decade later when seeking the council's permission to charge for its use, the area had become impassable and had been of no use to the inhabitants until their improvements. Powel also joined his father in 1726 in an enterprise called the Durham Company, which was intended to erect a furnace and other works for making and casting iron.[46]

Franklin shared characteristics with the entire committee: he was a prominent artisan, a serious technologist, and a well-off and influential citizen who promoted private and public undertakings. Although in 1748 he belonged to neither the Common Council nor the Provincial Assembly, Franklin had served as clerk of the assembly for more than a decade.

By February 1748 the ad-hoc public works committee had completed a proposal aimed at reclaiming the entire area of the original cove, extending to Third Street. It recommended developing a multiple-wharving system in the cove and creek that would include existing docks and landings. A sixty-foot dock would be built along the creek's main stem to its westernmost point. Two stretches of sloping beach of thirty and forty feet were to be left open on both sides of the main, northwestern branch for the landing of flats and small boats. The lower bank between Front Street and the Delaware would be raised above high tide and walled in with stone, and the channel would be widened to between sixty and eighty feet. The "common sewer" that flowed from the southwest into the Little Dock would be continued to the main stream, covering over the small tributary. Finally, the cove was to be regularly dredged as far as Third Street so that the bottom would be covered with water even at low tide.[47]

Few precedents existed in Philadelphia for a public works project of such size and scope, although Thomas Budd's 1698 design for the Dock certainly equaled the committee's plans, but comparable projects had been undertaken in other colonial cities. Boston's Long Wharf, built between 1710 and 1713, measured 1,600 feet. Nearly thirty years later, Newport's merchants, with a grant of town land from the city government, constructed a 50-foot-wide wharf that extended more than 2,000 feet into the channel. Newport's project differed from Boston's purely public effort by joining private and public resources. Yet neither project entered the city in the manner of Philadelphia's Dock. The New England cities thus avoided chafing effects such as those elicited by the committee's attempt to reorder the very center of Penn's town.[48] Philadelphia's efforts differed also in being born out of conflict, not the needs of commerce: the committee responded to the widely held belief that a polluted Dock would continue to degrade the city.

The Dock Creek restoration plan foundered precisely on the need to navigate between hesitant public authorities and entrenched private interests. The Provincial Assembly ignored the committee's proposal that "a tax be laid upon the city." Because the assembly controlled the municipal corporation's taxing authority and lacked sympathy for its proposed solutions, the Common Council was forced to approach the proprietor.[49]

In March, after discussing the matter with the assembly-appointed city assessors, the corporation selected the mayor, recorder, and several aldermen to approach the proprietor, Thomas Penn, for assistance. Penn expressed his concern for the "sickly state of the city," yet he questioned whether the "mud" deposited on the sides and bed of the Dock was really dangerous, since those waters had been polluted for many years "and yet no such fever was known until the year 1741." Penn advised that, if the mud there differed from that on the sides of the Delaware, then the tanyards should be removed. He left any decision about methods for removing the mud to the corporation, which, he said, was "on the spot." "If the Corporation or publick" wanted to restore the Dock, he insisted, those parties should pay for it or give up any rights to it and allow private owners to "clear and build upon it" and to receive the profits from "the landing of wood and other things on the bank."[50]

Having been rebuffed by both the assembly and the proprietor, the corporation declined the full responsibility for the area, requesting owners of land adjoining the Dock to clean up their own sites, with the sole incentive so being any profit that might result from their improvements. The Dock committee recommended, in turn, that the corporation agree to use its funds to build floodgates at the several bridges and to establish regular dredging of the watercourse.[51]

Students of Philadelphia's colonial city government have sometimes cited the corporation's lack of taxing authority as a reason for its failure to restore the Dock.[52] The record suggests, rather, a specific unwillingness to make a commitment to restoring the Dock, even if the financing scheme relied chiefly on private funds. From the beginning, Philadelphia's municipal corporation had regularly dealt with infrastructural matters, arranging for the repair of collapsed bridges, breaches in the streets, and overflowing sewers. Rarely did a civic leader deny responsibility for maintaining and regulating the several public wharves on the Delaware, the public landing at Blue Anchor Tavern, the Dock, the powder houses, or the stalls and storage buildings in the market areas along High Street and on Second Street below the Dock. To pay for this work, the corporation relied chiefly on revenues from fees, fines, and rents. Although these sources generally sufficed to pay for small repairs, the magnitude of the 1748 proposal to renovate the Dock called for far greater sums of money.

When additional means of funding are examined, however, and other commitments considered, the absence of taxing authority fails to account for the neglect of the Dock. In the same year that the ad-hoc committee put forth its engineering proposal, the municipal corporation raised a substantial sum toward defending the city from the French by guaranteeing the purchase of 2,000 lottery tickets. Defense efforts dominated extraordinary city and provincial expenditures for the next three decades, yet other projects received substantial sums drawn from money paid to the corporation for renting and leasing public property. In 1750 the corporation committed 700 pounds over several years for the newly established Academy of Philadelphia. It was not unusual for the Common Council to consider funding a new wharf, as it did in 1748. During the years following, the Provincial Assembly even allowed the city to raise funds by lottery for a landing in the Northern Liberties neighborhood and to pave streets in Philadelphia.[53]

Not only did the corporation possess these additional means of raising funds, but its income grew substantially between the 1720s and the 1770s. Its cash reserve amounted to more than 500 pounds by midcentury, which loaned at interest grew to 730 pounds by 1757. Revenues rose so rapidly during these years that by 1763 annual income was 640 pounds and the reserve balance stood at 1,000 pounds. During the 1760s and early 1770s, the corporation gave 300 pounds for a bridge and 500 pounds for a ferry across the Schuylkill north of Philadelphia.[54] For some time before the 1748 proposal, in short, the corporation had demonstrated that liberal values, not money, guided its administrative decisions: it simply lacked interest in the urban values the Dock represented. Through petitions and committee service, a number of individuals clearly expressed their belief in a civil order in which public rights balanced private desires. By action alone, city leaders demonstrated their commitment to a policy of allowing the individual choices of private property owners to determine the shape and character of the city. In the face of private property rights and competing claims, the corporation abdicated its public responsibility, instead relying on private enterprise to deal, or not, with the consequences of development.

The need for some decision had been made clear in the conclusion of the February engineering report: "The Nusance is of such a Nature . . . [that,] should it continue, may be of fatal Consequence in preventing the Growth and Increase of this City by discouraging Strangers . . . from coming among us, or filling our own Inhabitants with Fears and perpetual Apprehensions, while it is suspected to propagate infectious Distempers."[55] The defenders of the Dock had argued for amenities (i.e., open space through which to move more freely in the city and the ornamental qualities of the watercourse) and for utilities (i.e., a source of water to fight fires). Yet not even the association with disease was persuasive enough to force quick action. Having rejected the option of controlling land use by moving the tanneries outside the city in 1739, and thus avoiding a confrontation with private economic interests, the preparers of the 1748 report left the Dock's manufacturers in place, offering instead a pure technological solution. It was this response that made the 1748 proposal prescient.

The prescience of a pure technological solution became clear during the 1760s. The committee's makeup had attested to a growing body of experience and knowledge in construction and civil engineering, knowledge that the legislators of the 1760s would incorporate into a systematic treatment of the city's problems. The stature and character of the 1748 committee's members confirmed the foresight of local leaders whose experience could prove beneficial in responding to the city's environmental problems. Yet the committee's proposals became moot as buildings and streets continued to expand over the watershed throughout the 1750s. As settlement moved beyond Fourth Street, lots above the cove were sold and built over, both in the remaining marshy areas near

Spruce Street to the southwest and along the creek that fed the cove from the northwest. Under orders from the municipal corporation, the bulk of the hills surrounding the headwaters were used to fill and level the area above the cove and north of Spruce Street.[56]

By 1760 the natural features of the cove's watershed had been obliterated, with no open undeveloped marsh remaining, but even then the Dock itself still attracted defenders. In late January 1763 a group of petitioners made a final attempt to preserve the Dock. They reiterated previous claims, telling the Provincial Assembly that "the public Dock or Creek" endangered the health of citizens because of its use as a dump for "Carcases . . . Carrion, and Filth of various kinds." As earlier, the petitioners wanted to restore the Dock, yet this time they combined the notion of land-use restrictions from 1739 with the engineering approach of 1748. They also moved, as they had not done before, to save the town's water supply. By the 1760s the growing number of distilleries in the area around the Dock led the protesters to cite the "Number of Still-houses erected of late."[57]

The petitioners thought that the distilleries, being constructed mostly of wood, constituted fire hazards. Beyond that, the industry's processing operations brought more polluting wastes to the neighborhood of the Dock. Distilleries deposited their liquid "dregs or returns" in "wells . . . dug for that purpose." Like the content of privies, this liquid waste tended to mix with the water drawn from wells for domestic use. Some of the distilleries even emptied their wastes into the "public gutters" that fed the city's expanding drainage system.[58]

Clearly demonstrating their grasp of subterranean water flow, the petitioners wanted the manufacturers removed in an attempt to protect groundwater, just as they wished the Dock to be once again navigable by small craft transporting building materials and firewood and useful for supplying water to fight fires. Reminiscent of the 1748 report, the petition recommended that the Dock be "cleared out, planked at the Bottom, and walled on each Side."[59] The Dock would serve, in effect, as a combined canal and reservoir.

After receiving the petition, the assembly appointed a new committee to investigate and report. Like its predecessor, this committee took a favorable view of the Dock's potential, recommending it as a "public Utility" that should "be cleansed, and properly walled." The committee explicitly claimed the modified watercourse for the public, since it was unable to find "any Persons [with a] just and legal claim . . . to the said Dock . . . or the Streets laid out adjoining thereto."[60]

Once again, the assembly set aside the assertion of public ownership and charged private owners with making the necessary repairs on those sections of the walled watercourse adjacent to their properties. In 1763 a supplement to a comprehensive act of the previous year to regulate streets and sewers contained specific instructions for restoring the Dock as far as Third Street. Each property owner was to erect "a good, strong, substantial wall of good, flat stone from the bottom of the said Dock," the thickness, height, and depth to be specified later. If the residents did not complete the work within three months of receiving directions in writing, the commissioners would have the work performed and bill the owners.[61]

So slowly and ineptly did the city move on the restoration of the Dock that another supplement was passed in 1765 acknowledging that the attempts "to open, cleanse, repair, regulate and make navigable a certain watercourse . . . known by the name of the Dock" had failed to "answer the good purposes that were expected." Indeed, the attempt to command improvements had apparently been abandoned, since the 1765 supplement directed that the Dock be filled in between Walnut and Third streets "over the arch *now erected.*"[62]

The fate of the Dock was fixed. The act of building an arched conduit through the section above Walnut Street and covering it confirmed that the citizens no longer found the once-marshy stream-fed cove a "commodious Dock." After a century of ill use and grudging maintenance, the Dock had become the filthiest site in a habitat that was generally polluted with discarded waste and poor drainage, poorly protected by the fitful regulation of obnoxious industries located in the middle of the settlement. Residents later recalled that "few people at the time regretted the dock being arched over," since "at high water great patches of green mud floated on it" and the few fish that still entered the creek "soon floated belly up."[63]

As the city closed in, the creek had become no more than a link, though perhaps a major one, in a drainage system that was expanding along with the settled core. The cove and streams had become a contradiction in nature: a watercourse without a watershed. From the perspective of the comprehensive legislation passed in the Provincial Assembly during the 1760s, the Dock was an engineered structure, no more, no less.

THE URBAN TECHNOLOGY ACTS OF THE 1760S: THE SYSTEMATIC RESPONSE

Between 1763 and 1765, the first step had been taken toward arching and covering the channel that had been under construction since the

1600s. The second step came in 1784, when city regulators extended the stormwater drain from Walnut to Front Street, and the final one arrived in 1818, when the closed sewer was continued to the river. The initial step represented not a new understanding of the crisis by city leaders but rather a capitulation to the results of long neglect. Of more consequence was the community's long-standing awareness that the polluted Dock was one problem among many. Private privy pits and manufacturers' waste pits leaked their contents into water wells; processing industries polluted the air; citizens habitually threw dead animals on the commons; and practically everyone dumped garbage in the streets, empty lots, open sewers, and watercourses of the city. The systematic extension and intensification of infrastructural networks and municipal service became the only logical choice.

These acts clearly represented an expansion of public responsibilities after eighty years of governments' hesitating to take charge of the physical needs of the city. The response was in many ways modern, using technology to fix problems that were social and political. The 1760s legislation not only rejected the 1739 attempt to control and establish the location of industrial practices but also converted the Dock into the key element in a citywide drainage system.

The first comprehensive step appeared in 1762 with the passage of a seven-year act that, although it would be replaced in 1769, successfully codified much of the technical legislation of eighty years.[64] Its breadth was captured in the title: "An Act for Regulating, Pitching, Paving, and Cleansing the Highways, Streets, Lanes and Alleys and for Regulating, Making and amending the Watercourses and Common Sewers within the Inhabited and Settled Parts of the City of Philadelphia, and for Raising of Money to Defray the Expenses Thereof."[65] After dealing with specific problems regarding streets, drainage, and waste removal, the Provincial Assembly assigned responsibility for enforcement to the municipal corporation and to a group of commissioners to be elected by the freeholders. In its main regulatory sections, the act mandated programs to pave the streets, lanes, and alleys and to lay out and maintain stormwater sewers and watercourses. Although unmentioned in the 1762 act's title, and recognized in the 1769 title with the added words, "and for Other Purposes Therein Mentioned," the longest section established a system for removing solid waste and filth from the city.

Both the method and materials for the streets—usually stone surfaces laid with sand and gravel—were to be established by the commissioners, who were to give priority to streets "most used by the country in bringing their produce and effects to market." Similar instructions were included for sidewalks, or footways, the expense for which was to be borne by owners of property adjoining them. Along with the regulations already established for the Dock, other regulations stipulated that subterranean and surface stormwater drains be built through the settled parts of the city. Enabling authority was granted to a committee made up of the mayor or recorder, four aldermen, and four elected commissioners, who were charged both with laying out sewers on private land and compensating the owners fairly. The regulators were to determine the degree of descent of watercourses and to fine persons who obstructed the passage of waters through the sewers.[66]

A section on solid waste removal followed the several paragraphs that dealt with streets and the drainage system. Most of the work of carrying off the "mud, mire, dirt, and other filth" found on streets was to be performed by hired scavengers, or street cleaners. Porters, church sextons, and the caretakers of other institutional buildings were to sweep all waste dirt and soil into the street on Fridays for scavengers to haul away on that day or the day after. Special wastes, such as shavings, ashes, and dung, were to be set aside for the scavengers, with stiffer penalties set for noncompliance. Scavengers' fees were set by city administrators and were to be paid by business owners and tradespeople, with no charges attached to the removal of waste material "incident to common house-keeping." The final ten pages of the 1762 act dealt exclusively with sources of general funding, including the remains of previous lotteries and fees assessed on property, such as "houses, lands, tenements, rent-charges, bound servants and negroes."[67]

The waste removal regulations of the comprehensive act were considerably advanced in a 1763 act "to Prevent and Remove Certain Nuisances in and near the City of Philadelphia"—that is, to regulate the disposal of contaminating, or toxic, wastes. A list of nuisances included parts of buildings (e.g., porches, windows, and spouts and gutters) that interfered with passage on streets and sidewalks, but the act focused on industrial wastes: foul liquids, wastes from stills and boiling vessels used by distillers, renderings from soap boilers and tallow chandlers, and fat and grease from slaughterhouses. Organic wastes generated by the general community, such as the contents of privies and necessary houses and dead animals (cattle, sheep, hogs, and dogs), were designated as well. All such wastes were to be buried "a full or sufficient depth" either on the commons or "on or near any of the streets." Nothing was to be thrown "into the public water-course of the said city, called the Dock." In addition, the act set the depths of privies so as "to preserve the waters . . . wholesome and fit for use."[68]

Although the lawmakers provided no specific labels, the 1762 legislation had dealt mostly with inorganic waste, including sweepings of harmless material and household refuse, along with ash and manure, but not food waste. The 1763 act dealt with the disposal of potentially unhealthy or toxic and definitely unpleasant waste material, specifically carrion and unwanted and unused by-products from manufacturing processes. In contrast to its predecessors, the 1763 act held the businesses and individuals that produced waste responsible for removing it. The 1769 act incorporated all these concerns and added others. Besides regulating the size and placement of signs and sign poles, a final paragraph provided that the Dock below Second Street continue to be cleaned and repaired. The act also established two public landings on the Delaware to complement those on the Dock below Front Street.[69]

Philadelphia's leaders had at last responded in a comprehensive fashion to the long environmental crisis, in which the polluted Dock served to focus the problems with pollution that occurred throughout the city. After thirty years of makeshift engineering, the provisions of the 1760s acts reflected a now-established understanding of the links between pollution, infrastructure, waste removal services, and funding arrangements.[70] Again, the connection between ecological systems and settlement patterns appeared in a warning contained in a January 1769 petition. After reiterating the problems of economic losses to landowners in the area of the Dock and the greater chance of disease, the petitioners explained that these problems would worsen "as the vacant Parts of the City, from which the Water is conveyed to the said Sewer, [were] improved and built upon."[71]

Despite this understanding of the land's hydrological properties, the city's leadership had turned to mechanical solutions. Earlier in the 1760s, city leaders began a process that would convert the entire Dock into a sewer within fifty years. At the same time, they tightened the administration of city services and took steps to systematize an infrastructure of technology and services. Not only did the new comprehensive approach borrow from past legislative efforts, but the legislation relied less on individual landowners to initiate the task that would create a healthy and pleasant city. These public initiatives did not so much overturn the relative standing of public and private rights as accept the need for public authorities to work within a world shaped by private interests and individual acts. The shift came with the community's recognition that piecemeal fixes were inadequate when pervasive conditions called for a centralized, systematic response.

These steps were slowed and even halted by the distractions of the Revolution and the transformation of local and provincial governments during the 1770s and 1780s. But this procrastination does not belie so much as underscore their importance. Seen from the path leading to the Revolutionary years, the disastrous epidemics that struck Philadelphia at the end of the century appear as a response to past neglect as well as a stimulus to the building of a centralized waterworks. Endemic and epidemic disease killed 20 to 25 percent of the population between 1793 and 1797; had the city applied technological insights from the thirty years prior to the Revolution, such a death toll might not have been exacted.

Compared to the situation at the end of the century, Philadelphia's experience of urban technology between the 1730s and the 1760s was more complex because public use of natural advantages engaged in open contest with private rights to property development. Issues of technological choice and settlement design were complicated by ecological systems, intense environmental pollution, and the absence of established governing arrangements. During the nineteenth century, the situation became simpler with the acceptance of a fully mechanized habitat. Eighteenth-century Philadelphia offers a richer context for the study of settlement patterns, for it displays the process of making choices that resulted in the triumph of mechanization. With mechanization, the possibility of incorporating ecological systems into technological systems disappeared.

In their tight focus on the hardened patterns of the nineteenth- and twentieth-century city, historians of urban technology tend not to appreciate organic perspectives of city development such as Lewis Mumford's. This disdain has led some historians to find in Mumford's work "overarching but difficult-to-establish notions."[72] Because they observe concrete terrains served by pervasive mechanized urban infrastructures, complete with water-carriage sewage networks directed toward vast sewage treatment facilities and chemically based water treatment plants, they understandably have difficulty seeing the organic issues raised by the city-building experience.

Yet how difficult would it be to demonstrate Mumford's statement that "a characteristic feature" of the industrial era involved the "transformation of the rivers into open sewers"? Or the accompanying results: poisoned aquatic life, destroyed food, and unswimmable waters? Is it really overarching to state that some of the chief contributions of the nineteenth-century U.S. city—"water closets, sewer mains, and river pollution"—represented a "backward step ecologically, and so far a somewhat superficial technical advance"?[73]

A close look at Philadelphia during its formative century, when vital organic elements remained active forces within the city, renders Mumford's holistic approach not only entirely relevant but more helpful to gaining an understanding of the problems of modern settlement patterns. Because seventeenth-century capitalism "treated the individual lot and the block, the street and the avenue, as abstract units for buying and selling, without respect for historic uses, for topographic conditions, or for social needs," early cities were flattened and built over.[74] Obscured along with the topography was an alternative, environmentally sounder vision of the city.

The story of Dock Creek matters because it perfectly illustrates how a natural cove and stream system became a quasi-natural, quasi-mechanical entity: a planked, walled canal. This in turn became an element in an evolving urban technological system: a brick conduit for transporting sewage, liquid wastes, and stormwater. As an artifact of the process of mechanization, early Philadelphia raises fundamental questions with a clarity directly rooted in their seminal character. Eighteenth-century Philadelphia possessed an urban core not yet built over that provoked a long struggle in which the disposition of a natural utility and urban amenity was determined by a predominantly private economic order's inability to accommodate natural utilities.

The very persistence of the values behind mechanization illustrates how the extended struggle over the Dock was no simple issue of filling in a tidal cove and leveling a watershed in order to install a comprehensive drainage system. The loss of the Dock and creek reflects the narrow set of values that have shaped U.S. settlement patterns. Public ends are transformed by the aims of a private order, social and environmental goals are submerged in mechanistic solutions, and natural entities such as the Dock are relegated to memory and to the pages of antiquarian histories.

Carolyn T. Adams

6 | Industrial Suburbs

Environmental Liabilities or Assets?

RECENT SCHOLARSHIP ON AMERICAN SUBURBS has acknowledged that not all suburbs are the same, that they come in a wide variety of types and income levels. Researchers have turned increasing attention to the older suburbs, sometimes called "inner-ring suburbs," as their problems have worsened. For example, the Brookings Institution undertook a comprehensive, multiyear study of older suburbs, publishing the results in *One-Fifth of America: A Comprehensive Guide to America's First Suburbs.* That report defines first suburbs strictly as commuter communities, saying that the "places that developed before or during the rapid suburban expansion right after World War II . . . began as bedroom communities . . . [;] think of the Levittowns or of television character Rob Petrie's New Rochelle, NY."[1] According to the Brookings scholars, those first suburbs are now foundering in a "policy blindspot" with few state or federal tools to help them adapt to their new realities.

Whatever the treatment of those older bedroom suburbs, however, older *industrial* suburbs have received even less serious attention. In those rare instances when urbanists have acknowledged that industry helped shape the suburbs, they have concentrated on the shift of manufacturing after World War II while paying less attention to the industrial suburbs that began appearing in metropolitan regions long before that conflict—indeed, long before the twentieth century.[2]

Scholars who have studied Philadelphia's manufacturing history have shown that industrialization occurred there through the establishment of a series of industrial districts beyond the city's built-up center.[3] This development pattern defied the Chicago school's ecological model of urban change during the nineteenth and early twentieth centuries, which conceived of city growth as "a process of decanting the core," with concentric rings gradually expanding outward from a city's industrial center.[4] Instead, different components of Philadelphia's industrial economy grew simultaneously in multiple locations, some of them far from the city's center. Waterways were the key determinants of location in the earliest phase of industrialization, particularly the Delaware and the Schuylkill, two major rivers that marked the eastern and western edges of the early city. The region's rail lines exerted an important influence on industrial patterns somewhat later in the nineteenth century. Both waterways and railways moved raw materials and finished goods through the region, serving early manufacturing centers that lay beyond the boundaries of Philadelphia. This chapter will focus on such industrial districts built in the metropolitan area during the nineteenth century. Their fortunes rose and fell in some common patterns that by the mid-twentieth century had dramatically reduced their vitality.

These days, policy analysts take a bleak view of the viability of first suburbs. One widely read study of metropolitan conditions, after enumerating the serious challenges facing central cities, goes on to lament: "The problem is even worse for distressed, inner-ring suburbs. . . . Regional elites care about central-city decline because they have substantial investments in downtown businesses, hospitals, universities and museums. They have no such commitments to distressed suburbs. By themselves, these suburbs can do little to arrest their decline."[5] Suburban analysts regard aging industrial suburbs as the least fortunate of these older communities, suffering from multiple handicaps. Typically, aging industrial suburbs are dotted with abandoned factories sitting atop brownfields. Their housing stocks, home to factory workers in an earlier generation, were built in styles and sizes that have not been attractive to recent generations of suburban homebuyers.

This chapter, however, argues that because these older manufacturing suburbs are typically high-density communities, with housing in easy walking distance of small-scale commercial districts and rail transportation, they can contribute significantly to environmentally

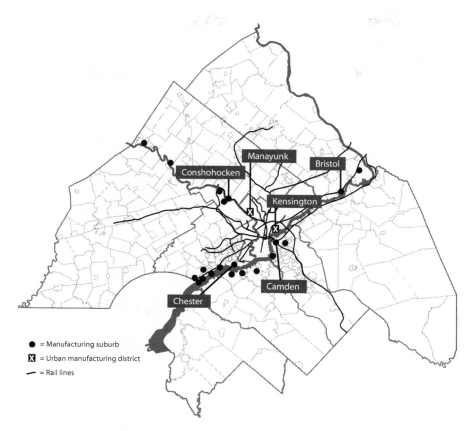

FIGURE 6.1. Districts historically devoted to manufacturing in the Philadelphia metropolitan area.

responsible growth patterns in the future. The potential is especially strong for manufacturing suburbs that were built along rivers because of the premium that real estate developers now place on waterfront locations. We see emerging signs that developers regard these older manufacturing districts as employment and residential centers of the future.

ONCE-THRIVING INDUSTRIAL CENTERS

To provide a sense of the places and manner in which these separate industrial districts sprang up, I will consider a half-dozen examples whose locations are identified in figure 6.1.

A little more than a mile upriver from the central Philadelphia wharves along the Delaware, the industrial district of Kensington flourished early in the nineteenth century. At first Kensington was home to diverse manufacturers producing everything from glass and pottery to wagons, machinery, and chemicals. Starting in the 1840s, textile trades began to dominate the area. Wool and silk mills clustered there, as did rug and lace factories, and later in the century carpet making came to dominate. The twentieth century brought a new specialty in hosiery.[6] Despite updating its product lines, however, Kensington's mills ultimately succumbed to competition from the southern United States and overseas. They now stand abandoned, surrounded by blocks of modest brick row houses that had been built originally for Irish, British, and German laborers. One author writing about Kensington in 1970 painted this early morning word picture of the neighborhood: "A pale winter sun shines wanly on rows of drab houses, almost all alike. The houses are soot-gray, as are the nearby stores, factories, bars and churches. Even at this early hour, the section looks tired." He pronounced this aging industrial neighborhood "Philadelphia's last large stronghold of the low-income white man."[7]

Directly across the Delaware River from Philadelphia, Camden secured its incorporation from the state of New Jersey in 1828, though it initially depended on the much larger economic engine of Philadelphia, in whose shadow it grew. Howard Gillette dates Camden's emergence as a more independent economic entity to the end of the Civil War, when the town's multiplying plants began producing carriages, woolen goods, and steel pens. In subsequent decades the Campbell Soup Company built its business on the Camden waterfront, as did the Victor Talking Machine Company and the New York Shipbuilding Corporation. By the early 1960s, however, local industries had declined so much that even the waterfront—once Camden's strongest economic asset—had become a dumping ground and an eyesore.[8] Its residential neighborhoods were blighted by abandoned buildings and contaminated sites. Not until the late 1980s, when the state of New Jersey began to take an interest in reviving Camden's faltering economy, did plans for large-scale redevelopment on the waterfront take hold. I will return to those plans later in this chapter.

Twenty-three miles northeast of Philadelphia, the small Pennsylvania borough of Bristol started as a ferry crossing on the Delaware River where passengers and goods could cross to Burlington, New Jersey. A canal connecting Bristol with upriver towns was built in 1827, after which manufacturing grew. Coal yards and warehouses appeared along the canal, followed by carpet and wool mills. Shipbuilding was another major contributor to the borough's economy. When the Merchant Ship-building Corporation arrived in 1917, shipbuilders and other shipyard workers poured into the town. At about that time, the Rohm and Haas Chemical Company established a major plant that remained a force in the borough's economy for many decades. As late as World War II, this Rohm and Haas plant manufactured Plexiglas and other acrylic products for use in the war, and the shipyards were converted to manufacturing aircraft. By the 1960s, however, those factories stood abandoned.

In the opposite direction from Philadelphia along the Delaware, fifteen miles south of Philadelphia, Chester became a successful mill town in the early 1700s. By the nineteenth century, Chester's diversified manufacturers were making ships, steel, iron, brass, cloth, carriages, barrels, shoes, and pottery. Chester's naval shipyard supplied the Union during the Civil War and made ships for the U.S. government in the twentieth century's two world wars. The Sun Shipbuilding and Dry Dock Company was sometimes described as a city in itself, sprawling along Chester's riverbank. It employed thousands, as did other major employers, such as the Scott Paper Company and Ford Motor Company. Chester's economy also relied on an oil refinery and a chemical manufacturing plant. In the 1960s Chester started losing its shipyard and automobile industry, and most of its manufacturing base would gradually go the same way. During the fifty years from 1950 to 2000, its population literally shrank by half as the area became known for its high unemployment, low-performing schools, and abandoned neighborhoods.

Not all the region's industrial enclaves were arrayed along the Delaware River. For example, Manayunk emerged by the 1830s as another thriving mill town on the banks of the Schuylkill River. It was known for the number and size of its textile mills, particularly its mechanized textile manufacturing. Located at a distance from Philadelphia's other textile districts, the cotton manufacturers in Manayunk could more easily equip their mills with power looms and other labor-saving devices, which were strongly resisted by hand weavers in Kensington and elsewhere.[9] Employees faced low wages, long hours, bad working conditions, and constant threats of replacement by machines, factors that led some to call Manayunk "the Manchester of America." Textile production dominated the economy of this district all the way up to the Great Depression, when the relocation of companies to the South and elsewhere began a slow erosion of its industry. One by one, the textile mills along the Schuylkill shut down, creating unemployment for long-time residents.

Conshohocken, ten miles farther up the Schuylkill River beyond Manayunk, prospered in the early nineteenth century because a canal built alongside the unnavigable river not only provided excellent transportation but also supplied the water power the area's early mills required. The town's dominant economic driver for most of its life was the iron industry. The first foundry was built in 1844; the largest and longest lived was the Alan Wood Steel Company, which survived from its nineteenth-century origins to the mid-twentieth century. Conshohocken drew a diverse laboring population. The Irish came to work in the mills and quarries, followed by Polish laborers later in the nineteenth century and then Italians. A second major employer was the Lee Tire and Rubber Company, whose factory was built in the 1890s. In the 1960s, however, Conshohocken's steel industry proved unable to compete against Japanese steel producers, and Lee Tire finally closed its doors in 1980. Those closures marked the end of the borough's manufacturing era.

Each of these places had a unique history that shaped its present-day character, yet they all shared some characteristics. Typically, these early towns were built on the same grid system used in Philadelphia. Indeed, outlying towns often adopted Philadelphia's system of using numerals to name streets running in one direction and tree designations, such as Walnut, Locust, and Spruce, for those running in the other.[10] All these towns spawned large factory buildings, most often located along freight rail lines. Their housing stocks were built originally for workers' families and were therefore smaller and more densely clustered than newer suburban housing. Nineteenth-century workers needed housing located within walking distance of factories since few could afford to pay daily transit fares. Many times, the housing units were built as row houses with shared walls. Small retail districts sprang up in walking distance, but these mom-and-pop retail districts have suffered from competition with retail malls and big-box stores.

Industrial suburbs shared social characteristics, too. Because they were working-class communities, their populations often lived in relative isolation from the wider economy. Without money for travel or entertainments, inhabitants lived a circumscribed existence, building dense networks of association involving family, friends, and neighbors. In the vocabulary of recent sociologists, they possessed social capital of the bonding, rather than the bridging, variety. Some close observers of these communities have warned against romanticizing the advantages of that solidarity. Writing about them in the early 1970s, one author and journalist noted that what they shared was their alienation from the American mainstream.[11]

MAPPING NINETEENTH-CENTURY INDUSTRIAL DECENTRALIZATION

The map in figure 6.1 shows the metropolitan area comprising the city of Philadelphia and eight surrounding suburban counties. Four of those suburban counties sit on the Pennsylvania side of the region, while four others are located across the Delaware River in New Jersey. The dots on the map identify twenty suburban communities that date from the nineteenth century and grew as industrial districts. Like Philadelphia, these communities lost much of their manufacturing base in the second half of the twentieth century. As recently as 2000, however, all twenty were still devoting 10 percent or more of their land area to manufacturing.[12] It seems reasonable to use 10 percent as a cutoff in categorizing these suburbs as industrial, since the city of Philadelphia as a whole currently devotes about 10 percent of its land to industrial uses. Interestingly, however, little of Philadelphia's current manufacturing goes on within its early industrial districts, such as Kensington and Manayunk (identified on the map by Xs), since they have lost almost all their industrial bases. Instead, twenty-first-century manufacturing is located in newer industrial parks, particularly in northeastern Philadelphia.

The map clearly shows how the region's two main rivers, the Delaware and the Schuylkill, shaped the locations of industrial districts in the nineteenth century. Even at the time of the American Revolution, the riverbanks of southeastern Pennsylvania were already dotted with small-scale manufacturing concerns, including paper mills, flour mills, textile mills, and ironworks. Some early manufacturers (e.g., iron makers) located near abundant supplies of timber for charcoal. Early textile mills used water power to turn their wheels.[13] The scale of these enterprises was small by the standards of the subsequent industrial revolution but large enough to foster small towns.

As industrialization advanced and factories increased in size, companies continued to locate on the city's outskirts. During the latter half of the nineteenth century, land values were rising so rapidly in industrial cities that cheaper suburban land provided a significant advantage to business owners. In 1915 Graham Romeyn Taylor analyzed manufacturing districts including Pullman, outside Chicago; Homestead, outside Pittsburgh; Norwood, outside Cincinnati; and Yonkers, outside New York. He attributed the rise of these industrial suburbs to "the impulse toward cheap land, low taxes, and elbow-room," along with their proximity to urban rail lines and labor markets. Taylor observed how the flight of factories was creating increasingly distant suburbs: "with households, small stores, saloons, lodges, churches, schools clinging to them like living tendrils, they [the manufacturers] set themselves down ten miles away in the open."[14]

Further attesting to the historical influence of waterways, a number of the rail lines represented in figure 6.1 parallel the rivers. The two rivers shaped subsequent transport routes because so much of the region's productive capacity was arrayed along their banks that it made sense for infrastructure to be built there even after water was no longer the primary means of transporting goods and people.

The map also clearly indicates how the pattern of scattered manufacturing settlements helped to create a governmental map that is fragmented into hundreds of small towns and boroughs, each one governing its own local affairs. The spidery web of boundary lines subdividing the region demarcates over 350 separate local governments contained within the two-state metropolitan area. Only once in the region's history was significant consolidation of small townships accomplished. In 1854 the Pennsylvania legislature approved consolidation of the small city of Philadelphia with thirteen surrounding townships, six boroughs, and nine districts, including the important mill towns of Kensington and Manayunk. That dramatic move enlarged the boundaries of Philadelphia to its current size. No subsequent effort to annex suburban territory has succeeded. Once, in the early twentieth century, Pennsylvania enacted legislation that would have created a metropolitan planning district extending twenty-five miles into the territory surrounding Philadelphia, but that legislation was repealed when courts ruled it to be inconsistent with the state constitution.[15]

The metropolitan area portrayed in figure 6.1 covers eight suburban counties spread across two states (some regional analysts define the metropolitan area even more broadly as encompassing parts of Delaware and Maryland). Every one of its more than 350 local governments operates independently for most public purposes. This means they rely heavily on their local tax bases to fund local services, a dependence that has compounded the problems facing older manufacturing districts. The revenue bases of these communities began stagnating when manufacturing plants closed down, causing unemployment. Specialized districts, such as Kensington and Manayunk, located inside the jurisdiction of Philadelphia had the advantage of being directly connected to the city's broader economy and tax base. Although they saw their fortunes decline as a result of economic shifts, they at least benefited from the job opportunities and the tax base that remained in the city, particularly in its downtown district. But industrial suburbs outside the city limits

TABLE 6.1. Selected Demographic Factors in the Philadelphia Area

	REGION	MANFG. SUBURBS	PHILADELPHIA
Population change, 1980–2010	+11.3%	−7.4%	−9.5%
Adults with bachelor's degree or better, 2009	32%	18%	22%
Homes at risk of foreclosure, 2009	7.4%	9.7%	11%
Hazardous waste sites within five miles of town center, 2003	158	273	740

Sources: U.S. Census Bureau, 2010 Census and American Community Survey; U.S. Dept. of Housing and Urban Development, Neighborhood Stabilization Program; U.S. Environmental Protection Agency, CERCLIS Database.

had no such advantage. As incomes and property values stagnated, they were forced to confront the decline by relying on their own resources. Some indicators of that decline are evident in table 6.1, which compares conditions in the manufacturing suburbs to those in the rest of the region. Those indicators portray the manufacturing suburbs as stronger than the city of Philadelphia yet weaker than the rest of the region.

The disadvantages portrayed in table 6.1 might seem to consign these older manufacturing suburbs to a bleak future, yet other indicators suggest they may be more resilient than one might have expected. In an era when the region's residents and businesses face higher energy costs and builders encounter increasing resistance to greenfield development, these older communities have advantages. They are more densely populated than other suburbs. In 2010, for example, the average population density for the region as a whole was 1,345 persons per square mile, whereas the manufacturing suburbs contained 3,790 persons per square mile.[16] Their high-density housing styles are smaller and more energy efficient than recent suburban housing types and may therefore be attractive to smaller households, an important consideration in a region experiencing significant shrinkage in household composition. Some of the smaller households consist of young singles or childless couples. Others are made up of older residents whose children have left home, a significant and growing population in the Philadelphia suburbs. Because the houses were built for industrial workers who walked to work and to purchase daily necessities, they typically possess main street commercial districts, an attractive feature in the current real estate market.

Industrial suburbs offer an additional asset: they are well served by mass transit, especially rail service, since railroads played a crucial role in transporting both goods and passengers to manufacturing centers. While suburban residents on average live two miles from the nearest commuter rail station, people who live in the manufacturing suburbs only need to travel two-fifths of a mile to the nearest train.[17] (Admittedly, the suburbs' present rail infrastructure is a mixed blessing. At some older industrial sites, freight rail lines exert a blighting influence.) As an added infrastructural advantage, these communities may include water and sewage systems with excess capacity because of the outmigration they experienced in recent decades, and other infrastructure as well is already in place.

Finally, it is increasingly difficult to build on greenfield sites. Government and nonprofit land trusts are putting their weight behind preservation of open space and encouraging developers to look elsewhere for building sites. Even when empty land is available, the approval process can take years—up to five in New Jersey and close to four in Pennsylvania. By contrast, a developer typically can be building on a brownfield site in a year or two. Typically, abandoned industrial properties sit on large flat parcels of land. As I discuss in more detail later on, sometimes they offer the added advantage of historically valuable structures that can be renovated to lend character to the redeveloped site.

NEW LIFE FOR OLDER INDUSTRIAL DISTRICTS

What signs of redevelopment do these faded manufacturing districts exhibit? In metropolitan Philadelphia, redevelopers have adopted two main strategies to take advantage of the physical assets and the character possessed by these gritty postindustrial places.

Creating Arts and Entertainment Destinations

A number of these older suburbs are being transformed into arts and entertainment districts. Artists gravitate toward these older places for the ample, inexpensive workspaces they can secure in funky buildings with high ceilings and large windows. The modest, inexpensive housing that typically surrounds old factories provides an additional attraction. Not all manufacturing buildings can be saved, but the large parcels on which they sit, once cleared, can accommodate entertainment venues such as concert halls, theaters, and even arenas. This combination has inspired developers of various kinds to try turning old manufacturing districts into centers of culture and commerce, making them destinations for visitors who can bring money into these communities. Such efforts are being initiated by different sponsors in different locations. Consider the following three examples, the first initiated by a community-based nonprofit; the second, by for-profit developers; and the third, by a quasi-public corporation.

In the old industrial neighborhood of Kensington, an ambitious community organization turned a nineteenth-century textile mill into the Coral Street Arts House, which combines living and working spaces for artists. The restoration preserved many original features of the building, respecting historical guidelines and placing the structure on the National Register of Historic Places in 2004. The building houses painters, writers, photographers, and graphic designers and includes exhibition space for their work. Expanding this effort to foster the arts in order to redevelop communities, the New Kensington Community Development Corporation (NKCDC) began working to create an "arts corridor" as a destination for visitors. This commercial stretch of thirteen blocks contains buildings and spaces reflecting a jumble of land uses and dating from the nineteenth century, from warehouses to small storefronts to littered, abandoned lots. The plan sought to use the buildings (many of which were vacant) and public spaces to create a coherent sense of place that would draw new residents, shoppers, and visitors. The community-based organization has identified several large industrial properties that could be converted to showrooms and galleries, the kind of uses that require loading docks and access for trucks and vans. A striking feature of NKCDC's planning is its open acknowledgment of gentrification as an element that must be taken into account. The row house developments they have recently built or renovated combine market-rate units with subsidized units on the same block to preserve housing options for working families with modest incomes. Rather than chase out downscale concerns, such as a local thrift shop, planners hope to capitalize on them to retain the area's authentic, slightly edgy character. By preserving open spaces, particularly those along the waterfront, the NKCDC has stressed public access and public amenities, thus preventing profit-making developers from capturing all the riverfront property.[18]

On the other side of Philadelphia, the transformation of the former mill district of Manayunk has proceeded much further, largely through the efforts of private investors rather than nonprofits or governmental agencies. While serving as that area's representative on the city council, Philadelphia's current mayor, Michael Nutter, remarked, "Manayunk is the greatest commercial corridor that the government never created."[19] One pivotal investor, Dan Neducsin, began acquiring properties on Main

Street, the neighborhood's principal commercial thoroughfare, in the late 1980s, when dozens of the street's buildings were boarded up. Over a period of almost twenty years, he bought more than fifty buildings, allowing him to design the strategy for redeveloping the area. He systematically went about making Main Street a commercial destination by leasing storefronts to galleries, antique shops, restaurants, and home decorating stores. The businesses ranged from tiny, one-of-a-kind shops to an outlet for Vermont handcrafted furniture from Pompanoosuc Mills housed in the oldest surviving mill in Manayunk, dating from 1822. Once it became clear that Neducsin was dramatically upgrading the historic commercial district, the city government supported his efforts by preventing demolition, requiring that the city's historical commission review any exterior changes, and controlling signage on Main Street. Developers helped organize large events to draw visitors, including an annual arts festival and an annual bicycle race attracting professional cyclists from around the world. Manayunk boosters managed to convince the race planners to include Main Street in the fifteen-mile loop that participants must cover ten times. Since Manayunk contains the steepest, most grueling segment of the race, the neighborhood attracts crowds every year. The commercial revival of Main Street has spilled over into the housing market, attracting a younger, higher-income residential population to nearby row houses, a trend that has drawn criticism from many observers, including the author of a 2006 study who lamented that "by turning Manayunk into a glitzy shopping and transient mecca, what made it real and interesting to the first gentrifiers has been lost."[20]

Quite a different strategy is being pursued by those who are redeveloping Camden's waterfront from industrial to leisure activities. Rather than pursue a revival based on the historically accurate preservation of nineteenth-century industrial structures, Camden planners have chosen to convert large parcels of land that were formerly occupied by major industrial operations to create tourist attractions. These conversions have been led by a quasi-public corporation, the Cooper's Ferry Development Association (CFDA), which was founded in 1984 to plan and carry out economic development projects on the Camden side of the Delaware River. Its strongest emphasis has been on redeveloping the waterfront as a destination for visitors. The main elements of the transformation over two decades have been a sixty-six-slip marina for recreational boaters adjacent to the Adventure Aquarium, which was built in 1992 as the cornerstone of Camden's waterfront revitalization; a concert amphitheater with both indoor and outdoor venues built in 1995 by a partnership between the state government of New Jersey and private concert promoters; a 6,500-seat ball park where a minor league team plays its games; and the permanent installation of the historic battleship the USS *New Jersey,* along with a museum. Each project required a large parcel of land that the CFDA helped to assemble, clear, and equip with the required infrastructure. Recently renamed the Cooper's Ferry Partnership, the organization reports that the Camden waterfront currently draws roughly two million visitors a year, a number that might increase if Camden succeeds in marketing its waterfront as a unified tourist destination with attractions across the river in Philadelphia.[21]

Creating White-Collar Employment Centers

In addition to creating arts and entertainment districts, some developers have sought to rehabilitate these older suburbs by refurbishing abandoned mills and factories as spaces for businesses that employ a white-collar workforce. The amenity value waterfront locations possess has fueled a growing interest among real estate developers seeking to rebuild these sites for corporate uses. Admittedly, brownfield contamination is a problem, but it also represents an opportunity. A number of such sites have already attracted substantial investment. Private developers are especially drawn to parcels where they can create a high reuse value relative to deeply discounted current land values. That is precisely the situation prevailing in abandoned waterfront sites contaminated by previous industrial uses. The projects of two developers will illustrate this trend. Michael and Brian O'Neill, two brothers who were among the first in this region to recognize the potential of suburban industrial sites, established a real estate investment company in the 1980s specializing in such sites. Their combined efforts during the last two decades have changed the character of several manufacturing suburbs.

The O'Neill brothers led Conshohocken's effort to revive its economic base after its factories closed, and they are accorded much of the credit for revamping the area from a smokestack borough to a white-collar job center. Their first major conversion in Conshohocken came in 1987, when they bought the old Lee Tire plant and transformed it into an office and light industrial complex called Spring Mill Corporate Center. That project helped to fuel a wave of office construction in Conshohocken and its emergence as a corporate center. Michael O'Neill then redeveloped a 1929 chemical plant, adding a two-story 40,000-square-foot office extension for the Quaker Chemical Company's corporate headquarters.

The project completely gutted the plant interior but preserved original elements, including wood beams and exterior brick walls. Brian O'Neill took a site that had historically been used to produce steel and plastics and transformed it into a $350 million, 707,000-square-foot complex of office space and multistory apartments and condominiums. Government subsidies played a part in the project: the U.S. Department of Housing and Urban Development gave O'Neill about $5 million in grants and loans for this brownfield redevelopment, and the state committed $2.5 million to include public open space along the riverfront. This and similar projects by the O'Neills and other developers resulted in a substantial real estate boom in Conshohocken. State tax records show that from 1995 to 2006, the total real estate value in Conshohocken nearly quadrupled, a rate of increase that exceeded the growth of the wealthiest of the region's suburbs.[22] While some old abandoned properties still sit on or near the riverbank, they are now interspersed with major new office complexes, along with restaurants, clubs, and other services for the office workforce.

Michael O'Neill undertook another brownfield reclamation in Chester, where he restored a landmark electricity-generating station that had once powered shipyards and other industries. Like many other coal-burning power plants, this one had been built near the river to profit from the relatively low cost of hauling coal by water. Constructed in 1916, when electricity was relatively new, its architecture was intended to convey solidity and permanence, much like banks and government buildings in the early twentieth century. Massive four-story columns were designed to resemble a Greek temple, suggesting that it would last for centuries. Because of their negative environmental impacts, however, such utilities are no longer allowed to operate near rivers, so that the building had been vacant since 1981. The PECO Energy Company was planning to demolish the nine-story generating station when O'Neill took an interest in it, appealing for government subsidies to make its restoration financially attractive. In 1999 city officials in Chester debated designating the area as a Keystone Opportunity Zone (KOZ) to help O'Neill buy the vacant property and turn it into a modern office building. Designating this property as a KOZ would mean that no tax revenues would flow to the city government until 2015. Despite that sacrifice of tax gains in the immediate future, local officials looked at the deal as a plus: "We had to ask if we were cheating ourselves of potential tax revenue.... Our take was, there was nobody there and there was nobody coming."[23] Paralleling the local government in its tax forgiveness, state government agencies contributed $11 million for environmental cleanup, new roads, and other improvements. The impressive neoclassical structure reopened in 2005, renamed "The Wharf at Rivertown," and close to 1,000 white-collar workers are employed there, mostly in computer, software, and financial firms.

Yet another project that illustrates the redevelopment potential of industrial suburbs occurred in Bristol, where Michael O'Neill's firm saw an opportunity in an abandoned factory dating to World War I. In 1917 W. Averell Harriman had moved rapidly to build the Merchant Shipbuilding Company to support the national war effort. Between 1917 and 1921 his shipyard had delivered forty cargo ships to the U.S. Shipping Board's Emergency Fleet Corporation. The shipyard had closed after the war's end, after which the plant had become a soap factory, eventually being acquired by the Purex Company, which manufactured soap and bleach products there until the plant closed in 1986. Some time after its closing, the local redevelopment authority acquired the abandoned plant and spent more than a million dollars to demolish some old structures and remove toxic metals from the soil.[24] Then the authority went looking for a developer. It found a buyer in O'Neill's firm, which bought the forty-four-acre site in 2003 and converted what had been a fabrication shop at the shipyard into offices. O'Neill said his company was able to buy sites "no one else [would] touch" because he and his team had learned over the last twenty-eight years how to deal with issues that old buildings and sites present. The developer's confidence in the project was based on its riverfront location: "it's the only office building in Bucks County with a view of the river."[25]

STRATEGIES TO REVIVE INDUSTRIAL SUBURBS

Many scholars studying American suburbs have emphasized the negative consequences of moving manufacturing out of cities and into the suburbs because of the contribution that industrial decentralization made to metropolitan sprawl following World War II. As manufacturing plants have increasingly chosen to locate on interstate highways, central cities have lost much of their economic base. Bruce Katz of the Brookings Institution dubbed this pattern "the exit ramp economy." Yet in regions such as Greater Philadelphia, where industrial decentralization antedated the age of automobiles and trucks, manufacturing suburbs could play a positive role in stemming sprawl and promoting smart growth.

In the preceding pages I have sought to show that old industrial suburbs have the potential for environmentally responsible redevelopment as employment, commercial, and residential nodes in an era when energy prices are soaring and environmentalists are seeking ways to encourage higher-density development. Suburban governments must find ways to expand their tax bases beyond conventional single-family housing, a land use that often requires more public service expenditures than it generates in taxes. The sizable parcels of land left behind by manufacturers, and sometimes the abandoned factory buildings as well, can be redeveloped at higher-than-average densities for either commercial or residential purposes, strengthening the local tax base while making responsible use of already existing infrastructure. As the previously adduced examples illustrate, those industrial suburbs with waterfront locations find themselves in a particularly privileged position in the current real estate market. What could governments do to encourage this redevelopment trend and expand it?

Brownfields Policy

Virtually all the redevelopment projects described here involved reclaiming brownfields. While we might think of brownfields as posing major disadvantages to developers, contamination often represents an opportunity instead. As mentioned earlier, private developers are especially drawn to parcels where they can create a high reuse value relative to deeply discounted current land values.

The redevelopments I have discussed benefited greatly from changes in state policies regarding remediation of contaminated sites. In the mid-1990s both Pennsylvania and New Jersey adopted regulatory changes to encourage brownfields reclamation. Like many other states, they streamlined the development process and reduced the liability that discourages developers from rebuilding on brownfields. In 1993 New Jersey passed a law adjusting pollution treatment standards, the Industrial Sites Recovery Act. This legislation set different standards for residential and nonresidential cleanups and allowed land owners to avoid removing toxins from a site and instead simply contain them, for example, by erecting fences or building impermeable caps to prevent wastes from seeping out of contaminated sites. Similarly, Pennsylvania's brownfields law, enacted in 1995, established flexible cleanup standards and offered a release from future liability to the owners of brownfield sites once they had met one of those remediation standards. Previously, businesses acquiring factories and warehouses had been responsible for restoring those sites to near-pristine conditions. In 1995, however, the state allowed developers to undertake less-stringent cleanup plans depending on the intended future use of the site. Without those legislative changes, combined with government subsidies to help pay for cleanups, it is doubtful that the building conversions described in this chapter would have taken place.

Transit Policy

Policy makers need to work harder to exploit the potential of older industrial suburbs for Transit Oriented Development (TOD). Unfortunately, vast parking lots surround all three of the previously mentioned redeveloped office complexes, which encourage employees to depend on automobiles. This is not always the developer's preference, but suburban zoning codes require developers to build as many as three parking spaces for every 1,000 square feet of office space. Developer contributions to public investments in TOD would make more sense than building such massive parking lots given the transit access these locations already possess.

Admittedly, the metropolitan planning agency for Greater Philadelphia is promoting TOD for suburbs. But the relevant agency, the Delaware Valley Regional Planning Commission (DVRPC), is not focusing its TOD efforts on older manufacturing suburbs. Only six manufacturing suburbs appeared on the DVRPC's list of forty-five places chosen as potential sites for TOD development.[26] Moreover, when the DVRPC launched its Classic Towns program to promote older suburbs (which it defined as towns that matured before auto dependence), it included only two manufacturing suburbs. Its other sixteen choices were all residential communities, which it regarded as easier "sells" to prospective homebuyers.[27]

Promoting Balanced Development to Spread Social Benefits

While developers generally seek to attract middle- and upper-middle-class residents to live and work in older suburbs, public officials are charged with bringing benefits to all their constituents, including those at lower income levels. I have argued that in older manufacturing suburbs, the smaller, more compact housing styles are likely to become more attractive for smaller households in an era of higher energy prices. The waterfront locations of these communities hold the same appeal to housing developers that they hold for offices and other commercial developers. Some of the redevelopment projects discussed here have already produced signs of social conflict between established residents and newcomers. The tensions generated by the population changes taking place in Conshohocken provide a good example. One newspaper report characterized the new Conshohocken as "a sometimes jarring mix of old and new: of rickety rowhouses and $500,000 condos, of retired plant workers and 20-something tech-heads, of summer soapbox derbies and Zagat-rated restaurants."[28] Empty-nesters and young professionals are encroaching on the established blue-collar population, creating competition for properties and for public space. The newcomers are attracted by the small town character of the place, which one new arrival described this way: "Conshohocken . . . [has] a main street; it's set up in neighborhoods on a grid. You have access to major cities and highways, but you don't need them to get anything you don't already have, really."[29]

Yet the jobs and lifestyle now available to white-collar professionals in Conshohocken are not necessarily improving the fortunes of long-established families. A recent report on redeveloping older industrial cities focused on public policies that can spread social benefits to citizens across different income levels instead of concentrating them among more affluent newcomers.[30] Among the most important such benefits are education and job training to equip longtime residents for participation in the economic revival of these old towns. (Table 6.1 shows that only 18 percent of adults living in the manufacturing suburbs held college degrees in 2009, a somewhat lower percentage than obtains either in the central city or in the metropolitan area as a whole.) Also needed are initiatives to link local small businesses to incoming developers.

To benefit existing residents, government must also pay attention to the housing stock. Much of this housing is in disrepair, and some of it is even abandoned or threatened with imminent foreclosure. With houses as with industrial parcels, when prices drop dramatically, the land and any structures on it become attractive targets for developers seeking to profit by rehabilitating and selling at market rates. One possible strategy that local governments might pursue involves creating land banks to take control of abandoned or foreclosed properties; these banks could then seek nonprofit developers to rehabilitate the properties as affordable housing instead of letting them be bought by private developers for redevelopment at market rates. Even more beneficial to current residents are programs that help existing homeowners and landlords to stabilize their situations. A recent policy brief on the housing stock in Philadelphia's working-class neighborhoods emphasized the financial, social, and environmental benefits that accrue when government provides grants to homeowners so that they can weatherize their houses and repair basic systems, such as furnaces, water pipes, electric lines, and roofs.[31] In addition, counseling and financial services can prevent foreclosures on properties occupied by households that need only a little help to stay in their homes.

In summary, private developers may be crucial to reviving the fortunes of older manufacturing suburbs, but public officials must take strategic actions to shape the development agenda. Which public officials are best situated to defend the public interest in these matters? A regional approach would produce the greatest benefits. Plans to clean up major brownfield sites that pollute the land and water, to promote transit-oriented development, to train underemployed suburban workers, and to stabilize older housing stocks are likely to be less effective if undertaken on a strictly local basis. The impacts of all those strategies are spread across local government boundaries, and action in all those domains depends heavily on state policies and subsidies. Ideally, the revival of these older communities should be taken up by metropolitan coalitions and organizations supported by state government.

PART III | Landscape Transformation in the Growing City

Adam Levine

7 | The Grid versus Nature

The History and Legacy of Topographical Change in Philadelphia

BEFORE ANY CITY CAN BE built, the landscape—as the city's literal foundation—must be reconfigured to support the structures to be sited above it. In Philadelphia this foundation building was undertaken mainly to accommodate the grid (or gridiron) street system. In laying out the grid, city surveyors and engineers oversaw the leveling of thousands of acres and the encapsulation of more than one hundred miles of streams in underground sewers, a process that took place over hundreds of years. An examination of this process, beyond exposing the original landscape and the scope of its transformation, also reveals some of the attitudes of eighteenth- and nineteenth-century city builders toward the natural environment and some of this work's consequences that continue to affect the city today.

THE ORIGINAL TOPOGRAPHY

Originally covering only 1,200 acres, Philadelphia today spreads out over 129 square miles, having annexed (under the 1854 Act of Consolidation) the twenty-nine other municipalities of Philadelphia County.

The city is bounded on the east by the Delaware River and bisected by a major Delaware tributary, the Schuylkill River, both under the influence of a tide that averages about six feet. Before urbanization, the landscape was laced with dozens of smaller spring-fed streams (called creeks or runs in the region's vernacular). Philadelphia straddles the "fall line," the geological boundary at which the hilly Appalachian piedmont tumbles down into the relative flatness of the coastal plain; as the streams tumbled down from the hills, the falling water provided abundant power for the city's early mills. The highest hilltops in the city stand over four hundred feet, with the coastal plain elevations ranging up to about fifty feet.[1] The city's lowest points can be found in its tidal marshlands. Although they are almost completely filled in today, these wetlands once covered thousands of acres, most near the confluence of the Delaware and Schuylkill rivers and smaller areas at various points along both riverfronts.[2]

When Philadelphia was founded in 1682 by William Penn, an English Quaker, the land's physical features helped define the city's boundaries.[3] The original two square miles of the city prior to consolidation were bounded by the Delaware and Schuylkill rivers on the east and west, Cedar (now South) Street on the south, and Vine Street to the north. The site chosen was drier and higher than the swampy land that covered large areas of land below South Street but less hilly than the land to the north. It also lay at the narrowest point between the two riverfronts.

Several small streams cut gentle valleys through this narrow strip of coastal plain. Dock Creek (the site of the city's first public landing) drained much of the original city on the Delaware River side, with tributaries reaching as far west as Broad Street. Pegg's Run drained the city's northeastern edge, emptying into the Delaware River north of Vine Street. Minnow Run, with its springs in higher ground north of the city, was the largest of several streams that drained into the Schuylkill, and Shackaminsing Creek ran south into the tidal marshlands of present-day South Philadelphia.[4] Instead of exhibiting the featureless, bulkheaded boundaries of today, the rivers originally had irregular shorelines, including marshlands and mudflats inundated with every high tide and sandy bluffs that may have stood as much as twenty-five feet above the water.[5]

THE GRID PLAN OF STREETS

William Penn had witnessed both an epidemic of plague and a destructive fire that had devastated London in the mid-1660s. The grid of streets that he and his surveyor, Thomas Holme, devised for the original city of Philadelphia was considered a "vast improvement over the narrow and winding thoroughfares of European cities of the period," which provided little open space or greenery and allowed fire and disease to quickly spread from house to house (see fig. 1.1 in chapter 1).[6] The plan set aside an eight-acre public square in each quadrant of the city and a ten-acre square in its center.

Penn's supposed desire that Philadelphia be a "green country town, which [would] never be burnt and always be wholesome"[7]—so often quoted that it has attained a mythic status—does not in fact stand up to more in-depth scrutiny. Penn formulated this utopian ideal while in England, before the site for the colony's site had been chosen, but as Harriet Roach reveals in an exhaustive pair of essays detailing Philadelphia's early planning and settlement, he and his subordinates willingly altered this goal according to geographic realities and the needs and desires of the town's first settlers.[8] In any event, for the purposes of this chapter, the founder's original intention is less important than the plan that was chosen and its impact on the landscape.

As the city grew, the grid of streets expanded with it, encouraging what one nineteenth-century observer considered the "avidity" of Philadelphia landowners "for converting every piece of ground to the greatest possible revenue."[9] A gridiron street plan served this avidity well, allowing the subdivision of property into uniform rectangles that allowed land owners to utilize every square inch of a lot. The city plan rarely made use of diagonal streets, which might have provided shortcuts from one place to another but would also have created awkward triangles of land as they cut corners across existing property lines. Streets that might have meandered along the irregular contours of the land, following a hillside or a stream and thus preserving the beauty of the natural topography, were likewise shunned. The City of Brotherly Love became a city of unlovely right angles: squares and other rectangles as far as the eye could see, with rarely a curve or hypotenuse in sight.

Writing in 1905, the pioneering city planner Andrew Wright Crawford complained about Philadelphia's rectilinear arrangement:

> Its system of regular blocks materially interferes with transit and causes a monotonous architectural effect. . . . It compels the citizen to run his latitude and longitude generally, instead of taking a direct or diagonal route. It is curious how we strain at a gnat and swallow a camel in city making. Recently the Mayor of Philadelphia suggested a fountain for the centre of the City Hall court-yard, which would compel a slight detour.

> There has already been opposition because of this detour, and yet the
> enormous detours compelled by the street system are passed over in
> silence; if attention is called to the matter, the right of property owners
> to lay streets so as to erect the greatest number of buildings is declared
> paramount.[10]

Several years later Crawford elaborated: "There is one great handicap
to good street planning. . . . This is the opposition of real estate operators. In order to build the greatest number of houses on a street, they
want it straight and rectangular. They don't care for the persons who
are to live in these houses afterwards, and still less do they care for the
good of the city as a whole."[11]

As urban development expanded north and south of the city boundaries, neighboring municipalities developed their own gridded street
systems. By design or by human error, the grids in each municipality
often deviated from the city grid, frequently forcing adjustments as
straight streets were extended outward from the city. These adjusted
lines tended to disregard long-standing property boundaries on which
the existing streets might have been based and sometimes ran smack
into existing buildings, resulting in damage payments to owners far in
excess of the sums they would have been due if some deviation in the
street lines had been allowed.[12]

The grid, combined with a tendency of builders to put every house
at the same distance from the curb, led Thomas Jefferson to comment
on the city's "disgusting monotony" in 1790.[13] In 1804 the British visitor
John Davis observed that the diagonal streets in Pierre L'Enfant's plan
for the District of Columbia would have prevented "the monotony" that
he claimed to characterize Philadelphia and went on to suppose that the
difference between the two plans lay in "the superiority of taste in a
traveled Frenchman over a homebred Englishman."[14] Charles Dickens
offered a more bemused view of Philadelphia in his *American Notes*,
originally published in 1842: "It is a handsome city, but distractingly
regular. After walking about it for an hour or two, I felt that I would have
given the world for a crooked street. The collar of my coat appeared to
stiffen, and the brim of my hat to expand, beneath its quakerly influence.
My hair shrunk into a sleek short crop, my hands folded themselves
upon my breast of their own calm accord, and thoughts of . . . making a
large fortune by speculations in corn . . . came over me involuntarily."[15]

This regularity came at the expense of the landforms over which the
grid was laid. The ruling axiom of a grid system of city planning might
be stated as follows: wherever the grid contradicts nature, nature loses.

In order to accommodate the unnatural rigidity of a rectangular system of streets, natural features had to be cut down, filled in, leveled, and buried, ultimately erased not just from view but from collective memory.

In the 1840s a visiting writer named Alexander Mackay appreciated the shortcut provided by the only diagonal the gridded city then contained, Dock Street. "So unlooked for an oddity in such a place put me on inquiry," Mackay wrote, "but nobody would tell me how it got there." The diagonal street followed the course of the former Dock Creek, which had been channeled into an underground pipe after the Revolution and apparently forgotten soon thereafter.[16]

Eventually observers began to notice what was being lost. A 1902 report from the City Parks Association of Philadelphia bemoaned the fact that the generous provision for open space in William Penn's original plan "had either been forgotten or ignored" as the city expanded, while "the other main feature of the plan, the straight streets and square blocks, without a curve, or a diagonal, seized hold of the public's mind with a grip that [was] apparently . . . little diminished by age. On goes the gridiron," the report exclaimed, burdening the city with "its severe mantle of unloveliness."[17]

THE REGULATION OF ASCENTS AND DESCENTS

The process of laying out and grading streets was called, in Philadelphia and elsewhere, "the regulation of ascents and descents," or "street regulation." Determining the rise and fall (commonly called the grade) of a particular street was necessary to provide proper drainage and to prevent flooding. It also ensured that the grades were shallow enough to be negotiated without too much effort by the horse-drawn transportation prevalent when most of the streets were laid out. On a more basic level, surveying the street lines was the only way to ensure that abutting property owners did not encroach on the public highways with their houses or other structures. Aesthetics were also a consideration, as part of a 1698 law relating to the appointment of regulators reveals: "The ornament of towns and the conveniency and health of the inhabitants . . . depend upon the due regulation of streets and landing places."[18]

The work of street regulation was done by "regulators," working first with the surveyor-general of the colony and later with the city surveyor, all of whom were appointed by various authorities at various points between the city's founding and its consolidation in 1854. The regulators and the surveyors were charged with laying out street and property lines and determining drainage patterns by fixing the rise and fall of each street prior to grading and paving. Executing these plans, however, was not so straightforward. For much of the eighteenth century, there seems to have been no direct responsibility for the "highways," as the streets were officially called. In 1762 the Pennsylvania colonial assembly passed an act creating a board of six city commissioners who were charged with facilitating the work, but they had no authority to raise money. In 1804 the mayor was given the authority to appoint a city surveyor and regulator, and a supplement to the Act of Consolidation of 1854 created an official surveys department for the enlarged city. The chief engineer and surveyor, along with twelve district surveyors serving various parts of the city, constituted the board of surveyors.[19] One of the board's first tasks was to draw up a "full, minute, and accurate survey of the whole city . . . designating how the same should be graded and leveled, so as most beneficially to accomplish the drainage and sewerage of the whole city," a task that took decades to even partially execute.[20] Eventually the surveys department was put in charge of planning, designing, and supervising the construction of the city's streets, sewerage, and bridges.

STREET REGULATION: AN ONGOING PROCESS

Street regulation is an ongoing process in any city: as the city expands, new infrastructure has to be designed and built to provide access and services to the new development. Even in the relatively small area of the original Philadelphia, street construction continued for more than 150 years after the city's founding, with the two square miles not being fully built up from river to river until the mid-nineteenth century.

To proceed with the least disruption, street regulation should be undertaken before any buildings have been erected along the street, thus allowing builders to place their structures at the proper grade, but this ideal was not always the reality in Philadelphia. More than a hundred years after the city's founding, the Common Council noted the continuing need "to ascertain the descents for the water and the courses it should run" in unimproved areas and to prevent encroachment of buildings within the street lines, to "save expence to the public for either removing of earth to or from the streets unnecessarily," which it said had "been the case for want of such previous regulation." This resolution also aimed to correct previous surveys that had resulted in "the squares of the city not laid out parallel to each other as originally intended by the Founder, to the great irregularity and blemish of the City" (a statement that perhaps reveals more about the views of city officials at the time than those of William Penn).[21]

As urban development spread, neighboring municipalities also appealed for help in street regulation. A 1787 act of assembly appointed commissioners to regulate the streets, lanes, and alleys of Southwark, just south of Philadelphia along the Delaware River. A preamble to this law noted: "Whereas the district of Southwark has become populous and the freeholders thereof are daily erecting buildings and making improvements therein, but for want of a public and general regulation of the streets, lanes and alleys, they are irregularly placed and there is danger that in time they will become a heap of confused buildings without order or design unless a remedy be speedily applied."[22]

In 1862 a committee of the board of surveyors reported on the Hestonville section of West Philadelphia, where 160 buildings had been built without the benefit of an approved plan of grade regulation:

> Nothing so mars the beauty of a place such as Hestonville, when it becomes solidly built, as irregularity in the height of the buildings, and . . . nothing so retards or dampens the desire to build as the uncertainty of the individual whether, after his building is finished and his means lavished upon it and the grades become arranged, he will find his building looms up in the street or buried to the first floor, rendering the improvement which was before his pride, an eyesore to the neighborhood and a disappointment to himself. When no grade plan exists, this must necessarily happen, as each individual builds, not with reference to the good of the whole, or the benefit of his neighbor, but in such manner as his own particular piece of ground seems to most favor.[23]

The full board adopted a resolution to order "the establishment of grades in this section, demanded alike as a matter of justice to the citizens and property holders and as a measure of policy by the City."[24]

In some cases, alluded to in the previously cited reports, streets were regulated a second time after supposedly "final" grades had already been fixed and buildings had already gone up. This might be done to improve drainage or, along the riverfront, to provide better access to bridges and wharves. If the revised cutting or filling was severe enough, the rough foundation of a basement might be uncovered or a first floor be buried partially or completely. Noted Watson in his *Annals*: "The house still standing at the southwest corner of Race and Water streets goes down three steps to the first floor, whereas it used to go up three or four steps, in the memory of some ancients; thus proving the raising of the street there.... On Front street nearby, the street is lowered full one story, as the cellar of the house on the northwest corner of Front and Race streets, now standing out of the ground, fully proves."[25] Neither case would be an attractive proposition to a property owner, nor would it be in keeping with the founder William Penn's supposed desire for a regular and blemish-free city.

GRADE REGULATION: DIVIDED RESPONSIBILITY

Further complications arose because the city and other municipal governments in the surrounding county were responsible for regulating the grade only of the streets themselves, from curb to curb. The responsibility for grading interior blocks bounded by these streets was left to the private owners, who would generally not go to the expense of filling up or cutting down their lots until they were ready to develop the property, which could be years after the streets were built. In cases where streets had been cut through surrounding higher ground, the results could be picturesque. The natural ground above the leveled roadway might be the site of an old house, or used for grazing cows or other agricultural purposes. Where the street embankments were raised above surrounding unfilled lots, however, the resulting causeways often acted as dams, with pools of stagnant water forming in the low ground behind them.[26]

While these so-called ponds might provide great sport as skating places in winter, in summertime they often became great health nuisances. From the founding of the city through much of the nineteenth century, the anticontagionist, or miasma, theory of disease held sway. Adherents of this theory claimed that illness could be spread by masses of contaminated air (called "miasmas"), with foul odors identified as the evidence of the contamination. Householders used the ponds to dump their garbage, kitchen wastes, dead cats, and dead dogs; even dead horses ended up in them. In hot weather, all these things would decompose into a malodorous stew that, according to the miasmists, threatened the health of the surrounding neighborhood.[27] In the first half of the nineteenth century, the Philadelphia County Board of Health maintained a "ponds committee" that handled many complaints, ordering property owners either to provide outlets for the stagnant water or to fill their lots to the grade of the surrounding streets and levying fines against those who refused to comply.[28]

THE PROCESS OF STREET BUILDING

At its simplest, leveling the ground along the line of a street is a matter of geometry, measuring and removing the volumes of material above the grade regulation and looking for nearby areas with equivalent depressed volumes to fill. It is not an exaggeration to say that millions of cubic yards of earth were moved in the city during this process, with much of the moving (even into the twentieth century) done by people and horses.

In one time-tested method for lowering land, a horse-drawn plow loosened the soil before gangs of men with shovels loaded it into carts.[29] As the nineteenth century progressed, increasingly sophisticated horse-drawn digging equipment came to include self-loading and self-dumping carts and a variety of drags, scrapers, scoops, and other machinery that facilitated grading work. To remove hard rock sometimes required blasting, or a temporary quarry might be set up to cut building stone from the site. Besides stone, deposits of sand and gravel could be harvested from street excavations, and in one case a large clay deposit, exposed while crews were leveling the western end of Spruce Street, was reserved for use in lining a new reservoir at the Fairmount Water Works.[30]

While mechanized construction equipment, such as steam shovels, came into wider use in the later nineteenth century (followed by steam- or gasoline-powered tractors to replace the pulling power of horses), old-fashioned methods often remained more economical. A 1919 treatise on highway engineering considered horsepower useful under certain conditions and described a typical crew that might have been familiar to road builders of 1819 or even 1719: "Where the material is loosened by means of plows and hauled in wagons, the average small grading gang may consist of 1 foreman, 3 laborers and 2 teams for plowing, 9 laborers for loading, 2 laborers for spreading, and a sufficient number of teams for hauling to keep the above force busy."[31]

In any cut-and-fill work, then and now, workers seek to minimize hauling by dumping surplus material from the cuts into the closest low spots. This sometimes meant that the material had to be stockpiled until a convenient low spot could be identified or that work in a given area sometimes had to stop until ongoing "improvements" came within hauling distance. In 1825 the city councils ordered that Rittenhouse Square (one of the five squares set aside on Penn's original city plan) be filled up to its proper grade, but no cuts undertaken that year were sufficiently close to accomplish this goal economically. A reverse situation occurred several years earlier, when the city commissioners reported that dumping the "considerable quantity of earth from street projects in the vicinity" onto Franklin Square would "lessen the expense of hauling considerably," but they lacked the city councils' authorization to do so.[32]

In the 1850s work done on two West Philadelphia streets so as to "to open, grade, and put [them] in suitable condition for travel" included the following charges: for the excavation of earth, $0.25 per cubic yard; for soft rock, $0.50; and for solid rock, $0.80. Removal of stumps over six inches diameter cost $2.00 each, with smaller stumps removed at no charge. The "average haul" was not to exceed 500 feet, with any "extra haul" paid for at the rate of $0.02 per hundred feet. Under this single contract, the contractors moved more than 32,000 cubic yards of rock and earth (which, to use a modern comparison, would fill 1,600 dump trucks the size of a tractor-trailer container).[33] Though the report omits the mode of hauling, a standard dump or tip cart used for such work would have carried only one to three cubic yards, and drag scoops much less, meaning that more than ten thousand circuits were made between the cut and the fill areas.[34]

RURAL LANDMARKS SUCCUMB TO URBANIZATION

By the end of the nineteenth century, the following scene (described in an 1895 newspaper article) became all too familiar as real estate developers devoured the consolidated city's suburban and rural districts:

> The march of that product of civilization called improvement has of late years been removing from the city many places of historic value.... One by one the landmarks of history are disappearing, living only in the recollections of gossips to become traditions to the next generation.... At present Somerville ..., at Twelfth and Cambria streets, is a scene of desolation and ruin. Here and there through the rubbish and undergrowth only the hacked stumps and bared roots remain of the beautiful grove that once sieved the sunlight and tendered shade to a well-kept lawn and graveled paths. The old yellow plastered house ... still stands, but even it will vanish in a few weeks, and on the ruins of the fine old seat will be built rows of modern houses, and the place so long almost deserted will in a little while be thickly populated.... The work of grading the property, which is about four feet above the street level, is now being done, and when completed streets will be cut through for the convenience of the houses to occupy the site.... Contractor John Stabler, who cut down the trees, has a force of men digging out a cut through the grounds for the purpose of laying a

siding track from the Pennsylvania Railroad, in order to haul away the soil in cars. About 120,000 cubic yards of earth will have to be removed before the work of building the rows of houses ... can be commenced. ... A well-known gentleman who resides in the neighborhood, and who witnessed the destruction of the fine grove of trees, said that the work was one bordering on vandalism, and expressed the opinion that the property should have been purchased by the city as a park.[35]

While records of the city's earliest landscape are sketchy at best, many nineteenth-century paintings, drawings, lithographs, and photographs (as well as articles like the one just quoted) provide a wealth of information. Beyond offering purely commercial views that in themselves constitute an invaluable record of change, several artists and photographers purposefully documented a landscape that they knew was quickly being lost. Augustus Kollner and David J. Kennedy, who both worked in the nineteenth century, painted watercolors of many rural scenes as they were about to be subsumed by urban development. Frank H. Taylor, a Philadelphia commercial artist who worked before and after the turn of the twentieth century, similarly documented the passing scenes in West Philadelphia. In the same time period, the physician and amateur photographer John Eckfeldt also documented the rapidly disappearing West Philadelphia farmsteads. Eckfeldt's camera occasionally captured scenes that Taylor also captured in watercolor, and his stark photographs clearly reveal what the painter omitted in order to prettify and romanticize the scenes: the farmsteads under siege, surrounded by ranks of row houses lined up like soldiers, biding their time. Some landholders held out longer than others, but inevitably they sold out to developers, and soon afterward the grid of streets and houses would occupy yet another plot of formerly open land.[36]

PROTECTING THE PUBLIC HEALTH: TURNING POLLUTED STREAMS INTO SEWERS

Regulating watercourses to provide efficient and effective drainage has been a local concern since the founding of the city and was the main impetus for the previously discussed regulation of ascents and descents. Drainage could be provided in a number of different ways. Streets were graded so that water flowing in gutters would drain from block to block to block until it emptied into the nearest creek or river. Ditches might be dug to carry excess water from a low spot to the nearest stream, and small streams themselves might be straightened or channelized to speed the flow of water away from built-up areas. Finally, underground brick sewers to carry off stormwater were built beginning in the first half of the eighteenth century. By the mid-nineteenth century, however, the entire consolidated city had only 37.5 miles of such sewers.[37]

As the grid expanded across the territory, surface streams became increasingly problematic. Streams on the outskirts of a developing area were often the means by which stormwater was carried off; once they were surrounded by buildings, however, these same streams could be liabilities. Potential property damage from storm flooding was a major concern. Construction and maintenance of bridges became a large expense, one made more burdensome by the exigencies of the grid, which, depending on the meanders of a particular stream, might require a straight street to cross that stream several times.[38] Furthermore, the stream valleys and floodplains rendered nearby property unsuitable for most building purposes (unless, perhaps, one wanted to erect a water-powered mill). These economic considerations alone made putting urban streams underground, in pipes beneath the streets, an attractive proposition.

From a health standpoint as well, streams were seen as a disadvantage in an urban neighborhood. In the coastal plain in which the original city and other parts of Philadelphia County were sited, the lower reaches of slow-moving streams were often surrounded by marshes and mudflats exposed twice a day by a low tide, exuding an unhealthy dampness and "miasmas" that were seen as potent sources of sickness. Additional health concerns arose as streams became polluted. Privy wells often drained into adjacent streams, adding their contents to the household wastes or dead animals dumped there. Even after steam engines became the power source for most factories in the nineteenth century, streams alongside industrial sites provided a convenient water supply for a variety of processes (such as soaking animal hides in a tannery or dyeing and bleaching in a textile mill) and an ideal sink for the water fouled by those processes.

By the mid-nineteenth century, several large brick sewers had already been built to encapsulate polluted streams in the city and neighborhoods to the north. Dock Creek had long been sullied by wastes from leather tanneries, slaughterhouses, and other industries along its banks, and authorities began covering it in 1765 by placing a brick arch over it. Pegg's Run, just north of Vine Street, was similarly polluted and similarly piped, that process beginning in the 1820s. In the 1840s, officials initiated the process of burying the polluted lower reaches of Cohocksink Creek, which had previously been channelized within the walls of a serpentine canal.[39] Three winding streets still mark the courses of these streams: Dock Street over the course of its eponymous creek, Willow Street over Pegg's Run, and Canal Street over the lower Cohocksink.

In 1866 Henry P. M. Birkinbine, chief engineer of the city's water department, bemoaned the industrial discharges polluting the Schuylkill River (then the city's main source for drinking water) and also noted the predicament of numerous smaller streams draining the city, many of which, he said, were "once bright and beautiful":

> [These streams] are now befouled by refuse from manufacturing establishments. [They] are being covered out of sight, one after another, as objects too loathsome to look upon, whose fetid waters would spread disease and death, were they not thus hidden. Is there no remedy for this? Shall our industry only tend to make the most beautiful and necessary of objects loathsome, or shall we, by the strong arm of the law, protect the purity of the water, and force manufacturers to find some other means of carrying away refuse matter?[40]

As I will show later, even as Birkinbine wrote these words, the city's surveys department was devising a drainage system that would make the city itself the most flagrant polluter of its own waterways.

INCREASING THE CITY'S WEALTH: TURNING UNPOLLUTED STREAMS INTO SEWERS

While polluted creeks were among the first to be put out of sight, relatively untainted streams were shunted into underground sewers as well. In 1809 the city surveyor, Reading Howell, completed a "general regulation of both street lines and drainage of the surface of a part of Philadelphia" covering the area from Fifth Street west to the Schuylkill River, which was mostly undeveloped at that time. This beautifully rendered survey filled in the details of the original 1682 street plan and remains today one of the most complete delineations of the various streams draining that section of the city. It seems, however, that Howell located the streams this accurately only in order to use them in his drainage scheme for the area.[41]

Part of that scheme called for the largest stream, Minnow Run, to be carried in a sewer under Mulberry (now Arch) Street to the Schuylkill River. In 1820 the city commissioners reported, "Until this sewer be constructed, it will be impracticable to improve either the public streets, or private property, to advantage." They recommended that the sewer be built to save money that would have to be spent bridging the creek at every street crossing and to allow "owners of lots to fill them up to the established regulation" so they might subdivide and develop their property.[42] This project took many years from proposal to implementation, but by 1840 Minnow Run had been piped underground, along with the several other smaller streams that once watered the original city.[43] The elimination of these streams removed the last impediments to the completion of the original city's street grid, and the low ground around their residual valleys, if not immediately filled in, was nonetheless ripe for "improvement."

After the mid-nineteenth century, the city-building process continued in the miles of surrounding rural territory annexed by Philadelphia under the Act of Consolidation. Wrote two historians of the period: "The compact limits of the city proper, amounting to two square miles, presented a territory which it was child's play to control and supervise, as compared with the one hundred and twenty-nine square miles of the city and county of today."[44] More than just a manifold increase in square mileage, consolidation incorporated within the city limits a much wider variety of topography than had existed within the limited confines of the original city, including steeper hills, a half-dozen major creeks with deep valleys, and large expanses of tidal marshland. Topographical considerations were not foremost on the minds of the citizens and politicians who pushed consolidation through the state assembly; the centralized provision of police and fire protection were higher up on the list. Nonetheless, city surveyors and other officials believed that the dual challenges of extending the street system and providing adequate drainage for this much-enlarged territory could be better met by a consolidated approach rather than the piecemeal efforts of thirty different municipal governments.[45]

Anticipating consolidation, in 1853 the city surveyor and regulator Samuel H. Kneass reported to the city councils that the only way to drain the streets and neighborhoods of this soon-to-be-enlarged territory would be to devise a system based on "the natural water courses and features of the country"—that is, following watershed boundaries instead of artificial municipal boundaries. In the same report, Kneass proposed the "gradual disuse" of the then-current system of waste disposal in privy wells, recommending instead "the introduction of water closets into dwellings as rapidly as the desires of the population [would] demand."[46]

It was up to Strickland Kneass, the first chief engineer and surveyor of the consolidated city, to implement his older brother's proposals. During a nearly twenty-year tenure that began in 1854, the younger Kneass vigorously advocated replacing privies with water closets connected to a water-carriage waste disposal system. This change involved shifting from sewers designed to drain only stormwater from the streets to combined sewers that would carry household and industrial wastes as well.[47] While the grid of streets continued to be laid out with no reference to natural topography, this new drainage system was designed strictly according to the landscape, mirroring watershed boundaries and converting miles of smaller, mostly unpolluted rural streams into sewers that ultimately emptied into the city's two rivers.

City officials justified this wholesale conversion in a number of ways, including as a means to protect the public health. In an 1866 example of this argument, Kneass reported that Mill Creek in West Philadelphia was "rapidly being changed from a spring run to a foul and fetid channel." While the dozen or so factories in the valley did dump their wastes in the stream, Kneass seemed to reference the pollution caused by the city's own plan to empty branch sewers, carrying wastes from the surrounding neighborhoods, directly into the creek. If the creek remained an "open channel," Kneass continued, it would become each year "more and more repulsive in its discharge, with its miasmatic effluvia pervading the entire atmosphere in its neighborhood." By this logic, since streams were designated as sewers on the city plan and thus destined to become polluted, piping them underground could be justified as a positive (if somewhat preemptive) benefit to public health.[48]

This somewhat tortuous reasoning makes sense only when one considers the prevalent belief that miasmas, carrying foul odors, could themselves cause epidemic disease. Abolishing privies that polluted (with their odors) the very households by which they sat, and adopting a system to flush their wastes into pipes and carry them away from populated areas, was deemed vitally important.[49] The resulting pollution of streams was seen as "an unpleasant but an inevitable incident of the increase of a city," as Strickland Kneass's successor, Samuel Smedley, told a newspaper reporter in 1887.[50]

Unfortunately, such a system of waste disposal, based on a mistaken theory of disease, produced the opposite of its intended result. Neighborhoods may have been less odorous, but by delivering true disease-causing agents (e.g., bacteria) into the drinking-water supply, combined sewers in Philadelphia and elsewhere caused soaring death rates from waterborne diseases, in particular typhoid fever. Water filtration and chlorination, which were fully implemented in Philadelphia by 1914, greatly lessened the incidence of waterborne illness, but raw sewage continued to pour into the rivers until the city's three sewage treatment plants were completed in the mid-1950s.[51]

More easily explained were the several economic justifications for creek-to-sewer projects. One such justification involved cost savings during construction. Sewage is more than 99 percent water, and like any liquid, it flows most efficiently and cheaply by gravity. Streams flow by gravity, in valleys carved out of the landscape over eons, so designing a sewer system that conformed to the natural watersheds—with tributary or "branch" sewers emptying into the "trunk" or "main" sewers that followed the creek beds—avoided the huge expense of excavating sewer trenches deep enough to provide that gravity flow.

Once these rural streams were piped underground and their valleys filled—in some cases forty feet or more above the original streambeds—marginal lands that had previously been unmarketable became potentially profitable. These sewer projects were generally accompanied by the extension of water pipes and gas lines and the grading of new streets above the sewer pipes. Trolleys, first horse-drawn and later electrified, ran on tracks built along the streets, adding to the value of land in the neighborhoods they traversed. This ready-made infrastructure proved a windfall for owners of adjacent real estate, who had to pay only a minimal amount based on their property frontage for the sewer construction and might also receive payment from the city for land taken by the new streets.[52]

By attracting new development (primarily residential housing), this primarily city-funded infrastructure quickly paid for itself in increased tax revenues. Successive city chief engineers hammered home this idea in their reports to mayors and city councils, often quantifying the returns and quick payback of previous projects in justification of proposed work. In an 1866 report requesting $700,000 for sewer construction, Strickland Kneass claimed that, if the sewer to drain Federal Street in South Philadelphia were built, "good authority" warranted the belief that "an investment of at least $500,000 [would] at once be made in the erection of new buildings." Referring to the area around Mill Creek, Kneass wrote that "the best and most ornamental class of residences," which he said were "eagerly sought for occupancy so soon as completed," had been built up to the edge of the ravine in which the creek flowed, which served as an effective barrier to investment on its western side.[53]

In 1869 construction began in that ravine on the first section of the Mill Creek sewer, at twenty feet in diameter then one of the world's largest. Work continued for the next thirty-five years, until the five-mile main stem of Mill Creek within the city limits and all its tributaries were put underground, providing sewerage for a watershed of about 5,000 acres (see fig. 7.1). By the late 1870s an even larger project had begun

Figure 7.1. Mill Creek sewer between 47th Street and Haverford Avenue, 1883.

in the watershed of Wingohocking Creek. This project took fifty years, but eventually twenty-one miles of streams were erased from all but the city's sewer maps. In these two valleys, as well as smaller creek-to-sewer projects and general extensions of the grid across once-rural land, the goal was the same: to open up "unimproved" rural land for urban development.

Writing in 1884, J. Thomas Scharf and Thompson Westcott decried the process of city planning: "Old landmarks and ancient contours are not respected, the picturesque yields to utility, and the face of nature is transformed to meeting the exigencies of uniform grades, levels and drainage. The Board of Health, the Police Department, the City Commissioners, and the Department of Highways have no bowels of compassion for the antiquarian and the poet. They are the slaves of order, of hygiene, of transportation, of progress."[54] By the early twentieth century land had become simply a commodity, to be put to the use that would yield the greatest income for the owner and for the city through tax revenues. By then, municipal engineers had become skilled at facilitating this transformation of raw land into finished neighborhoods. Unfortunately, today's city residents are now living with a variety of problems resulting from those decisions and will end up paying for whatever solutions the new breed of engineers manage to devise.

OUT OF SIGHT, OUT OF MIND

Philadelphia's population expanded dramatically in the second half of the nineteenth century, and as a result, so did the proportion of urbanized land. In this period, planning often took place far ahead of actual development, with many streets plotted out decades before they were built. This can make it difficult to discern, when looking at certain mid-nineteenth-century maps and atlases, what was real and what existed only on the drawing boards (or in the dreams) of the city engineers. Just as Thomas Holme's 1682 plan for the city ignored much of the original topography in order to depict a city more inviting for settlers, these nineteenth-century images could be considered oversized real estate brochures or representations of Manifest Destiny on a municipal scale.[55]

The most enthusiastic street extensions of the period can be found in *The Complete Atlas of the City of Philadelphia,* published in 1860 by Joseph H. Bonsall and Samuel L. Smedley, in which these two surveyors drew the street grid over almost every square inch of certain then-rural neighborhoods.[56] Such maps seemed to be advertising that the entire city was available for "improvement," with the original topography (too unimportant even to portray) viewed merely as an engineering challenge to be overcome. In creating their plans, Smedley and other surveyors took great care to draw the streets and blocks of their proposed urban neighborhoods exactly to scale. If they bothered to locate the existing streams at all, however, they usually depicted them as black squiggles no wider than the pen nib and easily erased. By blithely drawing street lines as if the natural landscape did not exist, these city engineers ensured that, in time, it did cease to exist.

Among the many legacies of this mode of city building, its destruction of the natural water cycle is perhaps the most apparent today. With urban watersheds now covered mostly by impervious surfaces, stormwater quickly drains into often undersized sewers, leading to frequent storm flooding in low-lying areas, as well as erosion and consequent loss of habitat where storm sewers empty into the city's few remaining natural streams and scour the banks and bottoms. The current sewer system captures and treats all sewage during dry weather, but to avoid overloading the treatment plants during rainstorms, the combined sewers are designed to discharge excess flow directly into the city's creeks and streams. The diluted sewage in these overflows now constitutes a

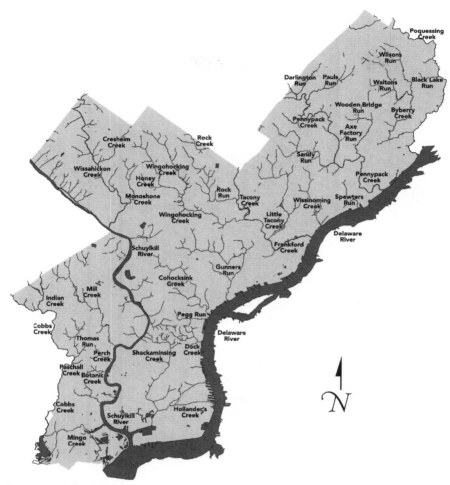

FIGURE 7.2. Philadelphia's surface streams prior to urbanization.

major source of stream pollution in Philadelphia and other urban areas (which is a somewhat backhanded tribute to the massive cleanup of industrial and sewage pollution accomplished in the past sixty years). Municipalities are under federal mandate to reduce the amount and frequency of these combined sewer overflows, but depending on the size of a city's system, necessary retrofits can cost millions or even billions of dollars. Another repercussion of the relandscaping of the city is the subsidence of filled land, which in Philadelphia led to the razing of nearly 1,000 homes in the Logan neighborhood around the Wingohocking Creek sewer and problems in other neighborhoods built on fill.[57]

By the early twentieth century, the view of city planners such An-

FIGURE 7.3. Philadelphia's remaining surface streams.

drew Wright Crawford began to filter into the consciousness of the city engineers. Newer sections of the city were in some cases designed with less avidity for wringing every possible dollar from the land and more sympathy toward the existing landscape and its use as an amenity. The city bought portions of the valleys of Pennypack, Tacony, and Cobbs creeks and set them aside as parkland. In the northeastern section of the city, much of which remained rural until the post–World War II housing boom, other smaller streams were left on the surface, with neighborhoods built around instead of over them. Unfortunately, this change in attitude came too late for most of the city's original topography. With valleys raised up, hills brought low, and streams buried out of

FIGURE 7.4. Philadelphia's streams captured in sewers.

sight and out of mind, the collective memory is as blank as the modern streamscape—a void that is ominous in both cases (see figs. 7.2, 7.3, and 7.4).

"I never knew where Mill Creek was until Tuesday morning," James Morris told a reporter after a 1961 collapse of the Mill Creek sewer exposed the stream flowing thirty feet beneath the street. "I moved in ten years ago, and often asked my neighbors why this is called the Mill Creek area, but nobody could tell me. Now I know."[58]

Michael J. Chiarappa

8 | Fed by the Adjoining Waters

The Delaware Estuary's Marine Resources and the Shaping of Philadelphia's Metropolitan Orbit

PHILADELPHIA'S ENVIRONMENTAL HISTORY, from William Penn's initial plan for the city and its surrounding area to the morphological adjustments that define this particular metropolis's postindustrial status, has taken shape as a layered legacy whose accretions—whether they speak of cultural affect, economic profit, or defilement of nature's bounty— are powerfully framed by the city's proximity to the Delaware Estuary. Radiating to consume parts of four states, the estuary's broad ecological relevance can belie its force as an inexorable tether of Greater Philadelphia's fortunes. Closer to Philadelphia proper, however, the natural resources of the marine environments of the Delaware River and Delaware Bay make the connection in far more conspicuous terms, for the city's sphere is positioned to draw sustenance, in the widest sense, from these two principal sections of the estuary and their adjoining tributaries.

Penn's promotional rhetoric for Philadelphia—"our intended Metropolis"—envisioned an urban setting ideally supported by its natural endowments: "Of all the many Places I have seen in the World, I remember not one better seated; so that it seems to me to have been appointed for a Town, whether we regard the Rivers, or the conveniency of the Coves, Docks, Springs."[1] His boosterism played to the strengths of the estuarine environment by casting the prospective metropolis of his "Holy Experiment" alongside glowing descriptions of waterborne bounty:

> Of the water, the Swan, Goose, white and gray, Brands, Ducks, Teal also The Snipe and Curloe, and that in great Numbers ... Of Fish, there is the Sturgeon, Herring, Rock, Shad, Catshead, Sheepshead, Ele, Smelt, Roach ... Of Shelfish, we have Oysters, Crabbs, Cockles, Concks, and Mushels; some Oysters six Inches long, and one sort of Cockles as big as the Stewing Oysters ... and of the Water, the Whale for Oyl, of which we have good store, and two Companies of Whalers, whose boats are built, will soon begin their Work ... to say nothing of our reasonable Hopes of good Cod in the bay.[2]

This characterization, along with others to follow bearing equal exclamatory force (Penn referred to the Delaware Bay's oysters as "monstrous"), fused the city's ecological imagination to the estuary's dispersed marine resources. These actions, both culturally and economically, set in motion a broadly affiliative urban matrix between Philadelphia and outlying areas that rimmed the estuary.[3] Additionally, Penn's role as a trustee for his fellow Quaker Edward Byllynge's vast holdings in West New Jersey gave him ample geographic perspective to appreciate the potential role of the Delaware Estuary's resources in fostering Philadelphia's urban orbit. His promotional utterances suggest Philadelphia as exerting a territorial influence over the estuary and its resources; a place appointed as nature's entrepôt, it would unite the best of what the city and its rural appendages offered. These reciprocating dynamics, reflected in the idealized urban geography of Penn's plan for a "green country towne," coalesced around the shared proprietary sentiment engendered by the "great River Delaware."[4] Ironically, Penn targeted the waterfront to symbolically lessen the disjunction between the city and its surrounding environs, designing what John Fanning Watson described as "a most graceful and agreeable promenade on the high bank of the riverfront, the whole length of the city," the intention being to give Front Street "an uninterrupted view of the Delaware and river scenery."[5] Such sentiment seemingly implies the maintenance of a pastoral ideal, but the ennoblement of "plantation work" in Penn's New World venture was scarcely informed by the land and water imagery of romantic stewardship. When Penn celebrated sturgeon "roasted or pickled" ("they eat like veal one way," he said "and sturgeon the other"), he was imposing on the Delaware Estuary's marine environment a practical intellectual framework designed to perfect nature. To this end, his inventories of the estuary's marine resources emerged from his membership in the Royal Society of London for Improving Natural Knowledge, a group with decidedly pragmatic views toward using nature and whose number included Isaac Newton, Christopher Wren, and John Locke.[6] While Penn's "graceful and agreeable promenade" did not materialize, the environmental implications of Philadelphia's nature-oriented urbanism brought clarity to the estuary's bioregional strength and recognition of an estuarine ecology that might serve as the cultural touchstone of a blurred urban/rural nexus stretching from the Delaware River's headwaters to the Delaware Bay's capes (see fig. 8.1).

So prompted, individuals and communities scattered throughout the Delaware Estuary—settlers whose aspirations were contingent on locating and using its bounty—began delineating the environmental contours of Philadelphia's emergent metropolitan sphere in terms of the broad reach of the river and bay's marine resources. Although a region not normally associated with the rise of European and American commercial whale fishing, the sighting of cetaceans at the estuary's southernmost reaches led Philadelphia's earliest promoters to prominently affix this marine mammal to the city's economic blueprint. Modest precedent in the region informed their optimism, as did the enticements of whale products in leveraging the Philadelphia area's economic and cultural position on the transatlantic stage.

Earlier Dutch settlement on the Delaware Bay at Swanendael (now the site of Lewes, Delaware) attempted to capitalize on the resource, achieving limited success but underscoring the profitability of whale oil in both European and American markets. At the dawn of the eighteenth century, Gabriel Thomas proclaimed, "The Commodities of Capmay-County . . . are Oyl and Whale-Bone, of which they make prodigious, nay vast quantities every Year, having mightily advan'd that great Fishery, taking great numbers of Whales yearly."[7] While Thomas's pronouncements and others similar to it are difficult to assess in terms of whaling's direct economic effects along the Delaware Estuary, any fanfare or projections for its success, notwithstanding their accuracy, said much about a maritime enterprise ideally placed at Philadelphia's doorstep. In the mix of extractive industries settlers planned for the Delaware Estuary, few bore the domestic and international cachet of harvesting whale oil, a product highly desirable as an illuminant and lubricant. Daniel Coxe, who never lived in the New World but for a time retained a controlling share of the Delaware Estuary's eastern flank[8] (i.e., the

FIGURE 8.1. Dock Street Fish Market, ca. 1909. Philadelphia had an officially recognized fish market at Market Street, between Water and Front streets, as early as 1764; this site was re-built in 1792 and again in the late 1850s. A fish market was also built in the city's Kensington section in 1810. The Dock Street Fish Market was built in 1898 when Delaware Avenue's width was increased by 150 feet, and this structure was destroyed by fire in 1908. The Dock Street Fish Market pictured here, a building formerly owned by the Pennsylvania Railroad, was ac-quired by the Fish Dealers Protective Association immediately following the blaze and was bounded by Dock and Spruce Streets (north–south) and Delaware Avenue and Front Streets (east–west). Courtesy of PhillyHistory.org, a project of the Philadelphia Department of Re-cords.

lands of West New Jersey) invested in whaling operations in Cape May County and developed plans for "a Magazine or Storehouse in [the] Dela-ware River for European Commodities."[9] Expressing sentiments simi-lar to Penn's and the individuals behind Pennsylvania's Free Society of Traders, who coordinated whale fishing from Philadelphia as early as 1683, Coxe envisioned a thoroughly modern metropolitan-rural corridor running the length of the Delaware Estuary, a combination of marine resources, alluvial lands, and transportation networks capable of ful-filling the production and exchange demands of a thriving entrepôt.[10] While not a Quaker, Coxe brought a planning mind-set to the Delaware Estuary that rivaled that of Penn and his cohort and exhibited a temper-ament Jeffery Dorwart claims "fit the mold of John Locke and other late seventeenth century British social and constitutional architects who sought to rationalize their world, create an orderly society, and experiment with their environment."[11] Prescient in his thinking, Coxe took his cue from whalers already operating on the estuary and recognized the value of a nonperishable marine product such as whale oil in advancing "a model mercantile and agricultural community," an ostensible prototype for a regional network of similarly conceived communities whose collective function would translate the Delaware Estuary into an environmental threshold for the Philadelphia area's innumerable local, regional, and international connections.[12]

While highly valued whale products provided a dramatic spark for the region's ecological imagination, each spring the ritual ascent of shad and sturgeon—coursing widely throughout the Delaware River and its namesake bay to reach their spawning grounds—became the basis of a shared fishing experience all along the estuary. This activity was more geographically immediate and pervasive than the peripherally located whaling operations. Gradually, as shad and sturgeon fisheries began to dot the estuary, these harvesting operations and their shoreline stages mapped and calibrated the Philadelphia area's use of the respective marine resources. Critical in this process was the identification and acquisition of suitable fishing places along the estuary's banks, particularly prime parcels situated on the Delaware River and the bay, as well as the Schuylkill River. Since both species proceed up the estuary during the spring spawning season, their arrival at particular sections occurred at different times between the months of March and June, with bay and downriver fisheries seeing the runs first. By the early eighteenth century, locally acquired knowledge of each species' habitats and biological dynamics was figuring prominently in fishing site selection, such information providing important criteria for choosing locations whose adjacent waters could accommodate the sweep of a large-haul seine, allow possible transshipment of the catch to Philadelphia or other desired markets, and serve agricultural and artisanal uses during nonfishing months. Such ideal features were touted in an advertisement for a "Plantation scituate in the County of *Glocester* in West-New-*Jersey* fronting the River *Delaware* . . . containing near 100 Acres of good Land and Meadow Ground, with a very good orchard, Dwelling House, and Kitchen." The seller boasted that the site was "a good Fishing-Place for catching Shad before the Landing" and remained "in good repair" and that it would be "very convenient for a Merchant or Tradesman," since it lay "about 12 Miles from *Philadelphia*."[13] A fortunate site owner or lessee, in addition to having "a good place for fishing" or "a Shad Fishery appurtenant" to his or her land, might enjoy the added benefit of "banked Meadow," that is, rich farmland reclaimed from marsh "banked in from the Tides," laden with nutrients from the estuary's marine environment.[14]

Eighteenth-century shad and sturgeon fishing operations quickly became attuned to their geographic proximity to the City of Brotherly Love, and informal discourse and the popular press made much of estuarine-dependent enterprises being "convenient to Philadelphia market" or "handy for Philadelphia market."[15] Qualitative pronouncements accompanied the marketing of both fish, but perhaps because their focus was an acknowledged international delicacy, sturgeon fisheries took greater pains in specifying the locations where fish were caught, the facilities where they were cured or pickled, and the methods or credentials used to guide the preservation process. The attentiveness given to the areas where sturgeon was harvested and cured was extended equally to naming those specifically authorized to market any given sturgeon operation's product. Edward Broadfield, honored by the Society of Arts and Commerce in London for producing the premier cured sturgeon in North America, made much ado in Philadelphia newspapers about the sites he worked on the Delaware River—Trenton, Bordentown, Gloucester in New Jersey, and Kensington (on Philadelphia's northern border)—and the merchants in the city who would market his product.[16] Having worked at the Lamberton sturgeon fishery just below Trenton prior to its being placed on the market in April 1765, Broadfield could vouch for the economic potential of its environmental endowments, which were said to include "great plenty of fish, also a pond made for preserving the fish alive . . . between the two greatest landings on Delaware River";[17] when offered for sale again in 1770, the site was touted as a place where "shallops constantly [plied] to and from Philadelphia."[18] With sturgeon from the Delaware Estuary being consumed not only domestically but in markets as distant as London, these environmental criteria bore significant qualitative weight as pickled *Acipenser oxyrhynchus* (Atlantic sturgeon) made its way from the water to the dinner table "put up" or "cured in the Baltick Manner."[19]

In 1769 New Jersey governor William Franklin announced that his state's General Assembly had passed an "Act to regulate the Method of taking Fish in the River *Delaware*"; this law highlighted the collective pressure exerted on both species and prohibited any entrapment device that would impede their upriver movement or "destroy or spoil any Spawn, Fry or Brood of Fish." It also instituted a minimum mesh requirement on haul seines to limit the taking of undersized fish or any other unintended by-catch.[20] Whether run by small-scale farmers or those who were more heavily capitalized, shad and sturgeon fisheries represented an important addendum to the colonial agricultural economy, a tradition that would carry on well through the nineteenth century. Shad, and to a lesser degree sturgeon, became so central to livelihoods throughout the estuary that the colonial legislatures of Pennsylvania and New Jersey enacted laws prohibiting or regulating the use of stationary entrapment methods, such as weirs, which were capable of adversely affecting catches farther up the Delaware and Schuylkill rivers and their tributaries. In order to facilitate equitable distribution of shad and maintain brood stock, the Pennsylvania legislature required haul seine operations on each side of the Schuylkill River to alternate the days and numbers of their respective sweeps—the process by which they set the seine net and hauled it to shore. Not to overstate the case, these regulations show some progressive thought entering into the management of these fisheries, though the measures were driven by economic efficiency and the desire to mitigate social tensions.[21] The prominent New Jersey politician Charles Read, of Burlington County, located just north of Philadelphia, had a thoroughly modern economic plan to place his shad and sturgeon fisheries alongside his considerable agricultural and industrial pursuits and spent time recording the details of manufacturing his haul seine, outlining ideas for making glue from sturgeon parts, and not surprising, designing "Fishing Waires."[22]

The regular arrival of shad and sturgeon at assigned times during spring months brought a measure of predictability whose economic benefits were not lost on the Delaware Estuary's earliest Euroamerican residents. This rhythmic phenomenon, wherein anadromous species undertake annual migratory spawning runs to the watery grounds of their birth, added a ritualized dimension to the harvest of these fish and a mythic renewal commonly associated with the anticipated environmental and economic rejuvenation of spring. For a society prominently motivated by the perceived providential design of the New World's natural resources, whether under colonial rule or in the newly found republic, the mythic value of these species made a culturally indelible, place-defining connection between their use and the Philadelphia area. In 1732 a number of Philadelphia's social and political elites organized the Colony in Schuylkill (later named the State in Schuylkill), generally regarded as America's first fishing and hunting club, where they began celebrating the arrival of shad by recreationally catching and preparing them at the organization's clubhouse along the river. Significant fanfare animated the club on "Gala Day," the first of May, where, by the late nineteenth century, freshly caught shad were subject to a "matter of some ceremony." In this instance, an elder organization member—the "Coroner," the inspector of the catch—permitted a "senior apprentice . . . the right to hold and turn the first shad" for his review, after which junior members were "allowed to learn the art of cleaning and splitting a shad properly" before nailing each fish to planks (thus the phrase "planked shad") and cooking them in front of an open fire.[23]

Other groups with similar social aspirations followed suit during the early nineteenth century. These fishing clubs included the Prospect Hill Fish House in Gloucester and the Tammany Hall Fish House just north of present-day Camden.[24] For the young Isaac Mickle, a member of one of Camden's native-born elite families, the clubs' activities were all too familiar when he made a diary entry in 1842 recording the satisfactions of a fishing party at his family's fish cabin on their farm; "We made eight or ten hauls," he said, commenting, "Between each haul we adjourned down to the dam to have music and refreshments." Fourteen days later he remarked: "Our *partie à peche* . . . gave so much satisfaction, that we resolved on having another to-day. . . . [We] made a dozen hauls and caught about that many fish; had plenty of music and dancing in the fish-cabin at our farm."[25]

At Fish House, the informal moniker for the State in Schuylkill, Philadelphia elites used shad to stage a sporting arena that subtly ritualized the affirmation, or extension, of social networks deeply enmeshed in the city's political and economic fabric. In this vein, the biological threshold of shad precipitated an environmental rite—one where a recreational harvest gave way to a feast of planked shad dripping in their own juice, accompanied by their roe delicately sieved into sauce (typically referred to as "shad roe")—that functioned critically in consummating the cultural temperament of the city's most influential citizenry. Not surprising, however, shad were not isolated to the mythmaking overtones of the State in Schuylkill's activities.[26] Not only did the species play a role in the ascendancy of the "Oldest Club in America," but shad gained further iconic status through a tradition of stories crediting it with having saved Washington's Continental Army from starvation at Valley Forge after the privations those troops endured during the winter of 1778. As John McPhee describes, members of Washington's encampment along the Schuylkill River may have dined on *Alosa sapidissima* (American shad) during the spring run of 1778, but accounts of shad stemming the demise of his army at its bleakest moment do not correlate with the times for the fish's arrival, when it could have achieved this feat. Instead, whether viewed as myth or legend, these written and oral narratives portray shad as "the deliverance of embryonic America, the finest hour of the founding fish," an "emotive account of the nation-saving shad . . . recommended by everything but sources."[27] These apotheosizing tendencies were not lost on *Harper's Monthly*'s writer Laura Spencer Portor when, in the early twentieth century, she was struck by the sign that greeted her at a fish market: "We Have Shad from the River Washington Crossed."[28]

Over the course of the nineteenth and early twentieth centuries, Americans viewed their natural resources as the liberating specter of a national temperament dedicated to the mutually reinforcing goals of economic and civic empowerment. The shad and sturgeon fisheries of the Philadelphia metropolitan area came squarely under the sweep of this environmental ethos. Fisheries devoted to both species, each having played a meaningful role in staking cultural, economic, and political claims to the Delaware Estuary's marine resources in the British colonial context, now became part of a working landscape infused with the ambitions and tensions of America's increasingly aggressive commercial society. This economic climate put new pressures on the Delaware Estuary's ecology in general and marine resources in particular; in the case of shad fishery, moreover, it introduced far more contentious relations among those exerting claims to participate in the enterprise. The legal standing enjoyed by shore-based haul seine fisheries, often simply labeled "shore fisheries," precipitated much of this tension. Unlike the activities of many who fished in alien waterborne contexts, out of sight or barely recognizable, to those on land, the sweep of the haul seine started and ended on shore, cultivating a connection between the terrestrial and aquatic worlds that fit more seamlessly into society's cultural map and, more specifically, conveyed a sense of dominion over submerged lands that comfortably conformed to the American pastoral paradigm. The area of water swept by a haul seine operation, known as a "pool" or "fishery," was in essence annexed to the adjacent land, providing the fishery owner with an exclusive private property, or riparian, right to its use.[29]

For a time, these privatized fisheries, particularly the New Jersey sites described by Bonnie McCay, "managed conflict and preserved rights of access to valuable fish resources to the propertied few."[30] While certain fishing locations were privatized, however, the fish themselves were not, and fishermen who lacked these sites and the entry they provided turned to gill nets to harvest waters beyond those reserved to riparian owners. Shore fisheries took umbrage at this development and viewed gill netters as impeding the arrival of shad at their onshore sites; to the former, whose fishing activity was confined to their landings, the gill netters' presumably unfettered movements breached conservation etiquette and undermined the equitable distribution of the resource. Furthermore, haul seiners, whose terrestrial orientation involved making "improvements" to their sites, tended to take a Lockean perspective on private property that, in their view, conferred on them a paramount claim to the resource. These episodes were emblematic of tensions that were festering as early as the mid-eighteenth century and that grew in scope as the Delaware Estuary became increasingly subject to industrial capitalism's volume-oriented production preferences. Such competing claims, particularly from manufacturers whose alterations to waterways often obstructed the migratory routes of shad and sturgeon, inevitably diminished the fish-producing capacity of the Delaware Estuary, as they had in New England, in other areas of the Middle Atlantic region, and in the South.[31]

Shad fisheries and shad fishing mediated a great many of the connections between Philadelphia and the Delaware Estuary, so vexations over use rights or access were an important undercurrent in one's geographic perception of the role marine resources played in sustaining the life of the city and its economic reach. Not resisting hyperbole, Samuel Howell, speaking on behalf of shore fisheries closest to Philadelphia in 1837, condemned gill netters as having "literally taken forcible possession of the river Delaware, under the plea of its being a common highway, and . . . virtually dispossessed the lawful owners of the fisheries of property which they considered secure, . . . as much their own as their farms": "The ingenuity of man, ever ready to evade restrictions that clash with his interests, has devised a mode of fishing by which all connexion with the shore is rendered unnecessary."[32]

This sentiment could not ward off the rise of gill netting for shad and sturgeon, particularly since pollution, artificial obstructions, greater fishing competition, and the natural configuration of the estuary demanded the versatility this entrapment method offered. Environmental and occupational changes were afoot, but these developments did not diminish the indissoluble historical relationship between shore fisheries and Philadelphia's multifaceted standing as the "principal market" for shad or detract from scenes where "immense numbers" of shad were sold at shore fisheries, "to which people flock[ed] from all quarters in wagons and boats."[33] Alluding to shore fishing's sublime effect as thousands of fish were being harvested, Howell remarked: "To see the water within the seine black with their backs and bristling with their fins . . . , to witness the animation and bustle of the fishermen, and behold their eagerness and anxiety to secure their booty, are circumstances calculated to excite in the spectator of such an enlivening scene, emotions of delight, and cause him to participate with the successful fisherman in all his joy and hilarity."[34] Near Philadelphia, haul seining for shad became a fusion of environmental and occupational spectacle, a vernacular pageant where a powerful metropolitan gaze publicly reckoned the cash nexus with both schooled and unschooled ideas of the species' ecological niche.

During the second half of the nineteenth century, gill netting for shad and sturgeon became most concentrated at locations along the Delaware Bay and in the lowest reaches of the Delaware River, sites where large-volume harvesting could be pursued away from upriver pollution and with potentially less conflict from haul seiners, to say nothing of removing competition with industry and shipping for valuable urban waterfront space. The proximity of these places—villages and towns such as Bayside, Hancock's Bridge, Salem, Pennsville, and Penns Grove in New Jersey and Port Penn, Bowers Beach, New Castle, and Delaware City in Delaware—to the lower Delaware River and upper Delaware Bay facilitated the crucial operation of setting nets with the incoming tide and hauling them just before the slack tides. In a commercial context where they were trying to chase higher profits while fish stocks were declining or only sporadically rebounding, shad and sturgeon fishers needed to live as close as possible to their fishing sites in order to efficiently respond to the estuary's physical forces and the biological imprint of their respective target species. The infrastructure of these locales assumed the guise of a modern commercial fishing community, replete with sufficient watercraft, entrapment gear, dockside arrangements, and housing. But significant changes had consumed each fishery by the end of the nineteenth century. Gill netting for shad overwhelmed the tradition of haul seining, but in an ironic nod to the city that shaped them, three such sites—Howells Cove, Gloucester, and Pea Shore—operated directly across from Philadelphia on the New Jersey shore during the late 1890s and were home to the most productive shad-seining operations in the United States at that time. By the 1880s and 1890s, moreover, the Delaware Bay, where sturgeon fishing had remained relatively slack for most of the nineteenth century, had become "the most prolific of all the sturgeon grounds ever developed in this country," a surge in production principally fueled by the demand for roe that was marketed as Russian caviar in Philadelphia and New York. The proximity of these urban markets to the Delaware Bay pushed this particular stock to the brink of extinction. When fishermen from the Delaware Estuary's most active sturgeon fishing communities met in Philadelphia at the turn of

TOPICAL SCENE AT HOPE CREEK
PHOTOGRAPH BY WM. J. S. BRADWAY

FIGURE 8.2. Shad fishermen mending their gill nets at Hope Creek, Lower Alloways Creek Township, New Jersey. Such net maintenance was vital for gill netters, who generally lacked the financial resources and infrastructure of shore fisheries and their use of haul seines. Author's collection.

the twentieth century to form the Sturgeon Fisherman's Protective Society, it was too late to stem the tide. The combined effect of pollution and fishermen who were unwilling to curb their catches meant that a type of fishing once productive enough to allow people to purchase caviar sandwiches was in the midst of its final days.[35]

On the bay and lower river, fishermen could transition from pursuing shad in March and April to targeting sturgeon in April, May, and June, working the same waters from the same New Jersey or Delaware site for the better part of four months. Transient and permanent residents often lived in one of the signature features of this working landscape, structures variously known as floating cabins, cabin scows, and cabin boats (see figs. 8.2 and 8.3). Fishing firms and individual fishers would tow these structures to protected shoreline locations where they assumed the function of floating villages adjacent to their fishing grounds. These harvesting operations were extensions of Philadelphia's economic sphere, and they maintained their role in it by quickly transferring shad to buy boats or to the docks for rail shipment or by rushing freshly caught cow sturgeon to butchering floats or wharves to have their roe processed into caviar. Collectively, this working landscape brokered

LOWER ALLOWAYS CREEK VIEWS NO. 64 PHOTOGRAPH BY WM. J. S. BRADWAY
VIEW AT HOPE CREEK DURING THE FISHING SEASON

FIGURE 8.3. The working landscape of the lower Delaware Estuary's shad and sturgeon fisheries at Hope Creek, Lower Alloways Creek Township, New Jersey. Sites such as these—in both New Jersey and Delaware—put fishermen in close proximity to the upper reaches of the Delaware Bay and lower reaches of the Delaware River's fishing grounds. From these locations, fishermen could efficiently transfer their catch to buy boats and rail connections bound to Philadelphia's markets. This image shows a place laden with skiffs, floating cabins, and entrapment gear. Author's collection.

routine harvesting and commodity exchange between Philadelphia and the fisheries; more systemically, however, and with the reciprocity of satellite relations, such landscapes struggled to endure into the early twentieth century through an environmental map keyed to shared occupational history, traditionally acquired ecological knowledge, and the increased flow of scientific information.[36]

When the U.S. Fish Commission was established in 1871, shad figured prominently in its plans to research, manage, and enhance (largely through artificial propagation) stocks of food fish deemed vital to the country's regional economic development. The federal government wasted no time in bringing the Delaware Estuary into a national discourse that justified engineering shad fishing to make it conform to, and ultimately uphold, the egalitarian ethos traditionally associated with shad harvests. In devising a federal template that would contribute to the enhancement of the Delaware Estuary's shad fisheries, Spencer F. Baird warned that chemical pollution, sewage, and the degrading effects of gas works were among numerous "improper interferences with the fish and the rights of the people at large" and underscored the futility of ameliorative efforts if states did not seriously undertake their mandated management roles.[37]

The U.S. Fish Commission had commenced systematic shad propagation efforts as early as 1872, and by 1886 the full weight of this program's scientific ambition was brought to the Delaware Estuary. Responding to the 1880 fisheries census, which showed a consistent decline in shad harvests between Connecticut and North Carolina, the commission dispatched its steamer *Fish Hawk* to the Delaware Estuary to conduct shad propagation. The *Fish Hawk* functioned as a floating hatchery and after 1887 became as regular a feature on the landscape as the fishers themselves. Working mainly in waters close to Philadelphia, the *Fish Hawk* crew relied on the area's well-known haul seine operations and gill netters for their supply of shad eggs and milt. This relationship fostered a valuable on-site exchange of information among the federal government, the region's state fish commissions, and the commercial fishing community. In the course of cultivating eggs, *Fish Hawk* crew members were able to assess the impact of water quality on fish mortality, particularly in water degraded by oil from Philadelphia's refineries, by traces of ammonia and sulfur from gas works, and by sediment disturbance from dredging around League Island.[38]

The U.S. Fish Commission's research on sturgeon propagation took place along the Delaware Estuary's fishing landscape between the late nineteenth and early twentieth centuries, but problems in simultaneously procuring cow sturgeon with ripe eggs and buck sturgeon with unspent milt made this project less successful than the shad propagation program. Ultimately, the commission extended the geographic reach of the Delaware Estuary's shad fisheries by exporting its eggs and fry to other estuaries along the East Coast. It also achieved this effect—through a concerted promotional campaign focusing on the Delaware River's shad fisheries and the artificial propagation schemes surrounding them—by exhibiting these activities at venues ranging from the 1893 Chicago world's fair to other less well-known U.S. international exhibitions during the late nineteenth and early twentieth centuries.[39]

Penn took delight in the size and taste of the Delaware Estuary's oysters ("They make a very rich broth," he wrote), and these impressions, coupled with the bold presence of Native American shell middens and stably affixed oyster beds, elevated the economic and nutritional standing of the resource in his metropolitan vision.[40] This assessment was not misplaced, and demand for oysters grew steadily, leading the New Jersey colonial legislature to enact its first oyster law in 1719. This law closed the colony's oyster grounds during the spawning season and restricted harvesting to boats owned by residents of New Jersey.[41] Philadelphia's oyster needs were scarcely inconvenienced by this measure since Pennsylvania's lower three counties (later the state of Delaware) lined the Delaware Bay and contained sufficient oyster beds to meet eighteenth-century demand. Also, oyster supply was likely ensured by Philadelphia merchants who either financed or had commercial relations with New Jersey oystermen, and the resources and will to vigilantly enforce the 1719 law remain open to question. Unlike many marine resources, oysters remain stationary after they attach themselves to a hard surface during their larval stage, and the accessibility rendered by their immobility was undoubtedly a source of economic and physical comfort given the exigencies facing eighteenth-century Philadelphians and their surrounding rural network. Eighteenth-century cartographers mapped the locations of the Delaware Estuary's prominent oyster beds to accommodate these emerging economic and environmental prerogatives.[42] Peter Kalm, a noted observer of the eighteenth-century North American environment, took stock of this dietary pattern and reported from Philadelphia on October 8, 1748: "The shore of Pennsylvania has a great quantity of the finest oysters. About this time the people begin to bring them to Philadelphia for sale. They come from that part of the shore which is near the mouth of the Delaware River. . . . Some men are seen with whole carts full of oysters crying them about the streets. . . . The usual way of preparing oysters here is to fry them on live coals until they begin to open."[43]

While Philadelphians gained a culinary attachment to Delaware Bay oysters, the loose enforcement of New Jersey's eighteenth-century oyster law allowed them to advance a financial stake as well. Working largely unfettered, Philadelphians grew accustomed to using sloops, schooners, and other watercraft to dredge bivalves from natural oyster beds in New Jersey and Delaware waters. Awash in an unceasing stream of economic boosterism and gradual progress in transportation improvements, early nineteenth-century oystermen working New Jersey's Delaware Bay confronted the implications of their resources being cast into America's mass-market revolution. On May 15, 1821, the *Independence*, a schooner based in Leesburg, New Jersey, used muskets to seize the Philadelphia oyster sloop *Hiram* and two other oyster boats from the city for illegally using an oyster dredge, harvesting during the closed season, and perhaps most offensive to this particular *posse comitatus,* not fulfilling the state's residency requirements before harvesting oysters. This incident, which took place in the Maurice River Cove section of New Jersey's Delaware Bay waters, generated two U.S. federal court cases, *Keen v. Rice* and *Corfield v. Coryell*, the former ruling that the captain of the *Independence* acted lawfully and the latter upholding New Jersey's right to dictate the terms under which nonresidents could harvest marine resources from its waters. Both cases, as Bonnie McCay has noted at length, affirmed a state's right to regulate marine resources as common property for the benefit of its citizenry and were thus early precedents in the gradual evolution of the public trust doctrine in the United States.[44] But these rulings did not dull the proprietary sentiment Philadelphians felt for Delaware Bay oysters (see fig. 8.4). By the mid-nineteenth century, John Fanning Watson was asserting the city's economic, cultural, and environmental ownership of the resource and its estuarine context, using such unambiguous references as "our own bay" and "our oyster beds in the bay."[45]

When New Jersey passed the Oyster Act of 1846, it offered a sweeping oyster management scheme for the entire state, most notably a host of legal protections to encourage oystermen to plant seed oysters on submerged grounds leased from the state. None of New Jersey's coastal waters could match the Delaware Bay's natural oyster growth or its sections suited to oyster cultivation, and legislation passed in 1856 provided a specific management framework for planting oysters in the Delaware Bay's Maurice River Cove.[46] Delaware Bay oyster planters were weary of seeing nonresidents poach oysters from the state's natural beds and were especially irked by predations taking place on the Maurice River Cove's planted grounds. Witnessing these beds chronically "plundered by persons not residing in this State," one commentator claimed, oystermen "endured these outrages with whatever patience they could muster, either not knowing what provisions for their protection had been made by . . . law, or fearing that that protection, when invoked, would prove inadequate."[47] Wanton disregard for the 1846 act engendered frustration throughout New Jersey's Delaware Bay region, and as an emerging consumer culture magnified the value of the bivalve, oyster planters and policy makers reckoned with management choices capable of balancing local and state territorial prerogatives, on the one hand, and pressures emanating from the far-flung proprietary impulses of regional and national markets, on the other.

These feelings escalated in the spring of 1869 when the New Jersey resident Gilbert Compton, a Delaware Bay oysterman, decided to "test" the 1846 act's efficacy by making a public spectacle on behalf of this collective sentiment. He proceeded by seizing the Philadelphia-based schooner *Rhoda L. Loper* from Maurice River Cove, averring it violated

FIGURE 8.4. Oyster cellar on Christian Street, Philadelphia, 1868. This oyster cellar, housed in a late seventeenth- or early eighteenth-century townhouse on Christian Street near where it intersects with Delaware River facing Front Street, is emblematic of the bivalve's enduring value in the diet of Philadelphians. Courtesy the Library Company of Philadelphia.

the 1846 act by employing a nonresident of New Jersey "to rake or gather clams, oysters, or shell fish" from the state's waters. Compton, taking his cue from a New Jersey tradition of executing citizen's arrests for violations of oyster law—a tradition used more for testing law than consistently enforcing it—delivered the vessel to Mauricetown and provided the local justices Samuel Cobb and Daniel Harris with documentation on the party's alleged transgressions. Benjamin Haney and Charles Scattergood, the vessel's owners, agreed that their crew did not meet residency requirements but contended that they legally purchased the oysters in question, the said oysters having been earlier planted and owned by New Jersey residents. To the aggrieved owners, their legal title to the oysters obviated the residency requirement. They argued that the state's residency requirements could be applied only to the state's natural growth; if applied to a nonresident's private holding of planted oysters, they were nothing less than a breach of the U.S. Constitution's guarantee "that the citizens of each state shall be entitled to all privileges and immunities of citizens in several states."[48]

Cumberland County's Circuit Court begged to differ and had powerful precedent on its side. Basing its decision on the 1825 federal court ruling in *Corfield v. Coryell,* the circuit court affirmed that, as custodian of its citizenry's common property interests, the state had the power to legislate the terms under which marine resources could be removed from its territorial waters. Specifically, a state's sovereign custodial authority over its common property resources gave the New Jersey legislature the power to use residency requirements to regulate the taking of any oysters, both natural growth and planted stock, from its waters. Haney and Scattergood may have owned the oysters, but they needed to hire New Jersey crews to remove them from the bay bottom.[49]

Emboldened by this ruling, New Jersey's Delaware Bay oystermen pressed for "more effective" enforcement power, leading the area's state legislative representatives, State Senator James H. Nixon and State Assemblymen Grosscup and House, to pen the provisions contained in the Oyster Act of 1871; in short, it amended the 1846 Oyster Act by instituting more elaborate legal oversight over Delaware Bay oystering.[50] New Jersey's oysters may have enjoyed historically entrenched common property protections reserved exclusively to the state, but they, not unlike resources that were touchstones of other states' financial self-interest, owed their economic ascendancy to commercial networks and capital freely flowing across state lines. Given their long-standing participation in the Delaware Bay oyster trade, Philadelphia oyster merchants bristled at the greater leverage New Jersey gained over the resource through the 1871 act and at seizures such as the *Loper* incident; taking issue with these developments, they accused the state of waging an "Oyster War" whose effect was "contrary to the comity of States."[51]

Notwithstanding the state's custodial authority over its oysters, New Jersey's policies could not escape scrutiny from participants in a regionally and nationally integrated economy whose accelerated pace helped drive the steady rise of oyster planting in Delaware Bay. Opposition to New Jersey's eligibility rules for vessels and personnel participating in its oyster trade became a public spectacle on Philadelphia's urban stage, with cries of "equal rights, equal government and equal protection" being commonplace on the Spruce Street docks where Maurice River Cove oysters were usually landed.[52]

With the courts offering little hope of a remedy to match this sentiment, Philadelphia's oyster establishment sought to rally support for its embattled position by striking a deep cultural chord. In a headline the *Philadelphia Inquirer* called the city's oystermen those "Who Built Up Cumberland County" and went on to portray them as the principal agents of Delaware Bay oyster planting's development:

> It has been about twenty years since planting in large quantities began in Maurice River cove. The peculiar adaptation of the cove was discovered by enterprising Philadelphians engaged in the business. When the trade was introduced here, the county of Cumberland, which now abounds in wealth, comfort, and a large population, was a perfect wilderness. After the people of our city had been engaged in this work for some time and found that the planting of the coves improved the oysters to such an extent that the Maurice river plants had eclipsed every oyster in the country, then the enterprising Jerseymen got at it. They began to move and settle in the county, and the trade, which our enterprising people had established there, has actually populated that district to the extent of forty thousand inhabitants. From a dense wilderness it has ripened into a flourishing and wealthy county.[53]

The historically charged content of this newspaper account evoked the privileged property concessions that the seventeenth-century philosopher John Locke assigned to those who "improved" nature and powerfully colored the city's expectation that its oystermen not be prohibited from directly gathering oysters from New Jersey's Maurice River Cove. Such an argument asserted Philadelphia's role in transforming nature, abetted lawfully by the U.S. Constitution's privileges and immunities clause, into an oyster market worth "millions of dollars" and couched New Jersey's regulations as an affront to economic claims secured by the republic's cultural and legal sensibility. Philadelphians readily took credit for supposedly "making Cumberland county both populous and wealthy" through oyster trade, but they did not want their differences with New Jersey to appear as a blatantly self-interested attempt to preserve economic hegemony over a section of a neighboring state or the lower reaches of the Delaware Estuary. Instead, they assuaged any legal qualms by claiming to be economically and culturally vested in Delaware Bay oystering, citing sole ownership of half the vessels used in the trade and shareholder status in two-thirds of those hailing from New Jersey ports. Philadelphians challenged the effect of New Jersey's public trust power on grounds that it abrogated social responsibility by denying employment to six or seven hundred city residents and compromised the welfare of three to four thousand women and children. To cast even darker aspersions on New Jersey's intent in exercising its public trust prerogative, the Philadelphia press portrayed the 1871 act not as a means to prevent poaching but as a cover to exclude the city in favor of lucrative New York City markets targeted by the soon to be completed Bridgeton and Port Norris Railroad. Each salvo in this dispute revealed growing pains in the application of public trust power, tensions precipitated by an unprecedented rise in the use of natural resources falling under the control of individual states. Such claims spelled new opportunities for New Jersey but threatened elements of Philadelphia's economic hegemony over the Delaware Estuary.[54]

Philadelphia's connection to the Delaware Bay's oysters was only minimally affected by these events. City residents were able to own oyster vessels, though the captains who operated them had to comply with the residency requirements stipulated in New Jersey and Delaware law, and eventually nonresidents were permitted to work as supporting crew. Those who scrutinized the industry on behalf of federal and state government did not overlook the implications of these loopholes. Ansley Hall, writing for the U.S. Fish Commission in 1892, reported that a "considerable number of the licensed vessels" were "owned in Philadelphia" and that the New Jersey captains who acted as legal agents of the vessel's operation became "nominal owners and proprietors of the oystergrounds occupied by them": "In this way," he said, "the law is evaded."[55] Earlier, the well-known oyster chronicler Ernest Ingersoll was more direct in deciphering the economic and legal effect of these machinations: "[The] whole region is dependent upon Philadelphia for its market, and hence, for a large part of the capital employed in carrying on the daily operations . . . more even than in New York, is the business centered and compact; or else it acts simply as a silent partner—a power behind the throne."[56] In 1904 Barton W. Evermann simply characterized the situation as one where "Pennsylvania capital" controlled "a considerable part of the oyster industry of New Jersey and Delaware."[57]

For years this commercial linkage rested on oysters' being trans-

FIGURE 8.5. Oyster processing facilities at Bivalve and Maurice River, New Jersey. These buildings and their surrounding landscapes significantly shaped the rise of oyster planting and
marketing on the Delaware Bay, as well as those networks linking the bivalve to Philadelphia's
metropolitan orbit. Courtesy Temple University Libraries, Urban Archives, Philadelphia, PA.

ported under sail to Philadelphia, but the arrival of the West Jersey
and Seashore Railroad (WJSRR) to the Maurice River Cove area in the
late 1880s provided regularly scheduled transit to the city in a more
direct route than that offered by the Central Railroad of New Jersey
(CRRNJ). These railroads operated oyster shipping stations on opposite
sides of the Maurice River, the CRRNJ's located at a venue named "Bivalve" on the river's west side and the WJSRR's, at one labeled "Maurice
River" on the east side. A variety of brokerages, with offices or representatives in Philadelphia, operated from these locales under the titles
of oyster shippers, wholesale dealers, and commission merchants (see
fig. 8.5).[58] While this commercial network made Delaware Bay oysters
a part of the faster-paced, volume-oriented rhythms of Philadelphia's
modern economic orbit around the turn of the twentieth century, the
public face of the bivalve was most evident in places where it was
cooked, eaten, or processed along the city's streets. Commentators suggest that rough oyster cellars and carts were steadily improving during

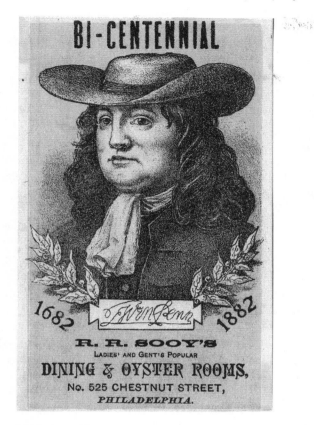

FIGURE 8.6. Trade card from R. R. Sooy's oyster restaurant on Chestnut Street, featuring a portrait of William Penn and noting the bicentennial of Philadelphia's founding. Author's collection.

the antebellum era, and by the end of the nineteenth century, the city abounded in oyster stands, oyster bars, and oyster dining rooms where amenities ranged from the extremely lean and modest to the refined and well finished.[59] Drawing on some of the strongest undercurrents of Philadelphia's cultural temperament, R. R. Sooy advertised his "Ladies and Gent's Popular Dining and Oyster Rooms" on Chestnut Street by using an image of William Penn bedecked with the word "Bi-Centennial" above his head and, below it, Penn's signature flanked by "1682" and "1882" (see fig. 8.6). Presaging the later pattern of Quaker images in advertising, here was Penn seemingly resurrected to once again extol the virtues of Delaware Bay oysters, only now with the added force of the city's mythic roots and two hundred years of its associated Quaker purity.[60]

When discussing the Delaware Estuary's oysters, sturgeon, and shad in *Natural Lives, Modern Times,* Bruce Stutz frames their iconic status in the late twentieth century as a function of their scarcity. Such environmental longing is certainly evident in the region's reaction to each species' crippled march toward the twenty-first century, whether it is a response to the devastating effects of the parasites *Haplosporidium nelsoni* (which causes MSX disease) and *Perkinsus marinus* (which causes dermo disease) on the estuary's oyster stocks since the late 1950s, to the biological impact of changing salinity levels, or to the pollution that decimated shad and sturgeon runs.[61] In actuality, however, the enshrinement of these resources began taking place a century earlier when problems first started looming; at the time, however, any potential resolution was blurred by a national ethos that revered its natural resources yet was culturally and economically driven to exploit them. This reverence/exploitation dualism, and the sometimes muted or contradictory statements it made on American environmental affairs, marked the Philadelphia metropolitan area's relationship with the marine resources of the Delaware Estuary. These cross-currents of American thought engulfed the region in a creative discourse where the fishing landscape—after it was environmentally compromised—became aestheticized in expressive formats ranging from academically inspired visual art and literature to the work of fishermen-poets to pictorial renderings prepared for the popular press and modern marketing schemes. Most conspicuous was a convergence of artistic energy that linked this occupational landscape to expressions of America's national and regional identity, regional or local romanticism, nostalgia, and the back-to-nature movement. Thomas Eakins's paintings and photographs of shad fishing at Gloucester, New Jersey—located directly across from Philadelphia—are among the most well-known efforts in this pattern, ably conveying the harvesting process and the public attention that accompanied it. In passages relevant to the way these paintings convey shad fishing's profound, uniquely regional and American affect, Kathleen Foster states that the artist was "proud of his heritage as an American and Philadelphian, and dedicated to his role as a national realist,"[62] while W. Douglass Paschall describes the context in which Eakins worked: "In April 1881 Eakins made the first of several photographic visits to the shad-fishing grounds of Gloucester, New Jersey, where steadily declining catches threatened the livelihood of local watermen as well as the seasonal picnics that had for many years lured Philadelphians across the Delaware River. Eakins's project to memorialize the humble fishermen—'subjects which he

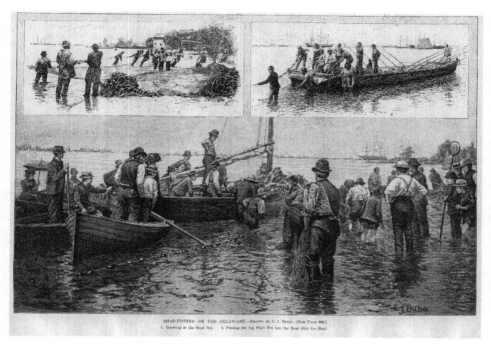

FIGURE 8.7. Montage from *Harper's Weekly*, April 10, 1890, showing shad fishing on the Delaware River. Author's collection.

has had in contemplation ever since his return to this country'—was reported by his knowing friend, the critic and Philadelphia Sketch Club president William J. Clark, Jr."[63]

While Eakins was painting and photographing, detailed engravings of haul seining for shad on the Delaware River appeared as montages in both *Harper's Weekly* (April 19, 1890; see fig. 8.7) and the *Illustrated London News* (October 20, 1883), and on April 30, 1881, *Harper's Weekly* ran a full-page engraving of Howard Pyle's *Shad-fishing on the Lower Delaware at Night,* which depicts drift netting for shad at night, when the fish are less likely to see the net's mesh. From either his perch on the Camden waterfront or while traversing the Delaware River on one of its ferries, Walt Whitman reveled in his observations of the shad fishery and, speaking of evening drift netters, remarked: "Of later May nights, crossing, I like to watch the fishermen's little buoy lights—so pretty, so dreamy—like corpse candles—undulating delicate and lonesome on the surface of the shadowy waters, floating with the current."[64] Although not sharing in the national spotlight, the Philadelphia-born George Emerick Essig (1838–1923), who trained at the Pennsylvania Academy of the Fine Arts and was eventually influenced by Edward Moran, joined in this artistic exchange and was arguably one of the most (if not simply the most) prolific visual artist of the Delaware Estuary during the later nineteenth and early twentieth centuries. In scenes spanning from Camden to the Capes, he showed himself to have been acutely sensitive to the actions of those who used the estuary's resources, and the precision of his etchings combined with the romantic grandeur of his luminist painting style conveys the coherence, the environmental fit, between this working landscape's signature features and the sublime ecology in which they were immersed.[65]

Similarly, Dallas Lore Sharp, a native of New Jersey's Delaware Bay region and a nationally recognized founding figure in America's back-to-nature movement, drew on the ritual power of annual shad and sturgeon migrations in his essay "The Sign of the Shad Bush" to awaken the nation's environmental sentiment in local settings that were touchstones of our first nature experiences.[66] Cornelius Weygandt, a University of Pennsylvania professor who brought his romantic, antimodern sensibility to a wide range of cultural topics in Pennsylvania and New Jersey, could not help but step into this chorus when he reflected on a meal of fried oysters he ate while visiting Fortescue, on New Jersey's Delaware Bay shore. To Weygandt, these fried oysters were nature's poetry drawn from "the bay just the afternoon before," humble "country fare" whose service "was a flow of the soul" from those "giving...of their experience of life, she who cooked the 'Fortescue Fries'; he who opened them." Largely reflecting the experiences of other Philadelphians, Weygandt's musings were emblematic of an expressive urge fostered by a local foodway whose reach brought him from "Finnelli's Single Dips" (oysters served "on Broad Street near Chestnut in Philadelphia's heart") full circle to their place of origin on the Delaware Bay.[67]

Local photographers, such as Graham L. Schofield and William J. S. Bradway, lived either in or near some of the area's finfishing and shellfishing communities, and this entry afforded them exceptional opportunities to participate in the visual dialogue that defined the regional identity and mythic appeal of these enterprises for those living amid the interconnected venues of the Delaware Bay and the Delaware River. When Schofield assumed ownership of the *Bridgeton Evening News* in 1927, his photography served to reinforce the newspaper's long-standing efforts to spatialize the memory of marine resource use throughout the estuary's urban/rural matrix. Such visual expressions were coupled to the newspaper's narrative strategy, an effort to bridge the collective memory of maritime life to a historical and public memory responsive to the environmental transformations sweeping the estuary. This was never more evident than on April 14, 1925, when the *Bridgeton Evening News* ran a headline proclaiming: "Gloucester's [N.J.] Shad Fleet Shrinks to One Rowboat: Two Fishermen, Where Once There Were 100, Cast Nets in the Oily Delaware."

For others, the expressive drive emanating from their environmental vantage point was far less public in scope yet, given the personal sentiment it widely represented, equally compelling in its effect. In 1920 the fisherman-poet George Pyle, of Bayside, New Jersey (a location also known as "Caviar" for the sturgeon roe processed there), typified this collective feeling in a fifteen-part poem that summarized the productivity, occupational culture, and afflictions of the shad and sturgeon fisheries. The work begins with this quatrain: "As I sat alone in my cabin / Thinking of days gone by / When sturgeon and shad were plentiful / And living was not so high."[68]

From the late seventeenth through the mid-twentieth century, the cultural and economic life of the Philadelphia metropolitan area, a dynamic urban/rural network, was significantly shaped by the Delaware Estuary's marine resources. Always conspicuous were the estuary's oysters, which found a ready place in the city's dining rooms, at oyster stalls on the streets, and in the city's numerous oyster bars or oyster saloons. The same can also be said of shad and sturgeon, whose ascents up the estuary each spring provided both a seasonal ritual and an anticipated dining experience. Market and sport hunting for waterfowl and other estuary-dependent migratory species represented yet another means by which Philadelphians and their rural cohort nutritionally, culturally, and economically sustained themselves through the Delaware River and the bay. By the mid-twentieth century, however, this tether had frayed. Ironically, the twentieth-century Quaker historian Frederick Tolles's statements on the seventeenth- and eighteenth-century Delaware Valley could not have stronger overtones for this environment and its marine resources: "The Delaware united West Jersey, Pennsylvania, and the Lower Counties (which eventually became the state of Delaware) into a single economic province, and linked it with the rest of the Atlantic Community."[69] Today, environmental historians are providing a narrative whose perspectives offer the possibility of a more informed rapprochement between this urban/rural matrix and the waters coursing through it. Notwithstanding the critiques of a fleeting tourist experience, heavy participation in both the Annual Shad Festival at Lambertville, New Jersey, and the Annual Bay Days Celebration at the oystering community of Port Norris, New Jersey, indicates a regional population seeking to place itself in the historical context of a river and bay that still exerts a grip on their lives, and in 2009 the Fishtown section of Philadelphia held its first shad festival. All these events are yet another expression of the way the Philadelphia area's environmental history is critically defined by the Delaware Estuary, and examining the myriad legacies that are intertwined in the commercial scale and cultural meaning of harvesting its valuable marine resources can build the framework of a narrative that will help facilitate a sustainable future.

Robert J. Mason

9 | Metropolitan Philadelphia

Sprawl, Shrinkage, and Sustainability

MAYOR MICHAEL NUTTER, ELECTED IN 2007, has said that he wants to transform Philadelphia from the workshop of the world into America's greenest city. Already Philadelphia is one of the country's most sustainable places—number 8, according to the organization Sustainlane.[1] This is no surprise: Philadelphia is energy efficient because it is densely populated and, by U.S. standards at least, well served by intra- and intercity public transportation. In the sprawl rankings (and there are several ranking schemes) the larger Philadelphia metropolitan region again achieves respectable scores.[2] For all their sins of overreduction and simplification, these rankings do highlight the energy, transportation, and infrastructural advantages that Philadelphia and other older cities have built up and that may greatly brighten their prospects in adapting to an era of higher energy prices and reduced greenhouse gas emissions.

This chapter provides a brief overview of Philadelphia's development history and then focuses on problems and prospects in the postwar era. While Philadelphia's story is in many ways similar to those of other aging industrial cities, it also is exceptional in several respects, among them the city's and region's early preeminence, traditionally high levels of residential rootedness and comparatively modest numbers of immigrants, two big Levitt developments, a recent resurgence in downtown population, a great number of higher-education institutions, and a location in the middle of "Megalopolis."

EARLY DEVELOPMENT

William Penn conceived of Philadelphia as a "greene countrie towne." Originally designed as a rectangle bounded by the Delaware and Schuylkill rivers, it was laid out according to a gridded street pattern and contained a central square (now home to its city hall) and four more public squares, one at each corner. Penn was not only a pioneering urban planner but also an early exurbanite. Though he never managed to spend much time there, his spacious and well-appointed retreat, Pennsbury Manor, was situated well up the Delaware River, beyond the farthest northeastern reaches of present-day Philadelphia. Today's reconstructed estate stands next to the Tullytown landfill, where much of Philadelphia's solid waste resides. A little farther west is Levittown, a monument to mass suburbanization.

During its first two centuries, Philadelphia grew rapidly, expanding well beyond its original rectangle. As the city grew into its role as "workshop of the world," new factories increasingly located away from the congested urban core, along the two rivers and later close to rail lines. Since the vast majority of employees walked to work, residential clusters developed around the plants, particularly between 1830 and 1860. As a consequence, the city grew more rapidly at the edges than at the core.[3] In addition, as railroad lines penetrated the city in the 1800s, they reconfigured the emerging social landscape by creating barriers and fragmenting the city,[4] just as expressways would do in the twentieth century.

Philadelphia's pattern of expansion only partly conforms to the classic Chicago school model of concentric expansion outward from a center. Perhaps it is best characterized as a hybrid case, with elements of concentric expansion and polycentric development, per the "Los Angeles school" and the earlier Harris and Ullman model that the LA school incorporates.[5] The city itself realized its current dimensions, growing from only 2 square miles to almost 130 in the municipal consolidation of 1854, a few decades before the wave of municipal annexations peaked in other major cities.[6] In 1860, 60 percent of the region's population lived in the city of Philadelphia.[7]

A regional fabric developed beyond the city, woven in the 1700s around small manufacturing centers and agricultural market towns, such as Chester, West Chester, Reading, Easton, Camden, Trenton, and Norristown. Surrounding farmlands and communities were linked to the city via regional networks of roads and later canals and railroads that transported coal, timber, agricultural products, and other resources.[8] Campbell's Soup, still headquartered in Camden, New Jersey, once consumed and condensed enormous quantities of local produce, in the process shaping the agricultural landscapes of southern New Jersey and neighboring states.

Although resource and trade demands transformed Philadelphia's hinterland during the nineteenth century, these developments produced no great flow of commuters into the city. Long-distance commuting was simply not yet practical for the masses. Through much of the century, commutes were expensive and time consuming, and early countryside and horsecar-supported suburban living was an option mainly for the elite.[9] Indeed, Philadelphia's earliest railroad suburbs established themselves in the 1830s on the famed Main Line, with a series of elite communities springing up directly to the city's west along the Pennsylvania Railroad. Though the Main Line area remains one of the country's wealthiest corridors, its exclusionary practices, both formal and informal, finally began to break down in the 1960s. Today's Main Line corridor, which contains a mix of exclusive homes, apartment buildings, small retail strips, and college populations, still stands as an example of transit-oriented development even in an era when many of its residents commute by car.[10]

By the mid-nineteenth century, as Philadelphia's middle class grew, so did early "suburbs," such as West Philadelphia, Spring Garden, and Mount Airy (after the 1854 municipal consolidation, they would become neighborhoods within the newly expanded city). Following the general Main Line model, these settlements were radially organized along streetcar lines oriented toward the central city.[11] Not until the very end of the nineteenth century, however, would medium to long-distance daily commutes become truly affordable and efficient for the middle class. In the 1890s streetcars were electrified, paved-street mileage grew exponentially, rail ridership soared, and bridges spanned the Schuylkill; as a result, modest but increasingly long commutes started becoming commonplace in Philadelphia as in other U.S. cities.[12] By the close of the trolley era, around 1920, about a quarter of America's nonrural population was living in suburbs, but this was just the precursor to the suburbanization of the "recreational automobile" and freeway eras.[13]

CAR CULTURE COMES OF AGE

By the turn of the twentieth century, Philadelphia's decentralization trajectory was well established, perhaps irreversibly so. Nineteenth-century Philadelphia had already established itself as a city of neighborhoods and single-family homes;[14] that its population would sprawl into single-family developments, especially once it became feasible for the middle class to move to the suburbs, seems like a logical progression. Together with cultural predispositions favoring dispersed settlement,[15] as well as other enabling factors I discuss later, widespread automobile ownership would provide the suburban synergy.

Philadelphia's population peaked in 1950. As far back as the late 1800s, however, the city was exhibiting core urban poverty surrounded by more affluent populations, an unevenness that would intensify dramatically through the 1900s.[16] By the early twentieth century, the automobile was starting to reshape settlement patterns nationwide. As early as 1920, population in Philadelphia's outlying areas was growing twice as rapidly as that in the central city; this was the case for Atlanta, St. Louis, and Cleveland as well.[17] Of course, the baselines for such measurements matter. The outlying areas had relatively lower populations, yielding a higher growth percentage figure; indeed, before World War II, the greatest absolute number of the Philadelphia region's housing starts still occurred within city limits.[18]

Newspaper and magazine ads of the 1920s linked shiny new cars with freedom, graceful living, and easy access to expansive new social networks stretching through the leafy suburbs. Two major Delaware River bridges were completed during that decade, and in 1936 a rapid transit connection to Camden started operation. In the early through mid-1950s, the Philadelphia sections of the Pennsylvania Turnpike were opened, a forerunner of the interstate highway system, into which the turnpike would be incorporated.

American cities experienced a wave of decentralization in the 1930s and 1940s.[19] In Philadelphia and other cities, however, sprawl was constrained (though hardly stopped) first by the Great Depression and then by World War II. Indeed, car culture was ascending in a major way as the nation emerged from the Depression, with surface parking increasing and property values steady or declining in the urban cores.[20] As early as 1941, more than 30 percent of those traveling into central Philadelphia did so by automobile.[21] The stage was set for returning military service members to unleash an incredible pent-up demand for a modern real-

ization of the Jeffersonian ideal: a single-family home in quiet surroundings with a sizable yard.

DEVELOPMENT CONSTRAINTS

The region's physical landscapes provide many opportunities for
sprawled development and relatively few constraints. While Philadelphia is hardly surrounded by an undifferentiated plain, the landscape is
one of rather modest relief, with some areas of steep slopes, wetlands,
and regular flooding that limit—or at least *should* limit—development.
The main initial obstacles to the spread of regional development to the
city's east and west were the Delaware and Schuylkill rivers, and they
had been spanned by multiple bridges by the end of the nineteenth
century. Rather few wooded areas remained even two centuries ago,
for most of the nonurban space had been converted to land for crops
or grazing.[22] Large tracts of active and abandoned farmland presented
nearly ideal opportunities for housing developments, with many landowners more than eager to make a profitable sale. The notion that farming might be the best use of regional lands was largely absent before the
1970s.

The main historical controls on sprawling development patterns,
such as they were, related principally to economic and mobility considerations. Before World War II, suburban development mostly clung to
rail lines and road corridors. Comprehensive regional planning schemes,
promoted by visionary thinkers of the 1920s and some of the New Deal
programs of the 1930s,[23] had limited practical effects, particularly in
Pennsylvania. Indeed, by the late 1920s, many planners had rather given
up on central cities, seeing virtue in making fresh, unencumbered starts
in the outlying areas. Increasingly, they were becoming convinced that
building more highways was the right prescription for coping with traffic congestion and in some instances even urban poverty.[24]

One of the few actions that could significantly affect future development patterns was the acquisition of regional parkland. Prior to World
War II, most parks were not created with the intention of managing
regional development. Instead, they were meant to provide recreation
opportunities, and in some cases, circumstances were simply fortu-
itous. When a wealthy benefactor was ready to sell (or give) land to a
local or state government, it often made sense to buy or take that land.
A regional park strategy was not in place; rather, opportunism was the
order of the day, and in large part, it still is. All told, parks and state

game lands, though they constitute a significant proportion of the land base in many parts of Pennsylvania, do not occupy enough acreage in southeastern Pennsylvania to greatly influence regional development patterns.[25] Fairmount Park, situated within the city, is a notable exception, especially its 1,800-acre Wissahickon Valley, which became part of the park system in the late 1860s.[26] The initial motivation for the acquisition was water-quality protection in the Schuylkill watershed, even though pollution continued unabated in the Manayunk area, along the Schuylkill's main stem.

New Jersey's portion of the metropolitan region presents a rather different story. Development there has been constrained by the creation of the Pinelands National Reserve, which is governed by a comprehensive regional plan adopted in 1981. Development restrictions apply in the Pinelands sections, inland from the Delaware River, of Burlington, Camden, and Gloucester counties, all part of the metropolitan area.[27] While much of the protected land is less than ideal from a developer's point of view, the restrictions have likely prevented it from being far more developed than it is. Indeed, plans put forward in the 1960s called for a sprawling Pinelands regional jetport, surrounded by a "garden city," that would have served the New York–Philadelphia region. Much earlier, in the late 1800s, the industrialist Joseph Wharton developed an elaborate scheme for delivering Pine Barrens water to Philadelphia, but he was thwarted by the New Jersey legislature, which passed a law prohibiting the conveyance of New Jersey's water out of state. The state ultimately acquired Wharton's land in 1950; it became the Wharton State Forest, which occupies most of southern Burlington County and is now part of the Pinelands National Reserve.[28]

BEYOND THE SEVEN-COUNTY REGION

Philadelphia, which is situated in the middle of the East Coast megalopolis,[29] is close to the New Jersey shore and northeastern Pennsylvania's Pocono plateau. Although Philadelphia's "shadow impacts" (i.e., its effects on land development beyond the metropolitan region) are not all that profound, they merit mention. Seasonal tourist migration to the shore, whether for the weekend or the summer, does generate major traffic congestion at peak times and is responsible for considerable residential development. But that development is constrained by the desire to be close to the water. Linear sprawl is in evidence, but much of that development takes the form of motels and multifamily condominiums.[30] In contrast to the usual fiscal and environmental problems associated with Philadelphia sprawl, the dangers facing these populations include vulnerability to rising sea levels and increased storm surges that may be brought on by a changing climate.

Like the New Jersey shore, the Pocono region was at first an elite retreat and later a seasonal destination for Philadelphia's middle-class residents. A site for family vacations, the Poconos also have served as a romantic getaway for couples, many of them on their honeymoons.[31] Second-home ownership by Philadelphians is substantial in the area, though in recent years it has been eclipsed by a surge of full-time residents, many of whom commute to New York City.

Extended commuting patterns also are directly affecting the Philadelphia metropolitan region. Travel to New York City is relatively efficient via rail, bus, and highway, and commuters concentrate in Mercer County, New Jersey, and in Philadelphia and Bucks County, in Pennsylvania. Commuters also travel from the region to Washington, D.C. But not all commutation is outbound; indeed, commuters come in from a wide area. Travel into the region from the west, particularly Lancaster County, has increased in recent years, posing new threats to that region's fertile agricultural lands. Berks and Lebanon counties, to Philadelphia's northwest, are increasingly represented in the regional commuter network as well.[32] Dispersed employment within the metropolitan region, discussed later, means that at least some of the region's jobs are not all that distant from those counties.

Philadelphia takes its water from the Delaware and Schuylkill rivers, with the intakes situated within the city's boundaries. Unlike many other cities, including Boston, Newark, New York, and Seattle, Philadelphia does not draw its water from distant reservoirs and thus is not a "hydrologic colonizer." But Pennsylvania is a member state of the Delaware River Basin Commission, which manages the river for multiple uses. The commission's preeminent responsibilities include ensuring adequate water for New York City, which draws most of its water from reservoirs in the watershed's upper reaches, and enforcing adherence to flow targets downstream.[33] The latter is particularly pertinent to Philadelphia given the narrowly avoided calamity during the early 1960s drought, when the Delaware Estuary's "salt front" advanced upstream to a point only a few miles south of the city's main drinking water intake.

POSTWAR SPRAWL

Philadelphia's peak population was recorded in the 1950 census, but that decennially defined event might better be described as a bump atop a plateau framed by a rapid population increase before 1920 and a dramatic decrease after 1970. As was the case in most metropolitan areas, Philadelphia's outward growth really gained steam after World War II, and this new growth was at a much lower density than the mainly urban growth that preceded it. The city, already quite built out except in its northeastern reaches, developed nine square miles of land between 1944 and 1954, while surrounding suburban counties developed sixty-one square miles. During that same period, Philadelphia added two square miles to its industrial tax base, while the suburban counties added sixteen.[34]

Figure 9.1 illustrates the spread of development through the region. While the 1930 map shows some early signs of spread along transportation corridors, the 1970 map reflects full-fledged low-density sprawl. Most remarkable is the relatively small increase in population between 1970 and 2005 accompanied by intensive land consumption. Only after 2000 did the land-consumptive intensity of Philadelphia's sprawl begin to slow a bit.

In Philadelphia, as elsewhere, postwar suburbanization was enabled by the car culture and promoted by such government policies and actions as subsidized home mortgages, the tax deductibility of mortgage interest and property tax payments, redlining and disinvestment in urban neighborhoods, and the development of the interstate highway system.[35]

As I noted previously, the Pennsylvania Turnpike had already reached Philadelphia and the Schuylkill Expressway was near completion when the 1956 Interstate Highway Act was passed. Though the city today is not girdled by beltways, the region is crisscrossed by numerous expressways, many of them handling traffic far in excess of their planned capacities. Interstate 95, which slices through the heart of the city and severs downtown from the waterfront, still lacks an interchange where it crosses the Pennsylvania Turnpike north of Philadelphia. Deemed obsolete the day the ribbon was cut in 1957, the mostly four-lane Schuylkill Expressway is variously referred to as "Thrill-kill," "Sure-kill," "Sure-crawl," and worse. In the region's western suburbs, I-476 (the "Blue Route") finally opened in the early 1990s after being slowed for decades by community opposition. Most of the interstate system's elements planned for the Philadelphia region did come to fruition, though a proposed expressway along the southern boundary of the city's business district was stymied by intense community opposition. Indeed, opposition to expressways mounted in the 1970s in many regions.[36] Unlike Boston, Seattle, or Toronto, Philadelphia does not have

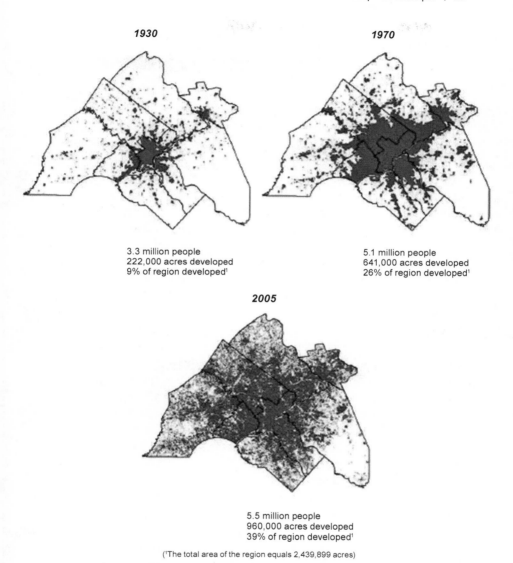

1930

3.3 million people
222,000 acres developed
9% of region developed[1]

1970

5.1 million people
641,000 acres developed
26% of region developed[1]

2005

5.5 million people
960,000 acres developed
39% of region developed[1]

([1]The total area of the region equals 2,439,899 acres)

FIGURE 9.1. Philadelphia regional development patterns. From the Delaware Valley Regional Planning Commission.

any expressways to nowhere, that is, projects stopped in their tracks by local opposition. Nor does it (yet) have firm plans to fully reconnect the city to its waterfront, the motivation behind Boston's "Big Dig," Manhattan's Hudson River Park, San Francisco's removal of the Embarcadero Freeway after the Loma Prieta earthquake, and the pending teardown of Seattle's Alaskan Way Viaduct.

The Philadelphia region is home to two Levittowns, monuments to the postwar revolution in large-tract, assembly-line, affordable housing production (or in Lewis Mumford's words, "instant slums").[37] Levittown, Pennsylvania, located on former farmland about thirteen miles northeast of central Philadelphia, got started in 1951. Interestingly, more than half its early inhabitants came from outside the region, notably from New York City and northeastern Pennsylvania.[38] And although Levittown was not exclusive economically, it was racially. After the first black family was driven out, Levitt reacted by saying, "We can solve a housing problem, or we can try to solve a racial problem. But we cannot combine the two."[39] Willingboro, New Jersey, is home to the other Levitt community. In 1957 township residents voted for a name change, making it another Levittown, but they then reversed the change in 1963.

A spatial revolution in retailing soon followed the housing revolution. Before the late 1950s, larger retailers were reluctant to establish themselves outside the center city. Indeed, early Levittowners would travel to Trenton to buy groceries,[40] something many Trentonites are unable to do in the city today. But the 1960s brought a shopping-center tsunami to the suburbs. Cherry Hill, New Jersey, five miles east of Philadelphia, became home to one of the early regional megamalls, the first enclosed shopping mall in the East. Opened in 1961 by the Rouse Company, it boasted a climate-controlled interior, free and easy parking, and indoor vegetation, all of which drew shoppers and assorted gawkers from well beyond the region. It also became a keystone for further regional commercial development. Indeed, the township itself, formerly Delaware Township, takes its current name from the shopping center. King of Prussia, northwest of Philadelphia, became another such subcenter,[41] today comprising an assortment of office and shopping facilities. Its first major shopping mall, opened in 1963, now ranks as one of America's largest shopping complexes. Malls in this first wave of development grew in scale and sales volume through the 1970s, as the region's inhabitants found themselves no longer depending on Center City (as downtown Philadelphia is known regionally) for most of their shopping. By 1972 combined retail sales in the seven suburban counties exceeded those in Philadelphia County by 17 percent. Employment dispersal was well underway during this era, with the suburban counties collectively eclipsing the city's share of metropolitan employment in the early 1970s.[42] Although significant fluctuations occurred along the way, these general housing, retail, and employment trends continued through the 1980s.

Toward the turn of the millennium, the region continued to grow, though slowly, while the city's population kept declining. Total developed land increased dramatically in growing suburbs (34.2 percent) and rural areas (41.1 percent) between 1990 and 2005.[43] Agriculture remains significant through parts of the region, with dairy and truck farms, nurseries, greenhouses, and some grain-production operations in Pennsylvania and New Jersey counties, as well as blueberry and cranberry production in Burlington County, New Jersey. Nonetheless, despite a raft of new state and local programs and funding designed to preserve agricultural land, farmland loss continued. Between 1990 and 2005, nearly 20 percent of agricultural lands were converted to other uses at an averaged rate of about twenty-three acres per day.[44]

Not surprisingly, land consumption per person, a basic sprawl indicator, has been increasing for decades; it grew by 13 percent from 1990 to 2005. Much of this increase is due to increased acreages per capita in the more rural areas; growing suburbs actually were becoming slightly denser during this period. Developed areas, by contrast, were seeing increases in land area per person, mainly because of population declines in these locales.

A critical dimension of urban sprawl is "job sprawl." Municipal-level data reveal that only 10–25 percent of "middle-suburb" residents commute to work in Philadelphia, and that number drops below 10 percent for the outer suburbs.[45] Between 1994 and 2001, and again between 2000 and 2005, the share of jobs in the core city continued to decline.[46] One distinct element of Philadelphia's job sprawl is the dispersed "pharmaceutical corridor" that reaches through and beyond various parts of the region, mostly (but not entirely) outside the central city.[47] Compared to other metro areas, the Philadelphia region exhibits highly dispersed employment with a somewhat less sprawling residential pattern. If anything, this disparity exacerbates the spatial mismatch between suburban jobs and urban job seekers. Yet even if the job-seeking population were to become increasingly suburban, the mismatch would not necessarily be alleviated; "automobility" is critical for most jobs, yet car ownership is much lower among the poor than among those of greater means.[48]

Joel Garreau's "edge cities" concept,[49] much heralded in the early 1990s, describes a national metamorphosis of the metropolis that seems to have peaked in the Philadelphia region. Garreau recognized King of Prussia, Warminster, and Cherry Hill, New Jersey, as edge cities: emerging concentrations of office and retail functions remote from core urban areas. But only King of Prussia remains a distinct edge city today, with the smaller, more established Lansdale seemingly emerging as a new edge city.[50] Today's region, in Lang's analysis, is the poster child for edgelessness; he refers to it as the "Edgeless Metropolis of the North."[51]

The nine-county Philadelphia region is a complex mosaic of 353 municipal governments woven into the Megalopolitan fabric that links it to other major eastern cities. Different researchers have developed different community-level typologies; they point to, among other things, fiscal distress and population loss in core urban areas and older inner suburbs at one extreme and low-density residential and commercial development in outlying affluent suburbs at the other.[52] Tax capacity, school systems, housing characteristics, employment opportunities, and equality and inequality are the principal issues that concern residents, planners, and elected officials; all too characteristically, however, they approach these matters from the parochial perspectives of their respective balkanized places. From the state and national political vantage points, though, the suburbs in Bucks and Montgomery counties constitute a critically important electoral swing district that has recently trended toward a more Democratic, metropolitan-friendly outlook.

CONFRONTING REGIONAL SPRAWL

A few opportunities to begin comprehensively addressing regional development patterns presented themselves early on, but little progress was made. In 1912 private individuals organized an association to foster cooperative planning among towns and boroughs near Philadelphia. Then, in 1913, the Pennsylvania legislature authorized the creation of the Metropolitan Planning Commission. Facing considerable local opposition, it was abolished after only two years. During the 1920s, when regional planning reached something of an apogee nationwide, the Regional Planning Federation of the Philadelphia Tri-State District was created. Its forward-looking 1932 report, released around the time when the state legislature authorized municipal zoning ordinances, broadly emulates the 1909 Burnham Plan for Chicago. The federation's plan called for open-space protection and anticipated a regional population as high as 15 million by 1980. But unlike New York City's Regional Plan Association, Philadelphia's organization did not survive. In 1952 Montgomery, Bucks, and Delaware counties formed the Southeastern Pennsylvania Regional Planning Commission. Philadelphia was not included.[53] Subsequent regional organizations include the nongovernmental, business-oriented PENJERDEL Council, formed in 1950; the Delaware River Port Authority, formed in 1951; the Southeastern Pennsylvania Transportation Authority, formed in 1963; and the Delaware Valley Regional Planning Commission (DVRPC), formed in 1965.

One of the first of the more recent waves of concern about sprawl and its impacts came in the late 1960s and early to mid-1970s, represented by a host of state and local-level efforts to more vigorously plan for and regulate residential and commercial growth, as well as by the landmark 1974 study *The Costs of Sprawl.*[54] Pennsylvania and Philadelphia were not national growth-management leaders during this era. The relevant regional planning entity, the DVRPC, conducts research and provides technical services for the nine-county region spanning Pennsylvania and New Jersey, but it wields little power, relying instead mainly on collaboration and consensus. Much of its work is oriented toward transportation planning.

Several boomlets of interest in metropolitan regionalism have emerged over the past decade and a half. Neal Peirce's *Citistates,* published in 1993, and Myron Orfield's *Metropolitics,* first published in 1997 and updated in 2002, are beacons. Peirce and Orfield both took their messages on the road, making presentations and attracting media attention in Philadelphia and other places. Regional-level studies also sounded alarms about sprawl: *The Costs of Sprawl in Pennsylvania* (2000), *Flight or Fight* (2001), and reports by the Pew Charitable Trusts and the Brookings Institution have focused attention on sprawl and metropolitanism in Philadelphia. Moreover, regional-level survey data reveal considerable public concern about growth, sprawl, and traffic congestion, if some ambivalence in deciding which level of government should confront it and how. Recently, working through Greater Philadelphia First and other channels, a diverse range of economic interests has sought to recast the larger region as a tourist and convention destination and build on its education, health-related, and other assets.[55]

In the 1990s sprawl began returning to the political agenda in a major way, and the "smart growth" approach has been advanced as a comprehensive policy response to the phenomenon.[56] This approach calls for, among many other things, concentration of development in and close to existing settlements. But this poses particular challenges for Philadelphia and other regions. For one thing, "smart growth" means many different things to different people. Outlying communities often try to hijack the agenda, focusing only on those aspects that would slow or stop growth locally while largely neglecting smart growth's urban revitalization elements. In the absence of a strong regional framework, this is precisely what has happened in the Philadelphia region. And Pennsylvania planners face additional particular challenges: each municipality must plan for the full range of land uses within its boundaries (including, for example, mining in urban centers), and until recently, the state's planning code did not allow for multimunicipal land-use planning. New Jersey's planning system is more robust, and New Jersey has a state plan as well as a court-enforced affordable housing mandate.[57]

In recent years both states have embraced collaborative, smart-growth, incentive-based planning approaches. Pennsylvania now supports multimunicipal planning, and its Growing Greener and Growing Smarter programs provide substantial funding for open-space and farmland protection. Over the past four decades, New Jersey's Green Acres program has provided billions of dollars for land acquisition. In addition, many localities, especially those that can afford it, have used ballot questions to raise funds for land acquisition, while local-level land trusts and watershed conservancies have worked collaboratively to protect farmland, open space, and ecologically critical lands. Between 1988 and 2008, voters approved 212 of 240 local ballot measures, authorizing more than $738 million in bonds and $128 million in new tax revenues and appropriations dedicated to open space protection; additional funding has come from statewide ballot measures and dedicated funding in Pennsylvania and New Jersey, substantial portions of which flow to the Philadelphia region. In 2004 the region had 35,815 acres of protected public lands, a 13 percent increase over 2000, with much of the funding for the acquisitions having come via ballot measures.[58]

ENCOURAGING SIGNS

With respect to environmental sustainability and sprawl, Philadelphia possesses compelling infrastructural advantages. As already noted, Smart Growth America's comprehensive sprawl study rates the Philadelphia region quite respectably. While its sprawling tendencies are far greater than those of New York, Jersey City, and Boston, it scores well with respect to street network accessibility, residential density, and mixed use, with homes, shops, and offices found next to one another. It rates somewhat less well, however, on "centeredness" of population and employment, affirming Lang's "edgelessness" characterization.[59]

There are encouraging indicators of urban vitality. Philadelphia's Center City has been rebounding since the 1990s, with a surge in the number of residential building permits issued between 2000 and 2005. Though the city as a whole continues to lose residents, downtown population concentration ranks behind only that of Manhattan and Chicago.[60] But beyond Center City, Philadelphia has a great deal of vacant and blighted land. Mayor John Street's Neighborhood Transformation Initiative, kicked off in 2001, brought considerable progress in removing blighted buildings and abandoned cars and in greening and redeveloping abandoned spaces. Still, the program has fallen far short of its early promise.[61]

The Philadelphia region is experiencing an upsurge in immigration. While Philadelphia has long lagged behind other large northeastern cities in its proportion of foreign-born residents, its fortunes changed after 1990. Cumulatively, the suburban counties are receiving more immigrants than the city itself, but the city remains the most common destination.[62] Though immigration's implications for regional development patterns are complex and not yet fully understood, the influx appears likely to be fostering population densification and urban revitalization.

The region's public transportation network has seen some significant enhancements in recent years, with the new and well-used Camden-Trenton River Line stimulating revitalization along that old commercial corridor. In addition, several projects in the planning stage promise further improvements: an extension of the PATCO high-speed line in southern New Jersey; restoration of rail service connecting Philadelphia to Reading; and transit-oriented development in the city and region facilitated by Pennsylvania's 2004 Transit Revitalization Investment District Act, which allows for value capture taxes to fund improvements around stations. The Philadelphia Water Department is implementing stormwater management regulations that will promote urban greening by essentially taxing imperviousness. The city also is considering various development and greening proposals, including a project to underground part of I-95, in a concerted effort to reconnect the city to its waterfront. And localities across the region are producing sustainability plans: the new Greenworks Philadelphia plan includes meaningful sustainability targets, Montgomery County has committed to robust sustainability targets, and Chester County has a forward-looking land-use plan in place.[63] While the initiatives are too numerous to list here, a note of general caution is in order: many of them fail to seriously address the regional context within which they are situated.

PHILADELPHIA'S METROPOLITAN MOMENT?

Quite possibly, the region has neared or even reached the limits to sprawl. First are the physical limits: most choice tracts are already developed or preserved. But beyond this, sustained higher energy prices and serious national, regional, and local commitments to reducing greenhouse gas emissions will limit further sprawl. Perhaps the area will not reach the level of McMansion abandonment that the planner Arthur Nelson forecasts for 2025,[64] but development will probably be much more constrained and contained by that time. The region's dual challenge will be to shape what it can of this emerging world and adapt to the externally driven changes over which it has rather little control.

Is this Philadelphia's "metropolitan moment," as a collection of articles in the *Philadelphia Daily News* proclaimed?[65] The view expressed therein may be rather optimistic, but a more sober, balanced assessment is offered by the DVRPC in its "Connections" long-range regional plan:

> Greater Philadelphia enjoys many advantages including a relatively low rate of transportation congestion; a superb transit system; a location in the middle of the northeast corridor; many traditional hometown communities; an affordable standard of living; a popular and growing park and trail system; numerous institutions of higher learning and advanced medical care; and abundant historical, cultural, natural, and scenic resources. At the same time, we face notable challenges such as increasing sprawl; a decreasing amount of open space; pockets of poverty, unemployment, and racial or ethnic segregation; a spatial mismatch between workers and jobs; disinvestment in many older centers; and an aging infrastructure that requires extensive reinvestment.[66]

The DVRPC has outlined an overarching regional vision that includes protecting 50 percent of the more than one million acres of land not currently protected and promoting denser, mixed-use "livable" communities. Similarly, the GreenSpace Alliance, whose members include major conservation organizations in southeastern Pennsylvania, has called for one acre of preserved land for each acre developed.[67]

Renewed optimism about a regional approach to environmental sustainability is being driven by a confluence of events, including growing interest in urban living among young folk and aging baby boomers, volatile energy costs, regional distribution of stimulus and other federal funding, and the prospect of new energy taxes or a cap-and-trade system for carbon emissions. While all these factors may not really herald that metropolitan moment, they are likely to at least move the region in that direction. One of the most vexing and often deliberately under-recognized challenges is that of intraregional equity. Few regions have gone so far as to create even weak forms of metropolitan governance or regional tax-base sharing.[68] Nor are many, if any, likely to adopt such approaches in the foreseeable future. But recent years have witnessed a proliferation of regional equity movements, with broad-based coalitions of business, government, labor, faith-based organizations, and other interests having achieved some successes in putting equity on the agenda in a meaningful way.[69] In the Philadelphia region, several regional equity coalitions are active in New Jersey, and a 2005 regional equity summit was held in Philadelphia. Moreover, the newly formed Philadelphia Metropolitan Caucus seeks to address such equity-related issues as regional workforce development.

If past is prologue, in the coming decades the Philadelphia region will adapt, following the lead of other regions in seeking to become more dense, more urban, more regionally connected, more outward looking, and less divided and unequal. Philadelphia has already made exemplary progress in its own right, while Pennsylvania and New Jersey are making strides in the areas of statewide planning, commitments to energy efficiency, and provision of affordable housing. What may really drive the region beyond incremental steps toward its metropolitan potential are sustained higher energy prices and meaningful limits on carbon emissions.

PART IV | Confronting the Ecologies of the Modern City

Anne Whiston Spirn

10 | Restoring Mill Creek

Landscape, Literacy, Environmental History, and City Planning and Design

THE MILL CREEK NEIGHBORHOOD OF West Philadelphia is a place of many puzzles. Within its street-grid of three-story brick row houses with small porches are other types of dwellings: a Georgian mansion, single-family homes on large lots, tiny row houses with stoops and no yard in front or back, and tall towers of concrete. The amount of open land in Mill Creek is striking, especially in contrast to the dense fabric of small row houses. Much open land is covered by rubble and grasses; in some places trees have grown twenty feet high. On some blocks, only one house or one small lot is vacant; in other areas, houses have sagging porches and crumbling foundations, and there are almost as many vacant lots as buildings. Blocks of vacant land and wasted structures border blocks of well-tended houses and gardens. Boarded-up storefronts speak of failed ventures, but other institutions, such as the numerous community gardens, flourish. Mill Creek is among the poorest neighborhoods in Philadelphia, yet it is home to many well-educated, middle-class residents; almost all are African American.

To those who can read this landscape, it poses many questions. Why is there so much vacant land? Do the size, form, and locations of abandonment exhibit any patterns? How did some parts of the neighborhood come to be so devastated, while others prosper? These are not trivial riddles. The answers reveal the nature of Mill Creek and are key to its future. When those who plan and build the city disregard the significance of these mysteries or fail to see them at all, they waste resources, make dangerous and expensive mistakes, and inflict grave injustice on all who live there.

The landscape of Mill Creek offers a catalog of the failures of twentieth-century urban policy, planning, and design. Some disastrous policies and projects deliberately aimed at insidious effects; most were well-intentioned but misguided. The Federal Housing Administration's guidelines for underwriters, spelled out in the 1930s, contributed to redlining, the banking practice of refusing to grant loans for the purchase of properties on the basis of location.[1] Redevelopment projects of the 1950s, such as the public housing towers inserted into this neighborhood of small-scale row houses, had devastating effects on the place they sought to improve and contributed to the racial segregation of a neighborhood where blacks and whites had lived next door to one another, in identical row houses, for at least a century. New parks, playgrounds, and streetscapes built in the 1960s cracked and sank within a few years of construction, and a public housing project built in the 1950s was recently demolished.

The critics of modernist urban planning and redevelopment are now legion. However, much recent development in Mill Creek is likely to produce similar results. Like their predecessors, those responsible for planning Mill Creek often treat symptoms and fail to address the underlying processes that produce them. Planners too often concentrate on narrowly defined problems and fail to see the connections among seemingly unrelated phenomena. Designers tend to focus on physical form and fail to account for the processes that will continue to shape their projects over time. Planners and designers alike see the devastation in Mill Creek but are blind to the blocks of well-kept homes and miss the fact that houses of one type are never vacant. They do not see the eighteenth-century mansion; it is on no map or tour of Philadelphia's historic houses. Such prejudice is not limited to top-down planners and designers. Nonprofit organizations dedicated to community reinvestment stress the neighborhood's liabilities and neglect its resources and the opportunities these afford. Even grassroots activists often concentrate on a specific local problem or a particular site and overlook how these fit into the larger neighborhood, city, and region.

Planning a neighborhood is both a spatial and a temporal undertaking, but planners' and designers' maps are usually static snapshots of current conditions, narrowly framed. Some problems, though manifest locally, reflect phenomena set in motion outside the neighborhood and must be resolved in that context. Some features of the built landscape are clues to forces that continue to exert a decisive influence, while others are artifacts of processes now defunct. Some are amenable to change, and others are not. Some are themselves dynamic agents that enable or constrain possibilities for subsequent development.

Restoring the Mill Creek neighborhood will require understanding how it came to be, how the built landscape evolved, which processes and actions fueled that evolution, when they did so, and which of its features have had a sustained impact on their surroundings. I use the word *landscape* in the original sense it had in English and Nordic languages—the mutual shaping of people and place—to encompass both the population of a place and its physical features: its topography, water flow, and plant life; its infrastructure of streets and sewers; its land uses, buildings, and open spaces.[2] The urban landscape is shaped by rain, plants and animals, and human hands and minds. Rain falls, carving valleys and soaking soil. Grasses, shrubs, and trees colonize abandoned land and produce new habitat. People mold landscape with hands, tools, and machines, through law, public policy, the investing or withholding of capital, and other actions undertaken hundreds or thousands of miles away. The processes that shape landscape operate at different scales of space and time: from the local to the national, from the ephemeral to the enduring.

READING THE LANDSCAPE OF MILL CREEK

The landscape of Mill Creek is a textbook of the culture and politics of American city planning and city building from the colonial period to the present. Market Street, the neighborhood's southern boundary, is Philadelphia's main east-west axis and one of its oldest routes, laid as a western extension of William Penn's grid plan of 1683 for the center of the city. The prevailing grid of streets in Mill Creek is an artifact of the nineteenth-century streetcar suburb. The principal thoroughfares, Lancaster and Haverford avenues, cut diagonally across the grid and pre-date it. Like Market Street, they once linked the city to its agricultural hinterlands; each points to a former ferry crossing on the Schuylkill River, one to Market, the other to Spring Garden. Lancaster Avenue was the nation's first turnpike and before that an Indian trail that followed a ridgeline.

Water-powered mills were operating along Mill Creek by 1711. A map of 1753 shows a saw mill near the creek's intersection with Haverford Avenue and another mill located near the creek's mouth, on the Schuylkill River.[3] When steam engines replaced waterwheels as a source of power, the size and rate of production expanded. By the middle of the nineteenth century, textile mills were prominent along Mill Creek. No longer tied to the stream as a source of power, factories still relied on its water for fire protection and production processes. The Good Intent Mill was built in 1808 at Forty-sixth and Market streets and then rebuilt in 1865. The Blockley Cotton Factory was built around 1819 one block upstream from Good Intent, at Forty-sixth and Haverford; it had a series of owners and was known successively as Eyre's Woolen Factory, Martha Blundin's Mills, and Andalusia or Longstreth's Mills. Like Good Intent, it produced cloth from raw wool and cotton (imported from the Carolinas), but the workforce was much larger: 250 hands in 1877, one-third men and two-thirds boys and girls.[4]

Wealthy eighteenth-century Philadelphians chose the outskirts of the city as sites for their country estates, such as Woodlands at the mouth of Mill Creek and Paul Busti's Blockley Retreat, a 240-acre farm established in 1794 that overlooked the creek upstream near the road to Haverford. In 1836 the Pennsylvania Hospital, located in downtown Philadelphia, bought Busti's estate to serve as a separate facility for psychiatric patients. The creek formed the boundary between the male and female wards and was an integral part of the grounds, which were designed as a pastoral landscape intended to provide a soothing environment. The Institute, as it was later known, pioneered humane methods of treatment for the mentally ill, for which it was recognized internationally. A group of Quakers founded a home for "colored orphans" on Haverford Avenue just east of the creek and across the street from the Busti mansion. This was among the nation's first institutions dedicated to the care of African American children.

The *Hopkins Atlas* of 1872 shows the creek, hospital, home for orphans, and mills within a grid of streets, houses, and platted (but undeveloped) properties. This was a landscape undergoing rapid change from countryside to streetcar suburb. The tiniest houses were clustered on blocks behind larger commercial buildings on Lancaster Avenue, as were slaughterhouses and stables. The interior of the neighborhood included large single-family homes, both free standing and attached, and modest row houses. Within six years, according to atlases from 1872 and 1878, many properties had changed hands, and large tracts under single ownership were split into smaller blocks of narrow lots filled with row houses, many with little or no yard. An African Methodist Episcopal church served African American residents. Although the neighborhood's residents were predominantly white, enumeration tables of the 1880 U.S. census record that "Blacks" and "Mulattos" lived side-by-side with "White" families.[5]

The *Bromley Atlas* of 1895 no longer shows the creek, and in it row houses have replaced the mill buildings at Forty-sixth and Haverford. There were stores on many corners, and several streetcar lines linked this residential neighborhood to downtown Philadelphia. Three decades later, almost all the land north of Haverford had been developed. After the 1870s, the dwellings built were row houses with porches; most were modest, and some were mean and without indoor plumbing, while others were more substantial. A new type of row house was introduced during the 1920s; each house had a front garden and, underneath, a garage that was accessed from the interior of the block via a common driveway. In 1923 Mill Creek Playground and Sulzberger Middle School, an imposing brick structure on Forty-eighth Street between Aspen and Fairmount, took up two of the last remaining open blocks. In the *Bromley Atlas* of 1927, the sinuous line of the sewer beneath blocks of row houses is the only visible trace of the former creek.

Today the seventeenth-century forest and the eighteenth- and nineteenth-century agricultural and industrial landscapes seem obliterated, but abundant traces remain. From the corner of Forty-sixth and Haverford, one can read several hundred years of history. A large block slopes upward toward the northeast. At one time split up into multiple blocks and covered by homes, the site was for many later years a grassy meadow with a grove of ash and ailanthus trees and is now home to a ball field, a church, and an apartment complex.[6] At the southeast corner of this block, on the site of the former home for "colored orphans," stand a church and the St. Ignatius Nursing Home, which serves elderly African Americans. On the northwest corner is an open lawn—the Blundin Mill site; one block to the south was the location of the Good Intent Mill, now also demolished. A high stone wall runs along the south side of Haverford Avenue, east to Forty-second Street and west to Forty-ninth; it was built in the mid-nineteenth century to enclose the Pennsylvania Hospital's buildings, gardens, and inmates. The western branch of the hospital still functions as a psychiatric facility, but the eastern property was sold and its buildings demolished in 1959 to make way for the towers of West Park, a public housing project. Uphill to the east, behind the stone wall of the old hospital, the roof of the Busti mansion remains visible. It is now the Lee Cultural Center, which sponsors African American cultural activities. Basketball courts and a playground occupy the former gardens. Downslope, in the valley where the creek once flowed through the Blockley Retreat and hospital grounds, stand an elementary school that was built in the 1960s and an enclave of townhouses constructed in the 1990s.

There are painful stories in Mill Creek, stories just as important to remember as stories of mills and mansions. By the late nineteenth century, the creek was polluted by wastes from slaughterhouses, tanneries, and households. In the 1880s it was buried in a sewer, its floodplain filled in and built over, but it still drains the stormwater and carries all the wastes from half of West Philadelphia and from suburbs upstream. Each new suburb built in the watershed poured more sewage and stormwater into the sewer. The size of the pipe—about twenty feet in diameter—is now too small for the quantity of sewage and stormwater it must convey after major rainstorms.

For more than sixty years the ground has fallen in, here and there, along the line of the sewer. The creek has undermined buildings and streets and slashed meandering diagonals of shifting foundations and vacant land across the urban landscape. Local newspapers have chronicled the long series of broken pipes and cave-ins.[7] In the 1940s forty-seven homes were demolished because they were "plagued with rats and filled with sewer vapor." In 1945 a neighborhood of small row homes built above the sewer on the site of the former Blundin Mill was destroyed when the sewer collapsed. In 1952 a thirty-five-foot cave-in on Sansom Street swallowed two cars, and porches of three homes crumbled into the crater. On July 17, 1961, the sewer caved in beneath Funston Street near Fiftieth. Three people died in the incident, which also destroyed 4 houses; ultimately 111 homes were condemned and demolished, leaving hundreds homeless and many others fearful of further collapse. "We haven't been ordered to leave. We're just too frightened to stay here," one person told a reporter. Months later, the *Philadelphia Evening Bulletin* described residents' complaints of sewer odors and their frustration at the city's slow response in repairing the thirty-foot chasm. By 1980 entire city blocks lay open within the buried floodplain. Young woodlands of ailanthus, sumac, and ash grew up on older lots, with urban meadows appearing on lots vacated most recently. Many community gardens in this part of West Philadelphia lie within the old floodplain of Mill Creek; older gardeners remember when buildings sank, their foundations undermined by subsiding fill.

Higher ground presents other types of vacant land, left behind by outwardly flowing capital and population. Vacant corner lots are common, the remains of the many corner stores that once served the neighborhood but fell victim to changing scales and modes of merchandising and the failure of new businesses to fill the gap. Individual scattered vacant lots appear here and there, "missing teeth" in otherwise intact blocks of homes, the consequences of isolated events such as deaths or fires. Some of these lots were once the sites of "heir houses," structures vacated after an owner died without leaving a clear title to the property; without active ownership, such homes fall into disrepair.[8] Others once had houses that were destroyed by fire, their owners perhaps lacking insurance and thus the resources to rebuild. For many years, businesspeople and homeowners in Mill Creek found it difficult or impossible to obtain fire insurance and mortgages. The Philadelphia Real Property Survey of 1934, a contributing factor to such insurance and lending practices, documented building age and condition, as well as the race, income, and education of residents. Because many of Mill Creek's houses were older, some in poor condition, some with flooded basements, and because its residents represented different races and ethnic origins (some with relatively low incomes), the survey gave its lowest rating, "D" or "red," to the entire neighborhood except for a few nonresidential blocks (the sites of a cemetery, a playground, and a school).

In 1945 Pennsylvania enacted enabling legislation for federally funded redevelopment under the Urban Redevelopment Law. Three years later, the city designated the Mill Creek neighborhood as a redevelopment area and hired the architect Louis Kahn to produce a plan. In 1950, following a sewer collapse near Forty-seventh and Fairmount streets, Kahn was again commissioned, this time to design the Mill Creek Housing Project on several square blocks near the cave-in. Newspaper articles from the 1950s through the 1960s record protests by residents who opposed public housing, particularly the high-rise apartment blocks. The public housing was built, as were playfields and ball courts on other blocks that had fallen in. Land directly over the sewer pipe remained open lawn or became parking lots, but much of the public housing was built on the buried floodplain. There have been no major cave-ins in recent years, but sinking streets, playgrounds, and parking lots, as well as shifting building foundations, continue to plague the area. The elementary school built on the corner of Forty-sixth and Haverford in the 1960s, for example, sustained structural damage in the 1990s.

Between 1950 and 1970, the overall population of the Mill Creek neighborhood declined by 27 percent. In 1950 the Bureau of the Census described the population as being about 27 percent Caucasian and 73 percent African American. By 1960 the white population had dropped to about 13 percent, falling to 4 percent in 1970, and to lower than 2 percent in 1990.[9] There are local reasons for these demographic changes, but they are also part of a much larger story. The city of Philadelphia as a whole lost population during this period. While six suburban counties around Philadelphia grew by as much as 12 percent in the 1990s, Philadelphia lost 9 percent of its population during the same period.[10] This is a local manifestation of a national phenomenon, a massive migration from central cities to suburbs and exurban areas that has reshaped American rural and urban landscapes, consuming farmland and forests and destroying urban communities in the process.

Given the outward flow of population and capital and the inward flow of sewage and groundwater, the abundance of vacant land and deteriorating or abandoned properties in Mill Creek is not surprising. Nonetheless, the single feature of the Mill Creek landscape that has had the most significant, persistent, and devastating effect is the least recognized: the floodplain of the creek itself and the hydrological processes that continue to shape it. Yet the strong pattern it creates—the band of open land and deteriorating buildings—is striking once recognized. Until recently another locus of widespread abandonment and deterioration lay outside the floodplain. The area between Forty-eighth Street and Lancaster Avenue was riddled with boarded-up houses and abandoned blocks of land. Until the early 2000s, it contained some of the oldest and smallest houses; now it contains some of the most recent housing projects.

Just as significant as the devastated areas are locales where little or no abandonment occurs. Perhaps these intact blocks of older homes are even more significant for their survival, given the strong destructive forces operating on Mill Creek's landscape. Residents have transformed small open lots into private gardens or off-street parking and larger ones into community gardens, such as Aspen Farms, at Forty-ninth and Aspen streets, which has often won the prize for "best community garden" in an annual citywide contest. In the neighborhood west of Forty-eighth Street, many homes have well-used front porches, some carpeted with plastic lawn and furnished with chairs and potted plants. Many residents of such blocks are longtime homeowners who belong to well-established social networks. Although small row houses of brick predominate, there are blocks of slightly more substantial row houses, many with fine architectural details: bands of elaborate brickwork on façades and ceramic tiles and parquet floors in the interiors. One type of block seems never to have vacancies, even when located on the buried floodplain: those composed of stone-faced, two-story row houses, each fronted by a garden and with a garage under the house.

Why did the area west of Forty-eighth Street, outside the buried floodplain, remain relatively intact while other parts of the neighborhood declined more radically? Blocks in this part of Mill Creek received the same rating of highest risk as the rest, and they were likewise subject to redlining. Their relatively good condition stems in large part from their distance from somewhat noxious land uses such as slaughterhouses and stables, which clustered near Lancaster Avenue. Another factor may be the scale, quality, and style of the area's homes, which are sufficiently large to accommodate the needs of modern families, though even the more substantial ones are small enough to maintain on a modest income. As the population has declined, the most desirable housing has remained attractive to homeowners and has been sustained, while the least desirable seems to have been abandoned more readily.

The landscape of Mill Creek is full of dialogues and stories, from epics to folklore to cautionary tales. It is rich in history; its features are landmarks of ideas, values, and change offering potential sources of pride on which to build the future. To read this landscape is to understand that nothing stays the same, that catastrophic shifts and cumulative changes shape the present. It permits the reader to see what is not immediate: the former store in a vacant corner lot; the future forest in today's meadow; water underground in a building's cracking foundation or slumping pavement. To read landscape is also to anticipate the possible, to envision, choose, and shape the future: to see, for example, the connections among buried, sewered stream, vacant land, and polluted river and to imagine rebuilding a community while purifying its water.

THE WEST PHILADELPHIA LANDSCAPE PROJECT

For the past twenty-four years, I have worked in and studied Mill Creek: first, from 1987 to 1991, as part of a larger landscape plan and "greening" project for West Philadelphia and then, since 1994, as the primary focus of my research on urban landscape planning and community development.[11] The first stage grew from my work on the role of urban nature in city design and planning.[12] I focused initially on vacant land as a resource to restore the urban natural environment and rebuild inner-city neighborhoods and then broadened my investigation to explore how urban planning and design might combine a comprehensive, top-down approach with a grassroots, bottom-up approach.[13]

Vacant urban land poses social, environmental, and aesthetic problems. It is a symbol of neglect and decay but can also be a resource for reshaping neighborhoods such as Mill Creek to serve the needs of their residents and to address regional problems. When Philadelphia's urban grid pressed westward from the city center into the rolling hills and valleys of West Philadelphia in the 1880s, row houses packed the narrow streets of Mill Creek. Vacant lots now relieve the former density and provide space for new uses and the opportunity to correct past mistakes. There is an impulse, particularly among Mill Creek residents and the local politicians who serve them, to build houses on vacant land, but there is no housing shortage in the city of Philadelphia, whose shrinking population and large proportion of aging homeowners mean that the surplus of houses will persist into the foreseeable future.[14] Without major shifts in national policies, this trend is unlikely to change.[15] Nonetheless, the residents have substantial investment in the neighborhood, which should be recognized and strengthened by infill construction on vacant land within and adjacent to well-maintained blocks of homes. In any case, houses should not be rebuilt on much of the vacant land in Mill Creek. Although the former creek bed is buried, the valley bottom still functions as a floodplain, so the soil is sometimes saturated. Consider, instead, alternative uses that can tolerate the conditions there, such as playfields, parking areas, large community gardens, orchards, and commercial nurseries. The West Philadelphia Landscape Project, in one of its key proposals, advocates managing the buried floodplain as part of a broad approach to planning the city's watersheds and as a strategy to secure funds to rebuild the neighborhood.

Normally, as rain falls in the Mill Creek watershed, it flows quickly across the paved urban floodplain to the sewer and then on to a treatment plant for cleansing before discharge into the Schuylkill River. A heavy rain, however, can produce more runoff than the system can handle, and some flows directly into the river—a combined sewer overflow. Such overflows are a significant source of water pollution, and the U.S. Environmental Protection Agency has threatened to fine the Philadelphia municipal government if they are not eliminated. A conventional solution utilizing "grey" infrastructure (e.g., new sewage treatment plants and underground storage tanks) would require billions of dollars, but there is an alternative approach: "green" infrastructure, which would save Philadelphia millions, if not billions, of dollars over the cost of conventional methods. For example, low-lying vacant blocks in Mill Creek could detain stormwater and thus eliminate combined sewer overflows from the watershed. Bringing the creek back above ground is no longer feasible, for it is now a sewer that carries waste as well as stormwater, but its reflected presence as a green ribbon of parks and playfields would recall the creek, protect houses from flooding, and provide local open space for a variety of public and private uses. Far from being radical, this proposal applies well-accepted watershed-planning practice to an urban watershed. In 1985 I made a similar proposal in Boston.[16] A few years later, the moment was opportune in Philadelphia, with ample time to lay the groundwork before the city planning commission produced its plan for West Philadelphia in 1994.

By the end of the first phase of the West Philadelphia Landscape Project, in 1991, my students, colleagues, and I had created a digital database with maps showing the neighborhood's demographics and physical features, made proposals for the strategic reuse of vacant urban land in the Mill Creek watershed, and designed dozens of gardens (including new common space for Aspen Farms). *The West Philadelphia Landscape Plan: A Framework for Action* provides an overview of the project during that initial period and describes the core recommendations.[17] The project is fundamentally academic, and there was no client in the conventional sense. Unbound by political expedience, the work enjoys no official standing. We carried out demonstration projects but had no authority to implement plans.

During the first phase of the project (1987–1991) and for years following, I hoped to convince the city's planning commission and water department that the buried creek was both a force to be reckoned with and a resource to be exploited. In 1991 my research assistants and I presented our work to the director of the Philadelphia City Planning Commission and the chief planner for West Philadelphia and gave them copies of the reports. An article in the *Philadelphia Inquirer* the following year summarized the proposals and urged the city to adopt them.[18] In 1993 *Living on Earth*, a program on National Public Radio, broadcast a story on the West Philadelphia Landscape Project. I was confident that the work would influence the city's plan for West Philadelphia. It did not.

When the city's *Plan for West Philadelphia* was published in 1994, it failed to mention the buried floodplain and the hazards it posed. In 1994 part of the Mill Creek neighborhood was designated a federal Empowerment Zone, and new housing and businesses were proposed for locations on the buried floodplain. That same year, the city donated a large parcel of vacant land for the construction of subsidized housing for first-time, low-income homeowners. This latter project, jointly sponsored by the city and the Nehemiah Corporation, was especially troubling. For one thing, the site lay on the buried floodplain. In addition, the project was designed as an enclave; not surprisingly, buyers of those homes report that they have little or no contact with the larger Mill Creek community.[19] Had the developers chosen a site on vacant land next to blocks of well-maintained homes, the new residents could have been integrated into the neighborhood and its existing networks of homeowners. This also would have bolstered those residents' previous investments of time, energy, and money.

I did not initially intend a long-term involvement in the West Philadelphia Landscape Project, but the city planning commission's disregard for the health, safety, and welfare of Mill Creek residents renewed my commitment. It also prompted new realizations that both sharpened and enlarged the questions my research sought to answer. Confronted with skepticism about the existence and dangers of the buried floodplain, I began to understand this resistance as a form of prejudice and a kind of illiteracy: the inability of public officials, developers, and even Mill Creek residents themselves to read the landscape.

I then organized my teaching and research to explore these issues. From 1994 to 2001 students in my classes at the University of Pennsylvania and at the Massachusetts Institute of Technology analyzed the urban watershed; demonstrated how stormwater could be collected in landscape projects that are also stormwater detention facilities; and created designs for wetlands, water gardens, and environmental study areas on vacant land in the Mill Creek neighborhood.[20] In 1995 my research assistants expanded and redesigned the digital database and converted it into a program that could run on personal computers (which were only then becoming sufficiently powerful). We hoped to make the database accessible to local organizations and residents.[21] When the West Philadelphia Landscape Project Web site was launched in early 1996, it featured the database, reports, and accounts of projects carried out from 1987 to 1991. Since then, it has been a showcase for ongoing work by myself and my students.[22]

In 1994 my students and I launched a program with a public school in the Mill Creek neighborhood to reach a broad spectrum of the Mill Creek population and also to bring together children and the elder gardeners with whom I had worked since 1987. What began as a community-based environmental education program organized around the urban water-shed grew into a program on landscape literacy and community development. In the process, I learned that the consequences of landscape illiteracy are far greater than I had imagined.

TEACHING AND LEARNING LANDSCAPE LITERACY: THE MILL CREEK PROJECT

From 1996 to 2001 hundreds of children at Sulzberger Middle School, together with dozens of my students at the University of Pennsylvania, learned to read the neighborhood's landscape; they traced its past, deciphered its stories, and told their stories about its future, some of which were realized. For tools they used their own eyes and imaginations, the place itself, and historical documents, such as maps, photographs, newspaper articles, census tables, and redevelopment plans. The program, named the Mill Creek Project, comprised four parts: reading landscape, proposing landscape change, building landscape improvements, and documenting these proposals and accomplishments. The first two parts were incorporated into my university classes and those at the middle school during the academic year; all four were integrated in a four-week summer program.

I chose to work with Sulzberger Middle School for several reasons. First, the school's location was ideal. Aspen Farms Community Garden is just a block away, and the gardeners were keen to participate. The school's front and back doors open on different worlds. The front doors look out on the high ground of the old floodplain terrace and face the small neighborhood of homes around Aspen Farms. The cafeteria and gym, opening to the rear about ten feet lower, are in the bottom-land, as is the playground and, across the street, the Mill Creek Housing Project (since demolished). Furthermore, children in sixth through eighth grades (typically, ages eleven through thirteen) are old enough to grasp relatively sophisticated ideas and to work on landscape construction projects yet young enough for an educational experience to inspire them to seek a high school curriculum that would prepare them for college. I was warned that many teachers in the Philadelphia school district shunned Sulzberger; its reputation seemed to stem from the students' weak performance on standardized tests (reported to be among the worst in the city's middle schools) and Mill Creek's status as one of the city's poorest neighborhoods. Reflecting the area generally, all the students (and most of the teachers) were African American. The principal was initially reluctant to work with me but was persuaded by the sponsorship of Penn's Center for Community Partnerships and the Aspen Farm gardeners. It took two years of small collaborations to lay the groundwork for a more ambitious program.

At the start of the first year of the expanded program, in the fall of 1996, a Sulzberger teacher told me that her students called their neighborhood "The Bottom." "So they already know it's in a floodplain?" I asked. "No," the teacher replied, "they mean it's at the bottom." Both meanings of the word can be read in the area around the Sulzberger Middle School: standing water after rain; slumping streets and sidewalks; vacant house lots strewn with rubble; whole square blocks of abandoned land, with men standing around street corners on a workday afternoon, jobless.

At the time, the school's environmental curriculum treated such topics as tropical rain forests and exotic wildlife at length while issues of local importance, including watersheds and plant succession, received scant attention or none at all. One popular science teacher took students once a year to an environmental study center in the suburbs to see and study "Nature." To change the teachers' and students' perceptions that the Mill Creek landscape was divorced from the natural world presented quite a challenge. It was equally hard to persuade students that the neighborhood had ever been different or that it might be changed.

In the fall of 1996 my students taught weekly workshops on Mill Creek and its urban watershed. They led a field trip to look for signs of the buried creek (slumping sidewalks, cracked walls, manhole covers). One eighth-grade teacher followed up with further assignments, including an essay on the buried creek, the problems it posed, and ideas for solutions. The students did what was asked, but the creek was not yet real to them. When my students spoke of designs for change, the children told them all the reasons the proposals would fail. "It won't happen"; "Someone will wreck it." Studying the history of the neighborhood· proved to be the key that unlocked the students' imaginations.

"You mean, there really was a *creek*!?" a thirteen-year-old exclaimed in April 1997 as she examined a photograph from 1880 showing the stream, a mill, and workers dwarfed by the huge sewer they were building, with new row houses in the distance. This breakthrough in her understanding came six months into the Mill Creek Project. The catalyst was a series of weekly classes taught by students in my seminar "Power of Place: Water, Schools, and History."[23] Each of my students led a group of six or seven eighth-graders in a series of six ninety-minute workshops. The sessions focused on particular time periods. There were no lectures and no secondary sources. At the end of every class, two eighth-graders from each group "reported out" by telling the rest of the class what they had discovered. The groups looked at different primary documents or emphasized different themes to provide a variety of topics for the reporting out.

My students brought in texts, tables of statistics, maps, and photographs and then asked the eighth-graders to describe and compare them. To help the children draw meanings from the documents, they posed successive questions. By breaking up big questions into smaller ones to which the schoolchildren could find answers, my students led them to develop hypotheses and then to find confirming evidence. Only after the children had identified potential explanations for their observations did my students relate background information they had gleaned from their own reading and from our seminar discussions. The idea was to encourage the children to form the habit of looking for significant detail, framing questions, and inferring possible answers. I hoped that having used this process in reading the documents describing the history of their neighborhood, the students would transfer it to reading the landscape itself.[24]

During the first class at Sulzberger, the Penn students introduced the concept of a primary document.

> "Where do the authors of your history textbook get the information they write about?" a Penn student asked.
>
> "From books."
>
> "And where do the authors of those books get their information?"
>
> "From other books?"
>
> "What about the sources for those books?"

One by one, the Penn students presented a timeline composed of selected events in the history of Mill Creek, each represented by a copy of a document from the period in which one of those events had occurred: a seventeenth-century map of the Delaware Valley showing a river in the midst of forest, an eighteenth-century engraving of a Leni-Lenape village, a map from 1872 showing several mills along Mill Creek, a photograph of the Mill Creek sewer under construction in the 1880s, Louis Kahn's plan for the redevelopment of the neighborhood in 1954, a newspaper report of the sewer's collapse in 1961, or the Empowerment Zone proposal of 1994. When we arrived at Sulzberger the following week, the eighth-graders had mounted the documents on red construction paper, laminated them under a protective coating of plastic, and posted all twenty in the hallway outside their classroom, where the display remained until the end of the school year, prompting much comment by teachers, parents, and other students.

The Sulzberger students' interest intensified as the time period under discussion got closer to the present. During the third class, they compared maps from 1872, 1886, 1895, 1910, and 1927, an activity that revealed the neighborhood's rapid development, and looked at photographs showing the construction of the Mill Creek sewer.[25] One student spotted the African Methodist Episcopal church and the home for "colored orphans" labeled on the map from 1872. "So there's more of us by then," she said quietly. The class on the 1930–1970 period was a turning point. My students were apprehensive, for they anticipated that the Sulzberger students would be angry to learn about the effects of redlining and urban renewal on the neighborhood. They asked the children to play the role of a neighborhood council in 1961; each group was a subcommittee charged with investigating an important issue. The groups presented their findings to the entire class and recommended actions, which then were discussed and voted on. One group investigated the origins of the 1961 cave-in and what was being done to prevent future catastrophes. They read newspaper articles, studied maps and photographs, and learned that the cave-in was one of many that had occurred along the Mill Creek sewer since the 1930s. A second group reviewed Louis Kahn's *Redevelopment Plan for Mill Creek* and his design for Mill Creek Public Housing. They were particularly impressed to learn that Kahn was a famous architect. The students marked up a copy of Kahn's plan and coded it with different colors to illustrate their recommendations that the neighborhood council should support some features and oppose others, such as the construction of high-rise apartment blocks and the conversion of many through streets to cul-de-sacs.

A third group investigated how homeowners and small businesses might obtain loans for mortgages and improvements. This group read the Home Owners Loan Corporation (HOLC) criteria for rating neighborhoods and studied the maps of Mill Creek in the *Philadelphia Real Property Survey* of 1934, which showed every block, except for a few occupied by cemeteries and schools, as highest risk, and they learned the meaning of redlining. The students' responses to the HOLC report, maps, and lending practices surprised me. They showed no anger. Instead, their faces registered surprise, then relief, and then determination to come up with an effective response: a citywide march on city hall, a petition, and the establishment of a community bank.

The students' energy carried over into the next class, which focused on the present and planning for the future. Staff members from the West

Philadelphia Empowerment Zone and the city planning commission and two gardeners from Aspen Farms visited the class. Sulzberger students asked the planners: "Why did you let those new houses be built on the buried floodplain? Did you warn the people who bought them?" "What are you doing about the Mill Creek sewer?" "What have you done about redlining?" "Why haven't you started a community bank?"

Between our weekly visits, the Sulzberger teachers involved in the project took the material we brought in and used it across the curriculum in social studies, math, science, and English. The principal teacher reported, for example, that the class spent an entire day analyzing census statistics from 1860 to 1990. They were particularly fascinated to learn that African Americans had lived in the neighborhood since at least 1860 and that many white people had lived there for most of the nineteenth and twentieth centuries. And, he said, they turned to their U.S. history textbook with greater interest than they had shown previously.

Landscape literacy entails more than reading; it means shaping landscape also. Each student made a proposal for transforming the creek from a liability into a neighborhood asset. The essays and drawings were reproduced at the end of the school year in a booklet with one-sentence reviews by the mayor of Philadelphia and city council members, among others.[26] At the end of April, the Sulzberger students, together with their Penn mentors, gave a public presentation on the history of Mill Creek, illustrated with slides and posters, at a symposium held at the University of Pennsylvania. After the presentation, someone in the audience asked what was the most important thing they had learned. One thirteen-year-old answered for the whole class: "We learned to be proud of our neighborhood," she said. "So many important things have happened there, and so many people have cared for it for hundreds of years. I want to stay there and help make it a better place."

At the beginning of the semester, Sulzberger students described their neighborhood in negative terms and said they would not live in Mill Creek if they had a choice. Only one student said she planned to attend college. Two months later, all but one student said they planned to attend college. The teacher reported that his students' performance in all subjects had improved dramatically. He attributed this to the Mill Creek Project—specifically, to the use of primary materials, which challenged the children and made history real for them, and to the project's ability to sharpen their perceptions of relationships between their own lives and landscape and the larger city, region, and nation.

Teaching and studying the history and landscape of Mill Creek also caused learning to become real for my Penn students.[27] Most were unprepared for what they observed: the sheer extent of devastation in the Mill Creek landscape, for example, and the high level of intelligence among the children. My students' weekly journals revealed their evolving understanding of race and place. After several visits to Sulzberger, many acknowledged their surprise that some of the Sulzberger students were smarter than they, and this led them to reflect on their own prejudice and privilege. They also reported that their experiences in Mill Creek challenged assumptions and theories asserted by texts they were reading for other courses.

The culmination of the year was a four-week summer program for Sulzberger students and teachers organized and led by four of my research assistants.[28] In the mornings, the group met either at Aspen Farms, where participants built a water garden and an outdoor classroom, or at Sulzberger, where they constructed a topographic model of the Mill Creek watershed and learned how to create a Web site. Two Sulzberger students from the eighth-grade class worked as junior counselors in the mornings and, in the afternoons, as research assistants at the university, where they wrote, illustrated, designed, and produced "SMS News," a series of Web pages that were posted on the West Philadelphia Landscape Project Web site.[29] The four participating Sulzberger teachers also spent afternoons at the university; one research assistant taught them Web authoring and how to use GIS (geographic information systems) software to map the neighborhood. At the end of the summer, one of these teachers was appointed to head the school's new computer program.

The Mill Creek Project continued in subsequent years with a similar format of weekly workshops led by Penn students during the academic year and a four-week summer program in July based at the school and at Aspen Farms.[30] In 1998 the Sulzberger principal and teachers decided to expand the program, and they wrote grant proposals that yielded the necessary funds. They established four small learning communities, each with ten teachers and about 250 students, one of which focused on the themes of regional watershed and local community. Each class was required to design and carry out a community service project every year: to identify problems in the community and to bring these problems and potential solutions to public attention. The computer teacher created an after-school computer club and worked with the staff of Penn's Center for Community Partnerships to secure grants for the purchase of equipment and software. Within two years members of the computer club were taking apart and building computers and writing computer code to adapt commercial software.

PUTTING MILL CREEK ON THE MAP

From 1998 on, Sulzberger Middle School and the Mill Creek Project received increasing local, national, and international recognition.[31] Staff at the School District of Philadelphia, politicians, and officers from national foundations visited the school and observed Sulzberger and Penn students in the classroom. The Sulzberger portion of the West Philadelphia Landscape Project Web site led Pennsylvania's governor to invite students from Sulzberger to make a five-minute presentation as part of his 1998 budget speech to the state legislature; the students' presentation was televised, as was the legislature's response, a long standing ovation. Later that year, the Philadelphia school district named Sulzberger "School of the Month" and produced a television documentary on the Mill Creek Project and the school's innovations. In 1999 Sulzberger was the subject of a report on NBC's *Nightly News*, a nationally broadcast television program. In 2000 President Bill Clinton visited the school.

Recognition for the Mill Creek Project and for Sulzberger teachers and students opened doors to other collaborations. In 1999 the Mill Creek Coalition, a group of neighborhood organizations, invited me to speak to their group about the creek and its impact on the community, and we embarked on a series of joint projects, including research on flooded basements and a course for residents on the history of Mill Creek's landscape.[32] From 1996 to 1999 the West Philadelphia Landscape Project Web site received over a million visits from individuals in more than ninety countries on six continents. Visitors to the project itself included public officials. In the fall of 1996, staff of the U.S. Environmental Protection Agency's regional water division, who were increasingly concerned about combined sewer overflows in Philadelphia, encouraged engineers at the city's water department to meet with me to discuss stormwater detention's potential to reduce this type of pollution.[33] At that time, the Mill Creek watershed did not even appear on the maps the water department was using but was subsumed under the much larger watershed of the Schuylkill River. The engineers agreed to put Mill Creek on the map as a special study area. In 1999 staff from the water department asked me to take a group of engineers on a field trip to Mill Creek. With nineteenth-century maps in hand, we walked and drove along the buried floodplain and looked at potential sites for stormwater detention projects. This trip resulted in the decision to design and build a demonstration project on a vacant block next to Sulzberger that would detain stormwater and also function as an environmental study area and outdoor classroom for the school. The water department applied for and obtained a grant to fund the project in 2000 and pledged to work with teachers and students at Sulzberger. They hired one of my research assistants to direct the project and in 2001 cosponsored the summer program on the urban watershed with Sulzberger Middle School.[34] Later that year the city's water department, housing authority, and planning commission submitted a proposal to the U.S. Department of Housing and Urban Development's Hope VI Program, asking for $34.8 million to redevelop Mill Creek Public Housing in a demonstration project that would provide an environmental study area for the school and integrate stormwater management measures to reduce combined sewer overflows. The proposal was successful, and the city cleared the site in November 2002 and broke ground on the $110 million project in August 2003.

In 2001 I was confident that things were going well for Mill Creek. I had moved from the University of Pennsylvania to the Massachusetts Institute of Technology in the fall of 2000 and continued to work with teachers at Sulzberger. Students in an MIT class traveled to Philadelphia, collected stories about the project from various participants, and redesigned the West Philadelphia Landscape Project Web site. In 2002 the computer teacher at Sulzberger visited MIT to discuss plans for further collaboration. Then, a few months later, the Commonwealth of Pennsylvania took control of the Philadelphia school district and granted responsibility for the management of Sulzberger, among other schools, to a corporation headquartered in New York. After trying to work with corporation staff that summer, the computer teacher and the other key teacher in the Mill Creek Program resigned in protest at certain new policies.[35] In October 2004 I learned that key aspects of the city's demonstration project in Mill Creek had been abandoned.

Putting Mill Creek on the map and keeping it there is not easy, whether the focus is the creek itself, the neighborhood, or the people who live there. Confronting these failures, I sometimes think of the children's initial skepticism about prospects for change: "It won't happen.... Someone will wreck it."

LANDSCAPE LITERACY, ENVIRONMENTAL JUSTICE, AND CITY PLANNING AND DESIGN

Mill Creek is shaped by all the processes at work in inner cities across the United States. The neighborhood was laid waste by the flow of water and capital and the violence of redevelopment and neglect. The correlation of a buried creek with deteriorated buildings and vacant lands in inner-city neighborhoods is not unique to Philadelphia; similar situations are found in Boston, New York, St. Louis, and many other U.S. cities.[36] But Mill Creek is typical of such neighborhoods, where the residents are predominantly low-income people of color. Known locally as "the Bottom," it is one of many such "Black Bottoms" in the United States. They are at the bottom economically, socially, and topographically. Here, harsh socioeconomic conditions and racial discrimination are exacerbated by health and safety hazards posed by a high water table and unstable ground.

Despite such conditions, the landscape and population of these communities embody resources as well as problems. In Mill Creek these resources are many and varied. Flourishing community gardens demonstrate the energy and determination of the gardeners who reclaimed them from abandoned lots; flowers planted along the sidewalk and bags of vegetables offered there express the gardeners' generosity. Blocks of homes sporting furniture on porches and identical flower boxes, with newly planted street trees lining the sidewalks, are signs of existing social networks. Inside Sulzberger Middle School, the drawings, models, and essays that decorate the halls speak of young people's intellects and vision. Lancaster Avenue, the stone wall that runs for blocks along Haverford Avenue, and the many different types of houses, from the Georgian mansion to the tiny row house, are landmarks that make the past visible and change tangible. Even vacant blocks and the buried floodplain are potential resources. To recognize resources is not to deny the problems but to see each in the context of the other.

These resources are readily apparent once the observer is prepared to see them. Someone who knows neither local history nor the broader canvas of U.S. urban history is unable to read many of the stories the landscape holds. One who assumes that the city has supplanted nature is not likely to see the effects of the natural processes that still shape its landscape; another who believes that the city has degraded nature is apt to see only pollution. Those who think the ravaged state of a neighborhood is the natural outcome of its occupation by an "underclass" whose members have lived in poverty for generations may see only devastation. Prejudice is reinforced by the tools professionals use. If those responsible for planning and designing a neighborhood rely on maps of those features they judge to be important and do not spend time there, their assumptions are not likely to be challenged. Mistakes that follow from misreading or failing to read significant features of the urban landscape can have terrible consequences.

Ten years ago I thought that landscape illiteracy would at worst produce environmental injustice in the form of physical hazards to health and safety. The Sulzberger students showed me that there is an even greater injustice than inequitable exposure to harsh conditions: the internalization of shame for one's neighborhood. This is a particularly destructive form of injustice. To feel both at home in a place and ashamed of it is harmful. It saps self-esteem and can engender a sense of guilt and resignation. Before the students at Sulzberger Middle School learned to read their landscape more fully, they read it partially. Without an understanding of the forces that shaped the neighborhood, many believed that the poor conditions were the fault of those who lived there, a product of either incompetence or lack of caring. Learning of all the historical reasons sparked a sense of relief. Once they had the knowledge and skill to read the landscape's history, these children began to see their home in a more positive light; to appreciate the effort and vision that places such as Aspen Farms represent; and to regard some adults, including the gardeners, as heroes. They came to consider the possibility of alternative futures and brimmed with ideas. Secure in their knowledge and their abilities to reason, they challenged public officials with confidence and impressed them with articulate proposals. To read and shape landscape is to learn and teach: to know the world, to express ideas, and to influence others.

Verbal literacy is commonly acknowledged as an essential skill without which a citizen cannot participate fully and effectively in a democratic society. Teaching literacy became a cornerstone of the U.S. civil rights movement of the 1950s and 1960s. The "Citizenship School," which began as a means to increase voter registration through the promotion of literacy, evolved into a forum for discussion and a catalyst for political action.[37] In 1999, when I first read about Myles Horton's work with civil rights activists and Paolo Freire's with adult literacy programs in Brazil, I was struck by the many parallels to my experience with landscape literacy in Mill Creek.

Freire designed literacy programs that were tailored to what he calls the "word universe" of the learners. To extract the words specific to the universe of particular people and a particular place and as a preparation for reading the word, he employed images of the surroundings. He found that "decodifying or *reading* the situations pictured leads [people] to a critical perception of the meaning of culture by leading them to understand how human practice or work transforms the world." He believed that people should learn to read in the context of the "fundamental moments of their common history" and proposed that texts of local history be created for that purpose from transcripts of taped interviews with older inhabitants. In *Literacy: Reading the Word and the World,* Freire and Donaldo Macedo describe literacy as a form of cultural politics that either "serves to reproduce existing social formations" or "promotes democratic and emancipatory change." They assert that knowledge of the world is a precondition for literacy and that understanding and transforming the world should be its goal. Reading, they say, "always involves critical perception, interpretation, and the *rewriting* of what is read." Macedo suggests that "emancipatory literacy" has two dimensions: "On the one hand, students have to become literate about their histories, experiences, and the culture of their immediate environments. On the other hand, they must also appropriate those codes and cultures of the dominant spheres so they can transcend their own environments."[38]

Studying their neighborhood's natural and built features brought the place alive for the Sulzberger students. The understanding of their own landscape also opened wider vistas. It introduced them to broader social, political, and environmental issues and promoted other learning. In Freire's terms, it enabled the "students to develop a positive self-image before grappling with the type of knowledge . . . outside their immediate world." Only after they had "a grasp on their world" could they "begin to acquire other knowledge."[39]

Like verbal literacy, landscape literacy is a cultural practice that entails both understanding the world and transforming it. While writers must be verbally literate, however, many professionals responsible for planning, designing, and building the city are not landscape literate. After six weeks of investigation into their neighborhood's history, the children were more literate than many professionals, and some of their proposals for the neighborhood were more astute. To be literate is to recognize both the problems in a place and its resources, to understand how they came about, what means sustain them, and how they are related. Such literacy should be a cornerstone of community development and of urban planning and design. To plan prudently is to transform problems into opportunities and liabilities into resources and to intervene at an appropriate scale. To design wisely is to read ongoing dialogues in a place, to distinguish enduring stories from ephemeral ones, and to imagine how to join the conversation. The stakes are high for those who must live in the places professionals help create. Like literacy, urban planning and design are cultural practices that can serve either to perpetuate the inequities of existing social structures or to enable and promote democratic change.

AFTERWORD

What was present in 2005, when the original version of this chapter was written, is now history, but the repetition of past mistakes persists even as visionary plans are put forward. Since 2005 the municipal government has built new houses on formerly vacant land in the Mill Creek neighborhood, including many on the buried floodplain of Mill Creek, and this initiative continues. In 2011 the Mill Creek Farm, which occupied city-owned land on the buried floodplain, faced eviction and replacement by new houses. The patterns of vacant land are no longer so clear as they were ten years ago, but what is worse, the opportunities for addressing the city's combined sewer overflow problem have been diminished. Ironically, this is occurring just as the city's water department has embarked on a visionary plan for reducing combined sewer flows using green infrastructure, as outlined in *Green City, Clean Water: Combined Sewer Long Term Control Plan Update* (2009). The U.S. Environmental Protection Agency finally approved the plan in spring 2012, and other cities are likely to follow Philadelphia's lead. The water department has already finished prototype projects, and, if implemented, the plan will be a national landmark. The proposal calls for a 30 percent reduction in the city's impervious surfaces in the next twenty-five years in order to capture the first inch of rain to fall in a storm. If the plan works, it will save the city billions of dollars. But will it work (physically), and can it be done (economically, politically)? Some city agencies must still be convinced.

To help test and refine the plan, my MIT colleague Jim Wescoat and I have used it as a case study in an MIT course on water, landscape, and urban design, with a focus on the ultraurban Mill Creek watershed. To study the entire watershed in 2010, we selected seven transects from the headwaters of Mill Creek to its mouth; in 2011, we selected seven separate subwatersheds. Collectively, the transects and subwatersheds represent the diverse conditions that exist in the watershed, with variations in topography, impervious surface, land use, ownership, and demographics. For each transect and subwatershed, our students developed a conceptual design and a plan for implementation and management. Together, these plans highlighted diverse challenges and opportunities, but in each case, the proposed designs captured the first inch of rainfall (and more). We plan to build on these findings. This work and more can be seen on the recently revised and expanded West Philadelphia Landscape Project website.

Diane Sicotte

11 | Saving Ourselves by Acting Locally

The Historical Progression of Grassroots Environmental Justice
Activism in the Philadelphia Area, 1981–2001

THIS CHAPTER OUTLINES THE SCOPE and historical progression of environmental justice issues and grassroots activism in the Philadelphia Metropolitan Statistical (MSA) area from 1981 to 2001. This area encompasses not just the city of Philadelphia but also the surrounding Pennsylvania counties (Bucks, Chester, Delaware, and Montgomery counties) and the New Jersey counties across the Delaware River from Philadelphia (Burlington, Camden, Gloucester, and Salem counties). Environmental justice activists address poor environmental and environmental health conditions facing any community that bears a disproportionate share of pollution from industrialization or technology or that is deprived of its fair share of clean and healthy environmental conditions.[1] Grassroots environmental justice activists are typically local people fighting for cleaner, safer conditions where they live, work, and play.

The Philadelphia area is characterized by early and extensive industrialization, high population density, high degrees of social inequality, and contentious race relations; all these are preconditions for conflicts over the distribution of environmental hazards.[2] Philadelphia, once the third largest city in the United States, was a nineteenth-century manufacturing powerhouse whose factories turned out textiles, locomotives, chemicals, petroleum, and steel.[3] As is true of other U.S. cities where industrialization occurred on a massive scale before the 1950s (e.g., Boston), the absence of controls on industrial air and water pollutants and shortsighted waste disposal practices degraded the area's environmental quality.[4] Since 1970 deindustrialization has greatly decreased manufacturing employment in Philadelphia and the surrounding counties while leaving behind a plethora of hazards to environmental health, including brownfields, illegal hazardous waste dumpsites, and toxic chemicals in the sediment of the Delaware and Schuylkill rivers. The area's environmental hazards include abandoned and hazardous industrial buildings, soil contamination, lead-based paint on the interior surfaces of worn-out old homes and apartments, and a concentration of waste disposal industries. These conditions disproportionately burden the poorest communities in the area, including the Bridesburg and Port Richmond parts of Philadelphia; Southwest Philadelphia; Camden City, New Jersey; and Chester City, Pennsylvania. Such communities have relatively few resources to cope with pollution as they also struggle with poverty, crime, ineffective public schools, and generally low levels of health.[5] Yet rural communities in the area also face well water contaminated with toxic chemicals, landfill expansion, power plants, and other environmental hazards.

One of the earliest U.S. environmental justice struggles waged by a grassroots group was triggered by the Love Canal disaster in upstate New York. In the late 1970s Love Canal residents discovered that their community was built on a huge dump filled with leaking drums of toxic chemical waste. Trapped in a situation that was destroying their health, residents quickly discovered that they would have to fight to get their contaminated homes bought out, their health problems investigated, and the dumpsite cleaned up. Lois Gibbs, a local housewife, formed the Love Canal Homeowners Association; after years of struggling, the group ultimately won a buyout, evacuation, and medical registry for residents.[6] This case expanded public awareness of both the health hazards of exposure to chemicals and pollutants and the inadequacy of environmental enforcement and protections for the public. It also set the stage for the growth of the antitoxics movement.[7] Around the same time, residents of a black community in Houston initiated a class-action lawsuit seeking to block plans to site a landfill in their neighborhood on the grounds of racial discrimination.[8] Because of his involvement in this case, the sociologist Robert D. Bullard began to ask whether racism had caused minorities to suffer disparate impacts from environmental hazards in the United States. Over the next twenty years, researchers working in a variety of scholarly disciplines discovered environmental inequities in many areas of the nation: essentially, black, Latino, and low-income people tended to live closer to sources of pollution, toxic waste disposal sites, and other environmental hazards.[9] Researchers further discovered that laws to protect the public from pollution were often applied inequitably and that in the Philadelphia area, disadvantaged people, blacks, Latinos, and those working in manufacturing lived near the most hazardous air polluters.[10]

In the 1990s economic globalization accelerated, accompanied by the transfer of hazardous industries, such as metal smelting, plastic manufacturing, silicon chip manufacturing, and toxic waste recycling, from wealthy industrialized countries to poorer ones.[11] These events signaled the shift of environmental inequalities from the local to the global scale, exacerbating already existing global inequalities in wealth and health.[12] Recent research has revealed that people in poorer African and Asian nations will bear a disproportionate share of the health and safety risks from climate change due to greenhouse gases even though they have contributed relatively little to discharging those gases into the atmosphere.[13]

Locally as globally, environmental hazards and harms tend to "roll downhill," to be visited on those with less social and economic power, yet researchers and the public tend to notice only large-scale or legally important cases, which reflect only a handful of the environmental justice issues in any area. One legally important environmental justice case in the Philadelphia area involved the spatial clustering of polluting waste and industrial facilities in and around Chester City, Pennsylvania, a case that tested civil rights law's ability to redress the disparate impact of such facilities on low-income African American residents. In another, a Camden City, New Jersey, group sought to prevent the construction of a local cement recycling facility, and a district court judge agreed with the group's argument.[14] Shortly thereafter, however, in *Alexander v. Sandoval,* the U.S. Supreme Court ruled that citizens can sue federal agencies only in a narrow range of situations involving intentional racial discrimination, and the Camden ruling was later set aside. *Alexander v Sandoval* cut off any further attempts by environmental justice groups to bring lawsuits based on the disparate impact of environmental hazards on racial minority groups.[15]

The focus on these few high-profile cases of environmental injustice reinforces the impression that little grassroots activism has occurred in the Philadelphia area. Many agree that the political ethos prevailing in the Philadelphia area over the last hundred-plus years has had a chilling effect on community activism. Politics there has been characterized as a "coercive and undemocratic political machine, which . . . accustomed residents to authoritarian politics." The result has been a fatalistic attitude about the possibility of change; where this attitude exists, environmental justice activists face a daunting challenge. As the former Philadelphia city council member David Cohen puts it: "My main hurdle was first to convince the people of South Philly that they could win this fight . . . [;] the people, particularly in South Philadelphia, were so convinced that it could not be won."[16]

Despite these dynamics, I have turned up 251 separate cases in which grassroots-level collective action took place on more than thirty different environmental justice issues in this area between 1981 and 2001; 199 different environmental justice organizations worked on the issues. Nonetheless, such organizations and associated activists in the Philadelphia area have limited their effectiveness by focusing on anti-toxics efforts rather than environmental justice more generally. Anti-toxics activists tend to define problems in terms of one particular facility or process and focus mostly or entirely on local targets.[17] Antitoxics campaigns and environmental justice activists often share the same goals, whether cleaning up toxins, enforcing existing laws against pollution, or preventing the construction of new hazardous facilities in their backyards. Environmental justice activists, however, define the problems more broadly; in their view, inequalities in exposure or proximity to environmental hazards stem from inequities in social class, race, or ethnicity that drive the unequal allocation of the risks and rewards of industrialization.[18] Although racially diverse communities have often found themselves engaged in antitoxics struggles, only in the late 1980s did Philadelphia area activists begin contending that minority and low-income communities were being targeted for the proliferation of hazardous facilities. Some argue that too narrow a focus on "environmental racism" keeps predominantly white communities from recognizing their local struggles as environmental justice issues.[19] Thus, the racial divisions characteristic of Philadelphia likely contribute to the fragmentation and disunity of purpose that characterize antitoxics grassroots activism.

METHODS FOR DISCOVERING AND ANALYZING LOCAL ACTIVISM

It is notoriously difficult to chronicle the extent of environmental justice activism. This type of activism, more than most others, involves local residents struggling with local officials over localized threats to environmental justice. Most environmental justice groups are made up of local, everyday residents who meet around someone's kitchen table; few have the luxury of keeping good records detailing their efforts. As a result, the history of environmental justice activism leaves relatively few traces.[20]

One way to find out about these localized struggles is to search for local newspaper stories about environmental justice controversies. Although this method has the advantage of turning up smaller, more obscure cases (thus coming as close as possible to encompassing the entire universe of environmental justice controversies in the area), it also has some important disadvantages. First, and perhaps most serious, it reveals only those environmental justice struggles that were reported in newspapers large enough to cover the entire study area but small enough to focus on local issues. The data is thus biased, disproportionately reflecting cases that occurred in a city close to media outlets, those that were especially dramatic and newsworthy, or those that went on for a long time.[21] Second, news stories do not always accurately report what happened, though recent research has shown that this concern might be overstated.[22] In some cases, it was possible to bolster accuracy by "triangulating" with other sources to verify or corroborate factual information from these stories.[23] Third, the actors in environmental justice struggles who are most visible to the press (e.g., activists connected with large national organizations or politicians taking action on local issues to win elections) are often not the people who were truly instrumental in the campaigns. To correct this bias, I did not count actions by local politicians or regulatory agencies as "instances of activism" even though these actions were central to the issues on which local activists worked. To get perspective on the political and social context for the environmental justice struggles taking place, I interviewed people who played prominent roles in the environmental justice movement in the Philadelphia area. Using this combination of methods, I discovered many instances of environmental justice activism, including some that had faded from the memories of local environmentalist groups.

Choosing the study area was relatively easy. The area in question encompasses eight suburban counties as well as Philadelphia and thus provides views of both urban and suburban environmental justice issues and activism.

A more difficult decision arose in determining which issues to include or exclude as involving environmental justice. Environmental justice activists work on a staggeringly wide range of issues, including (but not limited to) biopiracy, deforestation, disasters, environmental racism, food quality, globalization, inequitable siting of hazardous facilities, occupational health, oil and mineral extraction, pesticide exposure, transportation inequalities, unsustainable development, and water privatization.[24] Anyone researching such activism thus faces the additional task of drawing boundaries around a subset of many possible environmental justice cases. In the end, I narrowed my focus to those issues that involved removing, alleviating, or preventing a perceived threat to human health, safety, or quality of life caused by some aspect of the environment. Among the fifty-four different issues that qualified for inclusion were abandoned hazardous waste sites; air and water pollution; airport noise; geographic clusters of health problems attributed to toxins or pollution; fires, spills, and chemical accidents; sewage sludge; and facilities handling household, hazardous, and construction wastes.

Finally, I had to define the term *activist.* Only those local residents participating in some form of collective action on an issue taking place in their community (as well as their allies from state- or national-level groups working on a local issue) were defined as activists. Searching the *Philadelphia Inquirer's* online database for the word *environmental* turned up 24,493 stories published between January 1, 1981, and December 31, 2001. The search yielded 655 newspaper stories that mentioned grassroots collective action on issues that qualified under my definition of environmental justice issues. After reading each story, I extracted the most relevant pieces of information and stored them in a database for analysis; this information encompassed the name of the case; the type of issue, including a distinction between cases involving siting disputes and those that did not; the name of the environmental justice group involved; actions taken; stated or implied goals of the group; and the location of the facility or contamination.

HISTORICAL PROGRESSION OF ENVIRONMENTAL JUSTICE ACTIVISM, 1981–2001

I identified 251 cases of environmental justice activism in 1981–2001. On average, newspapers mentioned 12 new cases each year; in some years there were far fewer (e.g., 2 in 1997) and in other years, far more (27 in 1999). Only 78 (31 percent) of these cases involved siting issues; 173 (69 percent) involved pollution from an existing facility or other environmental health issue (e.g., pesticide use). Nearly half the siting cases involved residents' efforts to block an incinerator.

While many issues involved perennial environmental justice problems (such as dumping, air pollution, and water contamination), some major issues tended to surface at a particular point in time and then fade away, to be replaced by other issues. This historical progression illustrates four important factors. First, grassroots environmental justice and antitoxics activists have been effective in spurring progress concerning environmental problems in the Philadelphia area since the early 1980s. Second, progress was ecologically limited, with solutions all too often generating more environmental problems and new social controversies. Third, the relationship between increases in public awareness of the health risks associated with proximity to waste and pollution was often followed by the increased concentration of such hazards in poor, minority communities. Fourth, the rise in environmental justice activism by residents of communities suffering concentrations of hazards interfered with, but did not completely prevent, the introduction of new hazards.

The progression of issues that environmental justice activists addressed was driven by changes in the political and economic context for various technologies, including those relating to landfills, incinerators, and power plants; by the development of new laws and regulations governing the disposal of waste and the generation of energy; and by expansions in public awareness on issues such as pollution, toxic waste, and environmental racism. Thus, the early 1980s were characterized by a disproportionate number of cases in which neighborhood activists dealt with soil, water, and air pollution from landfills. From 1981 until 1994, activists were also consumed with preventing the construction of new incinerators nearby or addressing air quality and waste problems at existing ones. The number of cases involving the placement of all types of unwanted facilities dropped off sharply after 1994; during this time, activists were kept busy with ongoing problems such as air pollution, the illegal dumping of waste, and drinking water contamination. The mid-1990s, however, saw an increase in the number of cases in which residents of minority neighborhoods claimed that environmental racism had led to the selection of their communities as the sites for toxic facilities or processes. Such battles resurfaced in 2000 with a proliferation of proposals for new electric power plants.

CLEANING UP DANGEROUS LANDFILLS, 1981–1985

In the early 1980s, much environmental justice activism in the Philadelphia area coalesced around the issue of landfills. In 1981–85, 21 percent of these cases dealt with landfills; in 1986–2001, only 6 percent did so. Contamination from landfills, illegal dumps, and uncontrolled hazardous waste dumps were a particular problem in the Northeast, where intense industrialization had combined with high population density to place people too close to all types of waste. Landfills had become the most popular option for the disposal of all types of waste in the 1940s and 1950s, for land on the outskirts of cities was abundant and cheap. But before the 1970s, a "sanitary landfill" was often nothing more than household garbage dumped directly onto the ground and then covered with a layer of earth.[25] Many landfills also accepted hazardous industrial wastes, for the disposal of these wastes was subject to only inadequate oversight and regulation before the 1970s.[26] Under these conditions, hazardous chemicals and leachate (in this case, the toxic liquid produced by putrefying household garbage) migrated easily through porous soil and into the water table, contaminating well water, rivers, and lakes.[27] In addition to enduring contaminated water, people living near landfills were often plagued by fires, caused by either the routine burning of garbage or the accidental ignition of built-up methane gas; nauseating odors, blowing trash, noisy dump trucks, and the declining value of their homes further reduced their quality of life.[28]

In 1976 the EPA began dealing with regulations for the disposal of hazardous waste as mandated by the Resource Conservation and Recovery Act (RCRA), which had been passed that year. This act set federal standards for landfills and required the states to survey their dumps and either bring them up to standards or shut them down.[29]

By the 1970s more spectacular environmental health issues, such as disease, nuclear radiation, and the genetic and reproductive effects of pollution, were already serving as the focus for a small but growing proportion of protests over environmental issues in the United States.[30] Once the public recognized landfills to be toxic hazards, controversies inevitably arose. For the Philadelphia area of the early 1980s, these controversies concerned issues similar to those related to Love Canal, for they involved human exposure to hazardous chemical wastes (in these cases, wastes that had been dumped in landfills).

Between 1981 and 1985 environmental justice activists focused on twenty-eight landfill cases. Only six of these were siting cases; the other twenty-two dealt with contamination from existing landfills. During this five-year period, fourteen distinct environmental justice groups in the Philadelphia area mobilized around contamination from landfills in seventeen locations.

One of the worst offenders was the Lipari Landfill, located in Pitman, New Jersey. From 1958 until 1971, when the dump closed, its trenches

were filled with three million gallons of liquid industrial wastes, including solvents, paints, paint thinners, and formaldehyde.[31] In 1978 concerned neighbors formed the Pitman Alcyon Lake Lipari Landfill Community Association (PALLCA) and began agitating to get the site cleaned
up. After events at Love Canal spurred the creation of the Superfund
in 1980, the EPA ranked the Lipari Landfill as its highest priority for
cleanup in 1982 and fenced it off. The EPA planned to flush the site with
water, a strategy PALLCA members believed was inadequate and would
spread contaminants. Joined by national groups including the Citizens'
Clearinghouse for Hazardous Waste and the National Campaign against
Toxic Hazards, PALLCA continued to agitate for excavation of the site
and incineration of contaminants instead of flushing.[32] In 1986 PALLCA
held a rally to support the Superfund reauthorization and continued to
fight for a safe cleanup, pollution monitoring, and a health registry.[33]

On the Pennsylvania side of the Delaware River, Montgomery County
residents were trying to cope with the effects of Moyer's Landfill. Toxic
leachate from the landfill had been seeping into drinking water wells
as early as 1977, prompting Thomas O'Leary and his neighbors to begin
using bottled water for drinking. He joined approximately 450 families
who formed the Montgomery County grassroots group Lower Providence Concerned Citizens (LPCC), and together they began to pressure
the EPA to investigate the landfill. They repelled an effort to double the
landfill's capacity and succeeded in getting it closed to further dumping,
but there was still much left to do. The EPA had discovered that PCBs,
dioxins, solvents, paints, and low-level radioactive wastes had been
dumped there since the early 1940s; the liquid from the landfill contained these chemicals in concentrations high enough to place it on the
National Priority List for Superfund cleanup. The landfill endangered
many people: each time it rained, the noxious runoff carried the leachate into the Schuylkill River, the source of half of Philadelphia's drinking
water.[34] The LPCC continued to take an active role in shepherding the
cleanup of the site, which was finally finished in 2002.[35]

Groups protesting landfills often chose names that would create col-
orful acronyms (e.g., People United for a Klean Environment, or PUKE;
No Dumps in Clean Environments, or NoDICE). In Florence Township,
New Jersey, the Mansfield Environmental Committee protested the EPA's
ineffective cleanup of toxic contaminants at the FLR Landfill with street
theater. Residents dressed their children as angels, led their march with
two black hearses, and placed makeshift tombstones at the children's
feet.[36] At the Bethayres Landfill, in Montgomery County, Pennsylvania,

the Citizens' Landfill Task Force pressured the county's board of commissioners to enforce local laws, fine the owners of the landfill, and get the state environmental regulators to take action.[37]

The West Deptford, New Jersey, activist Beatrice Cerkez succeeded in rallying 1,000 of her neighbors to oppose the expansion of the noxious Kinsley Landfill, and together they succeeded in getting it shut down. But this victory gave rise to new environmental justice battles: as Gloucester County officials saw it, losing the old landfill meant building a new one, this time in South Harrison Township. It also meant building a new incinerator in West Deptford.[38] Both facilities faced opposition from the host communities.

INCINERATOR BATTLES, 1981–1994

In 1977 the state of New Jersey passed its Solid Waste Management Plan, giving each county responsibility for its own waste. The plan included a surcharge on all out-of-state waste, creating a problem for Philadelphia, which was accustomed to dumping 55 percent of its garbage in New Jersey landfills.[39] Four years later, the New Jersey Department of Environmental Protection (NJDEP) decided that, as of 1986, the state would no longer accept Philadelphia's garbage in its landfills at any price.[40] Congress expanded the RCRA in 1984 by passing the Hazardous and Solid Waste Amendments, which enacted more stringent requirements for hazardous waste disposal and for landfills.[41] Tougher regulations governing landfills, the New Jersey ban on out-of-state waste, escalating dumping fees, and the growing scarcity of cheap open land, combined with community resistance to the creation of new landfills nearby, produced a "waste crisis" for local politicians in the 1980s.[42] Although incinerators constitute just one waste disposal option among many, they have often been mistaken for a panacea during such urban crises.[43] Accordingly, local administrators in the Philadelphia area began to consider incinerators a feasible solution to the ever-rising tide of trash.[44]

The use of incineration for disposing household garbage was not a new strategy. Approximately 180 incinerators had been built in the United States from 1885 to 1908, but many had been abandoned because they performed poorly. Modern technologies, however, allowed incinerators to "mass burn" wet, unseparated garbage. An even more profitable (and energy-efficient) option was the "waste-to-energy" plant, as proponents called the new refuse-derived fuel (RDF) processing plants, which can create fuel pellets from separated garbage. This fuel can then

be sold and used to produce electricity. By the late 1980s, the incinerator industry was led by four large corporations whose interests were
aligned with those of municipal officials, EPA analysts, and investors.
Jerome Balter, formerly of the Philadelphia Public Interest Law Center,
recalls the context for incinerator siting battles: "Whether true or not,
there was a big scare that went out that everybody is running out of
landfill space, and the cost of landfilling is going to go sky-high. And that
was related to the advent of incinerators. And you had the development
of far more sophisticated incinerators than had previously existed, with
a good deal of money behind them to influence decision-making by
communities. We had that situation in Philadelphia."[45] But communities
chosen to host an incinerator feared the toxicity of its emissions, which
would include not only dioxins, furans (released from the burning of
plastics), and other carcinogens but also toxic metals and metalloids,
such as arsenic, cadmium, lead, and mercury.[46] Indeed, incinerators
solved one waste problem while creating another: ash residues containing such high concentrations of toxic metals and carcinogens that some
regulators argued the ash itself should be labeled "hazardous waste."[47]

Public opposition was already a serious problem for incinerator
projects everywhere in the early 1980s, when California environmental
regulators commissioned the infamous Cerrell study. Cerrell Associates
researchers examined demographic differences between communities
to minimize political opposition to incinerators. Their findings resulted
in the recommendation to build incinerators only in low-income communities. In particular, they concluded that facilities in rural areas
where residents had low educational attainments and were predominantly Catholic would meet little effective resistance.[48] In the end, however, this "path of least resistance" strategy failed in the face of widespread and vigorous opposition in nearly all communities.

From 1981 to 1994 the Philadelphia area saw thirty-eight separate
environmental justice campaigns against incinerators, making up 22
percent of all environmental justice activism cases there. Half these
incinerator cases involved existing incinerators of various types; the
other half involved community opposition to the proposed incinerators
slated to burn household garbage.

The longest battle occurred over the proposal to build a 2,250-ton
trash incinerator near the obsolete naval yard in South Philadelphia, a
project backed by Philadelphia's mayor, Wilson Goode.[49] A broad-based
and mulitracial coalition of neighborhood and environmental groups,
brought together by the Trash to Steam Alternative Coalition, mobilized
to fight the incinerator.[50] From 1983, when the incinerator was first pro-

posed, to 1988, when the project was killed, thousands of people turned out to distribute flyers criticizing the incinerator, give "sniff tours" of the existing hazardous facilities in South Philadelphia, and pack city council meetings voicing opposition to the proposal.[51] Despite perceptions that South Philadelphia activists were acting from narrow self-interest, simply crying "Not in My Back Yard" (NIMBY), activists from neighborhood associations in North Philadelphia and Northeast Philadelphia joined in, arriving in busloads to speak out against incinerators at a key city council meeting.[52] The coalition had politically powerful allies, including Councilman John Street (who later became mayor of Philadelphia) and especially Councilman David Cohen, whose sustained opposition activists identified as a key factor in the defeat of the incinerator. Cohen played a central role in persuading progressive black city council members to oppose the project.

The prelude to battles over building incinerators in Montgomery County was the passage of Pennsylvania's Solid Waste Management Plan (Act 97) in 1980. This act empowered all municipalities to draft their own waste management plans, but its ambiguous wording left room for debate about whether the term *municipality* referred to townships or counties.[53] Three new incinerators were proposed for Abington, Ardsley and Plymouth Township, all towns in Montgomery County, where County Commissioner Paul Bartle lobbied vigorously for the power to supersede local zoning regulations. In Plymouth Township he faced strong opposition from TRASH, Ltd., a grassroots environmental justice group. Incinerator proponents had the upper hand: the Pennsylvania Department of Environmental Resources (PADER) supported incinerators and Bartle's position on county control over waste management. Bartle also enjoyed a huge budget compared to Plymouth's, as well as support from nearby towns that had pledged to send their trash to the Plymouth incinerator. The activists in TRASH persisted, pressuring Plymouth Township officials to fight the county, holding rallies, and questioning the fairness of the decision to bring an incinerator to their town.[54] Ultimately, however, TRASH lost when the State Supreme Court ruled that the proposed incinerator was not subject to local zoning laws; the facility was built in Plymouth.[55]

Three new incinerators were proposed for Camden County, New Jersey, one each in Bellmawr, South Camden, and Pennsauken. The largest of these was slated for South Camden, where Father Michael Doyle of Sacred Heart Church and other neighborhood activists spoke out against the project, criticizing the choice of the poor, predominantly minority community as the site for a hazardous facility.[56] The incinerator already had the support of Camden's mayor. But South Camden residents were veterans of environmental justice battles; they had organized the South Camden Action Team (SCAT) to push for enforcement of odor regulations at the nearby municipal sewage treatment plant.[57] During the first three years of public hearings over the incinerator, SCAT members turned out to greet officials' assurances of the plant's safety with skepticism.[58] Another group—Citizens against Trash-to-Steam (CATS)—emerged and began pressuring the Camden City Council to ban the incinerator. When it refused, CATS began collecting signatures; 15 percent of registered voters would have to sign the petition if the group was to get the issue in a referendum.[59] Meanwhile, the New Jersey Department of Environmental Protection issued a permit for the incinerator.[60] Although CATS did succeed in passing a binding referendum, the state overrode it, and the incinerator was built in South Camden.[61] Protestors from the international environmental group Greenpeace scaled the incinerator's 366-foot smokestack and chained themselves to a truck to delay construction.[62]

The struggle to block the Pennsauken incinerator succeeded, perhaps because of the organizers' success in forming a coalition. The Pennsauken group Stop Incineration Now (SIN) was joined by Camden's CATS and Allied Citizens Opposing Pollution (ACOP), from nearby Burlington County, at protest rallies.[63] Unfortunately, as often occurs, success in keeping the incinerator out of Pennsauken resulted in a move to expand the South Camden incinerator, thus exacerbating environmental injustice there.[64]

Older garbage incinerators, such as Philadelphia's 1950s-vintage Northwest Incinerator, also caused problems. Since 1974 the Northwest Incinerator had been cited forty-eight times for violating air quality standards and had contaminated the nearby Manayunk Canal with leachate from its waste piles.[65] Members of the Germany Hill Civic Association began to defend their neighborhood by pushing the city to comply with the law.[66] With representation from the Philadelphia Public Interest Law Center, they succeeded in shutting the incinerator in 1988 but had to continue fighting to get 100,000 tons of ash hauled from the site.[67]

Another incinerator controversy erupted in 1981, this one pitting the residents of Logan Township, New Jersey, against the NJDEP. The Logan incinerator, operated by Rollins Environmental Services, burned hazardous wastes and was the site of two serious explosions, a fire, and the release of acids into the air; it also had only a temporary permit.[68] The township filed two lawsuits: one against the NJDEP to keep it from issuing the facility a permanent permit and the other against Rollins.[69]

The local group Americans for Environmental Action (AEA) pushed for a plant shutdown and was joined by NoDICE, a group that was protesting another hazardous waste incinerator planned for nearby East Greenwich.[70]

Environmental justice activists worked on significantly fewer incinerator cases after 1994; between 1995 and 2001, there were only three new cases involving incinerators. The decline in new incinerator construction was a national phenomenon driven by multiple factors, including inefficient power generation at waste-to-energy facilities, the growing use of recycling, and stricter air quality standards.[71] But the delays and political turmoil caused by environmental justice activists also played a major role in defeating incineration as a strategy for coping with waste.[72]

FIGHTING ENVIRONMENTAL RACISM AND ENVIRONMENTAL INJUSTICE, 1994–2001

The term "environmental racism" refers to disproportionately choosing predominantly minority communities as sites for polluting facilities, intentionally and unintentionally discriminating against people of color in environmental policy making and enforcement, and excluding people of color from environmental decision making and activism.[73] Environmental racism thus constitutes a specific type of environmental injustice. The phrases "environmental justice" and "environmental racism" began to trickle into the national consciousness in the early 1990s, after researchers and activists showed that those with minority racial or ethnic backgrounds had greater exposure to environmental hazards, often because of proximity to those dangers.[74]

In the Philadelphia area, neighborhoods with multiple environmental hazards tend to be places also struggling with a lack of economic opportunity; drug dealing, violent crime, and other social problems; and institutional neglect.[75] Not surprisingly, then, many of the groups most prominent in fighting environmental racism were neighborhood organizations already working on poverty, crime, and other issues. When facing the possibility of a new facility that would add toxic pollution to the list of local problems, they fought it vigorously.[76]

One such group was the Eastwick Project Area Committee (EPAC), an umbrella organization serving eleven different neighborhoods in Southwest Philadelphia. These neighborhoods had a long history of racial integration but had become predominantly minority in recent years. They lay in the city's largest industrial district, with many tracts of undeveloped and abandoned land already zoned for industrial use. They were also near the large Sunoco Refinery and the Philadelphia International Airport and downstream of the notorious Clearview and Folcroft landfills, both Superfund sites on the National Priority List. Formed over decades of multiracial neighborhood activism since the 1950s, EPAC enjoyed a formal partnership with the Redevelopment Agency of Philadelphia in decisions about zoning-change issues and thus wielded an unusual amount of power over land uses in its neighborhoods.[77] In the 1980s EPAC began a twenty-year fight to get the Clearview and Folcroft landfills on the Superfund's list and to force the cleanup of the lead, pesticides, and PCBs leaching from them.[78] In 1986 EPAC led residents in rejecting a new trash transfer facility, but PADER issued the firm a permit anyway. Soon afterward, EPAC was pushing for a cleanup of the piles of trash that had accumulated there.[79] The umbrella organization's insider status made it particularly effective in finding out about proposed projects early in the siting process; thus, between 1981 and 2001, it blocked a sewage sludge incinerator, a toxic waste incinerator, a nuclear waste storage facility, and several other waste-processing facilities proposed for the area.[80] It also partnered with Sunoco employees in an effort to get the refinery to use less hazardous materials and participated in a "bucket brigade" in which neighborhood activists took air samples of the refinery at the fence line so that they could determine the types and quantities of its emissions. They discovered that the refinery was violating its air permit by emitting toxic chemicals at levels higher than the law allowed.[81]

In Chester, Pennsylvania, the community group Chester Residents Concerned for Quality Living (CRCQL) had been complaining of the emissions and truck traffic from the Westinghouse Incinerator since its opening in 1991.[82] The incinerator had been built by Delaware County officials under a cloud of corruption and in direct competition with plans for another incinerator whose revenues would have gone directly to the city of Chester.[83] A predominantly black and poor community, Chester was already the location of the Delaware County Sewage Treatment Plant (DELCORA); proposals then on the table would have added an infectious medical waste sterilization facility (ThermalPure) and an incinerator for burning contaminated soil (Soil Remediation Systems). The CRCQL's members believed that their town had been singled out as a "toxic wasteland" because of environmental racism.[84] The group collected signatures on a petition against granting the ThermalPure plant a permit and gave them to PADER officials. With the help of the Philadelphia Public Interest Law Center, it succeeded in getting the permit invalidated by the Commonwealth Court. Afterward, however, the Pennsylvania Supreme Court used an obscure maneuver known as "King's Bench power" to invalidate the Commonwealth Court's decision.[85] The facility began operating in 1993 but was closed in 1996 when its original owners went bankrupt.[86]

The CRCQL began fighting the next facility, Soil Remediation Systems, and was joined by the Campus Coalition Concerning Chester (C-4), a group of Swarthmore College students.[87] Although PADER issued the facility a permit, the project fell through after CRCQL relentlessly pressured the Chester city government to deny it a building permit. The CRCQL protested efforts to expand operations at the trash incinerator, and its lawyer won settlement money from incinerator operators and DELCORA for air quality violations. The money was used to fund a lead poisoning prevention program.[88] But environmental justice struggles in Chester continued: a proposal to burn used tires for fuel at the Kimberly-Clark paper plant in Chester galvanized activists in the new group the Chester Environmental Partnership (CEP) in 1999 and again in 2001; both proposals were defeated.[89]

Activists fought environmental racism in Camden, New Jersey, as well. Several neighborhood groups had already been active in the fights against hazardous facilities: Camden Churches Organized for People (CCOP), CATS, SCAT, and South Camden Citizens in Action (SCCIA). The SCAT group formed to push for remediation of the foul smells emanating from the "huge, black mounds of sewage sludge" at the Camden County Municipal Authority (CCMUA) sewage treatment plant, located just two hundred yards from the Sacred Heart Elementary School.[90] The local parish's Father Michael Doyle participated in both SCAT and the CCOP and became involved in battles to clean up the CCMUA, to block a proposed new incinerator that would burn sewage sludge and garbage, and to find answers when Camden's privately supplied water was found to be contaminated with the carcinogen TCE.[91]

Having lost the battle against the municipal incinerator, Camden residents faced a new fight: a large cement recycling company, St. Lawrence Cement, wanted to locate a facility on state-owned land, which would have meant tax relief for the company. The plant was to process 848,771 tons of blast furnace slag a year, and its annual emissions were projected at 60 tons of fine dust.[92] Olga Pomar, of Camden Regional Legal Services, represented the SCCIA in the battle to keep St. Lawrence Cement out of Camden. The SCCIA filed a landmark lawsuit based on civil rights violations under Title VI of the Civil Rights Act, charging that Camden citizens had been subjected to environmental racism and discrimination.[93] This national-level case drew much attention and support from various groups including the NAACP, the Natural Resources Defense Council, and the Sierra Club.[94] In 2001 a judge ruled that the New Jersey Department of Environmental Protection had failed to conduct a "disparate impact analysis" before issuing the permit and issued an injunction halting construction on the facility. Later that year, however, the U.S. Supreme Court ruled in *Alexander v. Sandoval* that private citizens may not sue under Title VI on the grounds of unintentional disparate impact, invalidating the injunction. Today Camden residents live with the environmental impacts of St. Lawrence Cement, the incinerator, and many contaminated abandoned industrial sites.[95]

ELECTRIC POWER PLANTS, 2000 AND BEYOND

From 1981 to 1999 only one siting case involving an electric power plant was the target of environmental justice activism. Suddenly, in 2000, Philadelphia-area environmental justice activists found themselves fighting proposals for five new plants. Why did power plants suddenly come into vogue? The timing of these cases rests on the changes in the electric power market driven by the Federal Energy Regulatory Commission's 1996 deregulation decision, which opened electric utilities to free market competition and allowed separate pricing for the generation, transmission, and distribution of electricity. In the wake of its own sweeping deregulation, California was experiencing rolling blackouts, prompting nationwide fears of scarcity that some charged were being used to justify building new plants—a profitable venture, because the deregulated utilities now had a greater financial incentive to increase sales.[96]

Power plants that burn natural gas inflict fewer toxins on their neighbors than coal-fired plants do because they emit little sulfur dioxide or mercury; however, they emit nitrogen oxide, carbon dioxide, and methane, three greenhouse gases that contribute to global warming and are known respiratory irritants.[97] They too thus fall under the category of "locally unwanted land uses" (LULUs). Predictably, residents of predominantly white counties with pockets of affluence (such as Chester and Montgomery counties) managed to keep power plants out of their backyards far more effectively than could residents in counties with concentrated poor minority populations, such as Delaware County.

Three of the five proposed power plants were to be sited in Montgomery County. Panda Energy sought to establish the largest of these, a 1,000-megawatt plant, in Upper Hanover, Pennsylvania. Opposing them was the grassroots group Partners for Community Preservation (PCP), which retained a lawyer to block zoning approval. After a two-year battle, which included posting "Stop Panda!" signs along the highway, the PCP won when Panda Energy was denied zoning approval and the state's environmental protection agency denied it a permit, prompting Panda to give up on the plant.[98] Two 500-megawatt plants were proposed for Limerick, Pennsylvania, one to be built by Florida Power and Light and the other, by PowerWorks. Both plants were opposed by Concerned Citizens for Limerick's Future (CCLF).[99] Although Limerick Township officials approved the Florida Power and Light plant, a panel of judges reversed their decision on the grounds of inappropriate land use. The officials who approved the power plant were voted out of office, and neither plant was built.[100]

In 2001 the battle shifted to Chester County, where Intergen wanted to build a power plant in East Pikeland. Residents formed the group Partners in Shared Air and won the battle when supervisors turned down the proposal.[101]

The only power plant built in the area during this time was a gas-powered Florida Power and Light plant sited in Delaware County's Marcus Hook in 2000. Marcus Hook is very close to Chester City, so the Chester Environmental Partnership took the lead in campaigning against it.[102] The Marcus Hook case illustrates how an increase in public awareness of health risks associated with industry and waste is associated with increases in the concentration of unwanted facilities in minority communities.[103]

ECOLOGICAL PROBLEMS, CONTESTED SOLUTIONS, AND CONTINUING ACTIVISM

The historical progression of environmental justice issues and activism in the Philadelphia area illustrates the ecologically inescapable nature of the waste disposal problem and the politically inescapable nature of local residents' demands for environmental justice. First, antitoxics activism aimed at cleaning up contamination from the Lipari Landfill, Moyer's Landfill, and other similar unlined landfills showed that disposing of industrial waste and household garbage in such a manner was a foolhardy and toxic solution to the problem of waste disposal. Then, state environmental regulators and local administrators tried to partner with large incinerator corporations to find an energy-efficient and environmentally friendly solution to the waste crisis—but at the expense of air quality in the communities hosting the incinerators. They were thwarted everywhere by the efforts of community activists, who resisted placing new incinerators near their communities and pushed authorities to enforce environmental laws at existing ones. After heightened consciousness about environmental health increased resistance to siting hazardous facilities near places where people lived, people of color in low-income urban neighborhoods in the Philadelphia area began to organize against environmental racism, the force they argued was concentrating environmental hazards in their communities. Finally, deregulation spurred multiple attempts to build gas-fired electric power plants near residential spaces, all of which were vigorously resisted by their intended host communities.

Although most environmental justice activism was fragmentary and hobbled by a predominant single-issue focus, local people continued to work in grassroots groups on redressing these and many other serious environmental injustices. Air pollution; the contamination of drinking water with toxic chemicals; occupational health problems; and the aftermath of fires, accidents, and spills involving hazardous substances—all these things posed serious problems in the Philadelphia area throughout the 1980s and 1990s. Finding ecologically beneficial and politically palatable solutions to the problems of waste disposal and environmental equity remains a daunting task for state and local officials in the area. It will take an enormous amount of skill and will for community leaders to address the environmental problems of the past and present without creating new problems for the future.

Domenic Vitiello

12 | Planning the Food-Secure City

Philadelphia's Agriculture, Retrospect and Prospect

> Don't after foreign Food and Cloathing roam,
> But learn to eat and wear what's rais'd at Home.
> Kind Nature suits each Clime with what it wants,
> Sufficient to subsist th' Inhabitants.
> Observing this, we less impair our Health,
> And by this Rule we more increase our Wealth
>
> Benjamin Franklin,
> *Poor Richard's Almanack* (1748)

FOOD SECURITY HAS RECENTLY REENTERED the consciousness of people concerned with urban environments and communities.[1] Urban agriculture is increasingly viewed as a strategy for community and economic development that addresses social, ecological, and health problems simultaneously. It is heralded as a new way of building sustainable cities for the twenty-first century.[2] But planning for urban agriculture and food security is as old as the city itself. This is an important, if often overlooked, part of its environmental and planning history.

Food and agriculture are basic to environmental history. The need and desire to eat has shaped much of the drama of human history, from wars to colonization to great internal and international migrations. Cultural historians have developed a substantial literature on imperialism and the globalization of food systems. Environmental historians, however, have thoroughly studied agriculture only in rural settings of the United States. Few urban historians have researched food systems, and planning historians are just beginning to uncover the heretofore hidden history of planners' involvement in community gardens, farmland preservation, and food distribution and market reform.[3]

This chapter constitutes part of this broader effort to write a useful history for contemporary food system planners and to expand the scope of urban environmental history and policy. It briefly surveys Philadelphia's agriculture and food system planning from the city's initial development in the 1680s to today, examining in greater detail the food movements and metropolitan food planning of recent decades. Recapturing this history can do more than highlight continuity and changes in the city and region's food system. Following a tradition in planning history, it can also help us understand the precedents for current planning and policy and frame today's initiatives as part of a much deeper history of cities' struggles for local food security in a global economy and society. To this end, it concludes with an introduction to Philadelphia's emerging twenty-first-century food policy. The latter parts of this account relate some of the work I have done as a researcher and participant in Philadelphia's local food sector, making the contents a combination of history and reflection on contemporary practice.

PLANNING PHILADELPHIA'S FOODSHED

Even before he set foot in the New World, William Penn envisioned a food-secure city and a metropolitan food economy. His "Green Countrie Towne" would have large homes surrounded by gardens, with more extensive agriculture in the surrounding countryside (see fig. 12.1). On his arrival at the colony, Penn wrote back to investors in London, enumerating the edible wealth of the region. "The Fruits that I find in the Woods, are the White and Black Mulbery, Chestnut, Wallnut, Plumbs, Strawberries, Cranberries, Hurtleberries and Grapes of divers sorts."[4] Complementing these was "The Artificial Produce of . . . Wheat, Barley, Oats, Rye, Pease, Beans, Squashes, Pumkins, Water-Melons, Mus-Melons, and all Herbs and Roots that our Gardens in England usually bring forth." He went on at length about the many "Fish, Fowl, and the Beasts of the Woods . . . some for Food and Profit, and some for Profit only."[5] Food would be the foundation not only of colonists' survival but also of Pennsylvania's economic development.[6]

The proprietor was unsure whether it would "be best to fall to [re] Fining the Fruits of the Country, especially the Grape, by the care and skill of Art, or send for foreign Stems and Sets, already good and approved." Ultimately, he decided "to try both . . . and hope the conse-

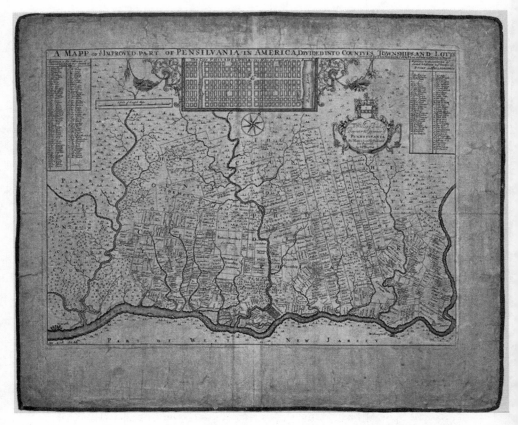

FIGURE 12.1. Thomas Holme, *A map of the improved part of the Province of Pennsilvania in America* (ca. 1687). In addition to showing the large agricultural estates plotted on this map, William Penn's surveyor Thomas Holme depicted two agricultural villages with smaller holdings arranged around towns at the right. Library of Congress, Geography and Map Division.

quence" would "be as good Wine as any European Countries of the same Latitude do yield."[7] The combination of native and imported species would help make a distinct American diet. But food exports would put Philadelphia on the world map.

In the 1730s Pennsylvanians began reaping the benefits of drought and agricultural shortages in Europe that sparked a wave of inflation lasting nearly a century.[8] With heightened demand for wheat and flour in countries from Ireland to the Mediterranean, and with migrants clearing land for farms and shipbuilders expanding merchant fleets, the Delaware Valley soon became the breadbasket of the Atlantic. As the geographer Carville Earle argues, "tobacco stunted the growth of towns" in the South since it was shipped directly overseas. But wheat helped grow towns into cities with diverse economies, spurring development of milling and packaging industries as well as wagon transport, warehousing, and shipping.[9]

Benjamin Franklin's generation recognized local agriculture as key not only to the region's food security but also to its economic development. A new set of civic institutions helped guide this growth. The American Philosophical Society established a committee on agriculture to consider problems such as wheat flies.[10] In the 1780s this committee helped spawn the Philadelphia Society for Promoting Agriculture, whose members tracked and tested agricultural improvements and displayed them at its fairs. These efforts led to the University of Pennsylvania's Faculty of Natural Sciences and Rural Economy, established in the early nineteenth century, though its plans for a veterinary school, pattern farm, and botanical garden saw only partial implementation.[11]

As frontier farms increasingly supplied staple grains for eastern markets, this education, research, and development aided the increasing specialization of Philadelphia's agricultural hinterland, particularly in higher-priced produce such as dairy goods, eggs, and vegetables. The pattern of regional dairies and market gardening feeding the city, with less-perishable bulk products imported from areas to the west, would persist to the mid-twentieth century. The rich, dark soils of Lancaster and Berks counties, in Pennsylvania, provided most of the region's dairy goods and much of its fresh vegetables. Pennsylvania's Adams County became its fruit belt.[12] The sandy soils of South Jersey's pinelands produced blueberries and cranberries, as well as tomatoes, in Vineland, Farmingdale, and other places whose names reflected these activities.

Although smokestacks and steam engines dominate popular images of the nineteenth-century city, agriculture supported most early industrialization. Farmers joined mechanics and scientists as members of the Franklin Institute, the region's foremost engineering society.[13] Beyond the gristmills, the factories of the nineteenth-century city processed cotton, tobacco, and forest products from the South, making Philadelphia a center of textile, chemical, and pharmaceutical manufacturing. Grain elevators and meatpacking plants dotted its rivers and railroad corridors.

As the United States became a global economic power in the Gilded Age, the city's agricultural hinterland expanded, and its food industries began to serve mass markets. Sugar refiners, such as Spreckels and Pennsylvania Sugar, and candy makers, such as Whitman's, ranked among the region's largest employers in the early twentieth century, processing sugar and cocoa from the tropics. Grains from the Midwest supplied giant bakeries including Freihofer, General Baking, National Biscuit (NABISCO), and Tasty Baking, which also processed the apples of Adams County and peaches from Pennsauken, New Jersey. The region's biggest food enterprise, Campbell's Soup, employed some 3,600 people in Camden by the 1920s, ensuring a national outlet for Jersey tomatoes and other vegetables grown nearby.[14]

Early professional planners sought to reshape the landscape of agriculture and food distribution in the early twentieth century city. Philadelphia's land-use patterns remained largely agricultural at the turn of the century, especially in the northeastern and northwestern sections of the city, where farms surrounded the industrial villages of Tacony, Frankford, and Manayunk. Some early planners advocated farmland preservation, and some, including Frederick Law Olmsted and George Waring, practiced "experimental agriculture." However, Philadelphia and other cities increasingly enforced their statutes limiting animal agriculture and passed new laws to reform food processing, warehousing, and public markets, such as those running down the centers of the city's wide avenues, including Girard, Spring Garden, and Second Street in Northern Liberties.[15] Planners built on the earlier critiques by Progressive Era reformers who had railed against the meatpacking industry, advocating the "redemption of the lower Schuylkill," to rid the central city of pollution from its largest slaughterhouses.[16]

As planners and their allies grappled with these transformations in the food system and the boom of urban populations, they became increasingly concerned with cities' "foodsheds" (a term coined in 1929 by W. P. Hedden in *How Great Cities Are Fed*). Following the pioneering study of the New York Mayor's Market Commission (1913), the National Municipal League published an alarming report on Philadelphia, *The Relation of the City to Its Food Supply* (1915).[17] The report's warnings about food safety and sustainability resemble those of early twenty-first-century critics concerned with food poisoning, meat production, and local supply chains.[18]

Other sorts of early planners and social workers integrated food into social programs. As did those in other cities, Philadelphia's settlement houses worked to improve immigrant neighborhoods by planting gardens, establishing community kitchens, and running cooking classes that promoted Americanization and a Progressive Era version of nutrition.[19] Philadelphia's Vacant Lot Cultivation Association, established in 1897, followed Detroit's "potato patches," another depression-era initiative to colonize undeveloped land with household and market gardens. Large-scale vegetable production in vacant and park spaces would reappear in the two world wars' Victory Gardens, as well as the public sector gardens programs of the Great Depression.[20] Herein lies the history of food in community development.

In the mid-twentieth century, however, this history of food planning exhibited an important break for reasons relating both to urban planning and development and to food systems. The most significant factor was post–World War II commercial agriculture's adaptation of chemical technologies developed for the war. Using fossil fuels, these technologies yielded the fertilizers, pesticides, and herbicides that, with mechanized irrigation systems, led worldwide food production to triple between 1950 and 1990, while farmland under cultivation expanded only 10 percent. In an era of cheap oil and natural gas, coupled with new chemical preservatives and, later, genetic modification of crops, food production, processing, and transportation became increasingly global in scale. The result was an industrial food system of unprecedented abundance, convenience, low cost, and geographic scope.[21]

In the context of this global food system, city planners seemingly had little reason to concern themselves with food production and distribution at the local level, with the possible exception of keeping roads well paved to ease the flow of trucking. Yet productivity came at a price, with depleted soils, lowered water tables, and crop yields that stopped rising in the early 1990s. Agriculture now depends on fossil fuels to such an extent that today approximately ten calories of hydrocarbon energy are consumed to produce each calorie of food on American plates. The average ingredient in a Philadelphian's meal is grown more than 1,500 miles away, as Americans feast on garlic from China, grapes from Chile, and spinach from California in a typical diet oblivious to time and space.[22]

In the second half of the twentieth century, planning and development produced sprawling metropolitan growth that further separated urban and suburban residents from their sources of food. Philadelphia's 1961 zoning code (in force for fifty years) included no land-use designation for agriculture, even though most of the city's vast northeastern section remained rural when it was drafted.[23] Farming seems to have had no legitimate place in the modern city projected by Edmund Bacon and his colleagues, a distinct departure from the visions behind Ebenezer Howard and John Nolen's garden cities, Frank Lloyd Wright's Broadacre City, and the goals sought by earlier generations of planners. Farms in the city became artifacts of a bygone era, waiting for a "higher and better use." Moreover, the agricultural hinterland was now largely divorced from the city, as the fruits and vegetables of South Jersey and southeastern Pennsylvania overwhelmingly fed into the global industrial food supply chain. Only at the end of the twentieth century would these trends begin to be combated and reversed.

PHILADELPHIA'S FOOD MOVEMENTS AND CIVIL SOCIETY

The food movements and institutions that emerged in the late twentieth century stem from diverse critiques of the global industrial food system. These critiques are not always consistent with one another, resulting in a fragmented set of local food initiatives. Some of these point the way toward a more sustainable metropolitan environment, while others highlight the economic and environmental injustices of U.S. cities today. Hunger, food access, and urban agriculture programs presently embody and reveal some of the cleavages and contradictions defining American society and environmentalism.

The local food movement of the late twentieth century largely exists within the mainstream environmental movement, growing out of the condemnation of industrial, chemical-based agriculture first popularized by Rachel Carson's *Silent Spring* and more recently by Michael Pollan's *Omnivore's Dilemma*.[24] It has given birth to what the sociologist Thomas Lyson dubbed "civic agriculture," which promotes organic, local, sustainable, and ethical food production, processing, distribution, consumption, and waste streams. The institutions and initiatives of this movement have succeeded in relocalizing food economies and limiting environmental impacts to a small extent.[25] Although they promote social inclusion and equity, in Philadelphia and other large cities these institutions have often struggled to wield significant influence outside high-income, high-wealth communities.

The most prominent early figure in Philadelphia's local food and civic agriculture movement was Judy Wicks, who established the White Dog Café in 1983.[26] Serving food from small family farmers in the region, the White Dog promoted local, organic, ethical, and equitable food systems. In 2001 it launched the Fair Food Project, largely to help small farmers remain on their land. Fair Food's programs have included farm-to-institution and farm-to-school local food sourcing; a farm stand at the Reading Terminal Market downtown; the Pigs in Grass Alliance, which supports humane pork production; and the publication of a local food guide. The White Dog and Fair Food are largely responsible for popularizing local food among middle-class diners and chefs across the city.[27]

Farmers' markets and "community-supported agriculture" ventures (CSAs) are among the most important instruments of civic agriculture and the local food movement, forging direct connections between small rural farms and urban markets. Two institutions founded in the late 1980s and early 1990s, the for-profit Farm to City and nonprofit Food Trust, coordinate producer-only farmers' markets, with vendors mostly from Lancaster and Berks counties. Sales at these markets have grown approximately 300 percent since the early 2000s, to roughly $2 million in 2008 and more in subsequent years, reflecting the fast-growing popularity of local food.[28]

Farm to City runs fifteen markets, all but one in wealthy communities, including one on Rittenhouse Square and another in Chestnut Hill. It promotes these markets as "providing a civilized and democratic gathering place."[29] Farm to City has also supported the development of CSAs, which provide capital to farmers each spring and distribute baskets of fresh produce to shareholders on a weekly basis throughout the growing season. Its Winter Harvest program has made this a year-round operation, though wintertime activities remain more limited than those of the summer months. Farm to City, Fair Food, and several partners opened the Common Market, a food distribution center for local food that represents an important model for scaling up localization of the region's food system. To date, it serves primarily large institutions, such as hospitals, expanding Fair Food's farm-to-institution program.[30]

Founded in 1992, the Food Trust has pioneered the development of healthy food retail in inner-city Philadelphia and nationally.[31] Although it operates large, lush farmers' markets at Headhouse Square, located in an affluent district, and the middle-class Clark Park, it is principally devoted to food access for poor people. Over half its more than thirty farmers' markets are in poor or working-class communities in the city and suburbs. The Food Trust's work bringing grocery stores to underserved neighborhoods, most notably the Fresh Food Financing Initiative, has expanded to New York, Illinois, and Louisiana and has become the basis of White House and USDA policy.

Public health studies initially concluded that supermarkets are the only meaningful way to transform "food deserts," neighborhoods that lack access to healthy food. However, planning and public health scholars have recently argued for a broader approach to fresh food retail.[32] To this end, the Food Trust's Corner Store Campaign has begun working with small stores, especially those near schools, to expand their offerings beyond Tastykakes and sugary sodas, in particular integrating fresh fruit and 100 percent juice for children's snacks.

Childhood obesity has become the focus of much food and health planning and policy debates, for disorders related to diet, such as diabetes and asthma, now present some of the most prevalent public health crises in the nation. Childhood hunger and obesity affect school and life outcomes. In response, the Food Trust has initiated programs with Greater Philadelphia's public schools, whose students make up its largest constituency. The organization runs a wide array of programs in the schools, promoting healthy eating for the region's roughly 200,000 children living below the federal poverty line. Other school-based initiatives include gardens and cooking classes, notably the Urban Nutrition Initiative (UNI) of the University of Pennsylvania. Students from UNI's program at University City High School operate a stand at Clark Park Farmers' Market, where they sell vegetables as well as smoothies prepared on their bicycle-powered blender.[33] Still other school programs involve attempts to expand participation in free and reduced-price school meals. These efforts aim to increase the flow of federal dollars into the region's food access systems, much like similar endeavors to boost participation in various programs that subsidize food for the poor, the elderly, and at-risk families.

In dealing with these other populations, a resourceful but perpetually stretched food relief sector scrambles to cope with hunger in one of the poorest cities in the United States. The food cupboards that grew up in the 1980s no longer constitute an "emergency" system, operating today as a regular part of unemployed, retired, and working poor people's food "shopping." The largest hunger relief institution in the region is PhilAbundance, which traces its roots to the Greater Philadelphia Food Bank, founded in 1981. In 2007 it gave away 24 million pounds of food, most of it diverted from the "waste" of industrial food manufacturers and distributors, reaching 65,000 people each week through food cupboards, homeless shelters, and social service agencies.[34] The region's other large food relief distributor is the Self-Help and Resource Exchange (SHARE), founded in 1986. Through churches, community centers, and other groups, it sells packages of meat, fresh vegetables and fruit, and staples at about half-price and requires two hours of community service (defined broadly) for each purchaser.[35] The Self-Help and Resource Exchange also gives food from the Emergency Food Assistance Program and state food purchase program to the city's 500 cupboards, while PhilAbundance sells to cupboards.

Although the distinctions between PhilAbundance and SHARE may appear modest, their respective emphases on industrial "reclamation" versus self-help represents one of the central lines of debate among antihunger professionals. They all generally agree, however, that existing public and private programs are sorely inadequate to the task of ending hunger.[36] A 2008 Drexel University study found that the maximum food stamp benefits leave the poorest Philadelphia families $3,000 short of being able to purchase the U.S. Department of Agriculture's minimum recommended diet.[37] Like other public and charitable assistance, anti-hunger programs do little to break cycles of dependence or address the root causes of poverty in the United States.

In recent decades community development professionals have point-ed to urban agriculture as a way to transcend these limits, to achieve food security by taking control of the means of food production. Urban agriculture professionals in cities of the Global South have realized this to some extent.[38] Urban farming remains in a more emergent, experi-mental phase throughout the Global North, however, where its econom-ics are different.[39] Its capacity to feed urban populations remains lim-ited, though Philadelphia is one of the most prominent centers of urban agriculture in the United States.[40]

Urban agriculture has been scaled up most in community gardens, which represent by far the greatest part of this sector. From the mid-1970s to the mid-90s, the Penn State Agricultural Extension and Penn-sylvania Horticultural Society ran different parts of one of the most robust community gardening support systems in the United States. It helped people take over vacant lots in declining neighborhoods, ulti-mately supporting some five hundred food-producing gardens (as well as flower gardens and recreational spaces). Yet these support programs were largely dismantled in the late 1990s and 2000s, for public and phil-anthropic funders lost interest during economic times when food was cheap and the city's real estate market was reviving.

The purpose of community gardens has varied in different eras, and like other parts of the local food system, gardens reflect a diversity of class interests. The majority of community gardeners in the late twen-tieth century came to Philadelphia in the Second Great Migration, with African Americans leaving the rural South for the urban North, and in the migration of Puerto Ricans following World War II, along with the influx of refugees and immigrants from Southeast Asia in the 1970s and 1980s. Like migrants in other cities, these people have gardened partly to preserve their agricultural and culinary heritage.[41] They have also gardened to feed low-wealth communities.

In 1994 the staff of Penn State's urban gardens programs tabulated $1,948,633 worth of vegetables and fruit grown in 501 community gar-dens.[42] When my colleagues and I replicated and expanded on this re-search in 2008, we found some 220 gardens still growing food and calcu-lated nearly $4.9 million worth of summer vegetables.[43] We found that

FIGURE 12.2. A small community garden in Southwest Philadelphia. Photo by Sarah Zuckerman.

the majority of gardeners in poorer communities distribute a significant proportion of their harvest to extended family, neighbors, fellow church members, and strangers who are hungry. Food from community gardens does not feed the city on a great scale, but it makes important contributions to local food economies, especially at the time of year when school meals are least available (see figs. 12.2 and 12.3).[44]

Community gardens have also been vehicles of gentrification. In changing Philadelphia neighborhoods, such as Spring Garden, Southwark, and Northern Liberties, new middle-class residents have found that gardens provide important quality of life amenities. Poorer residents who pushed drug dealers off vacant lots and replaced them with gardens report the arrival of wealthier residents and higher property taxes as unintentional consequences.[45] Quantitative proof came from research in the New Kensington section in the early 2000s, which found that gardens, street tree plantings, and other greening projects led by the Horticultural Society helped raise property values.[46] This helped shift the public policy logic for greening.

New Kensington is also home to Philadelphia's most famous and longest tenured urban farm. Greensgrow Farm, founded in 1997, grows specialty greens and heirloom tomatoes in hydroponic systems, raised

FIGURE 12.3. The city's fourth largest community garden, Glenwood Green Acres in North Philadelphia. Photo by Kevin Levy.

beds, and greenhouses on a three-quarter-acre site where a steel galvanizing plant once stood. It sells produce at its farm stand and to high-end restaurants, but it has turned a profit only by developing an extended CSA network and selling potted plants, primarily to middle-class consumers who value local food and local business.[47] Indeed, one side of Philadelphia's urban agriculture movement has been centrally focused on finding ways to make city farms into profitable concerns. The Somerton Tanks Farm (2003–2006) operated on a Philadelphia Water Department site as a test farm for the trademarked Small Plot Intensive (SPIN) method of farming, ultimately grossing close to $70,000 with one part-time and two full-time farmers in 2006.[48]

Another side of the urban agriculture movement is centrally concerned with food justice, an increasingly prominent part of the environmental justice movement.[49] Since 2005 Mill Creek Farm has built on the work of Anne Whiston Spirn by cultivating a site where row houses had collapsed into the Mill Creek sewer. Begun as a water department stormwater management project, the farm runs environmental education programs for neighborhood youth and sells produce to needy neighbors below market rates from its farm stand and its stall at a nearby Food Trust farmers' market. The farmers have informally supported the

Brown Street Community Garden, which occupies the other half of its site.[50] The farm and garden have faced possible displacement, however; for some two years the Philadelphia Housing Authority pursued plans to build on the site, perpetuating the perverse legacy of ignoring the ecological pitfalls of construction atop the city's underground creeks even after Spirn and others publicized the dangers.

A more decentralized food justice support organization is the Philadelphia Orchard Project (POP), which I helped establish in 2007. Planting permaculture orchards of fruit and nut trees, berry bushes, and useful perennials in vacant lots, schoolyards, community gardens, and other spaces owned by organizations in economically deprived communities, POP promotes "permanent agriculture" and community control of food production.[51] Older environmental and community organizations, such as the Urban Tree Connection and the faith-based drug-abuse rehabilitation program New Jerusalem Laura, have recently focused more of their work on food production and distribution.[52]

Many urban agriculture initiatives have straddled the realms of food justice and local food for the middle class. Teens 4 Good, a program of the Federation of Neighborhood Centers, works with public high school students to grow produce sold to upscale restaurants and at the Farm to City farmers' market at city hall.[53] Weavers Way Farm began informally in 2000 and hired full-time farmers in 2007. It initially served a middle-class clientele, growing crops at the Awbury Arboretum and selling them at the Weavers Way Coop Market in Mount Airy and later at the Headhouse Market (see fig. 12.4), but in 2008 it established a small farm at Martin Luther King High School. In 2009 Weavers Way expanded production at an adjacent homeless shelter and a CSA farm at Saul Agricultural High School, in Roxborough. Students at both schools are largely African American and live in working-class and poor communities. The project at Saul, one of only two large agricultural high schools in U.S. urban centers, is helping expand education and summer jobs in sustainable agriculture at an institution that primarily teaches traditional industrial agriculture.[54]

As urban agriculture matures in Philadelphia, initiatives in a range of communities have necessarily transcended their initial focus on a single site or market niche. This has generated networks of production, distribution, and sales, often combined with education and food access programs. In the words of one food systems scholar, they are "reweaving the food security safety net," mediating and integrating entrepreneurial and charitable activities.[55] Perhaps nowhere is this more evident than the City Harvest Program, a project of the Pennsylvania Horticul-

FIGURE 12.4. Weavers Way Farm at Awbury Arboretum in winter, with the Philadelphia Orchard Project nursery in the foreground. Photo by Domenic Vitiello.

tural Society, the Philadelphia Prison System, SHARE, and the Health Promotion Council. Since 2006, prisoners in the Roots to Re-entry program at the county prison's greenhouse have raised seedlings that are then distributed to community gardens, where plots are reserved to grow vegetables delivered to nearby food pantries at which nutrition educators teach people how to prepare healthy dishes (Mill Creek and Weavers Way Farm also participate). In 2009 gardeners recorded close to 13,500 pounds of fresh food donated through this program, plus more than 3,600 pounds from the prison's garden.[56] City Harvest has effectively institutionalized the generosity of community gardeners, building relationships between the mostly middle-class gardeners and their hungry neighbors.

In 2010 the Horticultural Society launched the City Harvest Growers Alliance, a project to develop a network of forty-five growers, some institutions and some individuals, with a variety of distribution outlets and production support infrastructure. The early members of this USDA-funded organization reflect the increasing diversity of urban agriculture in Philadelphia and other cities. Preston's Paradise coordinates a network of backyard farms in the Belmont section of West Philadelphia, organizing neighbors to cook, can, and eat together and selling produce from a cart in the neighborhood. The Baynton Street Farm, in German-town, started a small CSA for neighbors of its nearly two-acre site where an apartment building burned down. Two community gardens and two backyard gardeners also participated, as did Teens 4 Good; New Jeru-salem Laura, in North Philadelphia; the garden at the historic Grumble-thorpe house, in Germantown; and the new farm at SHARE's warehouse.

Philadelphia's civic agriculture and food security institutions have built one of the nation's leading local food sectors, though they still face tremendous challenges in one of the poorest and most food insecure cities in the United States. Significantly, in a departure from the early history of the region's food system, they have developed almost entire-ly in the absence of public sector involvement. Despite the presence of nationally recognized urban agriculture and food access programs, at the dawn of the twenty-first century the city government had no food policy. On city databases, community gardens and farms remained clas-sified as vacant land. The city had no zoning for agriculture and a cloudy vacant land policy. Except for the city's soup kitchen, homeless shelter, and youth-feeding programs, food security was not a subject of local policy and planning. In 2008, however, as oil reached $150 a barrel and consequent food inflation inspired a global food crisis, this began to change.

FOOD POLICY IN THE TWENTY-FIRST CENTURY

In 2008 Philadelphia's public sector planning and policy began to catch up to its social movements and civil society organizations work-ing on urban agriculture and food security. The quasi-public Delaware Valley Regional Planning Commission initiated a study of the region's food system that summer. In 2011 it released an action-oriented plan ad-vocating farmland preservation and strengthened metropolitan distri-bution systems, including indicators to track localization of the region's food system.[57] It is the first metropolitan planning organization in the United States to produce a sophisticated regional food plan.

At the same time, Mayor Michael Nutter's new Office of Sustainabil-ity responded to calls for a municipal food policy voiced by various local food advocates and institutions. In the fall of 2008 the mayor issued a municipal food charter, a statement of principles and goals for the local food system that advanced food security and food policy as a way to reduce the city's ecological footprint, promote economic security, and close waste loops. The following spring the office released a sustainabil-ity plan, *Greenworks Philadelphia*, with targets of fifty-nine new community gardens growing food, twelve urban farms, fifteen farmers' markets, and local food within a ten-minute walk for three-quarters of the city's residents by 2015.[58] The farms target was met sooner with the help of the Growers Alliance, and the city is likely close to the gardens target, thanks partly to the Horticultural Society's Garden Tenders program, which helps people organize and develop gardens. The Food Trust and Farm to City continue to expand farmers' markets, and local food continues to grow in popularity. The city's health department has launched an ambitious effort to transform the food available in public schools, corner stores, and food relief, though this is not part of *Greenworks*.

Unlike some other cities in North America, however, Philadelphia has not yet sorted out just what forms the "new urban agriculture" should take. Its sustainability plan, like many of this genre, is a numbers game that, at least in its local food section, does not tackle the more systematic problems that effective environmental planning must engage. Most planners, for example, have yet to account for urban agriculture as part of green infrastructure, including gardens' and farms' contributions to stormwater management and residents' ecological footprints. Philadelphia also lacks a strong land trust preserving community gardens, the key institutional mechanism supporting the leading urban agriculture sectors in Seattle, Chicago, and elsewhere. Philadelphia's parks and recreation, redevelopment, planning, and sustainability agencies have debated whether urban farming and gardening should be a long-term land use or, in the view of most departments, mainly an interim use paving the way for other forms of development. And while cities across North America are revising their zoning codes and passing "honey and eggs" ordinances to create a regulatory framework that supports a diverse urban agriculture sector, Philadelphia's comprehensive plan and zoning code pay only cursory attention to urban gardens and farms.[59]

More proactively, city government has denied urban farmers access to the city's best farmland. In the fall of 2010 the city council passed two bills outlawing "commercial farming" on the two largest farms in Philadelphia, the 76-acre Manatawna Farm, in Roxborough, and the 112-acre Fox Chase Farm. The paradoxical rationale, at least in the first case (Fox Chase was simply a copy-cat bill), was that the ten half-acre plots of market gardens that the Philadelphia Parks and Recreation Department sought to locate on part of the hay fields at Manatawna would disrupt the ecology of that farm. For a decade, however, the hay farming at Manatawna has been decidedly industrial, employing chemicals and a single farmer growing a low-value bulk crop. The attempt to replace a portion of this with small-scale, biodiverse, chemical-free agriculture roused a familiar cry in mostly white, affluent semi-rural areas such as Upper Roxborough, namely, invoking the protection of precious species to preserve the status quo. The potential victim in this case was the bobolink, a bird around which neighbors rallied in a successful campaign to prevent the transformation of even a small area of industrial farming to sustainable agriculture.

Philadelphia is thus a prime example showing how urban agriculture can evolve in ecologically irrational and socially inequitable fashion, especially in cities lacking strong public or private planning. Affluent and gentrifying neighborhoods are adding gardens, while less prosperous communities of color continue to lose community gardens as gardeners are displaced from the land or age out of gardening. In 2010 the city government's Aviation Authority declined to renew the lease for the city's largest community garden, Eastwick's ten-plus-acre, over-thirty-year-old Airport Garden.

Philadelphia is home not only to some of the leading nonprofit and private urban agriculture and community food security initiatives but also to some of the greatest local policy failures. The city's contemporary food policy is just emerging, though its concern for the multiple dimensions of food security reflects a longer, if discontinuous, history. Like those during earlier eras of food planning, the current policy embodies the many contradictions and tensions among economic development, environmental stewardship, and social equity. The project of bridging middle-class civic agriculture and food security in poor communities remains difficult. Rebuilding metropolitan food networks will take time and concerted effort on the parts of the public, private, and third sectors. Nonetheless, local food has at least been placed back on the table in the city's and region's planning and development, where it was for most of Philadelphia's history. It is undeniably vital for environmental justice and sustainability in the city's future.

Ann Norton Greene

13 | Wolves in the Wissahickon

Deer, Humans, and the Problem of Ecology in an Urban Park

THE LETTER TO THE *CHESTNUT HILL LOCAL,* a neighborhood newspaper, was yet another salvo in a "deer war" of more than a decade's duration, a conflict over managing deer in the Wissahickon Valley Park, a portion of Philadelphia's Fairmount Park that lies across the northwest section of the city. The author, a local animal rights advocate, had written similar letters and public statements over the years. She decried the "ongoing violence against deer" and described the park as "a deer slaughterhouse." She also likened it to a crime scene and a battlefield. "After 9 years, the total body count has reached 1,682 reported killed." In her view, deer were crime victims, butchered innocents and casualties of an illicit war.[1]

In 1999, after a several years of study and public meetings that followed three decades of growing alarm over the extent of deer damage in the Wissahickon Valley (which locals call simply "the Wissahickon"), the Fairmount Park Commission decided to reduce the number of deer through culling by a professional sharpshooter. There was a range of public opinion about the best way to manage the size of the deer herd, or whether it should be managed, though local animal rights advocates dominated public discussion of the issue. People questioned whether humans, not deer, were the problem, wondered whether culling would destroy the park's peace and beauty, worried about violence and public safety, and considered scientific evidence and opinion. The deer war became a window into larger concerns about urban nature, human-animal relations, and the meaning of ecology.

The late twentieth century saw the rising prominence of social conflicts over urban wildlife across the United States. It is not clear whether contacts between humans and wildlife actually had increased, people were simply more likely to demand that something be "done" about wildlife, or the rise of the animal rights movement had changed the context of such situations. It is clear that suburban and urban fringe neighborhoods, touted as a perfect mix of urban access and rural charm for humans, were also charming for wildlife with their lush lawns, tasty plantings, enticing garbage cans, delectable gardens, woodsy shelter, and predator-free spaces. Suburban expansion altered wildlife habitats as wildlife populations rose. When wildlife ceased to be charming landscape décor that certified the nonurban character of these neighborhoods, becoming instead a nuisance or threat, residents disagreed widely and vehemently over the proper response.

Of all the social conflicts over wildlife, ones involving deer were perhaps the most ubiquitous, volatile, and difficult—in the words of one veteran observer, "a politician's worst nightmare." Americans have an enormous affection for deer, but they do not agree on the appropriate way to share space with an animal viewed in a wide variety of ways: as wilderness symbol, valued wildlife, wild pet, pest, and even threat. For example, urban and suburban areas with dense road networks and rising deer populations have many deer-vehicle collisions. Nationally an average 1.5 million such collisions occurred each year in the mid-1990s, costing $1.6 billion in damages, injuring 29,000 people, and killing 200. In 2010 State Farm Insurance estimated 2.3 million reported collisions nationally. Records for the Philadelphia area are limited, but in the early 1970s, the number of deer killed on roads averaged 8 per year. Twenty years later, the yearly average was 185. The figure would have been higher had it included deer injured on the roads, and tabulations of car damage or human injuries would add still more information about the total costs. Other complaints include the rising incidence of Lyme disease and damage to gardens, landscaping, parks, crops, and forests. Estimate costs for deer-related damage to Pennsylvania agriculture were $90 million in 2007, with another $73 million in damage to forest products. Public officials have scrambled to manage deer in ways that address local problems while appeasing opponents of deer reductions.[2]

This chapter examines the history of the Wissahickon deer war to explore why it happened and what such knowledge might add to our understanding of the environmental history of Philadelphia. Controversies such as this reveal the different ways that people view urban nature. Though the conflict in the Wissahickon resembled those in other communities, deer wars are like Tolstoy's dictum about unhappy families: each is unhappy in its own way. Products of specific places, deer wars implicitly concern a question about belonging: are deer in the wrong place? Those places carry meaning, for people imbue the landscapes around them with their ideas about social and moral order. These values are tightly bound to places, and the relationship between the material and the moral landscape is seamless. William S. Lynn has written, "All human activity, including moral conflict, occurs at sites embedded in situations, making geographic context a constitutive element of all ethical problems." The ethical choices of the deer issue in the Wissahickon Valley, a landscape imbued with meaning for local residents, had everything to do with its setting in the social, historical, and material geography of northwestern Philadelphia.[3]

Like the Wissahickon, however, white-tailed deer have their own history; the Wissahickon deer war broke out at the intersection of those two histories. The history of environmental change in America, of environmental movements, and environmental policy and management over the last two centuries could be written as a history of whitetails. Questions about animals implicitly and inevitably raise deep and far-reaching questions about humans, all the more so when the animal involved is weighted with as much sentiment, value, and symbolism as deer are. Deer wars illustrate key aspects of twentieth-century environmental history: the expansion of the managerial state; questions of scientific, especially ecological, knowledge; suburbanization; changing attitudes about nature; and changing human-animal relations, including the growing influence of the animal rights movement. The story of the deer war adds animals into environmental history as historical agents and reflects broad historical changes in terms of local geography and history.[4]

THE NATURE OF DEER

In the Wissahickon, as in most places east of the Mississippi, to speak of deer is to speak of whitetails, or *Odocoileus virginianus.* One of five species of deer native to the United States, whitetails are by far the most widespread, appearing in almost every contiguous state as well as Canada, Mexico, and Central America. Whitetails in the Northeast usually weigh between 90 and 300 pounds, with females (does) weighing less on average than males (bucks). Whitetails measure thirty to forty inches high at the shoulder and six to nine feet in length. Mature whitetails have a solid reddish summer coat that changes to gray in the winter. They have white markings around the nose and eyes, inside the ears, on the chin and throat, inside the upper legs, and on the underside of the tail. The tail is four to eleven inches long and is raised, or "flagged," when the deer is alarmed or in flight, hence the name *whitetail.* Bucks grow and discard their antlers each year, starting with nubs of new antlers in the spring that grow rapidly until the fall. They scrape off the velvety tissue covering their antlers in the fall and shed them entirely in late winter (some females also grow small antlers).

Most Americans find deer physically appealing: the willowy legs, delicate cleft hooves, small head with a tapering nose on a long slender neck, huge dark eyes, and large diamond-shaped ears. Adding to their appeal, deer are usually elusive and mysterious. Like many prey animals, their extremely acute senses alert them to possible dangers in time to slip away. In addition, they are built to run, with long legs and a flexible spine that enables them to "bound" rather than gallop, leap up to nine feet vertically or thirty feet horizontally, sprint up to forty miles an hour, and achieve graceful, seemingly impossible feats of motion before disappearing among the trees.

Deer reproduce quickly, especially under favorable conditions. Does become pregnant in the fall; with an average gestation of 200 to 210 days, they give birth sometime in late spring. Fawns mature quickly and may be ready to mate in their second fall. Deer do not mate permanently; does and fawns live in small groups, and bucks tend to be solitary. Deer may appear to be living in herds when seen grazing in large numbers, but they lack the social organization or leadership structures characteristic of cattle and other true herd animals. Whitetails are quite sedentary, and the vast majority may live within a half-mile or so from their sites of birth.

Deer have what the anthropologist and natural historian Richard Nelson calls "natural virtuosity" because as a species they can occupy a wide range of habitats, hence the alacrity with which they have moved into urban fringes, tolerating and even appearing unconcerned about humans. The characteristics that make them highly adaptable include not only their acute senses, speed, small family groups, and high reproduction rates but also a ruminant four-chambered digestive system that can handle many different kinds of plants. The rumination process breaks down the plant material thoroughly, extracting a high percentage of the available nutrition. People who try to plant things that deer will not eat soon find out that a hungry deer will eat almost anything. Furthermore, deer can gorge on plants, stuffing their paunches quickly with barely chewed food and digesting it later when they are safely under cover. Gary Alt, a longtime head of deer management for the Pennsylvania Game Commission, notes, "Deer are second only to humans in their impact on a forest ecosystem."[5] In the rapidly changing landscape of the United States over the last four hundred years, deer have definitely been survivors.[6]

THE NATURE OF THE WISSAHICKON

The Wissahickon constitutes a section of Fairmount Park that lies along the Wissahickon Creek as it crosses northwestern Philadelphia to join the Schuylkill River at East Falls, about five miles upstream from Center City. Fairmount Park covers over 9,200 acres; the Wissahickon makes up 20 percent of this, comprising 1,841 acres, or approximately 3.3 square miles. The creek valley runs north by northwest from the confluence of the Wissahickon Creek and the Schuylkill River to the northern city boundary with Montgomery County. Over thousands of years, the creek has cut a narrow, deep gorge with steep hillsides and rocky outcroppings, intersected by the ravines of smaller tributaries. On a map of the city it forms a distinctive, slender strip of green across the dense neighborhoods that surround it: Manayunk, Roxborough, and Andorra flank it from south to north along Ridge Avenue on the west; Germantown, Mount Airy, and Chestnut Hill do the same along Germantown Avenue on the east; and the suburban community of Lafayette Hill bounds the top of the park across the city line. In addition to residential and commercial neighborhoods, several schools and colleges (including the city's agricultural high school farm) and other institutional properties line the park. Wissahickon Park also contains or abuts two equestrian stables, two nature centers, athletic fields, recreational pavilions, a restaurant, and historic buildings. City residents use the park heavily. Forbidden Drive, a hard-packed unpaved road cut into the steep creek banks and running the entire length of the gorge, is "forbidden" (hence its name) to automobile traffic and reserved for walking, running, biking, and horseback riding. Regularly used during the week, it becomes quite busy on weekends. There are numerous access points into the park.

Yet however accessible and utilized, the park is also oddly isolated. Most of the roads route traffic around rather than through it. Lincoln Drive swings around the southern foot of the gorge, and Church Lane links Ridge and Germantown avenues several miles north of it. There are only two ways to get across the gorge by car: the Walnut Street Bridge, high over the creek between Roxborough and Germantown in the southern portion of the park, and, four miles north, Bell's Mill Road, which goes through the park between Andorra and Chestnut Hill. There are only four places to drive a car in and park near the water: Wise's Mill Road, Bell's Mill Road, Valley Green Road, and Livzey Lane. The other roads into the park end at trailheads. While some sections of the park are always crowded, other areas feel quite remote and provide considerable solitude and quiet a relatively short walk from busy streets and neighborhoods. Wissahickon Park is an intimate local space, yet the geography of its deep gorge makes it feel vast and isolated, a wild island amid the tight geometry of the surrounding streets.

Wissahickon Park has proved to be a perfect place for deer, for it has everything deer like best: thick woods for cover and nearby water and edge environments of fields, lawns, and gardens that provide a constant buffet of delicious, nutritious plants without any hunters or predators at all. Because of its shape and location, it has a high ratio of edge environment to internal space. Additionally, it is just a short walk—across a few backyards, over local roads, or along the creek—from other equally safe and food-filled places.

CHRONOLOGY OF A DEER WAR

Deer had virtually disappeared from the Northeast by the end of the nineteenth century, but populations rebounded spectacularly in Pennsylvania during the twentieth century as a result of state game commission policies to increase them combined with habitat changes following the decline of timbering, which brought back forest environments. The 2010 state deer population was estimated to be around 1.5 million. Once rare, deer have become a common sight in urban hinterlands and protected forest areas. Evidence in Pennsylvania since the early twentieth century indicates that deer alter forest and other vegetation communities quickly. Because regeneration is slow, moreover, continued damage by deer alters the ecosystem both directly and, by changing habitat for other animals and plants, indirectly. Furthermore, these effects have implications for nutrient and mineral cycles, soil organisms, and soil erosion. The impact on birds is particularly severe when deer strip the vegetation from the floor, shrub level, and lower canopies of forests, which removes bird habitats. Deer are what is known as a "keystone" species because of their "significant impact on the diversity of species in ecosystems . . . [and] their potential for altering habitats through their herbivory."[7]

Deer impacts were noted in Wissahickon Park as early as the 1960s, and by the 1990s this had the Fairmount Park Commission (FPC) worried. Dr. Ann Rhoads, a botanist at the University of Pennsylvania Morris Arboretum in Chestnut Hill, made several public presentations about the broad implications of deer proliferation there, including one to the commission.[8] In 1991 the private group Friends of the Wissahickon, based in Chestnut Hill, voted unanimously to study the issue of vegetation damage and deer populations in and around the park. First organized in 1924, Friends of the Wissahickon (FOW) had from its beginning raised money for park improvements and maintenance to compensate for the city's chronic neglect and underfunding of the Fairmount Park Commission; it soon became the most powerful, influential group with respect to Wissahickon Park. At the same time, some of the socially prominent citizens appointed to the Fairmount Park Commission also participated in the FOW. Everyone knew the deer issue would be contentious; the FOW agreed to take point on finding a solution.

The dispute concerned two claims: that deer were damaging the park and that the park contained too many deer. Some FOW members, including a few on the conservation committee that was discussing the damage issue, had already objected to doing anything about the deer. The FOW decided to undertake a formal study. In 1993 it selected Natural Resource Consultants (NRC), a private firm located in Fort Hill, Pennsylvania, to evaluate the park's vegetation and recommend courses of action. The company submitted its final report at the end of 1996.

One of the NRC's first actions was conducting a deer count, since at that time all estimates of the park's deer population were informal. In 1994 NRC staff flew over the park in a twin-engine Cessna carrying a thermal imaging system to locate deer, but they found that even with this infrared tracking device, it was difficult to locate the deer in the park's many hilly, wooded regions. They had more success flying over the park by helicopter in February 1996, for a snowfall had made it easier to see the deer. At this time NRC staff counted a minimum of 159 deer in the park. This gave an average of 49 deer per square mile, though most deer were concentrated in the park's northern sections.

The NRC also studied the condition of the vegetation. In 1994 and 1995 its staff conducted a forest regeneration survey at four locations: the Andorra Natural Area; the west side of the creek north of Gorgas Lane; the stretch of the creek near Valley Green Inn; and the junction of Gypsy Lane and Lincoln Drive, near the Henry Avenue bridge. They selected circular sample plots with radii of six feet and recorded the species and sizes of seedlings and saplings within them. This survey established the kinds of trees the park contained and helped the researchers evaluate regeneration in terms of the needs of those species. The company also conducted a browse survey in the Andorra Natural Area, in the northwestern part of the park, in 1994. This area, one of the park's most dense and secluded regions, had already been identified as home to its highest concentrations of deer, and the researchers found significant evidence of damage there. Browse rates were at least 45 percent in this area (i.e., deer ate at least some of 45 percent of the plants growing there), and the overall browse rate was 60.5 percent. Greenbriers and rhododendrons had 100 percent browse rates, followed closely by azaleas, black birch, and mountain laurel. In the browse lines observed at Andorra, NRC staff saw "sign of overuse of vegetation by deer."[9]

The NRC emphasized how the park differed from other areas in the region. Though it was part of an archipelago of green spaces strung along the Wissahickon Creek's twenty-two-mile length and within its sixty-four-square-mile watershed, proximity did not make for a unified landscape: "Roadways and intense developments isolate the park from other forested areas and natural processes." Furthermore, the park was acting as a magnet for deer, which entered through the slender corridor of green spaces at the park's north border. Once in the park, deer tended to stay. It provided excellent food supplies for large numbers of deer, especially since the adjacent cultivated areas provided more nutrition than untended or uncultivated areas did. But the deer's ability to thrive in the park was misleading. Whatever their success in exploiting the park's environment, the Wissahickon was no forest primeval. As the NRC staff reported, "Despite its natural beauty and deceptively 'pristine appearance,' the Wissahickon valley is not typical of the ecosystems in which deer evolved." Furthermore, they noted, it was a "highly disturbed" environment.[10]

The consultants argued that if people wanted the Wissahickon to remain forested and to contain wildlife other than deer, deer damage would have to be reduced. The issue, however, went beyond simply determining the correct deer density and then shaping policy to achieve it. The NRC report refuted the widespread belief that the Wissahickon had an optimal carrying capacity that could be calculated and expressed as a specific number of deer per square mile. Furthermore, the report pointed out that carrying capacity could be understood in three ways: economically, as the density of animals necessary to produce a maximum sustained yield for profit; ecologically, as the number at which the local plants would keep the animals in a state of mutual self-sustaining equilibrium; and culturally, as the number of animals that can coexist with humans without causing conflicts.

Economic carrying capacity did not apply to the Wissahickon, and the NRC report contended that ecological carrying capacity was equally irrelevant. Many Americans believe that "left alone," every ecosystem rests in a state of harmonious, self-sustaining balance, allowing us to calculate precise carrying capacities for individual species. This ideal is often both the benchmark against which ecological damage is measured and the goal of repair and restoration efforts. For the Wissahickon, the articulated ideal state was usually the presettlement forest, imagined as pristine and unchanging until the Europeans arrived in the seventeenth century and started the historical clock ticking on environmental decline. Though at one point ecologists similarly believed that ecosystems develop until achieving such a stable state, or climax, they have since replaced this seemingly teleological view of biological change with a historical interpretation in which ecological change occurs randomly. There is no original ecosystem; the natural world is dynamic and historical, not static and ahistorical. Furthermore, not only had three centuries of disturbances (e.g., human usage; the introduction of exotic plants; and changes in air, water, and climate quality) made the goal of reestablishing the presettlement forest in the Wissahickon unattainable, but no one really knew what the presettlement forest had been like. It was impossible to unwind ecological change and discern a clear sequence of changes that led back to the presettlement ecosystem. No one could describe this ostensibly "natural" ecosystem; at best, they could determine whether existing conditions were healthy according to current ecological knowledge, which had some limits. The NRC report noted, "Ecologists' understandings of the dynamic process of plant ecology itself remains in its infancy," as does their "understanding how deer and [plant] systems co-evolve and interact."[11] Perhaps deer impact was simply part of natural, historical processes between deer and vegetation. Could damage that came from within the current ecosystem even be called damage? If left alone, would the deer self-regulate and reduce damage, or would deer damage transform the park into a different kind of landscape?[12]

Because the notion of ecological carrying capacity has little clear basis in history or science, the NRC report judged that decisions about the Wissahickon should begin with cultural carrying capacity. The area's ecosystem had changed in extraordinarily complicated ways, could not be restored to an unknown presettlement condition, and showed evidence of habitat degradation when measured in terms of vegetation damage, local extinctions, reduced wildlife diversity, slowed forest regeneration, and increased invasive and exotic species. What size deer population would produce a healthy ecosystem in the park? Was a healthy ecosystem in accordance with the values of the communities around it? What kind of place did people want Wissahickon Park to be, and what kind of relationship with deer did that mean? How many deer did people want?[13]

The report's conclusion listed the options for dealing with deer: doing nothing; mitigating damage through fencing and repellents; or reducing the population either by restoring predators, relocating deer through capture and transfer, introducing contraceptives, or killing. For those who wanted to maintain the Wissahickon as a forested landscape, doing nothing meant relying on the deer's capacity to self-regulate in some fashion. No one knows, however, whether deer populations ever self-regulate or what factors, if any, have limited deer populations historically. No one even knows how large past deer populations were, though wildlife biologists discount the widespread belief that current deer populations exceed presettlement levels.[14] Nor is the widespread belief in deer self-regulation warranted. It depends on Aldo Leopold's widely cited description of the deer irruption on the Kaibab Plateau in 1943, where a rapid increase in deer following the elimination of predators was followed by a dramatic population crash and then equilibrium, but little evidence indicates that this is how deer populations work in general.[15] Unhunted deer in Massachusetts's Quabbin Reservoir did not reach equilibrium but instead began to convert the forest into savannah. It was not clear that deer populations in the Wissahickon would self-regulate or that deer populations ever have been self-limiting. To do nothing was to allow the landscape of the Wissahickon to change, with the changes in park ecology at some point becoming irreversible and the forest giving way to savannah.

Another widely held belief is that predators, both human and animal, control deer populations—again, with reference to Leopold's Kaibab example. Not only are predation mechanisms not fully understood, however, but "predator/prey relations are extremely diverse. There is really no reason to believe that the characteristics that characterize one predator/prey system must hold for all, or even for the same system under different conditions."[16] It was not clear that the growth of the deer population was due to an absence of wolves, coyotes, and human hunters. In any event, predator restoration was not a viable solution in an urban setting where predators would, like the deer, wander over park boundaries into the surrounding neighborhoods, possibly threatening people, pets, and other animals, especially given that large numbers of predators might be necessary for meaningful deer control.

Damage mitigation and deer relocation were attractive solutions because they seem to offer humane ways of addressing the problem. Fencing provides the most common form of damage mitigation. It might be possible to fence private residences to protect them from deer, though it means swathing areas in expensive and unattractive wire fencing. Using fences to confine the deer into some areas of the park, however, would increase damage there. Relocation, too, initially sounds good but has a low success rate and causes high deer mortality. First, both capture and release are inordinately stressful to wild, sedentary animals. Individual deer are tied to such small ranges that placing them anywhere else is akin to dropping them onto a different planet. They become disoriented in the new settings and thus vulnerable to traffic accidents and predation. Then there is the difficulty of finding places to relocate urban deer. Given the enormous monetary damage the animals wreak on agriculture every year, few people living in or responsible for rural places welcome the addition of new deer, and most other protected forests have deer problems of their own.[17]

Contraception using PZP (porcine zona pellucida, an immunocontraceptive) is a benign and promising way of reducing deer populations, though the FDA has approved the drugs only for experimental cases. It has been most successful in small, isolated deer populations on islands and in other bounded areas. Current methods of deer contraception involve annually injecting the same individuals for several years, which requires sustained funding and public support. The long-term effects of using PZP are poorly understood; observed short-term effects include disruptions of the breeding season in ways that interfere with deer energy reserves, alter herd composition and social behavior, and cause late births and resultant high fawn mortality. Some researchers conclude that more direct methods of population reduction remain more effective.[18]

Mortality-based solutions take several forms: capture and euthana-

sia with nets or darts, professional sharpshooting, or some form of public hunting. While public hunts have been feasible in locations such as
the Quabbin Reservoir, proposals to hunt in an urban park raise significant issues of safety and management, as well legal issues, since hunting
is banned within city limits. And again, deer experience profound stress
when captured, whether the goal is relocation or euthanasia, raising the
same issue of potentially inhumane treatment in both cases. Culling by
official sharpshooters remains as the best way to quickly and humanely
limit the deer population.

To implement this option, it would be necessary to obtain a deer
control permit from the Pennsylvania Game Commission, which has
legal authority over all wildlife, not just game animals, and make the
necessary legal arrangements. With the well-organized and -funded
FOW continuing to take the lead on the issue and promising to help fund
deer control efforts, in late 1998 the city and the FPC applied to the state
game commission for a license to shoot up to one hundred deer in the
Wissahickon. At the same time, the FOW contacted the Humane Society of the United States for more information on deer contraception and
hired a communications consultant to help educate the public, through
pamphlets and speakers, about the ecological damage to the park and
the necessity of doing something about the deer.

For example, in January 1999 the group sponsored a public lecture by
Bryon Shissler, the author of the NRC report, at Chestnut Hill's Spring-
side School. Shissler reviewed the options for deer control and indicated
that the solution most likely to succeed was to have trained agents kill
a number of the deer. He explained the problems with reintroducing
wolves and coyotes into the park and the current limitations of deer contraception as an option. Shissler asserted presettlement deer density to
have been ten deer per square mile, noting that the park's density had
reached fifty-three per square mile. Deer were stripping the understory
in the park, exacerbating soil erosion, and causing rampant growth in
exotics such as Japanese honeysuckle, garlic mustard, and oriental bit-
tersweet. The FPC had largely avoided the issue, he said, because "the
idea of deer mortality makes anyone uncomfortable."[19]

The FPC finally received a permit to kill up to 125 deer and inaugu-
rated a cull in Wissahickon Park early in 1999. They hired the biologist
Anthony DeNicola to shoot the deer. DeNicola runs a nonprofit organization in Connecticut called White Buffalo, which carries out culls in
municipal parks. DeNicola sets up bait sites in late winter, when food
is most scarce, and shoots the deer with special ammunition that helps
him take down a deer in a single shot. He then removes the carcass and

any trace of blood. Because of delays in getting the permit, DeNicola got a late start and shot only 43 deer before the budding of spring foliage reduced the appeal of his bait sites.

In February the following year, the FPC received another permit and imposed a curfew to keep people out of the park at night when DeNicola was working. The cull was opposed by the newly organized Friends of the Animals of the Wissahickon (FOAW), an animal rights group. Group members demonstrated at the FOW office in Chestnut Hill and in Roxborough at Saul Agricultural High School, barraged local papers with angry letters, and disrupted the cull by infiltrating the park at night and preventing DeNicola from shooting. They also destroyed his bait sites with bleach and vandalized his car and equipment. The FPC called off the cull for that year, but in subsequent years it simply held the cull without announcement other than curfew signs posted at park entrances. Since 2002 the cull, which has continued every year, has been carried out by the wildlife services division of the USDA Animal and Plant Inspection Service.[20]

The FOAW and its supporters probably constituted a minority of opinion about deer policy, but its rhetoric, however intemperate, expressed critical themes about the relationships among humans, other animals, and environments generally and in Philadelphia in particular. The most overarching theme was the notion of the Wissahickon as "original" nature. Thus one person wrote that no one had a right to do anything to the deer because "the animals were here before the humans."[21] Nature, as represented by the park, was a place of peaceful coexistence and harmony.

Contrasting sharply with this view of the park was the idea of violence against the deer as an unnatural human activity. The cull was variously described as a slaughter, a massacre, bloodshed, genocide, and warfare. The park was called "Death Valley." The authors of the cull were compared to a "Balkan mass murderer," determined to murder deer. DeNicola, his supporters, and hunters of any kind were described as people motivated by the sadistic desire to inflict cruelty on helpless, innocent deer, individuals who took pleasure in killing does and fawns, destroying deer families, and leaving young deer wandering the streets. One aspect of this theme reflected concerns about urban violence. City Councilman Frank Rizzo Jr. announced that the deer policy sent "the wrong message: that it's acceptable to use a violent solution, killing, to solve a problem . . . with nature."[22]

Class issues related to the park emerged as well. Opponents alleged that the real reason for the deer policy was that "rich people" and members of the FOW who lived along the park did not want their gardens destroyed and got the FPC and FOW to act at their behest. In the words of one Mount Airy resident, "The old rich count the park as part of their estate. They think they can hunt deer in the park like they are Henry VIII."[23] Comments like this reflected the social history of northwestern Philadelphia, especially of Chestnut Hill, a traditional enclave of the wealthy WASP class. Members of this traditional social elite had long been members of both the FPC and the FOW.[24]

The conflict partly concerned the park's ecology, but the arguments often revealed a limited understanding of it. Assessments of vegetation damage and wildlife depletion were discounted by cull opponents, who denied that deer damaged the park; rather, they charged, the deer were being used as scapegoats, for the damage actually resulted from neglect by the FPC, disease, vandalism, weather, pollution, and dirt bikers. Even when shown specific foliage damage, the leaders of the FAOW dismissed it. Shown a rhododendron eaten by deer, one replied, "They haven't destroyed anything. They've sort of reshaped them, that's all. Leave them alone. Laissez-faire."[25] People who loved and defended the park did not know its plants; they could not see a browse line or recognize damage to plant life. "Being green" did not extend much beyond the notion that anything green must be healthy.

Many of those who did admit that the deer population might require reduction advocated the use of the deer contraceptive PZP and claimed that only the unwillingness of the FPC and FOW prevented this approach. David Pope, head of the FOW, repeatedly explained that the FDA had ruled PZP experimental, restricting its use and thus making it unavailable as an option. But to opponents of the cull, PZP would be a magic bullet instead of a real bullet, a technological fix that would make the whole problem of the deer vanish painlessly by means of a rational policy of birth limitation. The FOAW announced that it would seek funds to erect deer enclosures, thus confining the deer in order to make PZP an effective alternative.

WISSAHICKON HISTORY

These responses to the deer situation can be fully understood only in relation to the history of Wissahickon Valley Park and to the history of deer. The Wissahickon was part of the original Fairmount Park, established in 1868. In the middle of the nineteenth century, Philadelphia was one of several cities to establish a large park, among them New York City (Central Park was created in 1858). Philadelphia had acquired a much stronger and more centralized government in 1854 when an act of the Pennsylvania General Assembly combined all townships, districts, boroughs, and unincorporated communities in Philadelphia County, consolidating them into the city of Philadelphia. This gave city government control over safety, order, and public health in all these places; it also gave it the power to do things like create parks there. The act provided the city's governing classes with the political means of enacting their vision of the city's identity and future. The primary justification for the park was protecting the city's water supply by taking over the banks and local tributaries of the Schuylkill River, but a grand park encompassing the scenic river would symbolize the city's material and cultural prestige. The report on establishing the park declared, "No other city in the Union has, within its boundaries, streams which, in picturesque and romantic beauty can compare with the Wissahickon and the Schuylkill; and there are few, if any, which include within their limits landscapes which, in sylvan grace and beauty, surpass those which abound within the space we propose to appropriate. Nature herself has so adorned them that little remains for art to do, except skilfully, with cautious good taste, to open such paths as may develop the beauties of the ground."[26]

The goals of protecting the city's water supply against "filthy deposits and polluting drainage" and giving its residents the benefits of "breathing the fresh, free air in the midst of rural surroundings" led authorities to include the lower reaches of the Wissahickon Creek in the park as well.[27]

> It shall be the duty of said Park commissioners to appropriate the shores of the Wissahickon creek, on both sides of the same, from its mouth to the Paul's Mill Road, and of such with as may embrace the road now passing along the same; and may also protect the purity of the water of said creek, and by passing along the crest of the heights which are on either side of said creek, may preserve the beauty of its scenery . . . the grounds and creek hereby appropriated are declared to be part of Fairmount Park.[28]

When the Wissahickon gorge became part of Fairmount Park in 1868, it was already known as a unique scenic area and celebrated by writers, artists, and photographers. The actress Fanny Kemble described its beauties in her best-selling journal of 1835, as did Edgar Allan Poe in the 1840s; the latter called the stream a creek "of so remarkable a loveliness that, were it flowing in England, it would be the theme of every bard, and the common topic of every tongue."[29] Given how he and others extolled the beauty of the gorge, one might easily fail to realize that it was a major manufacturing and processing site until the late nineteenth century.

Its narrowness and 100-foot drop in elevation made the gorge an excellent source of waterpower. With agricultural products from southeastern Pennsylvania's rich farmlands funneling into Philadelphia, by the eighteenth century the creek had become an energy resource important to the city's economy. By the middle of the nineteenth century more than sixty mills lined its banks and many tributaries. They performed the vital economic functions of milling flour, sawing lumber, and making paper. In addition to describing the beauties of the gorge, Poe also referred to its banks being "parcelled off in lots . . . as building sites," to the selling of "water privileges," and to changes "wrought upon the brook and its vicinage . . . by the stern hand of the utilitarian."[30] Wagon roads wound down the steep hillsides and ravines to creek-side mills, and in the 1850s the Wissahickon Pike (the future Forbidden Drive) was built to carry goods down through the gorge toward Philadelphia.

How was this important industrial area was converted into parkland in 1868? By the middle of the nineteenth century, changes in Philadelphia's industrial economy had lessened the Wissahickon's importance to manufacturing and processing. Mechanization and steam technology reduced dependence on specific waterpower sites and, in combination with the development of railroads and efficient local horse transportation, permitted processing and production to be located in the city near wharves and railroad depots. The Schuylkill Canal generated greater waterpower than the Wissahickon Creek, and mills sprang up along it in Manayunk. These developments reduced the economic importance of the gorge's waterpower, thus facilitating the area's inclusion in the new park. Once the park was established, the Fairmount Park Commission began purchasing and tearing down the mills. The last operating mill on the Wissahickon Creek, the Wissahickon Paper Mill on Weiss Mill Road, owned by Charles Magarge and Company, closed in 1884.

Industrial change altered the social as well as the economic geography of nineteenth-century Philadelphia. After the Civil War, new urban, moneyed classes embraced a suburban ideal. Horse railways and steam railroads made it possible to work in the industrial city but reside in the greener fringe. Outlying villages were incorporated into the consolidated city and connected through public transportation. Especially along the east side of the Wissahickon gorge, where large estates bordered the park, Henry Houston and other developers laid out neighborhoods such as Chestnut Hill to attract affluent residents.

These wealthy classes were active in shaping Wissahickon Park, in part through service on the FPC. The Fairmount Park Commission had the authority to claim land from ridge to ridge but, having failed to do so at the beginning, was later forced to purchase land to establish the park's present boundaries around the Wissahickon gorge. Wealthy individuals residing in the neighborhoods near the park donated land. For example, residents of Chestnut Hill acquired land along Cresheim Creek to create a narrow arm that extended east from the Wissahickon, wrapping the park around two sides of Chestnut Hill between it and the rest of the city. Residents also donated money and adornments to Wissahickon Park and founded the Friends of the Wissahickon.

Ideas about Wissahickon Park were influenced by romantic era ideas about nature that became an important part of national culture in the nineteenth century. Industrialization and rapid urbanization transformed how U.S. citizens viewed the environment. The less they relied directly on nature, the more they viewed it as a place apart. Appreciation of nature became a sign of cultural and moral refinement and an important class marker. These nature beliefs included a reverence for wilderness that represented a significant change in Western culture. Romantic ideas had transformed the experience of wild nature from one of terror to one of sublime transcendence.

Romantic landscape paintings—such as those by Thomas Doughty, Thomas Cole, Frederic Church, and Albert Bierstadt—provided a visual lexicon of these ideal vistas, while romantic poets supplied the descriptive vocabulary. Sublime landscapes contained mountains, crags, chasms, ravines, waterfalls, and dramatic clouds. In addition, they were bathed in hazy, golden, slanting light and included deeply shadowed woods and stretches of calm water reflecting light, cloud, and crag. Sometimes they had the ruins of long-gone civilizations; the tumbled, overgrown stones amid an otherwise wild landscape provided melancholic reminders of the passage of time and the ultimate insignificance of humankind.

By the time Fairmount Park was founded, in 1868, middle- and upper-class Americans were well schooled to appreciate nature and the appropriate landscapes in a romantic vein, and the rugged Wissahickon gorge contained all the attributes of a properly sublime landscape. An 1871 article in *Scribner's Monthly* described the gorge as "enclosed by high hills whose bases creep down the very water's edge, and whose summits are crowned with lofty peaks and craggy rocks which bristle against the sky."[31] A late nineteenth-century Baedaker's travel guide went further, calling it "a miniature Alpine gorge" and thus linking it to some of the

most famously scenic and sublime areas in Europe, which formed traditional stops on "grand tours."[32] Speaking of the gorge's deepest part,
Poe said that "the windings of the stream are many and abrupt" and that
the creek appears as "an endless succession of infinitely varied small
lakes."[33] *Scribner's Monthly* declared, "There are not many such streams
as the Wissahickon, none perhaps in this country and few in the world,"
noting that the creek, which was sometimes "only a noisy brook running over pebbly bottoms," could change into "a flashing cascade leap-
ing from rock to rock with a shouting noise": "Then it widens out into
a sober river which flows into a peaceful lake, so quiet that down in its
depths the trees that meet above it are reflected with every delicate
outline of foliage."[34] This description recalls the contrast between grand
vista and precise foreground detail found in many romantic landscape
paintings. The *Atlantic Monthly* spoke of the "wild scenery" and "picturesque character" of the "tumbling stream shaded with dense foliage and
bordered by fern-clad, vine-hung rocks."[35]

The quality of light in the Wissahickon added to its sublime qualities. The depth of the gorge and its ravines makes for deep, shadowy
woods, slanting light, and dusky, haunting twilights. Poe advised his
readers to visit the creek only "amidst the brightest glare of a noonday
sun; for the narrowness of the gorge through which it flows, the height
of the hills on either side, and the density of the foliage, conspire to produce a gloominess, if not an absolute dreariness of effect."[36] Finally, the
place had ruins, even if they were in the process of being created as the
mills were torn down. To this day the area is dotted with the remains
of walls, abutments, buttresses, pillars, and steps, their stones toppled
and overgrown, while stones of the old mill roads lie underfoot. For the
romantics, a designation as "Nature" required a landscape to be a place
apart, unquestionably removed from the industrial world of human labor. Over time, the working past of the Wissahickon Creek was erased as
its industrial ruins were naturalized into the landscape of the park and
became elegiac symbols of the vastness of time.

Another way of erasing human work from the creek was to recall a
simpler, preindustrial past or to try to evoke its ancient presettlement
history. Thus, in 1901 a group of Colonial Dames led by Lydia Morris
(whose estate later became Morris Arboretum) erected a colonial-style
inn at Valley Green. In 1902 Sally H. and Charles W. Henry, a daughter
and son-in-law of Henry Houston, presented a statue of an Indian to the
park. After it was placed on a high rock overlooking the creek, local my-
thology bereft of historical accuracy transformed the figure into Tedy-
uscung, chief of the Leni-Lenape, surveying his lost wilderness domain.

The statue of the Indian was a kind of ruin, because it represented a timeless, wild nature of an imagined, ancient past. By linking the leisure landscape of the park to the Indians' primordial landscape and their allegedly more "spiritual" connection with nature, the statue helped elide the industrial landscape of work and production that had defined the gorge for nearly two centuries.

The Wissahickon thus became Nature, set apart from the human world, outside time and history, and identified with play rather than work.[37] It became a popular place for leisure activities of driving, picnicking, boating, and sleighing. Guidebooks emphasized the charm of its low-arched stone bridges, the drama of the deep pool and overhanging cliffs of Devil's Den, and the legends surrounding Mom Rinker's Rock or the Monastery. Henry Houston operated a large resort hotel in Chestnut Hill and created a lake (Lake Surprise) behind an old milldam on Cresheim Creek for boating, swimming, and ice skating.

DEER AND THE WISSAHICKON

Seventeenth-century European settlers described Pennsylvania's forests as teeming with deer. Coming from much more domesticated lands, where deer hunting had long been restricted, they were amazed at the abundance of game. Eastern woodland Indians burned the forests to create the edge environments attractive to deer. With colonists and Indians vigorously hunting deer for food and the transatlantic trade in hides, however, deer populations began declining. In addition, as European colonists pushed out Indian populations, they cleared rather than selectively burned the forests, creating a landscape different from the one the Indians had made. Pennsylvania instituted its first hunting restrictions in 1771, but deer populations declined further during the nineteenth century. Deer were most likely absent from the Wissahickon until the twentieth century. When Poe saw an elk in there in the 1840s, he at first thought it was part of his romantic fantasy about "the Wissahiccon of ancient days . . . when the red man trod alone, with the elk upon the ridges that now towered above." The elk was real enough, but not wild, merely "a pet of great age and very domestic habits [that] belonged to an English family occupying a villa in the vicinity."[38]

By the end of the century, deer were nearly gone from Pennsylvania. The deforestation of the state in the late nineteenth century had dramatically reduced deer habitats and made deer more vulnerable to hunters. In 1889 John Philips, a Pittsburgh industrialist on a hunting trip in Elk County, in the northern part of central Pennsylvania, killed what he feared was "the last deer in Pennsylvania."[39] Alarm over the disappearance of deer became part of the emerging conservation movement. Sport hunters from the middle and upper classes organized and lobbied for state regulation of game animals. Rejecting the practices of market hunters, which they saw as greedy and dishonorable, as well as those of "pot" hunters, which they saw as low class, they thought hunting should be regulated according to the "sportsman's code." This code entailed a group of elite ritualized masculine behaviors, drawn from aristocratic European hunting practices, that emphasized skill, honor, hardiness, appreciation of nature, and what the leading sportsman Theodore Roosevelt called "vigorous manliness." Deer were especially prized as game animals. Sportsmen lobbied for licensing, seasonal restrictions, and prohibitions against killing females. In Pennsylvania their efforts resulted in the establishment of the State Game Commission, as it was first called, in 1895. Deer became state property, scientifically managed to provide adequate numbers for continued hunting. The commission established game preserves and stocked them with whitetails in 1906.[40]

The FPC attempted to reestablish deer in the Wissahickon in 1914. Precisely why is unclear; the park commission may have been concerned about declining deer populations or else was responding to the Anglophilia of Philadelphia's upper class, many of whose members thought an English-style deer park would enhance the aristocratic Anglo-Saxon tone of the neighborhoods along the Wissahickon. Robert Glendenning, a Philadelphia broker, donated sixteen young deer, thirteen does and three bucks, which he had purchased from a private nature preserve in New Hampshire. The FPC hoped to have "a fair distribution of a real herd of the fleet animals throughout the wooded portions of the preserve." The deer arrived in February and were placed in a fenced two-acre tract at Gypsy Lane and Wissahickon (Lincoln) Drive. Later that spring they either escaped or were released and began living in the woods between the Wissahickon and Schoolhouse Lane.[41]

By the spring of 1915, it was reported that a pack of wild dogs was hunting the deer and had already killed four. Composed of feral dogs with "wolf instincts," it had formed shortly after the deer were released and now numbered more than two dozen. One newspaper report painted a violent picture: "Nearly every night the pack stalks the deer herd, and the woods resound with the yelping, snarling, and baying of the dogs. The deer have come lean and terror-stricken by the constant worrying." The dogs had not yet attacked people but seemed "very savage" and had eluded the park's guards. Commissioners considered arming the guards and having them shoot the dogs but dropped the idea out of fear that they might accidentally wound or shoot visitors to the park. The newspaper also mentioned that residents along Schoolhouse Lane were contacting the commission to complain that deer were raiding their gardens and eating shrubs and young trees.[42]

By the spring of 1916, residents of that neighborhood were demanding that the commission remove the deer. W. Worrell Wagner, who had an estate at Schoolhouse and Gypsy lanes, and his neighbors described the repeated destruction of gardens, flower beds, trees, hedges, and shrubs, despite the use of fencing (which the deer easily jumped) and repellent devices (which the deer learned to ignore.) Deer made almost daily visits to their properties in the spring and summer, though this was a matter of inference, not direct observation: "The general public has little opportunity to see the deer [which] confine their activities to early morning raids and appearances at dusk. The remainder of the time they are usually hidden in the woods." Wagner expressed his frustration: "One cannot shoot and kill without breaking the game laws; nor shoot to hurt without being liable to prosecution at the hands of the cruelty to animals societies; chasing by dogs also is illegal, I believe, so how am I going to get redress?" In a prescient statement that foreshadowed the deer question of the 1990s, the newspaper observed that this situation was "one requiring not a little thought": "[The FPC] must decide between the wishes of two sets of nature lovers, those who insist that the deer should be allowed to run at large regardless of damage and inconvenience to property owners, and those who appreciate just as fully the beauties of such an arrangement but know by personal experience its ill effects."[43]

The FPC decided later that month that the deer would be captured and removed from the park by a crew of expert trappers from the state. But one commission member, Theodore Justice, objected to this policy, stating that he had visited the residents along Schoolhouse Lane but "could find no trace of damage done" by deer. He suggested instead that the deer be driven up into the Wissahickon gorge. Apparently the capture effort was not entirely successful. Deer proved difficult to round up, and enormous amounts of time and efforts produced relatively poor results. Early in 1918 the *Philadelphia Record* reported that dog packs were still chasing deer in the park: "Apparently the only real appreciators of the herd of deer . . . are dogs. Theodore Justice, who urged acceptance of the deer, appears to be their only champion." Justice suggested having a "crack-shot ranger" shoot the dogs.[44]

DEER IN THE TWENTIETH CENTURY

The difficulties that the FPC encountered in confining, controlling, or corralling the deer in the Wissahickon were tied to events happening across Pennsylvania. Efforts to resuscitate the state's deer population proved perhaps too successful. Deer populations began to escalate, in part because of the growth of secondary forest and in part because of restrictions on hunting. By the 1920s Elk County, where John Phillips thought he had shot the "last" deer, had so many deer that they starved in huge numbers. Some areas were littered with rotting carcasses, and hungry deer were stripping the woods of plants, shrubs, and trees and causing extensive damage to crops.[45] By the 1930s wildlife managers had grown seriously alarmed about deer overpopulation in Pennsylvania, and they called for a balance between deer herds and deer habitats.

Efforts to limit deer populations encountered staunch opposition from hunters, especially when the game commission tried to hold doe seasons. Hunters wanted to shoot antlered bucks, in part because it is considered to be more masculine and in part because of long-standing prohibition in the "sportsman's code" against shooting does or "mother" deer. Hunters also expected to see a lot of deer when and where they liked to hunt. If they didn't, they complained to the game commission. Hunters are this commission's primary constituency and funding source, a fact that hobbles its ability to enact policies hunters do not like. In the 1990s wildlife managers would be saying the same things about balancing deer population and habitat that their predecessors had said in the 1930s, and with little more success.[46]

Meanwhile, material and cultural changes in American society fueled the upward spiral in deer populations. Deer proved quite able to adapt to suburban sprawl and exurban development, areas that resemble farms in their impact on deer nutrition. Deer populations, sensitive to food supply, continued to increase. At the same time, the traditional tool for deer management, hunting, was on the decline. There were fewer hunters, and as society urbanized, Americans grew more distant from the material realities of animals and food production and less understanding of hunting. Furthermore, as an emotional regard for wild animals increased and environmental consciousness grew, Americans "came to the consensus that, to be authentic, Nature must team with life—*wild*life, to be precise."[47]

Deer are wild without being overtly dangerous and have usually been viewed positively compared to the fear and revulsion directed toward wolves and other predators. Because deer can be quite tame around humans, they are perceived as a link between the human world and the wild. These attitudes have a long history. During the Middle Ages a complex symbolism that developed around deer portrayed them as "paragons of the animal condition" and representative of all animals. Deer were favored hunting animals among the nobility, integral to highly ritualized aristocratic hunting practices, which conferred an aura of nobility on them. Male deer, particularly harts, were frequently referred to as princes of the forest. Deer also enjoyed religious significance, figuring in miracle stories, symbolizing saints more often than any other wild animal did, and frequently used to stand for the crucified Christ. Over the centuries deer have come to symbolize harmlessness, vitality, innocence, love, and beauty; they are seen as swift, graceful, magical, ethereal, delicately feminine, and powerfully masculine.[48]

In the second half of the twentieth century, these traditional attitudes about deer were further intensified by a single cultural event: the movie *Bambi*. According to Ralph H. Lutts, "*Bambi* has played and continues to play a key role in shaping American attitudes about and toward deer and woodland life. It is hard to identify a film, story or animal character that has had a greater influence on our vision of wildlife."[49] Deer features are appealing to humans, but the cartoon fawn was even more so, with his huge head, large white eye patches, and enormous eyes with oversized pupils and long lashes. In a way that recalls Celtic and medieval images of deer, Bambi is referred to as "the little Prince," and his father is called "the Great Prince." The movie presents a woodland fantasy in which all the animals are friends and live in peace and harmony—except that the deer are somehow the aristocracy. Only humans disturb this idyllic world; they hunt the deer, kill Bambi's mother (offscreen), wound Bambi, and set the forest on fire, causing the woodland creatures to flee in chaos and terror. Bambi's suffering and his mother's death reference the medieval image of the wounded or dying stag as a symbol of the crucified Christ and also the medieval motif of the sobbing deer, who voices questions about social justice. The powerful archetypes employed in this film echoed and intensified the emotional attitudes about deer in the United States at the end of the twentieth century. They also do much to explain the emotionality of the opponents to deer control in the Wissahickon, such as the one who accused the city, FPC, FOW, and game commission of a "murderous conspiracy" to kill "Bambi's mother."[50]

WOLVES IN THE WISSAHICKON

The Wissahickon deer war demonstrated that place matters in these conflicts. At stake were definitions of the park as well as decisions about the deer. Responses to the deer question showed "overlapping imaginative geographies" to be at work, many different ways in which people assigned meaning to the park's spaces and boundaries. As the deer wandered and munched their way in and out of the park, they blurred the notion of a clear dichotomy between the human-built city and nature defined as "the world of original things . . . , the world [humans] have not made." This exposed the imaginative geography of the Wissahickon, in which arguments about the deer were also claims about controlling the character of northwestern Philadelphia's spaces.[51]

For example, some arguments about the deer expressed resentment against the traditional WASP elite based in Chestnut Hill and active in the FOW. When the FOW supported culling the deer, opponents charged that this was yet another case of the rich claiming the park as their own. Other concerns were safety and danger. Some opponents attacked the deer cull as the extension of violence into peaceful environs of the Wissahickon Park. The popular description of the park as an urban wilderness evokes its natural peace and beauty but also, in an older meaning of *wilderness*, its status as a dangerous, marginal place inhabited by uncontrolled beasts and beings. The park has porous boundaries with neighborhoods considered unsafe especially by those living in the more affluent neighborhoods of northwestern Philadelphia. Both isolated and accessible, it can be a dangerous place where criminals lurk. There really are some wolves in the Wissahickon. The presence of deer seemed to make the Wissahickon into the "right" kind of wild, while culling the deer reminded people of the larger problems of murder and violence in Philadelphia. As it happened, the institution of the cull and the most vigorous opposition to it, in 1998 and 1999, respectively, coincided with a sharp spike in Philadelphia's crime rate.[52]

A nearby deer war took a different form. In 2009 officials in the Valley Forge National Park announced that their deer herd had increased to nearly 1,300 and that a cull was necessary to save the park's landscape. They proposed reducing the herd by more than 80 percent, to between 165 and 185. Opponents there expressed the same abstract arguments about deer as had been expressed in the Wissahickon conflict, but significant differences altered the terms on which the battle was enjoined. Wissahickon is a city park, whereas Valley Forge lies in a suburban area and has a major highway running through it. Administered by the federal government, moreover, it ranks as one of the primary locations associated with the American Revolution. Thus, for example, when Friends of Animals and CARE (Compassion for Animals, Respect for the Environment) filed suit to stop the cull, they contended, "the National Park Service has abandoned its century-old mission to strive for parks in which conservation of nature is paramount," an argument not applicable to the Wissahickon as a city park. Different place, different kind of deer war.[53]

The modern economy has separated the majority of Americans from the places and production methods behind the commodities they consume. This has certainly altered their views of animals and their understanding of natural processes. Though animal rights advocates proved to be a minority, however noisy, they nonetheless expressed a popularly held view of nature as a place of balance and harmony. This included a romanticized view that death for wild animals is a gentle, kind fading away—a notion that dovetails with the animal rights focus on individual animals rather than species and on a human-centered notion of suffering. Thus opponents of the cull could argue that the deer would somehow self-regulate, not understanding that when limits on food supplies put pressure on deer populations, the result is a long-term process of rising mortality in which deer weaken, suffer, and die while continuing to give birth to weakened, vulnerable fawns. There proved to be a difference between environmental or "green" consciousness and ecological knowledge. Conflicts over deer involved a moral ecology of nature in competition with the biological ecology of a place. As Richard Nelson argues persuasively, "Deer are not merely a part of the scenery, not just works of natural artistry carrying on lives remote and disconnected from our own. We are bound together with deer in an intricate biological relationship centered around cultivated crops. . . . Deer are a fundamental part of our personal ecology."[54]

The conventional narrative of environmental history and environmentalism has been one of human harm to the natural world. In the Wissahickon, deer, part of that natural world, were identified as the agents of harm toward other parts of nature. Aldo Leopold wrote, "Just as a deer herd lives in mortal fear of its wolves, so does a mountain live in mortal fear of its deer." The ecosystem of the Wissahickon had come to fear the deer as well.[55] The deer question showed that as always, ideas about nature are rooted in particular places; the question of the deer was inseparable from this particular corner of the Philadelphia environment. Everyone involved in the conflict cared about the Wissahickon as a natural environment, but they understood the notion of natural environment in widely different ways, ranging from an ecosystem to a utopian refuge from twentieth-century society.[56] The conflict over the deer in the Wissahickon ended up being a debate over the history and meaning of the Wissahickon as "nature" within the city. The Wissahickon deer wars were very much a Philadelphia story.

I live in the section of Philadelphia described in these pages, a few blocks from the park. I drive the streets bordering the Wissahickon and walk its woods, encountering deer in the park, on the road, and occasionally in my own yard. I have learned to drive cautiously using high beams near the park at night. I have learned that when one deer is sauntering across the pavement, at least two more are likely to soon join it. I have learned to wait, since more often than not, a laggard deer will burst out of the woods and run frantically to catch up with the group, moving with a gait oddly both graceful and ungainly. As a farm child, environmental historian, and local resident, I have not been neutral on the subject of the deer; however, the process of researching and writing this chapter has informed and altered my views.

I called this chapter "Wolves in the Wissahickon" because when I began this project, wolves were my solution to the deer problem there. I argued that if humans are not willing to take on their responsibility as predators within the ecosystem, then we should bring back the wolves and the coyotes. Realistically, I knew that wolves and coyotes would not respect the boundaries of the park any more than the deer and that living near the park, my highly domesticated dogs, however feisty and courageous, would easily make a nice lunch or supper for serious canine predators. What I did not know was that the Wissahickon is an unsuitable habitat for large numbers of predators; bringing back wolves to the Wissahickon is ecologically untenable. Woods and deer do not a wolf habitat make. Nor was I any better than the FOAW at recognizing the plants of the Wissahickon, distinguishing between native and invasive species, or assessing damage to the understory. Pursuing this investigation made me realize the limits on my botanical and ecological knowledge. Perhaps my argument in favor of wolves in the Wissahickon really expressed my own desire to have "real" nature on my doorstep, one I imagine being truly authentic, albeit a kind of nature quite different from the one others imagine when they speak of the Wissahickon. Deer wars provide the opportunity to think about urban nature, helping us assess what kind of relationship we have with the natural world and how well we understand that world.

Notes

Introduction

1. Andrew Hurley, *Common Fields: An Environmental History of St. Louis* (St. Louis: Missouri History Museum Press, 1997), 1–3. For a broader discussion of the evolution of urban environmental history, see Joel Tarr's "Urban History and Environmental History in the United States: Complementary and Overlapping Fields," available at http://www.h-net.org/~environ/historiography/usurban.htm (accessed Mar. 12, 2012).

2. Andrew Isenberg, *The Nature of Cities* (Rochester, N.Y.: University of Rochester Press, 2006), xiv.

3. William Cronon, *Nature's Metropolis* (New York: Norton, 1991), 38.

4. Benjamin W. Labaree, William M. Fowler, John B. Hattendorf, Jeffrey J. Safford, Edward W. Sloan, and Andrew W. German, *America and the Sea: A Maritime History* (Mystic, Conn.: Mystic Seaport Museum, 1999), 23.

5. Alexis de Tocqueville, *Democracy in America* (New York: Harper Collins, 1969), 213–14; also available online at http://xroads.virginia.edu/~HYPER/DETOC/toc_indx.html (accessed Mar. 21, 2012).

6. John L. Cotter, Daniel G. Roberts, and Michael Parrington, *The Buried Past: An Archaeological History of Philadelphia* (Philadelphia: University of Pennsylvania Press, 1992), 3.

7. Ibid., 9, 14.

8. Ibid., 19.

9. Qtd. in ibid.

10. Ibid., 22.

11. Ibid., 32–35.

12. Richard Rhodes, *John James Audubon* (New York: Vintage, 2006), 34–35.

13. Charles Coleman Sellers, *Mr. Peale's Museum* (New York: Norton, 1980), 44–46.

14. Paul Semonin, *American Monster: How the Nation's First Prehistoric Creature Became a Symbol of National Identity* (New York: New York University Press, 2000), 23.

15. Sellers, *Mr. Peale's Museum,* 138; Thomas Jefferson to Charles Wilson Peale, January 16, 1802, in *Pennsylvania Magazine of History and Biography* 28 (1904): 138.

16. Qtd. in Rhodes, *Audubon,* 10.

17. Gary B. Nash, *First City: Philadelphia and the Forging of American Memory* (Philadelphia: University of Pennsylvania Press, 2002), 1.

18. Sam Bass Warner, *The Private City: Philadelphia in Three Periods of Its Growth* (Philadelphia: University of Pennsylvania Press, 1968), 21.

19. Warner, *Private City,* 49.

1. William Penn's Philadelphia: The Land and the Plan

1. William Penn, "Letter to the Free Society of Traders" (Aug. 16, 1683), in *William Penn and the Founding of Pennsylvania: A Documentary History,* ed. Jean R. Soderlund (Philadelphia: University of Pennsylvania Press, 1983), 318.

2. Nonetheless, there were physical problems to be overcome: "The site of the new city had serious disadvantages as a commercial entrepôt. It lay about a hundred miles up a tortuous river, full of shoals and shallows" (Mary Maples Dunn and Richard S. Dunn, "The Founding, 1681–1701," in *Philadelphia: A 300-Year History,* ed. Russell F. Weigley [New York: Norton, 1982], 5).

3. Thomas Holme, "A Short Advertisement upon the Situation and Extent of the City of Philadelphia and Ensuing Plat-form thereof, by the Surveyor-General" (1683), in *Penn and the Founding,* ed. Soderlund, 322.

4. William Penn to James Harrison (Aug. 25, 1681), in *Penn and the Founding,* ed. Soderlund, 77.

5. Mary Maples Dunn, "The Personality of William Penn," in *The World of William Penn,* ed. Richard S. Dunn and Mary Maples Dunn (Philadelphia: University of Pennsylvania Press, 1986), 3–14.

6. John A. Moretta, *William Penn and the Quaker Legacy* (New York: Pearson Longman, 2007), 34–36, 79–80; Joseph E. Illick, *Colonial Pennsylvania: A History* (New York: Scribner's, 1976), 2–9; David Hackett Fischer, *Albion's Seed: Four British Folkways in America* (New York: Oxford University Press, 1989), 573–77.

7. "The Charter of Pennsylvania" (Mar. 4, 1681), in *Penn and the Founding,* ed. Soderlund, 41–42.

8. Ibid., 41.

9. Ibid.

10. Ibid., 42.

11. Ibid., 45, 42; also see Hannah Benner Roach, "The Planting of Philadelphia: A Seventeenth-Century Real Estate Development I," *Pennsylvania Magazine of History and Biography* 92, no. 1 (Jan. 1968): 5–6.

12. Penn to Harrison, 77.

13. Sir John Werden to William Blathwayt (June 23, 1680), in *Penn and the Founding,* ed. Soderlund, 26.

14. Dunn and Dunn, "The Founding," 3.

15. Daniel K. Richter, "The First Pennsylvanians," in *Pennsylvania: A History of the Commonwealth,* ed. Randall M. Miller and William Pencak (University Park: Pennsylvania State University Press; Harrisburg: Pennsylvania Historical and Museum Commission, 2002), 10.

16. Ibid., 34–35; Gary B. Nash, *First City: Philadelphia and the Forging of Historical Memory* (Philadelphia: University of Pennsylvania Press, 2002), 26–27; Alan Taylor, *American Colonies: The Settling of North America* (New York: Penguin, 2001): 42–43; Alfred W. Crosby, *Ecological Imperialism: The Biological Expansion of Europe, 900–1900,* 2d ed. (New York: Cambridge University Press, 2004), 202–3.

17. Francis Daniel Pastorius, "Positive Information from America" (Mar. 7, 1684), in *Penn and the Founding,* ed. Soderlund, 359–60.

18. Penn, "Letter to the Free Society," 314.

19. Richter, "First Pennsylvanians," 17–18; Taylor, *American Colonies,* 189.

20. Penn, "Letter to the Free Society," 313.

21. Richter, "First Pennsylvanians," 28.

22. For a good discussion of this mutual incomprehensibility, see James H. Merrell, *Into the American Woods: Negotiators on the Pennsylvania Frontier* (New York: Norton, 1999), 145–49.

23. Susan E. Klepp, "Encounter and Experiment: The Colonial Period," in *Pennsylvania,* ed. Miller and Pencak, 58; Richter, "First Pennsylvanians," 37–38, 44; Taylor, *American Colonies,* 92–99.

24. Penn, "Letter to the Free Society," 314.

25. Wilbur Zelinsky, "Geography," in *Pennsylvania,* ed. Miller and Pencak, 390.

26. William Penn to John Aubrey (June 13, 1683), in *Penn and the Founding,* ed. Soderlund, 282; Penn, "Letter to the Free Society," 310–11.

27. Merrell, *Into the American Woods,* 23–24.

28. Penn to Aubrey, 282.

29. Penn, "Letter to the Free Society," 312.

30. Crosby, *Ecological Imperialism,* 157.

31. Richter, "First Pennsylvanians," 18.

32. Virginia DeJohn Anderson, *Creatures of Empire: How Domestic Animals Transformed Early America* (New York: Oxford University Press, 2004), 8–9, 45, 81.

33. Penn, "Letter to the Free Society," 312.

34. Zelinsky, "Geography," 393–94.

35. Richter, "First Pennsylvanians," 27; Taylor, *American Colonies,* 18.

36. See Soderlund, *Penn and the Founding,* 20.

37. "Deed from the Delaware Indians" (July 15, 1682), in *Penn and the Founding,* ed. Soderlund, 156–57.

38. George B. Nash, "City Planning and Political Tension in the Seventeenth Century: The Case of Philadelphia," *Proceedings of the American Philosophical Society* 112 (Feb. 1968): 54–55; Roach, "Planting of Philadelphia I," 7.

39. Thomas H. Keels, *Forgotten Philadelphia: Lost Architecture of the Quaker City* (Philadelphia: Temple University Press, 2007), 13; Hannah Benner Roach, "The Planting of Philadelphia: A Seventeenth-Century Real Estate Development II," *Pennsylvania Magazine of History and Biography* 92, no. 2 (Apr. 1968): 159–63.

40. Richard J. Webster, "Architecture," in *Pennsylvania,* ed. Miller and Pencak, 418.

41. Moretta, *Penn,* 127; Dunn and Dunn, "Founding," 18.

42. Keels, *Forgotten Philadelphia,* 9; Roach, "Planting of Philadelphia I," 18–20. For a conjectural map of Penn's first plan, see Sylvia Doughty Fries, *The Urban Idea in Colonial America* (Philadelphia: Temple University Press, 1977), 103.

43. William Penn, "Initial Plans for Philadelphia" (Sept. 30, 1681), in *Penn and the Founding,* ed. Soderlund, 83.

44. Ibid., 85.

45. Nash, "City Planning," 56–57. For a map of settlements on the Delaware and Schuylkill prior to Penn, see Roach, "Planting of Philadelphia I," 15.

46. John Andrew Gallery, *The Planning of Center City Philadelphia: From William Penn to the Present* (Philadelphia: Center for Architecture, 2007), 9, 50; Penn, "Letter to the Free Society," 308–24.

47. Qtd. in Spiro Kostof, *The City Shaped: Urban Patterns and Meanings through History* (New York: Bulfinch, 1991), 95.

48. Ibid., 103–15.

49. Leo Hollis, *London Rising: The Men Who Made Modern London* (New York: Walker, 2008); John W. Reps, *The Making of Urban America: A History of City Planning in the United States* (Princeton, N.J.: Princeton University Press, 1965), 163–64; Gallery, *Planning of Center City,* 9–10; Fries, *Urban Idea,* 96–98; Dunn and Dunn, "The Founding," 10. Penn had also been impressed by the ordered grid of Turin's city plan, which he had seen in the 1660s; see Moretta, *William Penn,* 130.

50. Fries, *Urban Idea,* 96–97.

51. Dell Upton, *Another City: Urban Spaces and Urban Life in the New American Republic* (New Haven, Conn.: Yale University Press, 2008), 119–20.

52. Roach, "Planting of Philadelphia II," 151–57.

53. Charles Dickens, *American Notes for General Circulation,* ed. John S. Whitley and Arnold Goldman (1842; repr., New York: Penguin, 1985), 145.

54. Dunn and Dunn, "The Founding," 7.

55. Kostof, *City Shaped,* 209–11, 220–21.

56. Holme, "Short Advertisement," 322.

57. John Andrew Gallery, *Philadelphia Architecture: A Guide to the City,* 3d ed. (Philadelphia: Center for Architecture, 1994), 74–75; George E. Thomas, with Patricia Likos Ricci, Richard G. Webster, Lawrence M. Newman, Robert Janosov, and Bruce Thomas, *Buildings of Pennsylvania: Philadelphia and Eastern Pennsylvania* (Charlottesville: University of Virginia Press, 2010), 82–83; Dunn and Dunn, "The Founding," 16. Philadelphia's city hall and Broad Street now stand two blocks west from the site Penn and Holme originally planned, to place the square at the true high

point between the two rivers. A few other subtle adjustments were made over the years to accommodate the grid to the lay of the land. See Upton, *Another City,* 139–40.

58. Fischer, *Albion's Seed,* 522–26; Soderlund, ed., *Penn and the Founding,* 4.

59. George B. Tatum, *Penn's Great Town: 250 Years of Philadelphia Architecture* (Philadelphia: University of Pennsylvania Press, 1961), 24–25.

60. Holme, "Short Advertisement," 322.

61. Reps, *Urban America,* 163.

62. Fries, *Urban Idea,* 97.

63. The blockhouse was converted to the First Swedes Church in 1677, before it was replaced by the present structure. See Keels, *Forgotten Philadelphia,* 12; Gallery, *Philadelphia Architecture,* 20; and Thomas, *Buildings of Pennsylvania,* 71.

64. Roach, "Planting of Philadelphia I," 30.

65. Gallery, *Planning of Center City,* 12.

66. Upton, *Another City,* 21–22. For a plan of Philadelphia's settlement pattern in 1794, see ibid., 23.

67. Keels, *Forgotten Philadelphia,* 17–18, 30–31. Brick market sheds replaced wood in 1720.

68. For the location of early buildings in Philadelphia, see the plan in James D. Kornwolf, with assistance of Georgiana W. Kornwolf, *Architecture and Town Planning in Colonial North America,* vol. 2 (Baltimore, Md.: Johns Hopkins University Press, 2002), 1173.

69. Gallery, *Philadelphia Architecture,* 22–23; Thomas, *Buildings of Pennsylvania,* 51–52.

70. Keels, *Forgotten Philadelphia,* 23–25; Gallery, *Planning of Center City,* 65; Thomas, *Buildings of Pennsylvania,* 12–14.

71. Upton, *Another City,* 115.

72. For the early development of wharves, see Roach, "Planting of Philadelphia II," 176–77.

73. Thomas, *Buildings of Pennsylvania,* 3, 37.

74. Ibid., 47–50; Gallery, *Planning of Center City,* 64; Gallery, *Philadelphia Architecture,* 21; Kostof, *City Shaped,* 150.

75. Lewis Mumford, *The City in History: Its Origins, Its Transformations, and Its Prospects* (New York: Harcourt Brace Jovanovich, 1961), 327.

76. Gabriel Thomas, *An Historical and Geographical Account of the Province and Country of Pensilvania and of West-New-Jersey in America* (London: A Baldwin, 1698), 5.

77. Keels, *Forgotten Philadelphia,* 19–21; Hugh Morrison, *Early American Architecture: From the First Colonial Settlements to the National Period* (New York: Oxford University Press, 1952), 514.

78. Gallery, *Philadelphia Architecture,* 12–13.

79. William Penn, *Some Fruits of Solitude: Wise Sayings on the Conduct of Human Life,* ed. Eric K. Taylor (Scottsdale, Pa.: Herald, 2003), 60.

80. Qtd. in Roach, "Planting of Philadelphia I," 9.

81. Moretta, *William Penn,* 119.

82. Dunn and Dunn, "The Founding," 7; Nash, "City Planning," 61; Roach, "Planting of Philadelphia II," 178–79.

83. Klepp, "Encounter and Experiment," 64.

84. Gallery, *Philadelphia Architecture,* 10.

85. Thomas, *Historical and Geographical Account,* 319.

86. An early example was the Townsend's Mill (1683) in East Germantown; see Keels, *Forgotten Philadelphia,* 16–17.

87. For a discussion of Penn's ideals for development of country farms, townships, and villages versus the actual development see Fischer, *Albion's Seed,* 577–84; Fries, *Urban Idea,* 95–96.

88. Edwin B. Bronner, *William Penn's "Holy Experiment"* (Philadelphia: Temple University Publications, 1962), 230–34.

89. Moretta, *William Penn,* 185–86, 241–43.

90. Ibid., 195.

91. William C. Kashatus, "William Penn's Legacy: Religious and Spiritual Diversity," *Pennsylvania Heritage* 37 (Spring 2011): 6–15.

92. Pastorius, "Positive Information," 360.

93. Moretta, *William Penn,* 128–29; Nash, *First City,* 39–44.

94. James Claypoole to Edward Claypoole (Sept. 23, 1682), in *Penn and the Founding,* ed. Soderlund, 180.

95. A reconstruction of Penn's barge is on display at the reconstructed Pennsbury Manor. See Larry E. Tise, *Pennsbury Manor: Pennsylvania Trail of History Guide* (Mechanicsburg, Pa.: Stackpole, 2002), 32.

96. Ibid., 24–27, 38–43; Thomas, *Buildings of Pennsylvania,* 171–72.

97. Thomas, *Historical and Geographical Account,* 320: Nash, *First City,* 20–21; Harry Ermerson Wildes, *William Penn* (New York: Macmillan, 1974), 314–16.

98. Tise, *Pennsbury Manor,* 32–37, 46. For a discussion of slavery at Pennsbury, see Wildes, *Penn,* 322–26.

99. Moretta, *William Penn,* 218; Fries, *Urban Idea,* 81–82, 90–93.

100. Soderlund, ed., *Penn and the Founding,* 19; Dunn and Dunn, "The Founding," 1.

101. Qtd. in Moretta, *William Penn,* 209–10.

102. Penn, *Solitude,* 80.

103. Originally commissioned by William Penn's son Thomas, the painting is now in the collection of the Pennsylvania Academy of the Fine Arts, Philadelphia. See Helmut von Erffa and Allen Staley, *The Paintings of Benjamin West* (New Haven, Conn.: Yale University Press, 1986), 206–8; Randall M. Miller and William Pencak, "Art," in *Pennsylvania,* ed. Miller and Pencak, 528–29; Nash, *First City,* 29–30.

104. Benjamin West to W. Darton (Feb. 2, 1785), qtd. in Staley, *Benjamin West,* 207. During the eighteenth century, the relationship between the Pennsylvania colonists and the Native Americans moved far from the peaceful ideals of Penn; see Francis Jennings, "Brother Miguon: Good Lord!" in *World of Penn,* ed. Dunn and Dunn, 198–210.

105. Carolyn J. Weekley, *The Kingdoms of Edward Hicks* (Williamsburg, Va.: Colonial Williamsburg Foundation, 1999), 53.

106. Peter Silver, *Our Savage Neighbors: How Indian War Transformed Early America* (New York: Norton, 2008).

107. Nash, *First City,* 302–3.

2. "Pro Bono Publico": Ecology, History, and the Creation of Philadelphia's Fairmount Park System

The author wishes to thank this volume's editors and those who assisted in the preparation of this chapter, including Theresa Stuhlman, Rob Armstrong, Mark Focht, Stephanie Craighead, Philip Price, Carol and Colin Franklin, Sam Katz, Harris Steinberg, Andrew Goodman, and Adam Levine.

1. "Voters OK Merger of Parks, Recreation: City Charter Is Amended," *Philadelphia Daily News,* November 5, 2008; Stephan Salisbury, "Strong Support for Parks-Recreation Charter Change," *Philadelphia Inquirer,* November 5, 2008.

2. The ex-officio members are the president of the city council and the executive director of the city planning commission or their designees, the water commissioner, the street commissioner, the public property commissioner, and the parks and recreation commissioner.

3. In addition to administering recreation centers, swimming pools, and playgrounds, the Philadelphia Department of Recreation also governed seventy-five properties classified on the department website as "parks" as well as historic buildings and sites such as the Betsy Ross House and Fort Mifflin. Nonetheless, although the department included these significant historic properties within its jurisdiction, it had no preservation management staff. See http://www.phila.gov/recreation/parks/Neighborhood__Parks.html (accessed Mar. 1, 2012).

4. The definitive nineteenth-century history of Fairmount Park (East and West parks and the Wissahickon) is Charles Keyser's *Fairmount Park: Sketches of Its Scenery, Waters and History* (Philadelphia: Claxton, Remsen and Haffelfinger, 1872), which appears in many editions. The only modern history of the entire Fairmount Park system is Esther Klein's *Fairmount Park: A History and a Guidebook* (Bryn Mawr, Pa.: Harcum Junior College Press, 1974). The founding of the Fairmount Park system is addressed by Theo B. White in his *Fairmount Park: Philadelphia's Park* (Philadelphia: Art Alliance Press, 1975). More recent studies include David Schuyler, *The New Urban Landscape: The Redefinition of City Form in Nineteenth-Century America* (Baltimore, Md.: Johns Hopkins University Press, 1988), 59–100; Elizabeth Milroy, "Assembling Fairmount Park," in *Philadelphia's Cultural Landscape and the Sartain Family's Legacy,* ed. Katherine Martinez and Page Talbott (Philadelphia: Temple University Press, 2000), 72–86; Elizabeth Milroy, "Images of Fairmount Park in Philadelphia," in *Thomas Eakins,* ed. Darrel Sewell (Philadelphia: Philadelphia Museum of Art, 2001), 77–94; and Michael Lewis, "The First Design for Fairmount Park," *Pennsylvania Magazine of History and Biography* 130, no. 3 (July 2006): 283–98.

5. George F. Chadwick mistakenly attributes this to Olmsted in *The Park and the Town: Public Landscapes in the Nineteenth and Twentieth Centuries* (New York: Praeger, 1966), 190.

6. *Third Annual Report of the Commissioners of Fairmount Park* (Philadelphia: King and Baird, 1871), 5.

7. Elizabeth Milroy, "'For the like Uses, as the Moore-Fields': The Politics of Penn's Squares," *Pennsylvania Magazine of History and Biography* 130, no. 3 (July 2006): 257–82.

8. Lawrence Lewis, *An Essay on Original Land Titles in Philadelphia* (Philadelphia, 1880), 137. See also Edward P. Allinson and Boies Penrose, *Philadelphia, 1681–1887: A History of Municipal Development,* Johns Hopkins University Studies in Historical and Political Science (Philadelphia: Allen, Lane, and Scott, 1887), 8–29.

9. The petition dates from 1805; see Historical Society of Pennsylvania, Philadelphia General Petitions. These improvements in turn prompted the city to landscape the other four public squares, bringing these in line with Centre Square as well as the small public garden south of the State House, first landscaped in the 1780s. See Elizabeth Milroy, "Repairing the Myth and Reality of Philadelphia's Public Squares, 1800–1850," *Change over Time* 1, no. 1 (Spring 2011): 52–78.

10. Initially the waterworks were powered by steam engines, but these proved unreliable. See Jane Mork Gibson, "The Fairmount Waterworks," *Philadelphia Museum of Art Bulletin* 84, nos. 360–61 (Summer 1988): 12–21.

11. The increase in "chills and fever" in upriver communities was noted by Charles V. Hagner in his *Early History of the Falls of Schuylkill, Manayunk, etc* . . . (Philadelphia: Claxton, Remsen, and Haffelfinger, 1869), 72–73.

12. Howard Gillette Jr., "The Emergence of the Modern Metropolis: Philadelphia in the Age of Its Consolidation," in *The Divided Metropolis: Social and Spatial Dimensions of Philadelphia, 1800–1975,* ed. William W. Cutler III and Howard Gillette Jr. (Westport, Conn.: Greenwood, 1980), 3–26.

13. Christine Boyer, *Dreaming the Rational City: The Myth of American City Planning* (Cambridge, Mass.: MIT Press, 1983), 9. See also David Schuyler, *The New Urban Landscape: The Redefinition of City Form in Nineteenth-Century America* (Baltimore, Md.: Johns Hopkins University Press, 1988).

14. This includes the surface area of the Schuylkill and other waterways. See 2010 U.S. Census Bureau data at http://www.census.gov/geo/www/gazetteer/files/Gaz_places_national.txt (accessed Apr. 26, 2011).

15. The consolidation act directed city councils "to obtain by dedication or purchase, within the limits of [Philadelphia], an adequate number of squares or other areas of ground, convenient of access to all its inhabitants, and lay out and maintain such squares and areas of ground as open public places, for the health and enjoyment of the people forever" (*A Further Supplement to . . . An Act to Incorporate the City of Philadelphia* [Philadelphia: Crissy and Markley, 1867], 37). See also Milroy, "Assembling Fairmount Park," 76.

16. [Andrew Miller], *The Sedgeley Park Scheme* (Philadelphia: Gibbons, Printer, 1857).

17. [William Saunders], "The Lemon Hill Park," *The Philadelphia Inquirer,* February 25, 1857.

18. [Andrew Jackson Downing], "A Talk about Public Parks and Gardens," *The Horticulturist* 3, no. 4 (Oct. 1848): 155–56; [Andrew Jackson Downing], "The New-York Park," *The Horticulturist* 6, no. 8 (Aug. 1, 1851): 347–48.

19. [Andrew Jackson Downing], "On the Moral Influence of Good Houses," *The Horticulturist* 2, no. 8 (Feb. 1848): 346–47.

20. When citizens raised only part of the purchase price, city councils voted to accept the deed to Sedgeley and take out a mortgage on the $65,000 balance; see

Fairmount Park Contribution (Philadelphia: privately printed, 1856) and "Extracts from Report of Committee on Fairmount Park Contribution," n.d., James Castle scrapbook, Historical Society of Pennsylvania. The Sedgley campaign is chronicled in *Sedgley Park, and Its Acceptance by the City of Philadelphia* (Philadelphia: Crissy and Markley, 1857) See also J. C. Sidney and A. Adams, *Description of Plan for the Improvement of Fairmount Park* (Philadelphia: Merrihew and Thompson, 1859). The history of the competition is recounted in Lewis, "First Design," 287.

21. In 1859 business leaders including Matthias Baldwin, Joseph Harrison, N. B. Browne, Evan Rogers, Horace Binney, and Fairman Rogers petitioned the city to acquire land on the west bank, including the former Solitude estate; see *Report of the Joint Committee of Water Works and City Property on the Extension of Fairmount Park* (Philadelphia: Crissy and Markley, 1859). For comparisons to the European parks, see *Speech of the Hon. James Miller on the Bill Authorizing the Purchase of Grounds on the West Side of the Schuylkill . . . for a Public Park . . . , March 20th, 1865* (Philadelphia: J. A. Wagenseller, 1865). In 1867 the bankers John Welsh and A.J. Drexel, the industrialist Joseph Harrison, and the newspaper publisher George Childs purchased the 140-acre Lansdowne estate and offered it to the city at cost; see "A New Park," *Philadelphia Age,* January 24, 1867.

22. The Reverend John W. Mears, *Water Supply of Our Great Cities* (Philadelphia: Published by Order of the Water Committee of the Councils [1866]), 17, qtd. in Sam Alewitz, *"Filthy Dirty": A Social History of Unsanitary Philadelphia in the Late Nineteenth Century* (New York: Garland, 1989), 106.

23. "The Park Extension," *Philadelphia Age,* February 21, 1867; "Appropriating ground for public purposes in the City of Philadelphia . . . ," act of March 26, 1867, P.L. 547, *Laws, Ordinances and Regulations Relating to Fairmount Park and Other Parks under the Control of the Fairmount Park Commission* (Philadelphia: Printed for the Commission, 1933), 9–13.

24. "A Supplement to An Act . . . 'Appropriating ground for public purposes in the City of Philadelphia . . . ,'" act of April 14, 1868, P.L. 1083, *Laws, Ordinances and Regulations,* 14–28; Frederick Law Olmsted and Calvert Vaux to the chairman of the Committee on Plans of the Park Commission of Philadelphia, December 4, 1867, Fairmount Park Commission Minutes, City Archives of Philadelphia, Record Group 149.1; repr. in Olmsted, *The Papers of Frederick Law Olmsted,* ed. Charles Capen McLaughlin, vol. 4, *The Years of Olmsted, Vaux and Company,* ed. David Schuyler and Jane Turner Censer (Baltimore, Md.: Johns Hopkins University Press, 1992), 231–32.

25. Cook's occupation is not known. The fountain is said to have been the first public water fountain erected in the city that was not part of the Fairmount waterworks. Benjamin Franklin had bequeathed one thousand pounds to the city and recommended that the accumulated capital be used to erect an aqueduct or pipeline to direct water from the Wissahickon. For more on this bequest, see J. Thomas Scharf and Thompson Westcott, *History of Philadelphia,* 3 vols. (Philadelphia: L. H. Everts, 1884) 3:1868; Benjamin Franklin, "Franklin's Last Will and Testament," in *The Complete Works of Benjamin Franklin,* ed. John Bigelow (New York: Putnam's, 1888), 10:223–24; Milroy, "Assembling Fairmount Park," 81–85.

26. Early improvements are detailed in the commission's first four annual

reports, published in 1869, 1870, 1871, and 1872. The secretary of the Philadelphia Sketch Club recorded that fellow members complained when their sketching excursions into the park were interrupted by baseball players. See secretary's notes, October 3 and 17, 1878, Philadelphia Sketch Club.

27. *First Annual Report of the Commissioners of Fairmount Park* (Philadelphia: King and Baird, 1869), 33–34.

28. Earl Shinn [Edward Strahan], *A Century After: Picturesque Glimpses of Philadelphia and Pennsylvania* (Philadelphia: Allen, Lane and Scott and J. W. Lauderbach, 1875), 48.

29. George Fenner, *Justice vs. Extraordinary Generosity* (Philadelphia: "Printed for Gratuitous Distribution," 1870), 7.

30. Thomas Cochran, "Fairmount Park: A Necessity for the Health and Recreation of the Present and Future Population of the City," *Philadelphia Evening Telegraph,* September 16, 1872; Newton Crane, "Fairmount Park," *Scribner's Monthly* 1, no. 3 (Jan. 1871): 231; Shinn, *A Century After,* 39–40.

31. Opinion of Thayer, P. J., 32 Leg. Int. 412, *Weekly Notes of Cases Argued and Determined in the Supreme Court of Pennsylvania . . . ,* 2 vols. (Philadelphia: Kay and Brother, 1876), 2:124–26. For Baltimore, see [Samuel Sloan], "The Philadelphia Park Extension and the City Water," *Architectural Review and American Builder's Journal* 1, no. 1 (July 1868): 45, 50.

32. Shinn, *A Century After,* 24.

33. Commissioner Joseph Harrison introduced plans for a public art museum in the park in 1871; see *Third Annual Report of the Commissioners of Fairmount Park* (Philadelphia: King and Baird, 1871), 79–80. Recent histories of the Centennial Exhibition include Bruno Giberti, *Designing the Centennial: A History of the 1876 International Exhibition in Philadelphia* (Lexington: University of Kentucky Press, 2002); Robert Rydell, *All the World's a Fair* (Chicago: University of Chicago Press, 1984), 9–37; Robert C. Post, *1876: The Centennial Exhibition* (Washington, D.C.: National Museum of History and Technology, 1976); John Maass, *The Glorious Enterprise: The Centennial Exhibition of 1876 and H. J. Schwarzmann, Architect-in-Chief* (Watkins Glen, N.Y.: American Life Foundation, 1973).

34. *Annual Report of the Commissioners of Fairmount Park* (Philadelphia: n.p., 1878), 34–35.

35. *Annual Report of the City Parks Association* (Philadelphia: n.p., 1889–90), 5. Philadelphians were inspired by the formation of London's Metropolitan Public Gardens Association in 1884; see Andrew Wright Crawford, "City Planning and Philadelphia Parks," *Annals of the American Academy of Political and Social Science* 35, no. 2 (1910): 76–77.

36. *Tenth Annual Report, City Parks Association of Philadelphia* (Philadelphia: n.p., 1898), 7–9.

37. *Thirteenth Annual Report of the City Parks Association of Philadelphia* (Philadelphia: n.p., 1901), 24–27. See also Andrew Wright Crawford, "The Comprehensive Park Movement in Philadelphia," *Charities* no. 32 (Aug. 6, 1904): 3–5.

38. For the complicated history of Philadelphia's water and sewage systems, see the website developed and maintained for the Philadelphia Water Department

by Adam Levine at http://www.phillyh2o.org (accessed Apr. 20, 2011). See also "Typhoid Fever in Philadelphia," *Medical Record* 55 (1899): 430; Michael P. McCarthy, *Typhoid and the Politics of Public Health in Nineteenth-Century Philadelphia* (Philadelphia: America Philosophical Society, 1987).

39. The ordinances governing the condemnation of land along these watersheds are listed throughout *Laws, Ordinances and Regulations Relating to Fairmount Park.*

40. Domenic Vitiello, "Machine Building and City Building: Urban Planning and Industrial Restructuring in Philadelphia, 1894–1928," *Journal of Urban History* 34, no. 3 (Mar. 2008), 411–21. See also David Brownlee, *Building the City Beautiful: The Benjamin Franklin Parkway and the Philadelphia Museum of Art* (Philadelphia: Philadelphia Museum of Art, 1989).

41. Ingrid Steffensen-Bruce, *Marble Palaces, Temples of Art: Art Museums, Architecture, and American Culture, 1890–1930* (Cranbury, N.J.: Associated University Presses, 1998), 106–9.

42. Multiple members of the Sellers, McMichael, and Widener families served; four generations of the Price family served on the commission from its founding to its demise.

43. "Mayor Wilson Dies," *New York Times,* August 20, 1939, 33.

44. *Report to the House of Representatives of the Commonwealth of Pennsylvania Covering an Investigation into the Books, Records, Management and Operation of the Fairmount Park Commission . . .* (Harrisburg, Pa., 1937), 27, at the Fairmount Park Historic Resource Archives.

45. The history of the bureau, later renamed the Department of Recreation, dates back to 1895, when city councils created a playground commission that was active until 1902. In 1907 the Children's Playground Association was established under the superintendent of schools. City councils created the Department of Recreation in 1911, but this was then absorbed into the Department of Public Works. See Robert Crawford, "The Philadelphia Experience," *Annals of the American Academy of Political and Social Science* 313 (Sept. 1957): 132–33.

46. Section 3-905 of the charter simply states that membership of the park commission will be expanded to include the recreation commissioner. Under section 3-915, three Fairmount Park commissioners were to be appointed to the ten-member Recreation Coordination Board. See Philadelphia Home Rule Charter, adopted by the electors, April 17, 1951, available at http://www.seventy.org/Files/Philadelphia_Home_Rule_Charter.pdf (accessed Apr. 22, 2011); R. Crawford, "Philadelphia Experience," 134.

47. "Fernhill Park Site Is Sought for Dairy Plant," *Philadelphia Bulletin,* March 12, 1961. See also Commissioners of Fairmount Park, *Ninety-Fourth Annual Report* (Philadelphia, 1961), 11. The Pulaski Highway project went through several iterations before being shelved in the early 1980s, yielding no resolution concerning how best to route traffic from the Betsy Ross bridge to I-95. See http://www.phillyroads.com/roads/PA-90 (accessed Apr. 20, 2011).

48. I am grateful to Mark Focht, executive director of Fairmount Park, for this information.

49. Robert N. C. Nix III, open letter to Fairmount Park supporters, May 2006,

available at http://www.fairmountpark.org/pdf/advisory_report/AR%20Cover%20Letter.pdf (accessed Apr. 20, 2011). Nix sent out the letter after receiving reports and recommendations from a specially appointed advisory group as well as from the Citizens for Better Parks and the Philadelphia Parks Alliance.

50. There had been three previous attempts to negotiate a lease between 2005 and 2008; the last vote among the commissioners was eight to four.

51. Philadelphia Court of Common Pleas, Orphans' Court Division, December 9, 2008, estate of Robert W. Ryerss, Deceased, O.C. no. 36 DE of 1896, control no. 081027. Among those leading the effort to acknowledge the ecological threat were members of the Society Created to Reduce Urban Blight (SCRUB); see http://www.urban blight.org/index.html (accessed Apr. 22, 2011).

52. Linda Lloyd, "Fox Chase Loses Appeal to Use Burholme Park," *Philadelphia Inquirer,* December 16, 2009. Fox Chase subsequently abandoned its plans to expand into the park. See Stacey Burling, "Fox Chase Drops Burholme Park Expansion Plan," *Philadelphia Inquirer,* January 16, 2010.

53. Data concerning Philadelphia's relative "greenness" and the distance of residents from parklands is from Philadelphia Parks and Recreation, *Green2015: An Action Plan for the First 500 Acres* (report prepared by PennPraxis for Philadelphia Parks and Recreation, Philadelphia, 2010), 8.

54. PaRC's mandate is described on the City of Philadelphia, Parks and Recreation, website at http://www.phila.gov/recreation/Commission_on_Parks_.html (accessed Mar. 1, 2012).

3. The Rise and Fall of Yellow Fever in Philadelphia, 1793–1805

1. The most outstanding example is a collection of essays: J. Worth Estes and Billy G. Smith, eds., *A Melancholy Scene of Devastation: The Public Response to the 1793 Philadelphia Yellow Fever Epidemic* (Canton, Mass.: Science History Publications, 1997). Also see the first synthetic work on the 1793 epidemic, John Harvey Powell, *Bring Out Your Dead: The Great Epidemic of Yellow Fever in Philadelphia in 1793* (Philadelphia: University of Pennsylvania Press, 1949).

2. Gilda Marie Anroman, "Infectious Disease in Philadelphia, 1690–1807: An Ecological Perspective" (PhD diss., University of Maryland, 2005). See also Susan Klepp, *Philadelphia in Transition: A Demographic History of the City and Its Occupational Groups, 1720–1830* (New York: Garland, 1989).

3. The tendency to point to the refugees reveals the larger tendency to focus solely on the 1793 epidemic. For example, see Powell, *Bring Out Your Dead,* 4–5.

4. David Geggus, *Slavery, War, and Revolution: The British Occupation of Saint Domingue, 1793–1798* (Oxford: Clarendon, 1982); David Geggus, "Yellow Fever in the 1790s: The British Army in Occupied Saint Domingue," *Medical History* 23 (1979): 38–58.

5. This has been established on the basis of genomic analysis; see Oyewale Tomori, "Yellow Fever: The Recurring Plague," *Critical Reviews in Clinical Laboratory Sciences* 41, no. 4 (2004): 397–98.

6. Thomas Monath, "Yellow Fever: An Update," *The Lancet: Infectious Diseases* 1, no. 1 (Aug. 2001): 12–13.

7. For the symptoms and course of the disease, see Tomori, "Yellow Fever," 408–9; and John C. Bugher, "The Pathology of Yellow Fever," in *Yellow Fever*, ed. George Strode (New York: McGraw-Hill, 1951), 141–42.

8. Jean Slosek, *"Aedes Aegypti* Mosquitoes in the Americas: A Review of Their Interactions with the Human Population," *Social Science and Medicine* 23, no. 3 (1986): 249–57.

9. Rickard Christophers, *Aedes Aegypti (L.), the Yellow Fever Mosquito: Its Life History, Bionomics and Structure* (Cambridge: Cambridge University Press, 1960), 57.

10. J. D. Goodyear, "The Sugar Connection: A New Perspective on the History of Yellow Fever," *Bulletin of the History of Medicine* 52 (1978): 5–21.

11. Christophers, *Aedes Aegypti,* 165–66.

12. Lord Cornbury, *Proclamation. 1702 Sept. 17* (New York: William Bradford, 1702).

13. Rene La Roche, *Yellow Fever, Considered in its Historical, Pathological Etiological, and Therapeutic Relations* (Philadelphia: Blanchard and Lea, 1855), 120.

14. Eve Kornfeld, "Crisis in the Capital: The Cultural Significance of Philadelphia's Great Yellow Fever Epidemic," *Pennsylvania History* 3 (1984): 189.

15. Benjamin Rush, *Letters of Benjamin Rush,* vol. 2 (Princeton, N.J.: Princeton University Press, 1951), 640.

16. There is considerable variance in the death tolls listed by secondary sources. Ellis Oberholtzer claims that 4,500 people died (*Philadelphia: A History of the City and Its People* [Philadelphia: S. J. Clark, 1911], 358); Kornfeld puts the number at 5,000 ("Crisis in the Capital," 189). Both estimates are based on the list of church burials, 4,042 in all, compiled by Matthew Carey in *A short account of the malignant fever, lately prevalent in Philadelphia* (Philadelphia: Matthew Carey, 1793), 112–16. The discrepancies appeared as historians attempted to ascertain the number of deaths omitted by Carey and the number of deceased who were not buried in any of the church cemeteries.

17. Richard Folwell, *Short history of the yellow fever, that broke out in the city of Philadelphia, in July, 1797: with a list of the dead; of the donations for the relief of the poor, and a variety of other interesting particulars* (Philadelphia: Richard Folwell, 1798), 64.

18. Thomas Condie and Richard Folwell, *History of the pestilence, commonly called yellow fever, which almost desolated Philadelphia, in the months of August, September & October, 1798* (Philadelphia: Richard Folwell, 1799), 29, 108.

19. William Currie, *A sketch of the rise and progress of the yellow fever, and of the proceedings of the Board of Health, in Philadelphia, in the year 1799* (Philadelphia: Budd and Bartram, 1800), 25.

20. K. David Patterson, "Yellow Fever Epidemics and Mortality in the United States, 1693–1905," *Social Science and Medicine* 34, no. 8 (Apr. 1992): 855–65.

21. Monath, "Yellow Fever," 13.

22. Susan Klepp, *Philadelphia in Transition* (New York: Garland, 1989), 336.

23. Ibid., 226.

24. Christophers, *Aedes Aegypti,* 516.

25. See Monath, "Yellow Fever."

26. For the lower range, 32,000 × 0.25 = 8,000, and 8,000 × 0.5 = 4,000; for the higher range, 40,000 × 0.25 = 10,000, and 10,000 × 0.5 = 5,000.

27. Klepp, *Philadelphia in Transition,* 228–29. Anroman elaborates on this idea with much more detail in "Infectious Disease," 147–55.

28. Robert B. Sullivan, "Heroic Therapy in the Age of Rush," *Bulletin of the History of Medicine* 68 (1994): 217–18; Mark Workman, "Medical Practice in Philadelphia at the Time of the Yellow Fever Epidemic, 1793," *Pennsylvania Folklife* 27, no. 4 (1978): 34.

29. For example, see K. F. Kiple and V. H. Kiple, "Black Yellow Fever Immunities, Innate and Acquired, as Revealed in the American South," *Social Science and History* 1 (1977): 419–36.

30. Benjamin Rush, *An account of the bilious remitting yellow fever, as it appeared in the city of Philadelphia, in the year 1793* (Philadelphia: Thomas Dobson, 1794), 95–97.

31. Isaac Cathrall, *A medical sketch of the Synochus maligna, or malignant contagious fever; as it lately appeared in the city of Philadelphia: to which is added, some account of the morbid appearances observed after death, on dissection* (Philadelphia: Thomas Dobson, 1794), 6.

32. William Currie, *A treatise on the synochus icteroides, or yellow fever; as it lately appeared in the city of Philadelphia* (Philadelphia: Thomas Dobson, 1794), 13–14.

33. Gary Nash, *Forging Freedom: The Formation of Philadelphia's Black Community, 1720–1840* (Cambridge, Mass.: Harvard University Press, 1988), 137.

34. Christophers, *Aedes Aegypti,* 474–75.

35. These numbers are drawn from Zachariah Poulson's *Poulson's Town and Country Almanac.* For temperatures in 1793, see the 1795 issue; for those in 1797, see the 1799 issue; and for 1798, see the 1800 issue. Poulson gives the temperature for every day at 3 p.m., which would approximate the high temperature for the day. Unfortunately, he does not record the low temperature, which would allow us to gauge when it got cold enough to kill off the mosquito.

36. In fact, with adequate documentation it is even possible to correlate the decline of yellow fever in each individual year with the contemporary weather reports. Unfortunately, 1793 is the only year for which comprehensive records of this nature survive. In the fourth edition of his authoritative account of the 1793 epidemic, Matthew Carey provides the temperatures at 7 a.m. and 2 p.m., which would approximate the lows and highs for every day of the epidemic, August through November. According to Carey's numbers, the temperature in Philadelphia at 7 a.m. did not drop below 43°F—the point at which *A. aegypti* dies—until October 16. Before that, the temperature never fell below 46°F, recorded on October 7. Carey also listed all the people who died during the epidemic and when they were buried. His data show the last burials for yellow fever victims occurred on November 6. Yellow fever has an incubation period of three to six days before the appearance of symptoms, and most patients die seven to ten days after the onset. If the last deaths occurred about sixteen days after the *A. aegypti* population in Philadelphia vanished, then the last victim would have died in late October or early November. After a few days to prepare the bodies, they were buried on November 6. Therefore, it must have been

the frost on the night of October 15 and the morning of October 16 that killed the remaining yellow fever mosquitoes.

37. Qtd. in Powell, *Bring Out Your Dead,* 23.

38. Ibid., 27.

39. Phineas Jenks, *An essay on the analogy of the Asiatic and African plague and the American yellow fever: with a view to prove that they are the same disease varied by climate and other circumstances* (Philadelphia: Hugh Maxwell, 1804), 33–34.

40. Condie and Folwell, *History of the pestilence,* 13.

41. About one hundred years would pass before Carlos Finlay, Walter Reed, and the U.S. Army Yellow Fever Commission definitively proved that *A. aegypti* transmits the disease. This is covered in depth in François Delaporte, *Histoire de la fièvre jaune* (Paris: Payot, 1989).

42. Powell, *Bring Out Your Dead,* 4–5.

43. Gary Nash, "Reverberations of Haiti in the American North: Black Saint Dominguans in Philadelphia," *Pennsylvania History* 65, no. 5 (1998): 48–50.

44. Condie and Folwell, *History of the pestilence,* 31–32.

45. Ibid., 43.

46. Donald Hickey, "America's Response to the Slave Revolt in Haiti, 1791–1806," *Journal of the Early Republic* 2, no. 4 (Winter 1982): 362.

47. These statistics were gathered from James Dun, "'What avenues of commerce, will you, Americans, not explore!' Commercial Philadelphia's Vantage onto the Early Haitian Revolution," *William and Mary Quarterly,* 3d ser., 62, no. 3 (July 2005): 478. The exception was 1794, when arrivals from Saint-Domingue made up 17.8 percent of all entries from foreign ports. Also see John Coatsworth, "American Trade with European Colonies in the Caribbean and South America, 1790–1812," *William and Mary Quarterly,* 3d ser., 24, no. 2 (Apr. 1967): 243–66.

48. Thomas Ott, *The Haitian Revolution, 1789–1804* (Knoxville: University of Tennessee Press, 1973), 65–66; Geggus, "Yellow Fever in the 1790s," 40.

49. Richard Grove, "The Great El Niño of 1789–1793 and Its Global Consequences: Reconstructing an Extreme Climate Event in World Environmental History," *Medieval History Journal* 10, no. 75 (2007): 88–89.

50. Ott, *Haitian Revolution,* 92–93; Geggus, *Slavery, War, and Revolution,* 375–81; for the Leclerc expedition and the number who died, see Pierre Pluchon, foreword to Pamphile Lacroix, *La Révolution de Haïti: texte intégral de l'édition originale* (Paris: Éditions Karthala, 1995), 19–20.

51. Hickey, "America's Response," 369–75; Tim Matthewson, "Jefferson and Haiti," *Journal of Southern History* 61, no. 2 (May 1995): 237–38.

52. For the development of Cuba in the late eighteenth and early nineteenth centuries, see Coatsworth, "Trade with European Colonies," 254; Clifford Staten, *The History of Cuba* (Westport, Conn.: Greenwood, 2003), 18–22; Geoff Simons, *Cuba: From Conquistador to Castro* (New York: St. Martin's, 1996), 131–32.

53. This information was drawn from *New American State Papers: Commerce and Navigation* (Wilmington, Del.: Scholarly Resources, 1973), 2:290, 3:13, 59, 91, 132, 189, and 229.

54. New Orleans, Savannah, Charleston, and Jamaica all hosted yellow fever epidemics. See John McLead Keating, *A History of Yellow Fever* (Memphis, Tenn.: Howard Association, 1879), 80. Keating provides a long list of all the places that yellow fever struck from 1702 until 1879.

55. Powell, *Bring Out Your Dead,* 67–69.

56. Copies of the law were printed in both newspapers that remained in circulation during the epidemic: *The Federal Gazette,* September 9, 1793; *Dunlap's American Daily Advertiser,* September 9, 1793.

57. This gradual accretion of power is evident from a look at the health laws of Pennsylvania. See State of Pennsylvania, *Compilation of the health-laws of Pennsylvania* (Philadelphia: Zachariah Poulson, 1798).

58. Condie and Folwell, *History of the pestilence,* 35–36.

59. Ibid., 38–39.

60. The origins and development of this view are discussed in James Riley, *The Eighteenth-Century Campaign to Avoid Disease* (New York: St. Martin's, 1987), 1–30.

61. Charles Rosenburg, *Explaining Epidemics: And Other Studies in the History of Medicine* (Cambridge: Cambridge University Press, 1992), 295.

62. Rush, *Letters,* 2:637.

63. Jean Devèze, *An enquiry into, and observations upon the causes and effects of the epidemic disease, which raged in Philadelphia from the month of August till towards the middle of December, 1793* (Philadelphia: Parent, 1794), 136–40.

64. Condie and Folwell, *History of the pestilence,* 7.

65. John Duffy, *The Sanitarians: A History of American Public Health* (Urbana: University of Illinois, 1990), 8–33; 41.

66. Martin Melosi, *The Sanitary City: Urban Infrastructure in America from Colonial Times to Present* (Baltimore, Md.: Johns Hopkins University Press, 2000), 30–31.

67. Sam Bass Warner, *The Private City: Philadelphia in Three Periods of Its Growth* (Philadelphia: University of Pennsylvania Press, 1987), 104–5.

68. Melosi, *Sanitary City,* 31.

69. Ibid., 29.

70. Elizabeth Drinker, diary entry for September 16, 1805, *The Diary of Elizabeth Drinker: The Life Cycle of an Eighteenth-Century Woman,* ed. Elaine Forman Crane (Boston: Northeastern University Press, 1994), 275.

71. K. David Patterson, "Yellow Fever Epidemics and Mortality in the United States, 1693–1905," *Social Science and Medicine* 34, no. 8 (Apr. 1992): 858.

72. Similarly, the construction of a waterworks system may have contributed to the decline of yellow fever in New York City. Like Philadelphia, New York had experienced several visitations of yellow fever in the 1790s and early 1800s. In 1798 alone, yellow fever claimed the lives of more than 2,000 New Yorkers. In response, state officials authorized the creation of a private water company, the Manhattan Company. Engineers working for the Manhattan Company quickly devised a way of bringing water from the Bronx River into the city via a network of wooden aqueducts. The New York waterworks began operation in November 1799. During its brief existence, the Manhattan Company never officially supplied more than one-third of the city's population with water, and unlike the Philadelphia waterworks,

the poor could not get water for free. But the city's residents did obtain free water from other sources. Because subscriptions to the Manhattan Company placed no limit on how much water a customer could access, citizens generously gave water to those without subscriptions. Moreover, the company gave free water to the ships on the waterfront, and shopkeepers gave water to their customers. Ready access to fresh water undoubtedly obviated the need for water barrels and other standing pools of water. The concomitant destruction of *A. aegypti* breeding grounds reduced the likelihood of yellow fever epidemics. After the waterworks opened, New York suffered only one serious epidemic, when yellow fever killed about 600 people in 1803. See Melosi, *Sanitary City*, 35; and Nelson Manfred Blake, *Water for the Cities: A History of the Urban Supply Problem in the United States* (Syracuse, N.Y.: Syracuse University Press, 1956), 55–62.

73. See, for example, Gordon S. Brown, *Toussaint's Clause: The Founding Fathers and the Haitian Revolution* (Jackson: University of Mississippi Press, 2005), 99–105; Philip Gould, *Barbaric Traffic: Commerce and Antislavery in the Eighteenth-Century Atlantic World* (Cambridge, Mass.: Harvard University Press, 2003), 155–89.

4. Bone Boilers: Nineteenth-Century Green Businessmen?

My thanks go to Adam Levine for comments on an earlier version of this chapter. Panel participants at the American Society for Environmental History, held in Houston in 2005, as well as Christine Meisner Rosen, Thomas Heinrich, and Pierre Desrochers, all offered helpful insights. I thank also the Beckman Center for the History of Chemistry at the Chemical Heritage Foundation and the Program in Early American Economy and Society at the Library Company of Philadelphia for fellowship support.

1. Deposition (or affidavit?) of Charles Cumming, June 23, 1853, in *Mary Ann B. Smith and Virginia Smith v. Charles Cumming* (hereinafter *Smith v. Cumming*), March Term 1851, no. 14, Court of Common Pleas, Proceedings in Equity, Philadelphia County, RG 20.19, Philadelphia City Archives and Records, (hereinafter abbreviated as PCAR). Most of the information here regarding Cumming's business is drawn from the case record; related court materials and various other business and legal materials that provide background on his business are cited specifically. While both "Cumming" and "Cummings" appear in records, I spell the name as "Cumming" throughout because he himself signed documents that way.

2. George Ord to Charles Waterton, September 23, 1848, George Ord Papers, American Philosophical Society, Philadelphia. Ord was condemning soap boilers and alkali manufacturers, and he put them all in the same category.

3. Joel A. Tarr, *The Search for the Ultimate Sink: Urban Pollution in Historical Perspective* (Akron, Ohio: University of Akron Press, 1996); Clay McShane and Joel A. Tarr, *The Horse in the City: Living Machines in the Nineteenth Century* (Baltimore, Md.: Johns Hopkins University Press, 2007); Martin Melosi, *Garbage in the Cities: Refuse, Reform, and the Environment* (College Station: Texas A&M University Press, 1981).

4. The miasma theory was not without its variations as well as outright critics.

And although John Snow put a significant hole in the theory with research on cholera victims in London, the miasmatic explanation was widely endorsed for many
decades by physicians and the general public. See John B. Osborne, "The Lancaster
County Cholera Epidemic of 1854 and the Challenge to the Miasma Theory of Disease," *Pennsylvania Magazine of History and Biography* 133, no. 1 (Jan. 2009): 5–28;
Charles E. Rosenberg, *The Cholera Years: The United States in 1832, 1849, and 1866*
(Chicago: University of Chicago Press, 1962).

5. Christine Meisner Rosen, "'Knowing' Industrial Pollution: Nuisance Law and
the Power of Tradition in a Time of Rapid Economic Change, 1840–1864," *Environmental History* 8 (Oct. 2003): 563–95.

6. For example, a commentator distinguished the "disposition of the carcasses"
of dairy cows as "another and distinct branch of business," adding, "[f]ormerly they
passed into the hands of the . . . bone boilers, but now they are transported across
the river [to New Jersey]. Their skins are then made into leather, their feet, oil, and
the little fat on the bones, into soap" ("New York Milk," *Valley Farmer,* Nov. 1, 1852,
384, quoting the *New York Journal of Commerce*).

7. On the legal doctrine "sic utere tuo ut alienum non laedas," see Rosen, "'Knowing,'" 567–68; William J. Novak, *The People's Welfare: Law and Regulation in Nineteenth-Century America* (Chapel Hill: University of North Carolina Press, 1996).
Smith v. Cummings, in A. V. Parsons, *Select Cases in Equity and at Law, argued and
determined in the Court of Common Pleas, First Judicial Circuit of Pennsylvania, from
1842 to 1851,* vol. 2 (Philadelphia, 1853), 92–103. The opinion of the court was handed
down on July 12, 1851.

8. Examining technical literature and trade periodicals from the late nineteenth
and twentieth centuries, Pierre Desrochers ("How Did the Invisible Hand Handle
Industrial Waste? By-product Development before the Modern Environmental Era,"
Enterprise and Society 8 [June 2007]: 348–74) finds that many Americans and Europeans recognized the value of residual chemical and solid substances generated in
manufacturing processes. In various industries, such as animal slaughtering, meat
processing, tanning, lumber milling, gas production, and soap making, manufacturers turned residuals into usable inputs within the same or related industries (357).
Technical writers described existing and evolving practices and also advocated for
even greater exploitation of "waste" in creative, efficient, and cost-effective ways.
"By-product use," Desrochers argues, "has always been a prominent feature of the
market system" and was encouraged by competitive pressures, cost considerations,
property rights, and the search for greater profits and efficiency (349). Christine
Rosen, in contrast, finds that litigation and regulation or threats of regulation were
the principal factors behind innovation in pollution reduction. Rosen examines
the meatpacking industry in New York and Chicago in the late nineteenth century,
chronicling ways that health and urban reformers pushed for changes to resolve the
stench, water, and solid waste pollution problems caused by animal processing. City
public health authorities advocated that centralized abattoirs be situated in less
populated neighborhoods. Large meatpacking houses initially resisted; only when
authorities flexed municipal regulatory and police powers, or when various parties
sued, did slaughtering and rendering businesses eventually recognize advantages

of concentrating their slaughtering operations in designated districts of cities. Butchers resisted, however, for they were "deeply conservative ... and unwilling ... to adopt new ways of doing business, including ones that would prove profitable by virtue of how they increased the efficiency of their operations" (Christine Meisner Rosen, "The Role of Pollution Regulation and Litigation in the Development of the U.S. Meatpacking Industry, 1865–1880," *Enterprise and Society* 8 [June 2007]: 297–347, quotation at 306).

9. Michal McMahon, "'Publick Service' versus 'Mans Properties': Dock Creek and the Origins of Urban Technology in Eighteenth-Century Philadelphia," chapter 5 of the present volume; McMahon, "'Small Matters': Benjamin Franklin, Philadelphia, and the 'Progress of Cities,'" *Pennsylvania Magazine of History and Biography* 116, no. 2 (Apr. 1992): 157–82; McShane and Tarr, *Horse in the City,* 155. In New York City, the Collect Pond was used as a dumping ground for slaughterhouse, tannery, and other waste until it was filled circa 1811; see http://www.nycgovparks.org/sub_your_park/historical_signs/hs_historical_sign.php?id=11238 (accessed Dec. 16, 2008).

10. McShane and Tarr, *Horse in the City,* 27–31.

11. Glue factories prospered in Philadelphia and New York City, two cities that emerged as centers of the leather trades. In New York City, the entrepreneur Peter Cooper, who later engaged in iron production and educational philanthropy, made a substantial fortune manufacturing glue beginning in 1827. Baeder, Adamson and Company established its glue-making firm in Philadelphia in 1828. Baeder, Adamson (variously Baeder, Adamson and Delaney) successfully diversified into sandpaper production (an item that required large quantities of sizing, or glue) and grew to be one of its largest manufacturers by the 1870s. In New York as well, carcass rendering on a large and often profitable scale emerged in the 1840s, frequently drawing the complaints of urban residents (Rosen, "'Knowing,'" 16).

12. Ann Norton Greene, *Horses at Work: Harnessing Power in Industrial America* (Cambridge, Mass.: Harvard University Press, 2008), esp. chapter 5; McShane and Tarr, *Horse in the City,* 36, 59–60.

13. Greene, *Horses at Work*; McShane and Tarr, *Horse in the City.*

14. J. Thomas Scharf and Thompson Westcott, *History of Philadelphia, 1609–1884,* 3 vols. (Philadelphia, 1884), 3:1762, using the population figures for the "city and suburbs."

15. See also Roger Horowitz, *Putting Meat on the American Table: Taste, Technology, Transformation* (Baltimore, Md.: Johns Hopkins University Press, 2006), chap. 2; Roger Horowitz, Jeffrey M. Pilcher, and Sydney Watts, "Meat for the Multitudes: Market Culture in Paris, New York City, and Mexico City over the Long Nineteenth Century," *American Historical Review* 109 (Oct. 2004): 1055–83.

16. Even as late as 1886 it was possible for those who ran roadside inns to do a profitable trade catering to cattle dealers who collected cattle from nearby farms; see *Gold v. City of Philadelphia*, 19 *Weekly Notes of Cases,* Sup. Ct. of Penna., 1887, 135–40.

17. Deposition of Jacob Knorr, [1859], no. 9, *Robt. Neely v. Stewart McClurg,* CP Equity, Box 1, ca. 1853+, Chester County Archives.

18. I. Smith Homans and I. Smith Homans Jr., *A Cyclopedia of Commerce and Commercial Navigation,* 2d ed. (New York, 1859), 1523; Edwin T. Freedley, *Philadelphia and Its Manufactures . . . in 1857* (Philadelphia, 1859), 65. Freedley suggests that in 1857 Philadelphians "consumed, among other things, 60,425 beeves, 11,930 cows, 100,479 swine, 303,900 sheep, *exclusive of meat brought in market wagons,*" suggesting that there was not much difference by 1857 between the number of cattle brought to Philadelphia's market and the number sold there.

19. Affidavit of Joseph J. Martin, in *The Philadelphia Stock Yards and Abattoir: The Testimony in Favor of their Location on the Schuylkill River above Market Street* (Philadelphia, 1875), 122, archived at the Library Company of Philadelphia.

20. The daily average cannot account for the seasonal variations in mortality among horses. Deaths of urban horses spiked in March and October. See McShane and Tarr, *Horse in the City,* 150.

21. Return of Charles Cumming, District of Penn, Philadelphia County, Pennsylvania, Manuscript Schedules, U.S. Census of Manufactures, 1850. Henry Gerker and Bodine, Baeder and Company, both in the seventh ward, Kensington, were the largest glue manufacturers in Philadelphia County (as measured by capital invested, value of products made, and number of employees). Unfortunately, the 1850 U.S. Census of Manufactures captured neither the plant from which Cumming was moving nor the operation near Kenderton, which he had not yet begun. For a graphic showing the glue works, see "[Charles Cummings Steam Glue Works,] Philadelphia, 1847," Print Department, Library Company of Philadelphia.

22. After midcentury much of the hair was imported from South American countries and presumably "cut from the animals while alive," which were "then let run" until they grew "another crop" (Horace Greeley et al., *The Great Industries of the United States* [Hartford, Conn., 1871 (1872 on title page)], 211–12, quotation at 212).

23. Freedley, *Philadelphia and Its Manufactures,* 218, 377; "Science Familiarly Illustrated: What Old Leather and Bones Are Good For," *Scientific American,* September 28, 1867, 167.

24. Greeley et al., *Great Industries,* 212.

25. Freedley, *Philadelphia and Its Manufactures,* 389–94; "Science Familiarly Illustrated," 167.

26. Freedley, *Philadelphia and Its Manufactures,* 144–46; "Working Farmer: Ground Bones," *New York Evangelist,* September 29, 1859.

27. See especially Bill for Injunction, March 17, 1851, *Smith v. Cumming*; Mary Ann B. Smith, Amended Bill, July 22, 1851, *Smith v. Cumming.*

28. Nicholas B. Wainwright, ed., *A Philadelphia Perspective: The Diary of Sidney George Fisher Covering the Years 1834–1871* (Philadelphia: Historical Society of Pennsylvania, 1967), 228–30. In 1851 the Kenderton neighborhood was located approximately between today's Seventeenth and Twentieth streets and Ontario and Pacific streets.

29. "Pennsylvania," vol. 1, p. 132, Feb. 22, 1850, manuscript, R. G. Dun and Co. Collection, Baker Library Historical Collections, Harvard Business School.

30. Answer of Charles Cumming to the Bill of Complaint [June 1851?], *Smith v. Cumming*; Bill of Indictment, No. 165, Nov. Sessions 1846, Court of Quarter Sessions,

Box A-6464, PCAR. (The bill is erroneously filed in the bills for the September sessions.)

31. *Smith v. Cummings*, in Parsons, *Select Cases*, 2:92.

32. Ibid., 2:101 (quoting Judge Parsons) and 102 (Judge Parsons quoting the answer of the defendant).

33. Ibid., quoting Judge Parsons. Parsons further remarked, "Numerous indictments, within the last few years, have been tried in the Court of Quarter Sessions of this county, for nuisances such as this is disclosed to be by the affidavits . . . ; and every Judge has ruled that the carrying on the business of '*bone boiling*' in a thickly populated part of the city or districts, was a nuisance *per se*" (101). The records of the Court of Quarter Sessions between December 1838 (when the series begins) and Parson's verdict of July 1851 reveal a total of five cases against bone boiling establishments, three of which named the same defendant. Cumming was found not guilty, the recidivist bone boiler was found guilty in two instances, and the disposition of the fifth case is unclear. (The fifth case involved an establishment that was not located in a populous area. A civil case for an injunction was subsequently filed in the Court of Common Pleas.) Parsons seems to have based his statement on an impression not supported by the facts. Most bills of indictment for this period survive, but they do not show that "every Judge" declared bone boiling in a populous neighborhood "a nuisance *per se*" (see Bills of Indictment, Court of Quarter Sessions, Philadelphia County); for the fifth case, see *Wickersham v. Woods*, Dec. Term 1853, no. 1, Court of Common Pleas, Proceedings in Equity, Philadelphia County.

34. Affidavit of William Warner, June 14, 1853, *Smith v. Cumming*; Equity Docket, March 1848 to June 1851, 120, PCCCP, RG 20.5, PCAR.

35. Answer of Charles Cumming [n.d.], and report of Peter Hay, July 12, 1852, in *Smith v. Cumming*; McShane and Tarr, *Horse in the City*, 28.

36. Affidavit of James R. White, May 5, 1852, *Smith v. Cumming*.

37. Undated entry [1852 or 1853] in the manuscript version of *Selections from the diary and correspondence of Joseph S. Elkinton, 1830–1905* (Philadelphia: [Press of the Leeds and Biddle Co.], 1913), Elkinton Family Papers, RG 5, Friends Historical Collection, Swarthmore College (this discussion of Wilson is omitted from the printed diary); E. Wilson, "Improvement in Methods of Rendering Lard," patented October 9, 1844, no. 3,784, U.S. Patent Office, available at http://patft.uspto.gov/net acgi/nph-Parser?Sect1=PTO2&Sect2=HITOFF&p=1&u=%2Fnetahtml%2FPTO%2F search-adv.htm&r=1&f=G&l=50&d=PALL&S1=00003784&OS=PN/00003784&RS= PN/00003784 (accessed June 25, 2009); Steve C. Gordon, "From Slaughterhouse to Soap-Boiler: Cincinnati's Meat Packing Industry, Changing Technologies, and the Rise of Mass Production, 1825–1870," *Industrial Archeology* 16, no. 1 (1990): 55–67.

38. Report of Peter Hay, July 12, 1852, *Smith v. Cumming*.

39. Cross-examination of James R. White, May 14, 1852, *Smith v. Cumming*; report of Peter Hay, July 12, 1852, *Smith v. Cumming*; affidavit of William A. Maupay, June 15, 1853, *Smith v. Cumming*; *Germantown Telegraph*, June 22, 1853.

40. Answer of Charles Cumming [n.d., June 1851?]. On the liberal economy, see Sean Wilentz, *Chants Democratic: New York City and the Rise of the American Working Class, 1788–1850* (New York: Oxford University Press, 1984).

41. Answer of Charles Cumming [n.d., June 1851?].

42. Ibid.; see also answer of Cumming to proposed amendments of original bill, July 25, 1851, *Smith v. Cumming.*

43. "Pennsylvania," vol. 1, p. 132, April 25, 1858, and Aug. 2, 1859, R. G. Dun Collection; *M'Elroy's City Directory,* 1858, 1861, and 1866; testimony of Charles Cumming and arguments by Brewster and Jones, "Notes of Testimony (taken on behalf of the City) in the matter of claims of Evan Prowattain and John McCrystal, for damages on the Wissahickon Creek, known as the 'Old Log Cabin,'" April–[Nov.], 1871, Fairmount Park Commission, Park Solicitor, files, 1871–1935, box A-978, PCAR.

5. "Publick Service" versus "Mans Properties": Dock Creek and the Origins of Urban Technology in Eighteenth-Century Philadelphia

1. See John Teal and Mildred Teal, *Life and Death of the Salt Marsh* (Boston: Little, Brown, 1969), esp. 19, for the utilities of the salt marsh. On the structures at the mouth of the cove, see Barbara Liggett, "Report on the Study of the Dock: Results of Archeological Examination, Philadelphia, Pennsylvania, 1975," draft MS, on deposit at the library of the American Philosophical Society, Philadelphia.

2. The fullest account of the Dock is Liggett, "Report on the Study of the Dock." Earlier accounts include John F. Watson, *Annals of Philadelphia, and Pennsylvania, in the Olden Time . . .* (1830), rev. Willis P. Hazard, 3 vols. (Philadelphia, 1909), 1:336–49; J. Thomas Scharf and Thompson Westcott, *History of Philadelphia, 1609–1884,* 3 vols. (Philadelphia, 1884), vol. 1.

3. Gary B. Nash, "City Planning and Political Tension in the Seventeenth Century: The Case of Philadelphia," *Proceedings of the American Philosophical Society* 112, no. 1 (Feb. 15, 1968): 60–64; Provincial Council of Pennsylvania, *Minutes of the Provincial Council of Pennsylvania,* October 18, 1700, vol. 2 of Samuel Hazard, John Blair Linn, William Henry Egle, George Edward Reed, Thomas Lynch Montgomery, Gertrude MacKinney, and Charles Francis Hoban, eds., *Pennsylvania Archives,* ser. 8, 8 vols. (Philadelphia: J. Severns, 1852), 10 (hereinafter cited as *Pennsylvania Archives*).

4. James T. Mitchell and Henry Flanders, comps., *Statutes at Large of Pennsylvania, from 1682 to 1801,* 16 vols. (Harrisburg, Pa.: C. M. Busch, 1896–1911), 11:298 (hereinafter cited as *Statutes at Large*).

5. For population data, see James T. Lemon, "Urbanization and Development of Eighteenth-Century Southeastern Pennsylvania and Adjacent Delaware," *William and Mary Quarterly,* 3d ser., 24 (1967): 502; Gary B. Nash, *The Urban Crucible: Social Change, Political Consciousness, and the Origins of the American Revolution* (Cambridge, Mass.: Harvard University Press, 1979), appendix, table 13, 407–8.

6. Richard C. Wade, *The Urban Frontier: The Rise of Western Cities, 1790–1830* (Chicago: University of Chicago Press, 1959), 24, 27–28; Lawrence H. Larsen, *The Urban West at the End of the Frontier* (Lawrence: University Press of Kansas, 1978), 3 (Larsen asserts the general influence of Eastern Seaboard cities on the urban West); John W. Reps, *The Making of Urban America: A History of City Planning in the United States* (Princeton, N.J.: Princeton University Press, 1965), 173–74. See also Henry Wright, "The Sad Story of American Housing," in *Roots of Contemporary American Archi-*

tecture: A Series of Thirty-seven Essays Dating from the Mid-Cenury to the Present, ed. Lewis Mumford (1952; New York: Dover, 1972), 326–27. Wade, Reps, and Larsen found in Philadelphia's grid a model for towns and cities along the moving frontier. Versions of the town plan—a one-by-two-mile rectangle broken by five squares, one located in the center and one in each of the quadrants—appeared in cities including Pittsburgh, Cincinnati, Lexington, Louisville, Kansas City, and Denver. The gridiron's influence extended, by Reps's account (125), even to the small, crossroads towns containing a central square intersected by a small grid of streets. On Philadelphia's wider influence, see Wade, *Urban Frontier,* 314, 316, and esp. 318–19.

7. For the waterworks, see Nelson M. Blake, *Water for the Cities: A History of the Urban Water Supply Problem in the United States* (Syracuse, N.Y.: Syracuse University Press, 1956), 18–43; for an account of an earlier centralized system, see Brooke Hindle, *The Meaning of the Bethlehem Waterworks* (Bethlehem, Pa.: Historic Bethlehem, 1977).

8. See Wade, *Urban Frontier*; Larsen, *Urban West*; Eric H. Monkkonen, *America Becomes Urban: The Development of U.S. Cities and Towns, 1780–1980* (Berkeley: University of California Press, 1988); and Blake, *Water for the Cities.*

9. In his early assessment of the field of environmental history, Roderick Nash explained that technology had "placed [the] tools in man's hands that allow him to sculpt the physical world"; see Nash, "The State of Environmental History," in *The State of American History,* ed. Herbert J. Bass (Chicago: Quadrangle, 1970), 250. Donald Worster places technology and its interaction with the environment alongside nature and ideology as one of the three central facets of the new environmental history; see Worster, "Transformations of the Earth: Toward an Agroecological Perspective in History," *Journal of American History* 76, no. 4 (Mar. 1990): 1090–91.

10. The historiography of city growth is summarized in Josef W. Konvitz, Mark H. Rose, and Joel A. Tarr, "Technology and the City," *Technology and Culture* 31 (1990): 284–94. For examples, see the special issues of the *Journal of Urban History* on technology and the city: 5, no. 3 (May 1979), and 14, no. 1 (Nov. 1987).

Michael Zuckerman has asserted that while New Englanders and Southerners were claiming primacy for their peculiar ideologies and principles, "men of the middle states were without incentives to such local consciousness. They simply held hegemony. Their principles and practices were increasingly inseparable from those of the emerging and expanding nation" ("Introduction: Puritans, Cavaliers, and the Motley Middle," in *Friends and Neighbors: Group Life in America's First Plural Society,* ed. Zuckerman [Philadelphia: Temple University Press, 1982], 5). For a synthesis of this literature, see Jack P. Greene, *Pursuits of Happiness: The Social Development of Early Modern British Colonies and the Formation of American Culture* (Chapel Hill: University of North Carolina Press, 1988).

11. Watson, *Annals,* 1:339.

12. Ibid.; *Minutes of the Common Council of the City of Philadelphia, 1704–1776* (Philadelphia, 1847), 412, 414, 422, 465, 500 (hereinafter cited as *MCC*); Judith Marion Diamondstone, "The Philadelphia Corporation, 1701–1776" (PhD diss., University of Pennsylvania, 1969), 108–9; Ellis Paxson Oberholtzer, *Philadelphia, a History of the City and Its People: A Record of 225 Years,* 4 vols. (Philadelphia: J. S. Clarke [1912]), 1:144.

13. Watson, *Annals*, 1:339; Richard Harrison Shryock, *Medicine and Society in America: 1660–1860* (Ithaca, N.Y.: Cornell University Press, 1960), 86–87, 91.

14. The following discussion of tanning relies chiefly on Dorothy Hartley, *Lost Country Life* (New York: Pantheon, 1979), 107, 201, 254–55; Peter C. Welsh, *Tanning in the United States to 1850: A Brief History* (Washington, D.C.: Museum of History and Technology, Smithsonian Institution, 1964); Jared van Wagenen Jr., *The Golden Age of Homespun* (Ithaca, N.Y.: Cornell University Press, 1953), 182–89.

15. Hartley, *Lost Country Life*, 254.

16. Samuel Hazard et al., *Pennsylvania Archives*, 3:2487.

17. Carl Bridenbaugh, *Cities in the Wilderness: The First Century of Urban Life in America, 1625–1742*, 2d ed. (New York: Knopf, 1959), 318.

18. *Pennsylvania Archives*, 3:2490.

19. *American Weekly Mercury*, September 6–13, 1739; *Pennsylvania Archives*, 3:2503.

20. Ernest S. Griffith, *History of American City Government*, vol. 1, *The Colonial Period*, vol. 1 (New York: Oxford University Press, 1938), 24; *Pennsylvania Archives*, 3:2501, 2503–4.

21. Morris's father-in-law, John Cadwallader, served on the Common Council in 1718 and in the Provincial Assembly between 1729 and 1734. After midcentury, Morris too served on the council. See Diamondstone, "Philadelphia Corporation," 298, 322, 365; Watson, *Annals*, 1:346.

22. The elder Hudson was sixty-seven in 1739. A wealthy man with property in England and a large slaveholder, Hudson was named a councilman in the original city charter of 1701; in 1705 he served as an alderman—one of a select group chosen from the councilors—and became mayor in 1725. Hudson's wife was a daughter of Samuel Richardson, a resident of the Dock Creek neighborhood and the founder of one of the more considerable Quaker families in the city. See Diamondstone, "Philadelphia Corporation," 298, 322, 365; Watson, *Annals*, 1:346. For the expansion of his tanyards above Third, see the unpublished map by Anna Coxe Toogood, archived at Independence National Historical Park, Philadelphia.

23. The debate appeared in 1739 in the *Mercury*, August 9–16 and September 6–13 and in a "postscript" dated September 13, as well as in the *Pennsylvania Gazette*, August 23–30. On "autumnal fever," see Martin S. Pernick, "Politics, Parties, and Pestilence: Epidemic Yellow Fever in Philadelphia and the Rise of the First Party System," in *Sickness and Health in America: Readings in the History of Medicine and Public Health*, ed. Judith Walzer Leavitt and Ronald L. Numbers (Madison: University of Wisconsin Press, 1985), 356.

24. For a fuller discussion of Franklin's provincial career and public philosophy, see A. Michal McMahon, "'Small Matters': Benjamin Franklin, Philadelphia, and the 'Progress of Cities,'" *Pennsylvania Magazine of History and Biography* 116, no. 2 (Apr. 1992): 157–82.

25. *American Weekly Mercury*, August 9–16, 1739.

26. Ibid.

27. Ibid.

28. Ibid.

29. Ibid., September 6–13, 1739; *Pennsylvania Gazette,* August 23–30, 1739. The charter is reprinted in *Ordinances of the Corporation of, and Acts of Assembly Relating to, the City of Philadelphia* (Philadelphia, 1851). See Diamondstone, "Philadelphia Corporation," 71; and Judith M. Diamondstone, "Philadelphia's Municipal Corporation, 1701–1776," *Pennsylvania Magazine of History and Biography* 90, no. 2 (Apr. 1966): 183–201.

30. *Pennsylvania Gazette,* August 23–30, 1739.

31. *American Weekly Mercury,* September 13, 1739; *Pennsylvania Gazette,* August 23–30, 1739.

32. The view that Sam Bass Warner Jr. asserted in his study of the growth of Philadelphia after the Revolution, *The Private City: Philadelphia in Three Periods of Its Growth* (Philadelphia: University of Pennsylvania Press, 1968), namely, that privatism existed "already by the time of the Revolution" (3), is amply supported in the specialized literature on Philadelphia. Warner errs, however, when he argues that, until the nineteenth century, "no major conflict [existed] between private interest . . . and the public welfare" (4). See Nash, "City Planning," 54–73; Gary B. Nash, *Quakers and Politics: Pennsylvania, 1681–1726* (Princeton, N.J.: Princeton University Press, 1968); Hannah Benner Roach, "The Planting of Philadelphia: A Seventeenth-Century Real Estate Development," *Pennsylvania Magazine of History and Biography I* 92, no. 1 (Jan. 1968): 3–47, 143–94; and Frederick B. Tolles, *Meeting House and Counting House: The Quaker Merchants of Colonial Philadelphia, 1682–1763* (Chapel Hill: University of North Carolina Press, 1948).

33. See the map entitled "Franklin's Philadelphia, 1723–1776," showing his residences and properties, in Benjamin Franklin, *The Papers of Benjamin Franklin,* ed. Leonard W. Labaree, Whitfield J. Bell, Jr., William Bradford Willcox, Barbara Oberg, and Ellen R. Cohn, 40 vols. (New Haven, Conn.: Harvard University Press, 1960), facing 2:456. Although the evidence supports Franklin's authorship, the *Gazette's* response represented the position of the original petitioners.

34. *American Weekly Mercury,* September 13, 1739.

35. Benjamin Franklin, *A Proposal for Promoting Useful Knowledge among the British Plantations in America* (May 14, 1743), in Franklin, *Papers,* 2:381.

36. *American Weekly Mercury,* August 9–16, 1739.

37. Ibid., September 13, 1739.

38. Francis qtd. in Watson, *Annals,* 1:341; Thompson Westcott, *"A History of Philadelphia . . . to . . . 1854,"* 210. Completed only to 1829, the partial manuscript was printed without pagination and never published. Page references refer to the paginated facsimile version held the library of the American Philosophical Society, Philadelphia.

39. Watson, *Annals,* 1:341; Oberholtzer, *Philadelphia,* 1:144; Westcott, "History of Philadelphia," 210; Scharf and Westcott, *History of Philadelphia,* 1:212.

40. Scharf and Westcott, *History of Philadelphia,* 1:212.

41. Bridenbaugh, *Cities in the Wilderness,* 399; Oberholtzer, *Philadelphia,* 1:144; *MCC,* October 19, 1747, 487–88.

42. Frank Willing Leach Collection, vol. 61, 71, Genealogical Records, Historical Society of Pennsylvania, Philadelphia; C. P. B. Jeffreys, "The Provincial and Revolutionary History of St. Peter's Church, Philadelphia, 1753–1783," *Pennsylvania Maga-*

zine of History and Biography 47, no. 4 (1923): 337; *MCC,* December 10, 1751, 553–54.

43. John W. Jordan, ed., *Colonial and Revolutionary Families of Philadelphia: Genealogical and Personal Memoirs,* vol. 1 (New York: Lewis, 1911), 30–31; Frederick B. Tolles, "George Logan, Agrarian Democrat: A Survey of His Writings," *Pennsylvania Magazine of History and Biography* 75, no. 3 (July 1951): 261–62.

44. Jordan, *Colonial Families,* 235; query, *Pennsylvania Magazine of History and Biography* 1 (1877): 358–59; Anne H. Cresson, "Biographical Sketch of Joseph Fox, Esq., of Philadelphia," *Pennsylvania Magazine of History and Biography* 32 (1908): 178. Of the six appointed members, only Warner failed to sign the report.

45. *MCC,* January 12, 1743, and August 17, 1744.

46. Ibid., January 28, February 14, and October 4, 1743; Jordan, *Colonial Families,* 110–11. The younger Powel omitted the second "l" from his name.

47. *MCC,* February 24, 1748, 494–96.

48. Bridenbaugh, *Cities in the Wilderness,* 171–72, 326.

49. *MCC,* February 24, 1748, 496.

50. *Pennsylvania Archives,* 5:244.

51. *MCC,* February 24, 1748, 495.

52. See Oberholtzer, *Philadelphia,* 1:145; Liggett, "Report on the Dock," 52.

53. *MCC,* January 18, 1748, 491–93, and July 31, 1750, 529–30; *Pennsylvania Archives,* 6:5397; *Statutes at Large,* 7:163–64.

54. Diamondstone, "Philadelphia Corporation," 223–30.

55. *MCC,* February 24, 1747, 496.

56. Watson, *Annals,* 1:341.

57. *Pennsylvania Archives,* 6:5384–85.

58. Ibid., 6:5384.

59. Ibid.

60. Ibid., 6:5397.

61. *Statutes at Large,* 6:238–40.

62. Ibid., 6:409–10 (emphasis added).

63. Watson, *Annals,* 1:347.

64. Charles S. Olton, "Philadelphia's First Environmental Crisis," *Pennsylvania Magazine of History and Biography* 98, no. 1 (Jan. 1974): 90–100, discusses in detail the legislation of the 1760s.

65. *Statutes at Large,* 6:196–214, 7:277–307.

66. Ibid., 7:198–202.

67. Ibid., 7:200–201, 204.

68. Ibid., 7:230–34.

69. Ibid., 6:230–32, 7:295–96, 304.

70. For the repeated use of the term "makeshift engineering" during another environmental crisis in late nineteenth-century Philadelphia, see Michal McMahon, "Makeshift Technology: Water and Politics in Nineteenth-Century Philadelphia," *Environmental Review* 12, no. 4 (Winter 1988): 20–37.

71. *Pennsylvania Archives,* 7:6308–9.

72. Konvitz, Rose, and Tarr, "Technology and the City," 288.

73. Lewis Mumford, *The City in History: Its Origins, Its Transformations, and Its Prospects* (New York: Harcourt, Brace, Jovanovich, 1961), 14, 459.

74. Ibid., 421.

6. Industrial Suburbs: Environmental Liabilities or Assets?

I wish to acknowledge Mark Mattson for designing the map (fig. 6.1) and Jason Martin for assisting with data analysis.

1. Robert Puentes and David Warren, *One-Fifth of America: A Comprehensive Guide to America's First Suburbs* (Washington, D.C.: Brookings Institution Metropolitan Policy Program, February 2006), 1.

2. See Robert Lewis, ed., *Manufacturing Suburbs: Building Work and Home on the Metropolitan Fringe* (Philadelphia: Temple University Press, 2004), chap. 1.

3. See Diane Lindstrom, *Economic Development in the Philadelphia Region, 1810–1850* (New York: Columbia University Press, 1978); P. Scranton, *Proprietary Capitalism: The Textile Manufacture at Philadelphia, 1800–1885* (Philadelphia: Temple University Press, 1983); and P. Scranton and W. Licht, *Work Sights: Industrial Philadelphia, 1890–1950* (Philadelphia: Temple University Press, 1986).

4. Richard Walker and Robert Lewis, "Beyond the Crabgrass Frontier: Industry and the Spread of North American Cities, 1850–1950," in *Manufacturing Suburbs*, ed. R. Lewis, 17.

5. P. Dreier, J. Mollenkopf, and T. Swanstrom, *Place Matters: Metropolitics for the Twenty-First Century* (Lawrence: University Press of Kansas, 2004), 215.

6. See P. Scranton, *The Philadelphia System of Textile Manufacture, 1884–1984* (Philadelphia: Philadelphia College of Textiles and Science, 1984).

7. P. Binzen, *Whitetown USA* (New York: Vintage, 1970), 79, 81.

8. H. Gillette, *Camden after the Fall: Decline and Renewal in a Post-Industrial City* (Philadelphia: University of Pennsylvania Press, 2005), 18, 125.

9. See Cynthia J. Shelton, *The Mills of Manayunk: Industrialization and Social Conflict in the Philadelphia Region, 1787–1837* (Baltimore, Md.: Johns Hopkins University Press, 1986); Scranton, *Proprietary Capitalism,* chap. 4.

10. Peirce Lewis and Ben Marsh, "The Physical and Cultural Landscapes of Central and Eastern PA," in *The Philadelphia Region,* ed. Roman Cybriwsky (Philadelphia: Association of American Geographers, 1979), 1–37.

11. Binzen, *Whitetown USA,* 10.

12. This observation is based on data from the Metropolitan Philadelphia Indicators Project, available at www.temple.edu/mpip/ (accessed Mar. 9, 2012).

13. Hugh Mason, "Early Industrial Geography of the Delaware Valley," in *The Philadelphia Region: Selected Essays and Field Trip Itineraries,* ed. R Cybriwsky (Philadelphia: Association of American Geographers, 1979), 74–80.

14. Graham Romeyn Taylor, *Satellite Cities: A Study of Industrial Suburbs* (New York: D. Appleton, 1915), 6, 1.

15. Ibid., 299, 316.

16. U.S. Department of Commerce, Bureau of the Census, *2010 Census Summary File 1* (Washington, D.C.: Bureau of the Census, 2011), 100-percent data.

17. This observation is based on data available from the Metropolitan Philadelphia Indicators Project at www.temple.edu/mpip/ (accessed Mar. 9, 2012).

18. See the New Kensington Community Development Corporation's website and specifically its riverfront plan at www.nkcdc.org (accessed Mar. 9, 2012).

19. Michael Nutter, qtd. in M. McDonald, "Balancing Boom on Main Street, Parking Woes, Taxes on Rise in Manayunk," *Philadelphia Daily News,* December 18, 1996.

20. G. A. Fisher, "The Gentrification of Manayunk" (master's thesis, University of Pennsylvania, Philadelphia, 2006), 64–65.

21. See the Cooper's Ferry Development Association's website, www.coopersferry.com (accessed Mar. 9, 2012).

22. A. R. Wood, "Razing at Riverwalk Can Begin," *Philadelphia Inquirer,* November 19, 2008.

23. D. Campbell, "Tension over Tax Deals," *Philadelphia Inquirer,* March 10, 2004.

24. J. Q. Sanders, "Reclaiming a Bristol Brownfield for Development," *Philadelphia Inquirer,* October 21, 2000.

25. H. Holcomb, "A Remake in Bristol," *Philadelphia Inquirer,* February 18, 2005.

26. Delaware Valley Regional Planning Commission, *Implementing Transit-Oriented Development,* vol. 2, *Station Area Profiles* (Philadelphia: DVRPC, December 2003).

27. See the Delaware Valley Regional Planning Commission website, www.classictowns.org (accessed Mar. 9, 2012).

28. P. Kerkstra, "The Conshohockens: New Neighborhoods Often Are at Odds with Long-Term Residents," *Philadelphia Inquirer,* November 24, 2003.

29. J. Q. Sanders, "At Heart of Changing Borough, Much Is Same," *Philadelphia Inquirer,* July 12, 2001.

30. Radhika Fox and Miriam Axel-Lute, *To Be Strong Again: Renewing the Promise in Smaller Industrial Cities* (Oakland, Calif.: Policy Link, 2008), available at http://www.policylink.org/atf/cf/%7B97C6D565-BB43-406D-A6D5-ECA3BBF35AF0%7D/ToBeStrongAgain_final.pdf (accessed Mar. 9, 2012).

31. Karen Black, *Effectively Preserving Philadelphia's Workforce Housing Stock* (Philadelphia: Women's Community Revitalization Project, 2009).

7. The Grid versus Nature: The History and Legacy of Topographical Change in Philadelphia

1. A comprehensive (if quaintly written) overview of Philadelphia's historical topography can be found in J. Thomas Scharf and Thompson Westcott, *History of Philadelphia 1609–1884,* 3 vols. (Philadelphia: L. H. Everts, 1884), vol. 1, chap. 1.

2. A discussion of the filling of marshlands and riverfront wetlands, while important to the understanding of Philadelphia's current topography, was omitted from this chapter because of space considerations. A wealth of material documents the city's historic wetlands; perhaps the best graphic depiction is Charles Ellet Jr.'s "Map of the County of Philadelphia from Actual Survey" (Philadelphia, 1843), available at http://www.philageohistory.org/rdic-images/view-image.cfm/ellet (accessed Mar.

12, 2012). Other worthwhile histories that document land making elsewhere include Nancy S. Seashores, *Gaining Ground: A History of Landmaking in Boston* (Cambridge, Mass.: MIT Press, 2003); William A. Newman and Wilfred E. Holton, *Boston's Back Bay: The Story of America's Greatest 19th-Century Landfill Project* (Boston: Northeastern University Press, 2006); Matthew Klingle, *Emerald City: An Environmental History of Seattle* (New Haven, Conn.: Yale University Press, 2007); and Kevin Bone, ed., *The New York Waterfront: Evolution and Building Culture of the Port and Harbor* (New York: Monacelli, 1997).

3. In this chapter, the benchmark for topographical change is the landscape that Penn and his contemporaries found on their arrival in the 1680s. Dutch and Swedish immigrants had settled around Philadelphia about fifty years before Penn, and Indians had lived there for millennia before that, but their effects on the landscape were minor compared to those of efforts undertaken after the founding of Philadelphia.

4. As with many other Indian names transliterated into English characters, Shackaminsing appears on old maps in a number of variations, including Shackhanson, Shackhausing, and Chickhausing. Dock Creek appears on many early maps of Philadelphia, although most show only the lower (probably navigable) reaches closest to the Delaware River. A detailed view of the upper reaches of Dock Creek and other streams draining preconsolidation Philadelphia is shown on a manuscript plan by Reading Howell, "A Ground Plat of the City of Philadelphia," completed in 1809; two copies are known, held by the Philadelphia Department of Streets and the Historical Society of Pennsylvania. For a 1796 map that details both streams and topography, see John Hills, "Plan of the City of Philadelphia and its environs," available at http://www.philageohistory.org/rdic-images/view-image .cfm/237-MP-019 (accessed Mar. 12, 2012).

5. John Fanning Watson, *Annals of Philadelphia and Pennsylvania in the Olden Time,* 3 vols. (Philadelphia: Edwin S. Stuart, 1905), 1:54–55.

6. George S. Webster, chief engineer and surveyor of Philadelphia, qtd. in Andrew Wright Crawford, "Recent City Planning in Philadelphia," *Charities and the Commons* 19 (Feb. 1, 1908): 1537.

7. Scharf and Westcott, *History,* 1:88.

8. Hannah Benner Roach, "The Planting of Philadelphia: A Seventeenth-Century Real Estate Development," *Pennsylvania Magazine of History and Biography I* 92, no. 1 (Jan. 1968): 3–47; Roach, "The Planting of Philadelphia: A Seventeenth-Century Real Estate Development," *Pennsylvania Magazine of History and Biography II* 92, no. 2 (Apr. 1968): 143–94. For a good summary of the arguments against the "green country town" idea and a wider discussion of the grid as an example of the desire for systematizing the world during the Enlightenment, see Dell Upton, *Another City: Urban Life and Urban Spaces in the New American Republic* (New Haven, Conn.: Yale University Press, 2008), chap. 6.

9. Watson, *Annals,* 1:233.

10. Andrew Wright Crawford, *The Development of Park Systems in American Cities,* Publications of the American Academy of Political and Social Science, no. 451 (Philadelphia: Academy of Political and Social Science, n.d.), 18, repr. from *Annals of*

the American Academy of Political and Social Science (Mar. 1905); available at http://www.archive.org/details/developmentofpar00crawrich (accessed Mar. 22, 2012). Crawford and others in the Philadelphia realized the limitations of the grid and devised a number of plans for diagonal streets, parkways, and other embellishments to the city plan in the first decades of the twentieth century; for a variety of political and economic reasons, however, most were never built. For a detailed study of Crawford and several contemporaries and their attempts to remake the city, see Jonathan Farnham, "A Bridge Game: Constructing a Co-operative Commonwealth in Philadelphia, 1900–1926" (PhD diss., Princeton University, 2000). Writes Farnham, "The diagonal was invested with enormous powers as it was promoted as the suture to reintegrate and restore the frayed fabric of the modern metropolis. On the diagonal, planners postulated, oppositions would meet and mingle in a thoroughly modern interchange. On the diagonal, incommensurable differences would run into sameness as goods of all sorts flowed in a frictionless exchange" (6).

11. Andrew Wright Crawford, "The Street: The Basic Factor in the City Plan," *Charities and the Commons* 19 (Feb. 1, 1908): 1497. This effort to commoditize the landscape was by no means limited to Philadelphia; rather, it transformed every town and city and, with the advent of factory farming, could even be said to have changed the face of America's farmland as well. About Seattle's transformation in the late nineteenth and early twentieth centuries, Matthew Klingle writes: "Driven by the imperatives of modernity and the engines of industrial capitalism, European and American invaders [as opposed to American Indians] tried to erase . . . the natural world. Their vision was to improve upon nature, to surmount it, to turn it into property" (*Emerald City,* 5).

12. For examples, see Road Petition Files 47-931 and 47-847, Record Group 21.26, Philadelphia City Archives.

13. Frederick D. Nichols and Ralph E. Griswold, *Thomas Jefferson, Landscape Architect* (Charlottesville, Va.: University Press of Virginia, 1978), 43.

14. Qtd. in Franz K. Winkler, "Mitigating the 'Gridiron' Street Plan," *Architectural Record* 29, no. 5 (May 1911): 379. L'Enfant considered grid street systems "tiresome and insipid" and said such plans could have their source only in "a mean continence of some cool imagination wanting a sense of the really grand and truly beautiful, [which is] only to be met where nature contributes with art and diversifies the objects" (qtd. in J. J. Jusserand, *With Americans of Past and Present Days* [New York: Scribner's, 1916], 168–69).

15. Charles Dickens, *American Notes for General Circulation* (London: Chapman and Hall, 1850), 68.

16. Qtd. in Upton, *Another City,* 119–20.

17. J. Rodman Paul and Andrew Wright Crawford, *Special Report on the City Plan by the City Parks Association of Philadelphia* (Philadelphia: City Parks Association of Philadelphia, 1902), 9.

18. John Hill Martin, *Martin's Bench and Bar of Philadelphia* (Philadelphia: Rees, Welsh, 1883), 142.

19. "Philadelphia City Archives Inventory," unpublished typescript, 231, 247, archived at City Archives reading room (also available in different format at http://

www.phila.gov/phils/Docs/Inventor/graphics/agencies/A090.htm [accessed Mar. 12, 2012]); Martin, *Martin's Bench,* 141; Edward F. Allinson and Boies Penrose, *Philadelphia: 1681–1887,* Johns Hopkins University Studies in Historical and Political Science (Baltimore, Md.: N. Murray, 1887), 32.

20. Allinson and Penrose, *Philadelphia,* 185. While much of the city was gridded out far in advance of development, some parts (including much of Northeast Philadelphia) retained a "rural" designation until the mid-twentieth century; only after World War II did urbanization finally reach these areas.

21. *Common Council Minutes,* June 2, 1794, 53–54, Philadelphia City Archives. The term "water courses" as used here and elsewhere refers to the mode by which the water was drained away from built-up areas, which could be the street gutters themselves, artificial ditches, natural streams, and eventually underground pipes.

22. *Statutes at Large of Pennsylvania,* vol. 12 (Harrisburg, Pa.: Harrisburg Publishing, 1908), 581–82.

23. Board of Surveyors Minutes, March 23, 1863, Philadelphia Department of Streets.

24. Ibid.

25. Watson, *Annals,* 1:233–35. While Watson's information (much of it anecdotal) needs to be viewed with some skepticism, his examples of the effects of street regulation on particular houses are supported by a wealth of visual information. For example, see Robert F. Looney, *Old Philadelphia in Early Photographs 1839–1914* (New York: Dover, 1976), 1, 4, 5, 101.

26. David J. Kennedy Collection, painting and manuscript K:V-36, Historical Society of Pennsylvania.

27. In retrospect, more dangerous than the stink that arose from these ponds were the clouds of mosquitoes that bred there, but the connection between mosquitoes and the spread of yellow fever, which killed thousands of Philadelphians in the eighteenth and nineteenth centuries, had yet to be made.

28. See, among many other examples, Philadelphia Common Council Minutes, January 26, 1803, and October 22, 1805; Philadelphia Board of Health Minutes, May 10, 1826, March 27, 1827, June 28, 1833, and July 19, 1833, both items at Philadelphia City Archives.

29. Jacob Cox Parsons, ed., *Extracts from the Diary of Jacob Hiltzheimer* (Philadelphia, William Fell, 1893), 62, 87. Hiltzheimer served as a Philadelphia city commissioner for three years in the 1780s, and his diary entries provide an enlightening if somewhat cryptic view of the prosecution of late eighteenth-century public works.

30. *City Commissioners' Report to City Councils,* December 31, 1819, 8, and March 6, 1827, 5, Historical Society of Pennsylvania.

31. Arthur H. Blanchard, ed., *American Highway Engineers Handbook* (New York: Wiley, 1919), 437.

32. *City Commissioners' Report,* February 13, 1826, 8, and February 1, 1822, 5, Historical Society of Pennsylvania.

33. *Journal of the Select Council of the City of Philadelphia: beginning Nov. 13, 1856, and ending May 7, 1857* (Philadelphia: Crissy and Markley, 1857), 148–54.

34. Blanchard, *American Highway Engineers,* 431.

35. Clipping dated August 2, 1895, no source noted, David J. Kennedy Collection, box 15, newspaper clipping scrapbook, 3, Historical Society of Pennsylvania.

36. The original work of Kollner, Eckfeldt, and Taylor, as well as black-and-white reproductions of many works by Kennedy and Taylor, can be found at the Free Library of Philadelphia, Print and Picture Collection. Kennedy's original paintings are at the Historical Society of Pennsylvania.

37. Carl Bridenbaugh, *Cities in the Wilderness* (New York: Ronald, 1938), 318; *Report on the Collection and Treatment of the Sewage of the City of Philadelphia* (Philadelphia: Department of Public Works, 1914), 109. Philadelphia now has more than 2,900 miles of sewers.

38. For example, Wyoming Avenue, laid out in the nineteenth century, required three bridges within about 2,000 feet to cross the meanders of Tacony and Frankford creeks. The avenue still crosses Tacony Creek, but an oxbow in Frankford Creek that necessitated two crossings was removed in the late 1940s as part of a flood control project.

39. For a historical study of Dock Creek, see Michal McMahon, "'Publick Service' vs. 'Mans Properties': Dock Creek and the Origins of Urban Technology in Eighteenth-Century Philadelphia," chapter 5 in the present volume.

40. *Annual Report of the Chief Engineer of the Water Department of the City of Philadelphia* (Philadelphia: William F. Geddes, 1867), 62.

41. See n. 6 for more on the Howell plan.

42. *City Commissioners' Report,* December 31, 1819, 4–5, Historical Society of Pennsylvania.

43. By 1840 various maps of Philadelphia, including one produced that year in London by the Society for the Diffusion of Useful Knowledge, were showing no trace of any creeks in the original city. The society's map can be viewed online at http://www.philageohistory.org/rdic-images/view-image.cfm/society-diffusion-phila-1840 (accessed Mar. 12, 2012).

44. Allinson and Penrose, *Philadelphia,* 78.

45. Ibid., 140–41.

46. Samuel H. Kneass, *Report on the sewerage and drainage of the city of Philadelphia made to the Select and Common Councils, May 9, 1853* (Philadelphia: Crissy and Markley, 1853), 5, 15. Kneass elaborated on his advocacy of water closets: "No one accustomed to the use of this comparatively modern improvement would ever consent to a return to the system now in use; it commends itself to favor in so many different ways, both in health and decency, that it is rather astonishing it makes way so slowly in a population so remarkable for general neatness and propriety as that of Philadelphia."

47. Most Philadelphia privy wells were brick-lined pits, dug in the backyard and topped by an outhouse, into which human excreta were deposited. The introduction of water closets using several gallons of water per flush overwhelmed the holding capacity of privies in Philadelphia and elsewhere and was a major factor in the shift to water carriage as the means of waste removal. For an overview, see Joel A. Tarr, "Decisions about Wastewater Technology, 1800–1932," *The Search for the Ultimate Sink* (Akron, Ohio: University of Akron Press, 1996), 111–30.

48. *Journal of the Common Council of the City of Philadelphia for the Year 1866* (Philadelphia: King and Baird, 1867), vol. 2, appendix 15, 19–20,

49. Wrote one historian about the same decision-making process in eighteenth- and nineteenth-century London: "It was a kind of madness, the madness that comes from being under the spell of a Theory. If all smell was disease, if London's health crisis was entirely attributable to contaminated air, then any effort to rid the houses and streets of miasmatic vapors was worth the cost, even if it meant turning the Thames into a river of sewage" (Steven Johnson, *Ghost Map* [New York: Riverhead, 2006], 121).

50. "Battle of the Sewers," *Philadelphia Inquirer,* January 26, 1887.

51. The health implications of sewage pollution of rivers and streams is addressed on a local level by Michael P. McCarthy in *Typhoid and the Politics of Public Health in Nineteenth-Century Philadelphia* (Philadelphia: American Philosophical Society, 1987). For a national overview of water pollution and many other problems, see Martin V. Melosi, *The Sanitary City* (Baltimore, Md.: Johns Hopkins University Press, 2000).

52. It is also true that from the latter part of the nineteenth century through the 1930s, corrupt politicians and their favorite contractors typically raked a measure of graft off the top of any large infrastructure project and often directed these improvements so they would most benefit property owned by themselves or their cronies. While this seems to explain much of the affinity for the grid and the rigidity with which it was applied, research into land ownership and political connections necessary to prove this point falls beyond the scope of this chapter. For more on this subject, see Domenic Vitiello, "Machine Building and City Building: The Planning and Politics of Urban and Industrial Restructuring in Philadelphia, 1891–1928," *Journal of Urban History* 34, no. 3 (Mar. 2008): 399–434; and Peter McCaffery, *When Bosses Ruled Philadelphia* (University Park: Pennsylvania State University Press, 1993).

53. *Appendix to the Journal of the Common Council of the City of Philadelphia for the year 1866* (Philadelphia: King and Baird, 1866), vol. 2, appendix 15, 17–19.

54. Scharf and Westcott, *History,* 1:5–6.

55. On the original plan for Philadelphia, Thomas Holme "drew in only a rough approximation of topography, leaving out such worrisome details as the numerous streams that zigzagged through the area and the marsh banks along the Schuylkill that would impede building of roads or houses immediately adjacent to that river" (Elizabeth Milroy, "'For the like Uses, as the Moore-fields': The Politics of Penn's Squares," *Pennsylvania Magazine of History and Biography* 130, no. 3 [July 2006]: 260). In the first use of the phrase, John L. O'Sullivan wrote in 1845 that it is "our manifest destiny to overspread the continent allotted by Providence for the free development of our yearly millions" (qtd. in Wayne Andrews, ed., *Concise Dictionary of American History* [New York: Scribner's, 1962], 580). Substitute *city* for *continent* and *thousands* for *millions* and this statement seems to reflect the view of Philadelphia city engineers in the second half of the nineteenth century.

56. This atlas and many others can be viewed online at http://www.philageo history.org.

57. A good summary of the history of sewerage in Pittsburgh, which has many

parallels to Philadelphia, can be found in Joel A. Tarr and Terry F. Yosei, "Critical Decisions in Pittsburgh Water and Wastewater Treatment," in *Devastation and Renewal: An Environmental History of Pittsburgh and Its Region,* ed. Joel A. Tarr (Pittsburgh: University of Pittsburgh Press, 2003), 64–88. The unstable ash used to fill the Logan neighborhood was collected and dumped under contract to the city by a local trolley company; see Harold E. Cox, *Utility Cars of Philadelphia 1892–1971* (Forty Fort, Pa.: Harold E. Cox, 1972), 76–79 (also available at http://www.phillyh2o.org/backpages/WingohockingAshCars.htm [accessed Mar. 12, 2012]). Depth of fill in Logan and elsewhere in Philadelphia is detailed in a study made in 2000 by Peter G. Chirico and Jack B. Epstein, *Geographic Information Systems Analysis of Topographic Change in Philadelphia, Pennsylvania, During the Last Century,* U.S. Geological Survey Open-File Report 00-224, digital publication (CD); also available at http://www.phillyh2o.org/backpages/USACE_USGS_SinkingHomesPhiladelphia.htm (accessed Mar. 12, 2012).

58. "Mill Creek's Families Bid Homes Good-By," *Philadelphia Evening Bulletin,* July 21, 1961.

8. Fed by the Adjoining Waters: The Delaware Estuary's Marine Resources and the Shaping of Philadelphia's Metropolitan Orbit

1. William Penn, "A Further Account of the Province of Pennsylvania (1685)," in *Narratives of Early Pennsylvania, West New Jersey and Delaware,* ed. Albert Cook Myers (New York: Scribner's, 1912), 260; William Penn, "Letter to the Society of Free Traders (1683)," in *Narratives of Early Pennsylvania,* ed. Myers, 239–40.

2. Penn, "Letter to the Society," 229.

3. William Penn to the earl of Sutherland, July 28, 1683, qtd. in John F. Watson, *Annals of Philadelphia and Pennsylvania,* vol. 1 (Philadelphia: J. B. Lippincott, 1868), 44–45.

4. Richard S. Dunn, "Penny Wise and Pound Foolish: Penn as a Businessman," in *The World of William Penn,* ed. Richard S. Dunn and Mary Maples Dunn (Philadelphia: University of Pennsylvania Press, 1986), 42–45; John Andrew Gallery, *The Planning of Center City Philadelphia from William Penn to the Present* (Philadelphia: Center for Architecture, 2007), 9; Penn, "Letter to the Society, 226.

5. Watson, *Annals,* 166.

6. Jean Soderlund, ed., *William Penn and the Founding of Pennsylvania, 1680–1684: A Documentary History* (Philadelphia: University of Pennsylvania Press, 1983), 282–83.

7. Gabriel Thomas, "An Historical Description of the Province and Country of West-New-Jersey in America (1698)," in *Narratives of Early Pennsylvania,* ed. Myers, 352.

8. Jeffery M. Dorwart, *Cape May County, New Jersey: The Making of an American Resort Community* (New Brunswick, N.J.: Rutgers University Press, 1992), 13.

9. G. D. Scull, "Biographical Notice of Doctor Daniel Coxe of London," *Pennsylvania Magazine of History and Biography* 7 (1883): 328, qtd. in Dorwart, *Cape May County,* 17.

10. Penn, "Letter to the Society, 229, 240–41; Thomas, "Historical Description," 345–46, 352; Dorwart, *Cape May County,* 12–18.

11. Dorwart, *Cape May County,* 13.

12. Ibid., 17.

13. *Pennsylvania Gazette,* May 17–24, 1739, in *Extracts from American Newspapers, Relating to New Jersey* (hereinafter *American Newspapers*), vol. 1, *1704–1739,* in *Documents Relating to the Colonial History of the State of New Jersey* (hereinafter *New Jersey Colonial Documents*), vol. 11, ed. William Nelson (Paterson, N.J.: Press Printing and Publishing, 1894), 567–68.

14. *Pennsylvania Gazette,* June 10, 1762, in *American Newspapers,* vol. 5, *1762–1765,* in *New Jersey Colonial Documents,* vol. 24, ed. William Nelson (Paterson, N.J.: Call Printing and Publishing, 1902), 43–44; *Pennsylvania Gazette,* June 2, 1748, in *American Newspapers,* vol. 2, *1740–1750,* in *New Jersey Colonial Documents,* vol. 12, ed. William Nelson (Paterson, N.J.: Press Printing and Publishing, 1895), 448; *Pennsylvania Gazette,* February 1, 1759, and February 12, 1761, in *American Newspapers,* vol. 4, *1756–1761,* in *New Jersey Colonial Documents,* vol. 20, ed. William Nelson (Paterson, N.J.: Call Printing and Publishing, 1898), 322, 529–30. For more on the banking meadow or marshland that rims the Delaware Estuary, see Kimberly R. Sebold, *From Marsh to Farm: The Landscape Transformation of Coastal New Jersey* (Washington, D.C.: National Park Service, 1992).

15. *Pennsylvania Gazette,* October 5, 1752, and December 18, 1755, in *American Newspapers,* vol. 3, *1751–1755,* in *New Jersey Colonial Documents,* vol. 19, ed. William Nelson (Paterson, N.J.: Press Printing and Publishing, 1897), 194–95, 567.

16. *Pennsylvania Journal,* May 21, 1767, and *The Pennsylvania Gazette,* October 1, 1767, in *American Newspapers,* vol. 6, *1766–1767,* in *New Jersey Colonial Documents,* vol. 25, ed. William Nelson (Paterson, N.J.: Call Printing and Publishing, 1903), 371–73, 459–60; *Pennsylvania Gazette,* May 2, 1754, and *New York Mercury,* June 16, 1755, in *American Newspapers,* vol. 3, 356–57, 505–6.

17. *Pennsylvania Journal,* March 21, 1765, in *American Newspapers,* vol. 5, 505–6.

18. *Pennsylvania Chronicle,* May 28–June 4, 1770, in *American Newspapers,* vol. 8, *1770–1771,* in *New Jersey Colonial Documents,* vol. 27, ed. William Nelson (Paterson, N.J.: Press Printing and Publishing, 1905), 158–60.

19. *The New York Mercury,* June 16, 1755, in *American Newspapers,* vol. 3, 505; *Pennsylvania Gazette,* October 9, 1766, and October 1, 1767, in *American Newspapers,* vol. 6, 226, 459; *Pennsylvania Gazette,* December 19, 1765, in *American Newspapers,* vol. 5, 689.

20. *Pennsylvania Gazette,* December 14, 1769, in *American Newspapers,* vol. 7, *1768–1769,* in *New Jersey Colonial Documents,* vol. 26, ed. William Nelson (Paterson, N.J.: Call Printing and Publishing, 1904), 583–86.

21. John McPhee, *The Founding Fish* (New York: Farrar, Straus and Giroux, 2002), 152.

22. Carl Raymond Woodward, *Ploughs and Politicks: Charles Read of New Jersey and His Notes on Agriculture* (New Brunswick, N.J.: Rutgers University Press, 1941), 399–403.

23. Robert Adams Jr., "The Oldest Club in America," *Century* 26 (Aug. 1883): 547–50; George Parsons Lathrop, "A Clever Town Built by Quakers," *Harper's Monthly Magazine* 34 (Feb. 1882): 330.

24. Philip Chadwick Foster Smith, *Philadelphia on the River* (Philadelphia: Philadelphia Maritime Museum, 1986), 106–7.

25. Philip English Mackey, ed., *A Gentleman of Much Promise: The Diary of Isaac Mickle, 1837–1845,* vol. 2 (Philadelphia: University of Pennsylvania Press, 1977), 292, 295.

26. Susan A. Popkin and Roger B. Allen, *Gone Fishing: A History of Fishing in River, Bay and Sea* (Philadelphia: Philadelphia Maritime Museum, 1987), 7–11; Adams, "Oldest Club in America," 547–50.

27. McPhee, *Founding Fish,* 173, 175.

28. Laura Spencer Portor, "Shad," *Harper's Monthly Magazine* 143 (July 1921): 256.

29. Bonnie J. McCay, *Oyster Wars and the Public Trust: Property, Law, and Ecology in New Jersey History* (Tucson: University of Arizona Press, 1998), 84–94.

30. Ibid., 84.

31. Gary Kulik, "Dams, Fish, and Farmers: Defense of Public Rights in Eighteenth-Century Rhode Island," in *The Countryside in the Age of Capitalist Transformation: Essays in the Social History of Rural America,* ed. Steven Hahn and Jonathan Prude (Chapel Hill: University of North Carolina Press, 1985), 25–50; Theodore Steinberg, *Nature Incorporated: Industrialization and the Waters of New England* (Amherst: University of Massachusetts Press, 1994), 166–204; John T. Cumbler, *Reasonable Use: The People, the Environment, and the State, New England 1790–1930* (New York: Oxford University Press, 2001), 79–101; Harry L. Watson, "'The Common Rights of Mankind': Subsistence, Shad, and Commerce in the Early Republican South," *Journal of American History* 83 (June 1996): 13–43.

32. Samuel Howell, "Notice of the Shad and Shad Fisheries of the River Delaware," *American Journal of Science and Arts* 32 (July 1837): 139.

33. Ibid., 136.

34. Ibid., 138.

35. Charles H. Stevenson, "The Shad Fisheries of the Atlantic Coast of the United States," in U.S. Commission of Fish and Fisheries, *Report of the Commissioner for the year ending June 30, 1898,* pt. 24 (Washington, D.C.: Government Printing Office, 1899), 220, 234, 236; Walter Sheldon Tower, "The Passing of the Sturgeon: A Case of the Unparalleled Extermination of a Species," *Popular Science Monthly,* October 1908, 367–69; Inga Saffron, *Caviar: The Strange History and Uncertain Future of the World's Most Coveted Delicacy* (New York: Broadway, 2002), 91–105; "Demand for Caviare: American Production Falling Off," *Fishing Gazette* 10 (Dec. 7, 1893): 12. The Sturgeon Fisherman's Protective Society was also known as the Sturgeon Fisherman's Protective Association, and it assisted state fish commissions with propagation efforts; see "Sturgeon Fishing in the Delaware River," *Fishing Gazette* 20 (June 27, 1903): 517.

36. John N. Cobb, "The Sturgeon Fishery of Delaware River and Bay," in U.S. Commission of Fish and Fisheries, *Report of the Commissioner for the year ending June 30, 1899,* pt. 25 (Washington, D.C.: Government Printing Office, 1900), 369–80; "The Sturgeon and Caviar Industry at Penns Grove, New Jersey," *The Way It Used to Be: Salem County Cultural and Heritage Commission* 2 (July 1989): 11–13; Stevenson, "Shad Fisheries," 233; "The Shad Fishing Industry in Salem County," *Salem Standard and Jerseyman,* March 1, 1922; Clem Sutton, interview by author, tape recording, Greenwich, N.J., July 31, 1991.

37. U.S. Commission of Fish and Fisheries, *Report of the Commissioner for 1872*

and 1873, pt. 2 (Washington, D.C.: Government Printing Office, 1874), xvii–xviii, xxxiv–xxxvi, xlviii–lix, lxxxi–lxxxiii.

38. U.S. Commission of Fish and Fisheries, *Report of the Commissioner for 1887,* pt. 25, *Miscellaneous Documents* (Washington, D.C.: Government Printing Office, 1891), xxxv, xlix–li; John J. Brice, "A Manual of Fish-Culture, Based on the Methods of the United States Commission of Fish and Fisheries," in U.S. Commission of Fish and Fisheries, *Report of the Commissioner for the year ending June 30, 1897,* pt. 23 (Washington, D.C.: Government Printing Office, 1898), 142–58; W. deC. Ravenel, "Report on the Propagation and Distribution of Food-Fishes," in U.S. Commission of Fish and Fisheries, *Report of the Commissioner for the year ending June 30, 1896,* pt. 22 (Washington, D.C.: Government Printing Office, 1898), 33–34; idem, *Report of the Commissioner for the year ending June 30, 1902,* pt. 28 (Washington, D.C.: Government Printing Office, 1904), 39–40; idem, *Report of the Commissioner for 1886,* pt. 14 (Washington, D.C.: Government Printing Office, 1889), xlvi; "The United States Fish Commission," *Fishing Gazette* 20 (May 23, 1903): 401–2.

39. Tarleton H. Bean, "Report of the Representative of the United States Fish Commission at the World's Columbian Exposition," in U.S. Commission of Fish and Fisheries, *Report of the Commissioner for the year ending June 30, 1894,* pt. 20 (Washington, D.C.: Government Printing Office, 1896), 177–96; "Sturgeon and Caviar," *Fishing Gazette* 22 (June 15, 1904): 520; "Sturgeon," *Fishing Gazette* 20 (Feb. 21, 1903): 156; "Propagating Sturgeon," *Fishing Gazette* 20 (June 27, 1903): 519; U.S. Commission of Fish and Fisheries, *Report for June 2, 1902,* 17–18; idem, *Report for June 30, 1898,* xxiv.

40. Penn, "Letter to the Society," 229.

41. William Stainsby, *The Oyster Industry of New Jersey* (Trenton, N.J.: The Unionist-Gazette Association, State Printers, 1902), 8–9; Ansley Hall, "Notes on the Oyster Industry of New Jersey," in U.S. Commission of Fish and Fisheries, *Report of the Commissioner for the year ending June 30, 1892,* pt. 27 (Washington, D.C.: Government Printing Office, 1894), 498–99.

42. William Faden, map entitled "Province of New Jersey, Divided into East and West, commonly called, The Jerseys, December 1, 1778," 2d ed. (repr.; Newark, N.J.: Barton, 1976, in the collections of the New Jersey Historical Society). See also charts of the Delaware Bay and Delaware River by James Turner (1756) and Joshua Fisher (ca. 1775) presented in Morrison H. Hecksher and Leslie Greene Bowman, *American Rococo, 1750–1775: Elegance in Ornament* (New York: Harry N. Abrams, 1992), 61–62.

43. Adolph B. Benson, ed., *Peter Kalm's Travels in North America: The English Version of 1770* (New York: Dover, 1964), 90–91.

44. McCay, *Oyster Wars,* 21–29.

45. John F. Watson, *Annals of Philadelphia and Pennsylvania,* vol. 2 (Philadelphia: J. B. Lippincott, 1868), 471.

46. "An Act for the preservation of clams and oysters," in *Acts of the Seventieth Legislature of the State of New Jersey* (Trenton, N.J.: Phillips and Boswell, 1846), 179–85; "An Act to authorize the planting of oysters on lands covered with water, in Maurice River Cove, in the county of Cumberland, and for protecting the same," in *Acts of the Eightieth Legislature of the State of New Jersey* (New Brunswick, N.J.: A. R. Speer, 1856), 364–67.

47. "The Oyster War," *Bridgeton New Jersey Patriot,* May 19, 1871.

48. Ibid.

49. Ibid. Judge Van Syckle allowed Haney and Scattergood a second plea and, maintaining his earlier ruling, provided further elaboration for his decision. This opinion of the Cumberland Circuit Court was reported under "The Oyster Cases," *New Jersey Patriot,* July 28 1871.

50. "An Act for the better enforcement in Maurice River Cove and Delaware Bay, of the act entitled 'An act for the preservation of clams and oysters,'" *Acts of the Ninety-Fifth Legislature of the State of New Jersey* (Morristown, N.J.: Vance and Stiles, 1871), 642–46; "The Oyster War."

51. "The Oyster War."

52. "An Oyster War," *Philadelphia Inquirer,* April 18, 1871.

53. Ibid.

54. "The Oyster Trade, A New Depot—Bridgeton and Port Norris Railroad," *New Jersey Patriot,* August 11, 1871; "An Oyster War"; "The Oyster War"; "Oyster Cases."

55. Hall, "Notes on the Oyster Industry," 504–5.

56. Ernest Ingersoll, *The History and Present Condition of the Oyster Industry: The Tenth Census of the United States* (Trenton, N.J.: John L. Murphy, State Senate Printer, 1882), 154.

57. U.S. Commission of Fish and Fisheries, *Report for June 30, 1902,* 477.

58. Christopher T. Baer, William J. Coxey, and Paul W. Schopp, *The Trail of the Blue Comet: A History of the Jersey Central's New Jersey Southern Division* (Palmyra, N.J.: West Jersey Chapter, National Railway Historical Society, 1994), 154–63; Don Wentzel, "The Bridgeton and Port Norris Railroad," *South Jersey Magazine* 9 (Winter 1980): 6–9; Don Wentzel, "Cumberland and Maurice River Railroad," *South Jersey Magazine* 15 (Summer 1986): 2–6; Donald B. Wentzel, "The Maurice River Branch," in *West Jersey Rails II,* ed. William J. Coxey (Haddonfield, N.J.: West Jersey Chapter, National Railway Historical Society, 1985), 2–5; Hall, "Notes on the Oyster Industry," 506–7.

59. Watson, *Annals,* 1:240.

60. Jackson Lears, *Fables of Abundance: A Cultural History of Advertising in America* (New York: Basic, 1994), 157–58, 171. Images of oyster dining rooms or oyster saloons are presented in Robert E. Looney, *Old Philadelphia in Early Photographs, 1839–1914* (New York: Dover, 1976), 27, 110, 124.

61. Bruce Stutz, *Natural Lives, Modern Times: People and Places of the Delaware River* (New York: Crown, 1992), 79–80, 83–86, 198–201, 306.

62. Kathleen A. Foster, "Eakins and the Academy," in *Thomas Eakins,* exhibition catalog, ed. Darrell Sewell (Philadelphia: Philadelphia Museum of Art, 2001), 95. In curating the 2001 exhibition "Thomas Eakins: American Realist" (Philadelphia Museum of Art, Oct. 4, 2001–Jan. 6, 2002) and editing the accompanying publication *Thomas Eakins,* Darrell Sewell assembled some of the most contemporary thought on Eakins's paintings and photographs of shad fishing at Gloucester, New Jersey, as well as the most comprehensive published catalog of these images

63. W. Douglass Paschall, "The Camera Artist," in *Thomas Eakins,* ed. Sewell, 245.

64. Walt Whitman, *Specimen Days* (Boston: David R. Godine, 1971), 83.

65. Marion Grzeesiak, *A Certain Slant of Light: Marines and Seascapes by George*

Emerick Essig (Oceanville, N.J./Philadelphia: Noyes Museum/Philadelphia Maritime Museum, 1993), 8–17.

66. Dallas Lore Sharp, *The Lay of the Land* (Boston: Houghton Mifflin, 1908), 105–13.

67. Cornelius Weygandt, *Down Jersey: Folks and Their Jobs, Pine Barrens, Salt Marsh and Sea Islands* (New York: D. Appleton-Century, 1940), 68, 71.

68. George Pyle, "Bayside Thirty-Five Years Ago, May 26th, 1920," *The Way It Used to Be: Salem County Cultural and Heritage Commission* 2 (July 1989): 14.

69. Frederick B. Tolles, *Quakers and the Atlantic Culture* (New York: Macmillan, 1960; repr., New York: Octagon, 1980), 117.

9. Metropolitan Philadelphia: Sprawl, Shrinkage, and Sustainability

1. SustainLane, "SustainLane Presents: The 2008 US City Rankings," available at SustainLane, http://www.sustainlane.com/us-city-rankings (accessed Mar. 9, 2012).

2. The most detailed and insightful sprawl rankings, including summaries of other rankings, are provided by Reid Ewing, Rolf Pendall, and Don Chen in *Measuring Sprawl and Its Impact* (Washington, D.C.: Smart Growth America, 2002).

3. William W. Cutler III, "The Persistent Dualism: Centralization and Decentralization in Philadelphia, 1854–1975," in *The Divided Metropolis: Social and Spatial Dimensions of Philadelphia, 1800–1975*, ed. William W. Cutler III and Howard Gillette Jr. (Westport, Conn.: Greenwood, 1980), 251; Eugene P. Ericksen, "Work and Residence in Industrial Philadelphia," *Journal of Urban History* 5 (1979): 150; Peter O. Muller, *Contemporary Suburban America* (Englewood Cliffs, N.J.: Prentice-Hall, 1981), 20, 29–30; Sam Bass Warner, *The Private City: Philadelphia in Three Periods of Its Growth*, 2d ed. (Philadelphia: University of Pennsylvania Press, 1987), 59–61.

4. Jeffrey P. Roberts, "Railroads and the Downtown: Philadelphia, 1830–1900," in *Divided Metropolis*, ed. Cutler and Gillette, 47–50.

5. Carolyn Adams, David Bartelt, David Elesh, and Ira Goldstein, *Restructuring the Philadelphia Region: Metropolitan Divisions and Inequality* (Philadelphia: Temple University Press, 2008), 2–3.

6. Howard Gillette Jr., "The Emergence of the Modern Metropolis: Philadelphia in the Age of Its Consolidation," in *Divided Metropolis*, ed. Cutler and Gillette, 3–25; Kenneth T. Jackson, *Crabgrass Frontier: The Suburbanization of the United States* (New York: Oxford University Press, 1985), 138–56; Muller, *Contemporary Suburban America*, 38.

7. Warner, *Private City*, xv.

8. Steven Conn, *Metropolitan Philadelphia: Living with the Presence of the Past* (Philadelphia: University of Pennsylvania Press, 2006) 10–12, 100, 119, 165–74; David J. Cuff, William J. Young, Edward K. Muller, Wilbur Zelinsky, and Ronald F. Abler, *The Atlas of Pennsylvania* (Philadelphia: Temple University Press, 1989), 92, 96–97; Cutler, "Persistent Dualism," 251; James T. Lemon, *The Best Poor Man's Country* (Baltimore, Md.: Johns Hopkins University Press, 1972); Diane Lindstrom, *Economic Development in the Philadelphia Region, 1810–1850* (New York: Columbia University Press, 1978), 93–151.

9. Muller, *Contemporary Suburban America,* 23–24, 28–29.

10. Peter O. Muller, Kenneth C. Meyer, and Roman A. Cybriwsky, *Metropolitan Philadelphia: A Study of Conflicts and Social Cleavages* (Cambridge, Mass.: Ballinger, 1976), 36–38. See also Jackson, *Crabgrass,* 87–102.

11. Conn, *Metropolitan Philadelphia,* 123.

12. Charles W. Cheape, *Moving the Masses: Urban Public Transit in New York, Boston, and Philadelphia, 1880–1912* (Cambridge, Mass.: Harvard University Press, 1980), 173–74; Robert M. Fogelson, *Downtown: Its Rise and Fall, 1880–1950* (New Haven, Conn.: Yale University Press, 2001), 45; John Henry Hepp IV, *The Middle-Class City: Transforming Space and Time in Philadelphia, 1876–1926* (Philadelphia: University of Pennsylvania Press, 2003), 168–204; Muller, *Contemporary Suburban America,* 30–38.

13. Muller, *Contemporary Suburban America,* 38–58.

14. Conn, *Metropolitan Philadelphia,* 127–29; Cutler, "Persistent Dualism," 270; Donna Rilling, *Making Houses, Crafting Capitalism: Builders in Philadelphia, 1790–1850* (Philadelphia: University of Pennsylvania Press, 2001). Though the home ownership rate declined substantially in Philadelphia during the 1990s, it remains high compared to that of other cities (Brookings Institution, "Philadelphia in Focus: A Profile from Census 2000," available at http://.brookings.edu/reports/2003/11_living cities_philadelphia.aspx [accessed Mar. 9, 2012]).

15. See, for example, Robert M. Fogelson, *Bourgeois Nightmares: Suburbia, 1870–1930* (New Haven, Conn.: Yale University Press, 2005); Dolores Hayden, *Building Suburbia: Green Fields and Urban Growth, 1820–2000* (New York: Pantheon, 2003); Robert J. Mason, *Collaborative Land Use Management: The Quieter Revolution in Place-Based Planning* (Lanham, Md.: Rowman and Littlefield, 2008), 195; Witold Rybczynski, *Last Harvest: From Cornfield to New Town* (New York: Scribner, 2007), 141–46.

16. Muller, *Contemporary Suburban America,* 34–35; Warner, *Private City,* 56, 171–75.

17. Cutler, "Persistent Dualism," 254.

18. Warner, *Private City,* xv.

19. Fogelson, *Downtown,* 218–48; Warner, *Private City,* 192–93.

20. Jackson, *Crabgrass,* 172–89; Muller, *Contemporary Suburban America,* 39.

21. Fogelson, *Downtown,* 251.

22. Cuff et al., *Atlas,* 93.

23. Mason, *Collaborative Land Use,* 22–23.

24. Mark S. Foster, *From Streetcar to Superhighway: American City Planners and Urban Transportation, 1900–1940* (Philadelphia: Temple University Press, 1981), 70–73, 108–9.

25. Cuff et al., *Atlas,* 222; Delaware Valley Regional Planning Commission (DVRPC), *Connections: The Regional Plan for a Sustainable Future* (Philadelphia: Delaware Valley Regional Planning Commission, 2009), 22–29.

26. Philadelphia Parks and Recreation, "The Fairmount Park System: For the Health and Enjoyment of Citizens," Fairmount Park, available at http://www.fair mountpark.org/HistoryIntro.asp (accessed Mar. 9, 2012).

27. DVRPC, *Connections,* 22–29; Mason, *Collaborative Land Use,* 95–102.

28. Mason, *Collaborative Land Use,* 23, 76–79.

29. Jean Gottmann, *Megalopolis: The Urbanized Northeastern Seaboard of the United States* (Cambridge, Mass.: MIT Press, 1961).

30. Conn, *Metropolitan Philadelphia*, 139–49.

31. Ibid., 149–56; Lawrence Squeri, *Better in the Poconos: The Story of Pennsylvania's Vacationland* (University Park: Pennsylvania State University Press, 2002).

32. Tom Infield, "The New Western Pioneers," *Philadelphia Inquirer*, December 11, 2007.

33. Mason, *Collaborative Land Use*, 92–98.

34. Cutler, "The Persistent Dualism," 254.

35. Peter Dreier, John Mollenkopf, and Todd Swanstrom, *Place Matters: Metropolitics for the Twenty-First Century*, 2d ed. (Lawrence: University Press of Kansas, 2004), 103–51; Jackson, *Crabgrass*, 190–218, 248–51; Muller, *Contemporary Suburban America*, 90–91; H. V. Savitch, "Encourage, Then Cope: Washington and the Sprawl Machine," in *Urban Sprawl: Causes, Consequences and Policy Responses*, ed. Gregory D. Squires (Washington, D.C.: Urban Institute Press, 2002), 147–52.

36. Muller, *Contemporary Suburban America*, 52.

37. Conn, *Metropolitan Philadelphia*, 135; Adam Rome, *The Bulldozer in the Countryside* (Cambridge: Cambridge University Press, 2001), 15–43; Rybczynski, *Last Harvest*, 157–66.

38. Muller, Meyer, and Cybriwsky, *Metropolitan Philadelphia*, 39.

39. Conn, *Metropolitan Philadelphia*, 136.

40. Muller, *Contemporary Suburban America*, 49.

41. Adams et al., *Restructuring* 27–29; Muller, Meyer, and Cybriwsky, *Metropolitan Philadelphia*, 49–52; Muller, *Contemporary Suburban America*, 163–66.

42. Cutler, "Persistent Dualism," 258–59; Muller, *Contemporary Suburban America*, 52–61, 124–28.

43. Delaware Valley Regional Planning Commission (DVRPC), *Tracking Progress Toward 2030: Regional Indicators for the DVRPC Long Range Plan* (Philadelphia: Delaware Valley Regional Planning Commission, n.d.), 16.

44. DVRPC, *Tracking Progress*, 16.

45. Metropolitan Philadelphia Indicators Project, *Sprawl: The Dispersal of Employment* (Philadelphia: Metropolitan Philadelphia Indicators Project, 2007), 2.

46. Brookings Institution Center on Urban and Metropolitan Policy, *Back to Prosperity: A Competitive Agenda for Renewing Pennsylvania* (Washington, D.C.: Brookings Institution, 2003), 35; DVRPC, *Tracking Progress*, 27.

47. Conn, *Metropolitan Philadelphia*, 15–16.

48. Adams et al., *Restructuring*, 43, 54–55; Muller, *Contemporary Suburban America*, 110; Rachel Weinberger, "Men, Women, Job Sprawl, and Journey to Work in the Philadelphia Region," *Public Works Management and Policy* 11 (2007): 177.

49. Joel Garreau, *Edge City: Life on the New Frontier* (New York: Doubleday, 1991).

50. Adams et al., *Restructuring*, 43–46; Metropolitan Philadelphia Indicators Project, *Sprawl*, 3.

51. Robert Lang, *Edgeless Cities: Exploring the Elusive Metropolis* (Washington, D.C.: Brookings Institution, 2003), 71.

52. Adams et al., *Restructuring*, 19–26; Nancy Greene Leigh and Sugie Lee, "Phila-

delphia's Space In Between: Inner-Ring Suburban Evolution," *Opolis* 1 (2002): 13–32; Muller, *Contemporary Suburban America,* 66–82; Myron Orfield, *American Metropolitics: The New Suburban Reality* (Washington, D.C.: Brookings Institution, 2002).

53. Cutler, "The Persistent Dualism," 267–68. This is symptomatic of the failures of city-suburban cooperation during that era; see Conrad Weiler, *Philadelphia: Neighborhood, Authority, and the Urban Crisis* (New York: Praeger, 1974), 52–54.

54. Fred P. Bosselmann and David Calllies, *The Quiet Revolution in Land Use Control* (Washington, D.C.: Council on Environmental Quality); Mason, *Collaborative Land Use,* 17–42; Real Estate Research Corporation, *The Costs of Sprawl* (Washington, D.C.: Real Estate Research Corporation, 1974).

55. On regionalism during this period, nationally and locally, see Adams et al., *Restructuring,* 6–7, 37–42; Clarion Associates, *The Costs of Sprawl in Pennsylvania* (Denver, Colo.: Clarion Associates, 2000); Conn, *Metropolitan Philadelphia,* 87–95; Jerome I. Hodos, "Globalization, Regionalism, and Urban Restructuring: The Case of Philadelphia," *Urban Affairs Review* 37 (2002): 358–79; Robert J. Mason, "Confronting Sprawl in Southeastern Pennsylvania: New Options for Communities," *Temple University Environmental Law and Technology Review* 23 (2004): 24; Metropolitan Philadelphia Policy Center, *Flight or Fight: Metropolitan Philadelphia and Its Future* (Philadelphia: Metropolitan Philadelphia Policy Center, 2001); Myron Orfield, *Metropolitics: A Regional Agenda for Community and Stability* (Washington, D.C.: Brookings Institution/Lincoln Institute of Land Policy, 1997); Orfield, *American Metropolitics*; Myron Orfield, "Politics and Regionalism," in *Urban Sprawl,* ed. Squires, 237–54; Neal Peirce, *Citistates: How Urban America Can Prosper in a Competitive World* (Washington, D.C.: Seven Locks, 1993); Jonathan Saidel, Brett H. Mandel, Kevin J. Babyak, and David A. Volpe, *Philadelphia: A New Urban Direction,* 2d ed. (Philadelphia: Saint Joseph's University Press, 2005), 291–308; Peter A. Tatian, G. Thomas Kingsley, and Leah Hendey, *Comparative Analysis of Philadelphia Conditions and Trends* (Washington, D.C.: Urban Institute/Pew Charitable Trusts, 2007); Basil J. Whiting and Tony Proscio, *Philadelphia 2007: Prospects and Challenges* (Philadelphia: Pew Charitable Trusts, 2007).

56. Robert W. Burchell, Naveed A. Shad, David Listokin, Hilary Phillips, Anthony Downs, Samuel Seskin, Judy S. Davis, Terry Moore, David Helton, and Michelle Gall, *The Costs of Sprawl-Revisited* (Washington, D.C.: National Academy Press, 1998); Mason, *Collaborative Land Use,* 174–94.

57. Adams et al., *Restructuring,* 45, 107–8; Mason, "Confronting Sprawl," 23–40; Mason, *Collaborative Land Use,* 187–91; New Jersey State Planning Commission, *Communities of Place: The New Jersey State Development and Redevelopment Plan* (Trenton: New Jersey State Planning Commission, 2001); Stephan Schmidt, "From Pro-Growth to Slow-Growth in Suburban New Jersey," *Journal of Planning Education and Research* 27 (2008): 306–18.

58. DVRPC, *Regional Indicators,* 39; Mason, *Collaborative Land Use,* 199–233; William D. Solecki, Robert J. Mason, and Shannon Martin, "The Geography of Support for Open-Space Initiatives: A Case Study of New Jersey's 1998 Ballot Measure," *Social Science Quarterly* (2004): 624–39; DVRPC, *Connections,* 26–29; Trust for Public Land LandVote Database, "Summary of Measures by State, 1988–

Present," Trust for Public Land, available at https://www.quickbase.com/db/bbqna2qct?a=dbpage&pageID=10 (accessed Mar. 9, 2012).

59. Ewing, Pendall, and Chen, *Measuring Sprawl,* 9–12.

60. Adams et al., *Restructuring,* 26–27; DVRPC, *Regional Indicators,* 28.

61. Adams et al., *Restructuring,* 98–99; Mark Alan Hughes, "Dirt into Dollars: Converting Vacant Land into Valuable Development," Brookings Institution (2000), available at http://.brookings.edu/articles/2000/summer_metropolitanpolicy_hughes .aspx (accessed Mar. 9, 2012); Jennifer Lin, "Blight Unbeaten: Despite Mayor Street's Plan, Thousands of Dangerous or Uncondemned Sites Remain," *Philadelphia Inquirer,* September 3, 2006.

62. Audrey Singer, Dominic Vitiello, Michael Katz, and David Park, *Recent Immigration to Philadelphia: Regional Change in a Re-Emerging Gateway* (Washington, D.C.: Brookings Institution, 2008); Weiler, *Philadelphia,* 26–28.

63. Chester County Planning Commission, *Linking Landscapes: A Plan for the Protected Open Space Network in Chester County, PA* (West Chester, Pa.: Chester County, 2002); City of Philadelphia, *Greenworks Philadelphia* (Philadelphia: Mayor's Office of Sustainability, 2008); Delaware Valley Regional Planning Commission (DVPRC), *Demographics of Transit Zones* (Philadelphia: Delaware Valley Regional Planning Commission, 2009); Delaware Valley Smart Growth Alliance, "Recognized Projects," Delaware Valley Smart Growth Alliance, available at http://www.delaware valleysmartgrowth.org/projects.htm (accessed Mar. 12, 2012); Montgomery County Greenhouse Gas Reduction Task Force, *Greenprint for Montgomery County: Climate Change Action Plan* (Norristown, Pa.: Montgomery County, 2007).

64. Christopher B. Leinberger, "The Next Slum," *The Atlantic,* March 2008, 70–75.

65. *The Metropolitan Moment* appeared as a twelve-page insert on April 28, 2009, in the *Philadelphia Daily News,* the "Peoples' Paper." It can be viewed online at http://www.philly.com/philly/news/20090428_The_metropolitan_moment.html (accessed Mar. 12, 2012).

66. DVPRC, *Connections,* 9.

67. Ibid., 8; Greenspace Alliance, "Regional Greenspace Priorities of Southeastern Pennsylvania: Executive Summary," Greenspace Alliance, available at http://www.regionalgreenplan.org/execsum.htm (accessed Mar. 12, 2012).

68. Orfield, "Politics and Regionalism."

69. Dreier, Mollenkopf, and Swanstrom, *Place Matters,* 216–309; Jeffrey R. Hening, "Equity and the Future Politics of Growth," in *Urban Sprawl,* ed. Squires, 325–50; Manuel Pastor Jr., Chris Benner, and Martha Matsuoka, *This Could Be the Start of Something Big: How Social Movements for Regional Equity Are Reshaping Metropolitan America* (Ithaca, N.Y.: Cornell University Press, 2009).

10. Restoring Mill Creek: Landscape, Literacy, Environmental History, and City Planning and Design

The original version of this chapter was published in *Landscape Research* (July 2005) and reprinted in *Justice, Power, and the Political Landscape,* ed. Kenneth Olwig and Don Mitchell (London: Routledge, 2009), 107–25, as "Restoring Mill Creek: Landscape Literacy, Environmental Justice, and City Planning and Design." The current

version expands on the history of Mill Creek and includes an update on developments since 2005.

Many debts are incurred during a project of such long duration, and it is impossible to acknowledge them all here. A list of sponsors and participants appears on
the West Philadelphia Landscape Project website, http://www.wplp.net/. The initial support of the J. N. Pew Charitable Trusts from 1987 to 1991 made possible the
foundation from which all later activities grew. Without the support of the Center
for Community Partnerships at the University of Pennsylvania, the work with Sulzberger Middle School would not have been possible; aid ranged from the provision
of vans for ferrying students back and forth to seed grants for curriculum development to support for research assistants. Those interested in learning more about
the center, whose leadership in promoting academically based community service
has received international recognition, should consult its website, http://www
.upenn.edu/ccp/. I am grateful to Kenneth Olwig for editorial suggestions on a previous version and would also like to acknowledge Cynthia Ott, who assembled a rich
archive of historical material, first as a student and then as a research assistant, and
who cowrote a paper that we presented on the Mill Creek Project at the American
Historical Association in 1998.

1. The racial composition of a neighborhood was one of several criteria used
for assessment. For an excellent discussion of research on redlining, both historical
and current, see A. E. Hillier, "Spatial Analysis of Historical Redlining: A Method-
ological Approach," *Journal of Housing Research* 14, no. 1 (2003): 137–67.

2. Landscape is not a mere visible surface, static composition, or passive back-
drop to human theater. Landscape associates a place with all who dwell there, past
and present. The Danish *landskab,* German *Landschaft,* and Old English *landscipe*
combine two roots. In all three, the first means both a place and the people living
there (earth, country, nation). *Skabe* and *schaffen* mean "to shape"; the related noun-
forming suffixes *-skab* and *-schaft,* as in the English *-ship,* indicate association or
partnership (see V. Dahlerup, V. *Ordbog over det danske sprog* [Copenhagen: Nordisk,
1931]; J. Grimm and W. Grimm, *Deutsches Wörterbuch* [Verlag von S. Hirzel, 1885]; and
J. B. Jackson, *Discovering the Vernacular Landscape* [New Haven, Conn.: Yale University Press, 1984]). Still strong in Scandinavian and other Germanic languages, these
original meanings have all but disappeared from English.

3. N. Scull and G. Heap, "A Map of Philadelphia and Parts Adjacent" (1753). Residents' occupations listed in the tax assessor's ledger of 1785 for residents of West
Philadelphia are those one would expect to find in a community of farms and rural
estates: farmers, gardeners, smiths, wheelwrights, millers, weavers.

4. Hexamer, *Hexamer's General Surveys* (Philadelphia: E. Hexamer and Son, 1872–
87).

5. Living in row houses on Lex Street in the blocks north of the home for colored
orphans, for example, were households of white, black, and mulatto families, most
with husband, wife, and children and many with boarders. Some of these residents
were immigrants from Scotland and Ireland, but most were native to Pennsylvania.
The men worked as laborers, drivers, millworkers, and bill posters. Most women

kept house or worked as laundresses. See U.S. Bureau of the Census, *Tenth Census, 1880,* Enumeration District 504 (Washington, D.C.: Government Printing Office, 1883), 20–21.

6. A fire hydrant amid the grove of trees was a clue to the houses that once stood here and to the pavement and pipes that still lay beneath the soil. The natural processes of plant succession that shaped the original forest drove the growth of the grove. The baseball field replaced the grove, but in the fall of 2010 the field was overgrown with weeds, on its way to becoming forest once again.

7. See H. Hillman, "Urban Redevelopment and the Mill Creek Neighborhood: 1930–1975" (unpublished paper, University of Pennsylvania, 1997). These articles were collected and compiled by Heather Hillman for my seminar "The Power of Place: Water, Schools, and History."

8. "Heir house" is a vernacular term explained to me by Frances Walker, a longtime resident of Mill Creek.

9. The population of Hispanic origin was lower than 1 percent in 1990.

10. M. Diaz, "Philadelphia Loses 9% of Its Population," *Philadelphia Inquirer,* July 1, 1999. Philadelphia's population grew slightly between 2000 and 2010.

11. The first phase, from 1987 to 1991, was a collaboration with the Pennsylvania Horticultural Association's Philadelphia Green program and the Organization and Management Group.

12. See A. W. Spirn, *The Granite Garden: Urban Nature and Human Design* (New York: Basic, 1984); Spirn, "Urban Nature and Human Design: Renewing the Great Tradition," *Journal of Planning Education and Research* 5, no. 1 (1985): 39–51; Spirn, "Landscape Planning and the City," *Landscape and Urban Planning* 13 (1986): 433–41; and Spirn, "Reclaiming Common Ground: Water, Neighborhoods, and Public Spaces," in *The American Planning Tradition: Culture and Policy,* ed. R. Fishman (Washington, D.C./Baltimore, Md.: Woodrow Wilson Press/Johns Hopkins University Press, 2000), 297–314.

13. A. W. Spirn, *The West Philadelphia Landscape Plan: A Framework for Action* (Philadelphia: Department of Landscape Architecture, University of Pennsylvania, 1991).

14. T. Ferrick, "Graying Homeowners, a New City Woe," *Philadelphia Inquirer,* September 15, 1997.

15. For specific recommendations for change in public policy, see Spirn, *West Philadelphia Landscape Plan.*

16. See Spirn, "Reclaiming Common Ground."

17. In addition to this report and the built projects, there are five additional reports. A. W. Spirn and D. Marcucci's *Models of Success: Landscape Improvements and Community Development* (Philadelphia: Department of Landscape Architecture, University of Pennsylvania, 1991) describes examples of successfully executed projects and draws lessons for similar projects that could be undertaken in West Philadelphia. Spirn and M. Pollio's *"This Garden Is a Town"* (Philadelphia: Department of Landscape Architecture, University of Pennsylvania, 1990) explores community gardens as models for neighborhood-based planning. Spirn and M. Cameron's *Shaping the Block* (Philadelphia: Department of Landscape Architecture, University of

Pennsylvania, 1991) focuses on the block as a significant unit of neighborhood and explores how residents can reshape their blocks to better support their needs. Spirn and Pollio's *Vacant Land: A Resource for Reshaping Urban Neighborhoods* (Philadelphia: Department of Landscape Architecture, University of Pennsylvania, 1991) describes the diverse types of vacant urban land that occur in West Philadelphia and how they can be reclaimed for a variety of uses. Spirn and R. Cheetham's *West Philadelphia Digital Database: An Atlas and Guide* (Philadelphia: Department of Landscape Architecture, University of Pennsylvania, 1996) is an introduction to the digital database.

18. T. Hine, "Surroundings: A Long-Buried Creek in West Philadelphia," *Philadelphia Sunday Inquirer,* November 15, 1992.

19. J. L. Cummings, D. DiPasquale, and M. E. Kahn, "Measuring the Consequences of Promoting Inner City Home Ownership," *Journal of Housing Economics* 11 (2002): 330–59.

20. Many of these can be seen by visiting the course portion of the WPLP website, http://www.wplp.net (accessed June 6, 2011), and the Web pages for my studio class "Transforming the Urban Landscape," which I taught in 1996, 1997, and 1998 http://web.mit.edu/wplp/course (accessed June 6, 2011).

21. Examples of maps and other information from the digital database are available online at http://web.mit.edu/wplp/wpdd/wpddhome.htm.

22. Visit the WPLP website, www.wplp.net. To see the original site, click on the link to 1997. The site was redesigned by my students at MIT in 2002; to see their version, click on the link to 2002.

23. The title of the class was a deliberate reference to the title of Dolores Hayden's *Power of Place: Urban Landscapes as Public History* (Cambridge, Mass.: MIT Press, 1995), which was a required text.

24. The five students enrolled in the seminar for the spring 1997 semester spent the first seven of the fourteen weeks preparing for their visits to the Sulzberger classroom. Each student researched one of five periods in the neighborhood's history from precolonial times to the present, found primary sources, and used secondary texts to put the history of the neighborhood into the context of region and nation. The secondary literature included S. B. Warner, *The Private City: Philadelphia in Three Periods of Its Growth* (Philadelphia: University of Pennsylvania Press, 1987); K. T. Jackson, *Crabgrass Frontier: The Suburbanization of the United States* (New York: Oxford University Press, 1985); and Hayden, *Power of Place.* The seminar students presented papers early in the semester and then used them to design a class session at Sulzberger in the second half of the semester. These papers served as the foundation for work in subsequent years; see C. Ott, "Pre-colonial, Colonial, and Early Industrial Eras in Mill Creek's History" (unpublished paper, University of Pennsylvania, 1997); C. Lane, "Mill Creek History: Industrial and Early Modern Eras: 1860–1930" (unpublished paper, University of Pennsylvania, 1997); Hillman, "Urban Redevelopment"; P. Tepwongsiriat, "Mill Creek in the Edge City Period: 1970s–Present" (unpublished paper, University of Pennsylvania, 1997); and B. Seider, "U.S. Census: West Philadelphia and Mill Creek, 1860–1990" (unpublished paper, University of Pennsylvania, 1997).

25. Ott, "Pre-colonial"; Lane, "Mill Creek History."

26. The name of the report is *Power of Place: Essays about Our Mill Creek Neighborhood*. The texts and drawings are available on the WPLP website, as are the reflections of Sulzberger teacher, Glen Campbell; see http://web.mit.edu/wplp/sms/pub.htm (accessed June 6, 2011).

27. Those enrolled in my urban studies seminar typically included undergraduate, master's, and doctoral students. Initially the students in the class were white or Thai; in later years, the course's ethnic and racial diversity broadened to include Hispanic, African American, and Asian American students.

28. Martin Knox, one of the research assistants who led the summer program in 1997, spoke in 2002 with my MIT students. His reflections are available online at http://web.mit.edu/4.243j/www/wplp/s-knox.html (accessed June 6, 2011).

29. SMS News is available online in the Sulzberger (SMS) part of the WPLP website at http://web.mit.edu/wplp/sms/smsnews/smsnew.htm (accessed June 6, 2011).

30. More information about and illustrations of the Mill Creek Project are available online at http://web.mit.edu/wplp/sms/millc.htm (accessed June 6, 2011).

31. Some of these are described West Philadelphia Landscape Project website.

32. For a description of these activities, see http://web.mit.edu/wplp/project/mccoal.htm and http://web.mit.edu/4.243j/www/wplp/s-cornitcher.html (accessed June 6, 2011).

33. Joe Piotrowki, associate director of the EPA's Water Division, Region 3, describes the EPA's role in the project at http://web.mit.edu/4.243j/www/wplp/s-piotrowski.html (accessed June 6, 2011).

34. My former research assistant, Sarah Williams, and Joanne Dahme, watersheds programs manager at the Philadelphia Water Department, describe their experiences with this program at http://web.mit.edu/4.243j/www/wplp/stories.html (accessed June 6, 2011).

35. Reportedly, the final straw came when the new management decided to distribute equipment in Sulzberger's computer lab to other schools that did not have as many computers.

36. Spirn, "Landscape Planning"; Spirn, "Reclaiming Common Ground."

37. M. Horton and P. Freire, *We Make the Road By Walking: Conversations on Education and Social Change* (Philadelphia: Temple University Press, 1990).

38. P. Freire and D. Macedo, *Literacy: Reading the Word and the World* (Westport, Conn.: Bergin and Garvey, 1987), 36, 45, 141, 36, 47.

39. Ibid., 128.

11. Saving Ourselves by Acting Locally: The Historical Progression of Grassroots Environmental Justice Activism in the Philadelphia Area, 1981–2001

1. Robert D. Bullard, ed., *The Quest for Environmental Justice: Human Rights and the Politics of Pollution* (San Francisco: Sierra Club Books, 2005), 1–2.

2. Carolyn Adams, David Bartelt, David Elesh, Ira Goldstein, Nancy Kleniewski and William Yancey, *Philadelphia: Neighborhoods, Division and Conflict in a Postindustrial City* (Philadelphia: Temple University Press, 1991), 30–55.

3. Elizabeth Geffen, "Industrial Development and Social Crisis 1841–1854," in *Philadelphia: A 300-Year History,* ed. Russell F. Weigley (New York: Norton, 1982), 307–62; Theodore Hershberg, "Free Blacks in Antebellum Philadelphia," in *The Peoples of Philadelphia: A History of Ethnic Groups and Lower-Class Life, 1790–1940,* ed. Allen F. Davis and Mark H. Haller (Philadelphia: University of Pennsylvania Press, 1973), 111–34.

4. Adam Levine, "Sewers, Pollution and Public Health in Philadelphia," *Pennsylvania Legacies,* May 2000, 14–17; Craig E. Colten and Peter N. Skinner, *The Road to Love Canal: Managing Industrial Waste before EPA* (Austin: University of Texas Press, 1995), 147–66.

5. Howard Gillette, *Camden after the Fall: Decline and Renewal in a Post-Industrial City* (Philadelphia: University of Pennsylvania Press, 2006), 147–70; Michael Greenberg and Dona Schneider, *Environmentally Devastated Neighborhoods: Perceptions, Policies and Realities* (New Brunswick, N.J.: Rutgers University Press, 1999), 10–30, 79–86.

6. Adeline G. Levine and Rose K. Goldsen, *Love Canal: Science, Politics and People* (New York: Simon and Schuster, 1982); Lois Marie Gibbs, *Love Canal: The Story Continues* (Vancouver: New Society, 1998), 19–66.

7. Robert Gottlieb, *Forcing the Spring: The Transformation of the American Environmental Movement* (Washington, D.C.: Island, 1994), 218–61; Andrew Szasz, *Ecopopulism: Toxic Waste and the Movement for Environmental Justice* (Minneapolis: University of Minnesota Press, 1994), 69–102.

8. Robert D. Bullard, *Dumping in Dixie: Race, Class and Environmental Quality* (Boulder, Colo.: Westview, 1994): xiii–xvii.

9. Michael T. Ash and T. Robert Fetter, "Who Lives on the Wrong Side of the Environmental Tracks? Evidence from the EPA's Risk Screening Environmental Indicators Model," *Social Science Quarterly* 85, no. 2 (2004): 441–61; Robert D. Bullard, Paul Mohai, Robin Saha, and Beverly Wright, "Toxic Waste and Race at Twenty: Why Race Still Matters after All These Years," *Environmental Law* 38, no. 2 (2008): 371–11; Rachel Morello-Frosch, Manuel Pastor Jr., Carlos Porras, and James Sadd, "Environmental Justice and Regional Inequality in Southern California: Implications for Future Research," *Environmental Health Perspectives* 110, supp. 2 (2002): 149–54; Evan J. Ringquist, "Assessing Evidence of Environmental Inequities: A Meta-Analysis," *Journal of Policy Analysis and Management* 24, no. 2 (2005): 223–47.

10. Jeremy Mennis, "Using Geographic Information Systems to Create and Analyze Statistical Surfaces of Population and Risk for Environmental Justice Analysis," *Social Science Quarterly* 83, no. 1 (2002): 281–97; Jeremy Mennis, "The Distribution and Enforcement of Air Polluting Facilities in New Jersey," *Professional Geographer* 57, no. 3 (2005): 411–22; Diane Sicotte and Samantha Swanson, "Whose Risk in Philadelphia? Proximity to Unequally Hazardous Industrial Facilities," *Social Science Quarterly* 88, no. 2 (2007): 515–34.

11. Jennifer Clapp, *Toxic Exports: The Transfer of Hazardous Wastes from Rich to Poor Countries* (Ithaca, N.Y.: Cornell University Press, 2001); Boy Luthje, "The Changing Map of Global Electronics: Networks of Mass Production in the New Economy," in *Challenging the Chip: Labor Rights and Environmental Justice in the Global Electron-*

ics Industry, ed. Ted Smith, David A. Sonnenfeld, and David Naguib Pellow (Philadelphia: Temple University Press, 2006), 17–30; David Naguib Pellow, *Resisting Global Toxics: Transnational Movements for Environmental Justice* (Cambridge, Mass.: MIT Press, 2007), 97–146, 185–224.

12. Daniel Faber, *Capitalizing on Environmental Injustice: The Polluter-Industrial Complex in the Age of Globalization* (Cambridge, Mass.: MIT Press, 2008), 1–12.

13. W. Neil Adger, Jouni Paavola, and Saleemul Huq, "Toward Justice in Adaptation to Climate Change," in *Fairness in Adaptation to Climate Change,* ed. Adger, Paavola, Huq, and M. J. Mace (Cambridge, Mass.: MIT Press, 2006), 1–19; Jonathan A. Patz, Diarmid Campbell-Lendrum, Tracey Holloway, and Jonathan A. Foley, "Impact of Regional Climate Change on Human Health," *Nature* 438, no. 17 (2005): 310–17.

14. Luke Cole and Sheila Foster, *From the Ground Up: Environmental Racism and the Rise of the Environmental Justice Movement* (New York: NYU Press, 2001), 34–53; Olga Pomar, "Toxic Racism on a New Jersey Waterfront," in *Quest for Environmental Justice,* ed. Bullard, 125–42.

15. Melissa Toffolon-Weiss and J. Timmons Roberts, "Toxic Torts, Public Interest Law and Environmental Justice: Evidence from Louisiana," *Law and Policy* 26, no. 2 (2004): 265–66.

16. Qtd. in Edward J. Walsh, Rex Warland, and D. Clayton Smith, *Don't Burn It Here: Grassroots Challenges to Trash Incinerators* (University Park: Pennsylvania State University Press, 1997), 176.

17. Sherry Cable, Tamara Mix, and Donald Hastings, "Mission Impossible? Environmental Justice Activists' Collaborations with Professional Environmentalists and with Academics," in *Power, Justice and the Environment: A Critical Appraisal of the Environmental Justice Movement,* ed. David N. Pellow and Robert J. Brulle (Cambridge, Mass.: MIT Press, 2005), 55–75.

18. David N. Pellow, Adam Weinberg, and Allan Schnaiberg, "The Environmental Justice Movement: Equitable Allocation of the Costs and Benefits of Environmental Management Outcomes," *American Behavioral Scientist* 14, no. 4 (2001): 423–39.

19. Michael K. Heiman, "Race, Waste and Class: New Perspectives on Environmental Justice," *Antipode* 28, no. 2 (1996): 111–21; Eric J. Krieg and Daniel R. Faber, "Not So Black and White: Environmental Justice and Cumulative Impact Assessments," *Environmental Impact Assessment Review* 24 (2004): 667–94.

20. Szasz, *Ecopopulism,* 69–70.

21. Thomas Gladwin, "Patterns of Environmental Conflict over Industrial Facilities in the United States, 1970–78," in *Resolving Locational Conflict,* ed. Robert W. Lake (New Brunswick, N.J.: Rutgers University Press, 1987), 14–44.

22. David G. Ortiz, Daniel J. Meyers, N. Eugene Walls, and Maria-Elena D. Diaz, "Where Do We Stand with Newspaper Data?" *Mobilization: An International Journal* 10 (2005): 397–419.

23. Catherine Marshall and Gretchen B. Rossman, *Designing Qualitative Research,* 4th ed. (Thousand Oaks, Calif.: Sage, 2006), 202–8.

24. Bullard, *Quest for Environmental Justice,* 1–20; David Naguib Pellow and Robert J. Brulle, "Power, Justice, and the Environment: Toward Critical Environmental Justice Studies," in *Power, Justice and the Environment: A Critical Appraisal of the En-*

vironmental Justice Movement, ed. Pellow and Brulle, (Cambridge, Mass.: MIT Press, 2005), 1–19.

25. Louis Blumberg and Robert Gottlieb, War on Waste: Can America Win Its Battle with Garbage? (Washington, D.C.: Island, 1989), 15.

26. Szasz, Ecopopulism, 12–13, 16.

27. Colten and Skinner, Road to Love Canal, 94, 114–17.

28. Greenberg and Schneider, Environmentally Devastated Neighborhoods, 83, 90–91.

29. Blumberg and Gottlieb, War on Waste, 63–65; U.S. Environmental Protection Agency, 25 Years of RCRA: Building on the Past to Protect Our Future (5305W), available at http://www.epa.gov/osw/inforesources/pubs/k02027.pdf (accessed Feb. 29, 2012.).

30. Gladwin, "Patterns of Environmental Conflict," 22.

31. U.S. Environmental Protection Agency, "Lipari Landfill NPL Site Fact Sheet" (Dec. 14, 2007), available at http://www.epa.gov/superfund/sites/nplfs/fs0200557 .pdf (accessed Mar. 12, 2012).

32. Anemona Hartocollis, "Report Expected to Assail Cleanup Plan for N.J. Dump," Philadelphia Inquirer, November 8, 1985, B4.

33. Kitty Dumas, "When Home Is Along a Toxic Lake," Philadelphia Inquirer, January 22, 1986, G2.

34. Marc Kaufman, "When It Rains: Complaints about Moyer's Landfill Pour In," Philadelphia Inquirer, January 8, 1982.

35. U.S. Environmental Protection Agency, "Moyer's Landfill: Current Site Information" (Feb. 2007), available at http://www.epa.gov/superfund/sites/nplfs/ fs0301226.pdf (accessed Mar. 9, 2012); Ginny Wiegand, "Battling on a Newfound Front, Former Union Man Fights County on Dump and Jail," Philadelphia Inquirer, September 11, 1986, B1.

36. Edward Power, "Parade Protests Dump as Citizens Go to Streets," Philadelphia Inquirer, February 2, 1981, B1.

37. C. S. Manegold, "This Landfill Brews Unrest over Its Odor," Philadelphia Inquirer, June 13, 1983, N2.

38. Ellen O'Brien, "She Dumped the Dump: Beatrice Cerkez Will Have Her Moment in the Sun Tomorrow as the Last Empty Trash Truck Pulls Away from Kinsley Landfill," Philadelphia Inquirer, February 5, 1987, D1.

39. Matthew Purdy, "'Trash Can' of the Valley: They're Putting on the Lid," Philadelphia Inquirer, August 7, 1983, B4.

40. Jack Severson, "A County Is Saying 'No' to Phila's Trash," Philadelphia Inquirer, July 28, 1986, C1.

41. Environmental Protection Agency, 25 Years of RCRA.

42. Joseph A. Slobodzian, "Kean's Waste Plan Has its Critics, but Is Mainly Cheered," Philadelphia Inquirer, January 13, 1985, G1.

43. Martin V. Melosi, "The Viability of Incineration as a Disposal Option: The Evolution of a Niche Technology, 1885–1995," Public Works Management and Policy 1, no. 1 (1996): 31–42.

44. George Anastasia, "All That Trash Wouldn't Go to Waste under City's Energy Conversion Plan," *Philadelphia Inquirer,* April 18, 1982, F3; Vernon Loeb, "Goode on TV, Asks Support for Trash-to-Steam," *Philadelphia Inquirer,* June 26, 1986, A1.

45. Jerome Balter, interview by the author, July 10, 2007.

46. Paul E. Connett, "Municipal Waste Incineration: A Poor Choice for the Twenty-First Century" (paper presented at the Fourth Annual International Waste Management Conference, Amsterdam, November 24–25, 1998).

47. Blumberg and Gottlieb, *War on Waste,* 8, 27, 33–34, 41, 48, 109–14.

48. Cerrell Associates and J. Stephen Powell, *Political Difficulties Facing Waste-to-Energy Conversion Plant Siting* (Sacramento: California Waste Management Board, 1984).

49. Jane Eisner, "Hearing on Trash Plant Set: Unit Would Make Shipyard's Steam," *Philadelphia Inquirer,* February 22, 1983, B1.

50. Walsh, Warland, and Smith, *Don't Burn It Here,* 140, 162–80.

51. Robin Clark, "It Was Familiar Opposition to a Familiar Proposal," *Philadelphia Inquirer,* April 14, 1988, B7; Dick Pothier, "Tour Takes a Whiff of South Phila," *Philadelphia Inquirer,* December 9, 1986, B2; William W. Sutton, "Council to Open Hearing on Trash Plant Today," *Philadelphia Inquirer,* November 12, 1986, B1.

52. Robin Clark, "It Was Familiar Opposition to a Familiar Proposal," *Philadelphia Inquirer,* April 14, 1988, B7.

53. Russell E. Eshelman, "State Lags on Trash Crisis, Commissioners Are Told," *Philadelphia Inquirer,* June 20, 1985, H14.

54. Howard Manly, "Transfer Solid-Waste Powers to County Level, Bartle Urges," *Philadelphia Inquirer,* March 10, 1986, H12.

55. Walsh, Warland, and Smith, *Don't Burn It Here,* 143–50, 155–56.

56. Julia Cass, "Plan for Incinerator in Camden Draws Fire," *Philadelphia Inquirer,* October 26, 1981, C3.

57. Gillette, *Camden after the Fall,* 105–6.

58. Andrew Maykuth, "Camden's Leaders Are Pushing Idea of a Trash-to-Steam Plant," *Philadelphia Inquirer,* November 11, 1984, B1; Andrew Maykuth, "Trash Plan in Camden Is Debated: Some Are Hostile to Trash-to-Steam," *Philadelphia Inquirer,* January 13, 1985, B1; Andrew Maykuth, "Hearing Is Divided over Camden Plant," *Philadelphia Inquirer,* May 29, 1987, B1.

59. Patrisia Gonzales, "Trash-Plant Foes Threaten to Seek Vote," *Philadelphia Inquirer,* September 11, 1987, B6.

60. Inga Saffron, "Trash-to-Steam Plant in Camden Is Approved," *Philadelphia Inquirer,* December 9, 1987, A1.

61. Andrew Maykuth, "Trash Plant in Camden Wins Ruling," *Philadelphia Inquirer,* November 17, 1988, B6.

62. "Six Incinerator Protesters Plead Guilty to Trespassing," *Philadelphia Inquirer,* June 2, 1990, B2.

63. Andrew Maykuth, "Protest Assails Incinerator Set for Pennsauken," *Philadelphia Inquirer,* Jan. 26, 1988, B3.

64. Gillette, *Camden after the Fall,* 111.

65. Bob Drogin, "City Signs Pollution Pact with State," *Philadelphia Inquirer,* April 5, 1983, B1.

66. Roger Cohn, "Rep. Rocks Asks for Probe of Incinerator," *Philadelphia Inquirer,* April 3, 1981, B5.

67. Linda Lloyd, "Unwanted Neighbor Gets Happy Goodbye," *Philadelphia Inquirer,* July 8, 1988, B1.

68. Gregory R. Byrnes, "Dump Site Permit Is Extended," *Philadelphia Inquirer,* September 24, 1981, B4J.

69. David O'Reilly, "Logan Township Drops Suit against Treatment Plant," *Philadelphia Inquirer,* January 8, 1983, B4.

70. Kitty Dumas, "Burning of Waste Attacked: 25 Protest Test in Logan Twp," *Philadelphia Inquirer,* Oct. 1, 1986, B1; Ellen O'Brien, "Chemical Plant an Odd Sort of Catalyst for Logan," *Philadelphia Inquirer,* December 19, 1986, B1.

71. Melosi, "Viability of Incineration."

72. Blumberg and Gottlieb, *War on Waste,* 80–81; Mark Dowie, *Losing Ground: American Environmentalism at the Close of the Twentieth Century* (Cambridge, Mass.: MIT Press, 1996), 133–35; Szasz, *Ecopopulism,* 149.

73. Benjamin F. Chavis, *Unequal Protection: Environmental Justice and Communities of Color* (San Francisco: Sierra Club Books, 1994), xi–xii.

74. Dorceta Taylor, "The Rise of the Environmental Justice Paradigm," *American Behavioral Scientist* 43, no. 4 (2000): 508–80.

75. Greenberg and Schneider, *Environmentally Devastated Neighborhoods,* 98–99; Pomar, "Toxic Racism," 130.

76. Gillette, *Camden after the Fall,* 105–11, 145–68, 171–75.

77. Diane Sicotte, "Don't Waste Us: Environmental Justice through Community Participation in Urban Planning," *Environmental Justice* 3, no. 1 (2010): 7–11; Guian McKee, "Liberal Ends through Illiberal Means: Race, Urban Renewal and Community in the Eastwick Section of Philadelphia, 1949–1990," *Journal of Urban History* 27, no. 5 (2001): 547–83.

78. Mark Jaffe, "Despite Leaching, Delco Landfill Unlikely to Receive Superfund Money," *Philadelphia Inquirer,* May 24, 1984, B6; U.S. Environmental Protection Agency, "Lower Darby Creek: Current Site Information" (Apr. 2007), available at http:// epa.gov/reg3hwmd/npl/PASFN0305521.htm (accessed Mar. 23, 2012).

79. Bill Miller, "Garbage Pops up Elsewhere," *Philadelphia Inquirer,* November 20, 1988, N6.

80. Sicotte, "Don't Waste Us."

81. South and Southwest Philadelphia Bucket Brigade, *What's in Our Air?* (unpublished report, n.d.)

82. Susan Q. Stranahan, "State Approves Infectious Waste Plant for Chester," *Philadelphia Inquirer,* July 24, 1993, B1.

83. Walsh, Warland, and Smith, *Don't Burn It Here,* 71–83.

84. Stranahan, "State Approves," B1.

85. Cole and Foster, *From the Ground Up,* 44–47; Emilie Lounsberry, "Court Assailed for Case Takeover," *Philadelphia Inquirer,* August 4, 1995, B1.

86. Dan Hardy, "Seeking to Reopen Chester City Plant: An Infectious-Waste Sterilization Facility Shut Down in '96," *Philadelphia Inquirer,* December 3, 1998, B1.

87. Robert Moran, "Students Cry Foul on Waste Plants," *Philadelphia Inquirer,* April 23, 1996, B2.

88. Dan Hardy, "Permit Changes Are Requested for Chester Incinerator," *Philadelphia Inquirer,* February 5, 1999, B2; Cole and Foster, *From the Ground Up,* 36, 39, 44–47, 52.

89. Dan Hardy, "A Request to Test-Burn Tires Raises Concern in Chester," *Philadelphia Inquirer,* December 5, 1999, ML1; Dan Hardy, "Kimberly-Clark Moves to Burn Tires for Fuel," *Philadelphia Inquirer,* September 11, 2001, B9.

90. Eric Harrison, "South Camden Residents Protest Sewage Odor at Meeting," *Philadelphia Inquirer,* Nov. 29, 1983, B8; Andrew Maykuth, "Change in Camden's Sewage Treatment Cheered," *Philadelphia Inquirer,* April 6, 1984, B2.

91. Dwight Ott, "In Camden, Demanding Clean Water," *Philadelphia Inquirer,* April 18, 1989, B5.

92. Gillette, *Camden after the Fall,* 106–7, 171–72.

93. Pomar, "Toxic Racism," 134–35.

94. Will Van Sant, "Others Joining Cement Plant Case," *Philadelphia Inquirer,* July 26, 2001, B1.

95. Pomar, "Toxic Racism," 134–35.

96. Julie Sze, *Noxious New York: The Racial Politics of Urban Health and Environmental Justice* (Cambridge, Mass.: MIT Press, 2007), 154, 158–59.

97. U.S. Environmental Protection Agency, "Electricity from Natural Gas" (Dec. 18, 2007), available at http://www.epa.gov/cleanenergy/energy-and-you/affect/natural-gas.html (accessed Mar. 12, 2012).

98. Leslie A. Pappas, "Activists Are Selling Causes–and More," *Philadelphia Inquirer,* April 2, 2003, B1; Jacob Quinn Sanders, "Denial of Permit Stirs up New Arguments," *Philadelphia Inquirer,* November 8, 2001, MC2.

99. Kathryn Masterson, "Proposal for Power Plants Go Forward," *Philadelphia Inquirer,* March 14, 2000, MC1; Benjamin Wallace-Wells, "Proposal Hits a Nerve in Town: Some in East Pikeland Fear a New Plant on the Horizon," *Philadelphia Inquirer,* February 8, 2001, B1.

100. Gaiutra Bahadur, "Judges Overturn Limerick Power Plant Approval," *Philadelphia Inquirer,* October 3, 2002, B1.

101. Benjamin Wallace-Wells, "East Pikeland Supervisors Reject Plan for Power Plant," *Philadelphia Inquirer,* May 23, 2002, B3.

102. Michael Stoll, "Generator Plan Raises Concerns: Marcus Hook Residents Are Worried about Pollution," *Philadelphia Inquirer,* February 18, 2000, B1.

103. Juliana Maantay, "Zoning Law, Health, and Environmental Justice: What's the Connection?" *Journal of Medicine, Law and Ethics* 30, no. 4 (2002): 572–93; Robin Saha and Paul Mohai, "Historical Context and Hazardous Waste Facility Siting: Understanding Temporal Patterns in Michigan," *Social Problems* 52, no. 4 (2005): 618–48.

12. Planning the Food Secure City: Philadelphia's Agriculture, Retrospect and Prospect

1. Food security is typically defined as a state in which all people enjoy stable access to safe, nutritious, culturally appropriate food.

2. See, for example, "Food and Planning," special issue, *Progressive Planning: The Magazine of Planners Network* 158 (Winter 2004); special issue on planning for community food systems, *Journal of Planning Education and Research* 23, no. 4 (Summer 2004); Samina Raja, Brandon Born, and Jessica Russel, *A Planners Guide to Community and Regional Food Planning: Transforming Food Environments, Facilitating Healthy Eating,* APA Planning Advisory Service report no. 554 (Chicago: American Planning Association, 2008); Kimberley Hodgson, Marcia Caton Campbell, and Martin Bailkey, *Urban Agriculture: Growing Healthy, Sustainable Places,* APA Planning Advisory Service report no. 563 (Chicago: American Planning Association, 2011).

3. Rural agricultural histories include Donald Worster, *Under Western Skies: Nature and History in the American West* (New York: Oxford University Press, 1992); and Geoff Cunfer, *On the Great Plains: Agriculture and Environment* (College Station: Texas A&M University Press, 2005). William Cronon's *Nature's Metropolis: Chicago and the Great West* (New York: Norton, 1992) and Richard Walker's *Conquest of Bread: 150 Years of California Agribusiness* (New York: New Press, 2004) are exceptional in their focus on agriculture's role in urbanization. Recent literature on imperialism and the early globalization of food includes Kenneth Kiple, *A Movable Feast: Ten Millennia of Food Globalization* (New York: Cambridge University Press, 2007); Mark Kurlansky, *Cod: A Biography of the Fish That Changed the World* (New York: Walker, 1997); and Virginia Scott Jenkins, *Bananas: An American History* (Washington, D.C.: Smithsonian Institution Press, 2000). The planning history literature on food systems includes Laura Lawson, *City Bountiful: A Century of Community Gardening in America* (Berkeley: University of California Press, 2005); Laura Lawson, "The Planner in the Garden: A Historical View of the Relationship of Planning to Community Garden Programs," *Journal of Planning History* 3, no. 2 (May 2004): 151–76; Gregory Donofrio, "Feeding the City," *Gastronomica* 7, no. 4 (2008): 30–41; and Joe Howe, Katrin Bohn, and André Viljoen, "Food in Time: The History of English Open Urban Space as a European Example," in *Continuous Productive Urban Landscapes: Designing Urban Agriculture for Sustainable Cities,* ed. Viljoen, Bohn, and Howe (London: Elsevier, 2005), 95–107.

4. William Penn, "Letter from William Penn to the Committee of the Free Society of Traders, 1683," in *Narratives of Early Pennsylvania, West New Jersey and Delaware, 1630–1707,* ed. Albert Cook Myers (New York: Barnes and Noble, 1912), 227.

5. Ibid., 228.

6. This account of the region's economic development is based partly on Domenic Vitiello, "Engineering the Metropolis: The Sellers Family and Industrial Philadelphia" (PhD diss., University of Pennsylvania, 2004); Vitiello, *Philadelphia Capital: America's First Stock Exchange and the City It Made* (Philadelphia: University of Pennsylvania Press, 2009); and Vitiello, "Reading the Corps of Discovery Backwards: The Metropolitan Context of Lewis and Clark's Expedition," in *"The Shortest*

and Most Convenient Route of Communication": Lewis and Clark in Context, ed. Robert Cox (Philadelphia: American Philosophical Society Press, 2005), 12–51.

7. Penn, "Letter from William Penn," 228.

8. Anne Bezanson, Robert D. Gray, and Miriam Hussey, *Prices in Colonial Pennsylvania* (Philadelphia: University of Pennsylvania Press, 1935); David Hackett Fischer, *The Great Wave: Price Revolutions and the Rhythm of History* (New York: Oxford University Press, 1996), 117–56.

9. Carville Earle, *Geographical Inquiry and American Historical Problems* (Stanford, Calif.: Stanford University Press, 1992), 88–152. See also David Meyer, *The Roots of American Industrialization* (Baltimore, Md.: Johns Hopkins University Press, 2003).

10. *Early Transactions of the American Philosophical Society: Published in the American Magazine during 1769* (Philadelphia: American Philosophical Society, 1969), 127.

11. Simon Baatz, *"Venerate the Plough": A History of the Philadelphia Society for Promoting Agriculture, 1785–1985* (Philadelphia: Philadelphia Society for Promoting Agriculture, 1985), 21–26.

12. S. W. Fletcher, *Pennsylvania Agriculture and Country Life, 1640–1940,* 2 vols. (Harrisburg: Pennsylvania Historical and Museum Commission, 1950).

13. Election of Board of Managers, February 16, 1824, Franklin Institute, Minutes of the Board of Managers.

14. Philip Scranton, "Large Firms and Industrial Restructuring: The Philadelphia Region, 1900–1980," *Pennsylvania Magazine of History and Biography* 116, no. 4 (Oct. 1992): 419–66.

15. Donofrio, "Feeding the City."

16. "Sellers et al. vs. The Pennsylvania Railroad Company et al.," Court of Common Pleas of Philadelphia County, December term, 1874, 1–2, testimony archived at the Library Company of Philadelphia; John Frederick Lewis, *The Redemption of the Lower Schuylkill* (Philadelphia: City Parks Association, 1924).

17. Cyrus Miller, John P. Mitchell, and George McAneny, *The Report of the Mayor's Market Commission of New York City* (New York: Little and Ives, 1913); Clyde King, *The Relation of the City to Its Food Supply* (Philadelphia: National Municipal League, 1915).

18. W. P. Hedden, *How Great Cities Are Fed* (Boston: D.C. Heath, 1929); Donofrio, "Feeding the City."

19. Richard Juliani, "Social Reform through Social Service: The Settlement Movement in South Philadelphia," *Pennsylvania Legacies* 7, no. 2 (Nov. 2007): 22–29.

20. Lawson, *City Bountiful*; Lawson, "The Planner in the Garden."

21. Lester Brown, *Plan B 2.0: Rescuing a Planet under Stress and a Civilization in Trouble* (New York: Norton, 2006); Dale Allen Pfeiffer, *Eating Fossil Fuels: Oil, Food, and the Coming Crisis in Agriculture* (Gabriola Island, British Columbia: New Society, 2006); Kenneth Deffeyes, *Beyond Oil: The View from Hubbert's Peak* (New York: Hill and Wang, 2005); Danielle Murray, "Oil and Food: A Rising Security Challenge" (report by the Earth Policy Institute, Washington, D.C., 2005).

22. David Pimentel and Mario Giampietro, "Food, Land, Population and the U.S. Economy" (report by the Carrying Capacity Network, Washington, D.C., 1994); Martin Heller and Gregory Keoleian, *Life Cycle-Based Sustainability Indicators for Assessment of the U.S. Food System* (Ann Arbor: Center for Sustainable Systems, University of Michigan, 2000), 40.

23. Philadelphia Zoning Code, 1961 (with successive overlays, none of which include zoning classifications for agriculture or community gardens).

24. Rachel Carson, *Silent Spring* (Boston: Houghton Mifflin, 1962); Michael Pollan, *The Omnivore's Dilemma: A Natural History of Four Meals* (New York: Penguin, 2006).

25. Thomas Lyson, *Civic Agriculture: Reconnecting Farm, Food, and Community* (Medford, Mass.: Tufts University Press, 2004); C. Clare Hinrichs and Thomas Lyson, *Remaking the North American Food System: Strategies for Sustainability* (Lincoln: University of Nebraska Press, 2007).

26. Portions of this account of Philadelphia's local food sector are adapted from Domenic Vitiello, "Growing Edible Cities," in *Growing Greener Cities: Urban Sustainability in the Twenty-First Century,* Eugenie L. Birch and Susan Wachter (Philadelphia: University of Pennsylvania Press, 2008), 259–80.

27. Author's interviews with Bob Pierson, July 10, 2006; author's interview with Ann Karlen, November 25, 2008; see also http://www.whitedogcafefoundation.org/fairfood.html (accessed Jan. 13, 2009).

28. http://www.thefoodtrust.org (accessed Jan. 13, 2009); *Food Matters* 2, no. 2 (Fall 2006); Ann Karlen, presentation at the Urban Sustainability Forum, January 18, 2007; Pierson interview; Karlen interview.

29. http://www.farmtocity.org (accessed Jan. 13, 2009).

30. Pierson interview; Karlen interview.

31. http://www.thefoodtrust.org (accessed Jan. 13, 2009); see also Tracey Giang, Allison Karpyn, Hannah Burton Laurison, Amy Hillier, and R. Duane Perry, "Closing the Grocery Gap in Underserved Communities: The Creation of the Pennsylvania Fresh Food Financing Initiative," *Journal of Public Health Management and Practice* 14, no. 3 (2008): 272–79; "The Need for More Supermarkets in New York" and "The Need for More Supermarkets in Chicago" (reports by the Food Trust, Philadelphia, 2008).

32. "Examining the Impact of Food Deserts on Public Health in Detroit" (report by Mari Gallagher Research and Consulting, June 2007); "Examining the Impact of Food Deserts on Public Health in Chicago" (report by Mari Gallagher Research and Consulting, July 2006); Kimberly Morland, Ana Diez Roux, and Steve Wing, "Supermarkets, Other Food Stores, and Obesity: The Atherosclerosis Risk in Communities Study," *American Journal of Preventive Medicine* 30, no. 4 (Apr. 2006): 333–39; Samina Raja, Changxing Ma, and Pavan Yadav, "Beyond Food Deserts: Measuring and Mapping Racial Disparities in Neighborhood Food Environments," *Journal of Planning Education and Research* 27, no. 4 (2008): 469–82; Sarah Treuhaft and Allison Karpyn, *The Grocery Gap: Who Has Access to Healthy Food and Why It Matters* (Oakland, Calif: PolicyLink, 2010).

33. http://www.urbannutrition.org (accessed Jan. 13, 2009).

34. http://www.philabundance.org/about/faqs.asp (accessed Jan. 19, 2009).

35. http://www.sharefoodprogram.org/about_spa.htm (accessed Jan. 19, 2009).

36. Mark Winne, *Closing the Food Gap: Resetting the Table in the Land of Plenty* (Boston: Beacon, 2008); author's interview with Steveanna Wynn, September 10, 2008.

37. Julie Thayer, Carolyn Murphy, John Cook, Stephanie Ettinger de Cuba, Rosa DaCosta, and Mariana Chilton, "Coming Up Short: High Food Costs Outstrip Food Stamp Benefits" (report for C-SNAP and Philadelphia Grow Project, Boston/Philadelphia, September 2008). These figures are based on a family of four.

38. Rene van Veenhuizen, ed., *Cities Farming for the Future—Urban Agriculture for Green and Productive Cities* (Ottawa: International Development Research Centre, 2006); Mustafa Koc, Rod MacRae, Luc J. A. Mougeot, and Jennifer Welsh, eds., *For Hunger-Proof Cities: Sustainable Urban Food Systems* (Ottawa: International Development Research Centre, 2000); Luc Mougeot, *Agropolis: The Social, Political and Environmental Dimensions of Urban Agriculture* (London: Earthscan, 2005).

39. Gail Feenstra, Sharyl McGrew, and David Campbell, *Entrepreneurial Community Gardens: Growing Food, Skills, Jobs, and Communities* (Davis: University of California, Dept. of Agriculture and Natural Resources, 1999); Jerome Kaufman and Martin Bailkey, "Farming Inside Cities: Entrepreneurial Urban Agriculture in the United States" (working paper, Lincoln Institute of Land Policy, Cambridge, Mass. 2000).

40. Portions of the remainder of this chapter are based on informal interviews and observations from the author's planning and community development work with a variety of urban agriculture organizations in Philadelphia, including efforts conducted as the founding president of the Philadelphia Orchard Project, as a member of the Weavers Way Farm Committee, and in a comprehensive survey of community gardens in the city during the summer of 2008, which was supported in part by the Pennsylvania Horticultural Society and Penn State Cooperative Extension.

41. Lawson, *City Bountiful*; Lawson, "Planner in the Garden"; Elisa Ludwig, "A World of Gardeners," *Philadelphia Inquirer,* August 28, 2008.

42. This research is reported at http://www.cityfarmer.org/Phillyurbag9.html (accessed Jan. 19, 2009).

43. Domenic Vitiello and Michael Nairn, *Community Gardening in Philadelphia: Harvest Report* (2009), available at https://sites.google.com/site/urbanagriculturephiladelphia/ (accessed Feb. 27, 2012).

44. Domenic Vitiello and Michael Nairn, "Everyday Urban Agriculture: From Community Gardening to Community Food Security," *Harvard Design Magazine* 31 (Winter 2010): 94–100.

45. Michael Nairn, "Keeping the Community in Community Gardening: Aquí Estamos y No Nos Vamos," *Progressive Planning* (Winter 2007): 4–6; Domenic Vitiello, "Twenty-First Century Urban Renewal in Philadelphia: The Neighborhood Transformation Initiative and Its Critics," *Progressive Planning* (Winter 2007): 1, 7–10.

46. Susan Wachter and Grace Wong, "What Is a Tree Worth? Green-City Strategies and Housing Prices," *Real Estate Economics* 36, no. 2 (2008): 213–39.

47. Author's interview with Mary Seton Corboy, March 30, 2005; http://www.greensgrow.org (accessed Jan. 12, 2007).

48. Author's interview with Roxanne Christensen and Nancy Weissman, August

28, 2006; *SPIN Overview* (Philadelphia: Institute for Innovations in Local Farming, 2005); Peter Van Allen, "Back to Basics: Farms Sprouting in Philadelphia," *Philadelphia Business Journal,* July 2004; Urban Partners, *Farming in Philadelphia: Feasibility Analysis and Next Steps* (Philadelphia: Institute for Innovations in Local Farming, 2007).

49. Gerda Wekerle, "Food Justice Movements: Policy, Planning, and Networks," *Journal of Planning Education and Research* 23, no. 4 (2004): 378–86.

50. Anne Whiston Spirn, "Restoring Mill Creek: Landscape Literacy, Environmental Justice and City Planning and Design," chapter 10 in the present volume; http://www.millcreekurbanfarm.org (accessed Jan. 12, 2007); author's interview with Johanna Rosen and Jade Walker, September 24, 2006; Jesse Smith, "The Plot Thickens," *Philadelphia Weekly,* July 19, 2006.

51. http://www.phillyorchards.org (accessed Jan. 19, 2009); Virginia McGuire, "Replacing Neglect with Peach Trees," *New York Times,* September 2, 2007; Virginia Smith, "Orchards Crop Up around the City," *Philadelphia Inquirer,* November 10, 2008.

52. http://www.urbantreeconnection.org (accessed Jan. 19, 2009).

53. http://www.greatsettlements.org/Teens-4-Good.page (accessed Jan. 19, 2009).

54. Students in the author's class, City Planning 653—Community and Economic Development Practicum, drafted a partnership plan for the Weavers Way CSA at Saul.

55. Patricia Allen, "Reweaving the Food Security Safety Net: Mediating Entitlement and Entrepreneurship," *Agriculture and Human Values* 16 (1999): 117–29.

56. Data provided by Eileen Gallagher, Pennsylvania Horticultural Society (in the author's possession).

57. http://www.dvrpc.org/planning/food.htm (accessed Jan. 19, 2009).

58. *Greenworks Philadelphia* (Philadelphia: Mayor's Office of Sustainability, 2009); see target 10.

59. Details of the Nutter administration's policy efforts in urban agriculture are related in Kimberley Hodgson, Marcia Caton Campbell, and Martin Bailkey, *Urban Agriculture: Growing Healthy, Sustainable Places,* APA, Planners Advisory Service report 563 (Chicago: American Planning Association, 2011). The Philadelphia case study in this report was authored principally by Domenic Vitiello.

13. Wolves in the Wissahickon: Deer, Humans, and the Problem of Ecology in an Urban Park

1. Bridget Irons, letter to the editor, *Chestnut Hill Local,* February 14, 2008, 4. For background on the conflict, see William Ecenbarger, "The Bambi Battle," *Philadelphia Inquirer,* March 27, 2010, B1.

2. Theresa L. Goedeke and Ann Herda-Rapp, "Introduction," in *Mad about Wildlife: Looking at Social Conflict over Wildlife,* ed. Herda-Rapp and Goedeke (Leiden, the Netherlands: Brill, 2005), 2, 3, 11; Natural Resource Consultants, Inc., "Development of Deer Management Recommendations for the Wissahickon Valley, Philadelphia, Pennsylvania" (final report for the Friends of the Wissahickon, Philadelphia, Dec. 20, 1996; hereinafter abbreviated as NRC report), 173; Michael Conover, *Resolving*

Human-Wildlife Conflicts: The Science of Wildlife Damage Management (Boca Raton, Fla.: Lewis, 2002), 101–2; NRC report, 7; "Driver Beware: Deer Collisions Peak in Mating Season," *New York Times,* November 9, 2010, available at http://www.nytimes .com/2010/11/10/us/10deer.html (accessed May 19, 2011); "Audubon Pennsylvania Presents Comments before Senate Committee," available at http://www.qdma .com/forums/archive/index.php/index.php?t-9019.html (accessed May 19, 2011); Bob Frye, *Deer Wars: Science, Tradition, and the Battle over Managing Whitetails in Pennsylvania* (University Park: Pennsylvania State University Press, 2006), xv; Ryan D. Hubbard and Clayton K. Nielsen, "Cost-Benefit Analysis of Managed Shotgun Hunts for Suburban White-tailed Deer," *Human-Wildlife Interactions* 5, no. 1 (Spring 2011): 13.

3. James D. Proctor, "The Spotted Owl and the Contested Moral Landscape of the Pacific Northwest," in *Animal Geographies: Place, Politics and Identity in the Nature-Culture Borderlands,* ed. Jennifer Woloch and Jody Emel (New York: Verso, 1998), 193; William S. Lynn, "Animals, Ethics and Geography," in *Animal Geographies,* ed. Woloch and Emel, 273.

4. Harriet Ritvo, *Noble Cows and Hybrid Zebras: Essays on Animals and History* (Charlottesville: University of Virginia Press, 2010), 3–5.

5. Quoted in Frye, *Deer Wars,* 4.

6. Richard Nelson, *Heart and Blood: Living with Deer in America* (New York: Alfred A. Knopf, 1998), 19, 19–27.

7. Ecenbarger, "Bambi Battle," B1; Nelson, *Heart and Blood,* 27.

8. *Chestnut Hill Local,* March 10, 1997.

9. NRC report, 123.

10. Ibid., 9, 17.

11. Ibid., 22.

12. Ibid., 30

13. Allen T. Rutberg, "The Science of Deer Management: An Animal Welfare Perspective," in *The Science of Overabundance,* ed. William J. McShea, H. Brian Underwood, and John H. Rappole (Washington, D.C.: Smithsonian Institution Press, 1997), 50.

14. Thomas R. McCabe and Richard E. McCabe, "Recounting Whitetails Past," in *Science of Overabundance,* ed. McShea, Underwood, and Rappole, 18.

15. H. Brian Underwood and William F. Porter, "Reconsidering Paradigms of Overpopulation in Ungulates: White-Tailed Deer at Saratoga National Historical Park," in *The Science of Overabundance,* ed. McShea, Underwood, and Rappole, 185, 193.

16. David L. Mech, *White-tailed Deer Ecology and Management* (Harrisburg, Pa.: Stackpole, 1984), 189, qtd. in NRC report, 41.

17. Nelson, *Heart and Blood,* 168.

18. Conover, *Resolving Human-Wildlife Conflicts,* 193, 204, 205; Marrett D. Grund, "Survival Analysis and Computer Simulations of Lethal and Contraceptive Management Strategies for Urban Deer, *Human-Wildlife Interactions* 5, no. 1 (Spring 2011): 29.

19. Larry Fish, "Deer vs. Parks: A Sticky Issue," *Philadelphia Inquirer,* January 28, 1998.

20. Frye, *Deer Wars,* 123–26; Barbara Boyer, "Activists Demonstrate against Plan for Deer," *Philadelphia Inquirer,* January 31, 2000; Peter Mazzaccaro, "Protestors Call

for an End to Deer Killing," *Chestnut Hill Local,* February 3, 2000; Peter Mazzaccaro, "Protestors Object to Park Curfew," *Chestnut Hill Local,* February 24, 2000; Shug Davis, Bridget Irons, Barbara Riebman, letter to the editor, *Chestnut Hill Local,* February 24, 2000.

21. Karen Janjanin, letter to the editor, *Philadelphia Inquirer,* February 9, 1998.

22. Qtd. in "Activists Demonstrate against Plan for Deer," *Philadelphia Inquirer,* Jan. 29, 2000, B3.

23. Helen Harvey, letters to the editor, *Chestnut Hill Local,* March 9 and May 18, 2000; Mazzaccaro, "Protestors Call."

24. John McArthur Harris, *Wissahickon Anthology,* archived at Chestnut Hill Historical Society Archives, box 1999.712, files 1.1–8.

25. Frye, *Deer Wars,* 125.

26. *Report of the Committee on Plans and Improvements by the Commissioners of Fairmount Park upon the extension of the Park* (Philadelphia: King and Baird, 1868), 5–6.

27. *First Annual Report of the Commission of Fairmount Park* (Philadelphia: King and Baird, 1869), 17.

28. Ibid., 56.

29. Edgar Allan Poe, "Morning on the Wissahiccon" (ca. 1843), *Collected Works of Edgar Allan Poe,* ed. Thomas Olive Mabbott, vol. 3 (Cambridge, Mass.: Belknap, 1978), 863.

30. Ibid., 863, 865, 866.

31. Newton Crane, "Fairmount Park," *Scribner's Monthly,* January 1871, 236–37.

32. Qtd. in T. A. Day, comp., *The Wissahickon* (Philadelphia: Garden Club of Philadelphia, 1922), 9; William Cronon, "The Trouble with Wilderness," in *Uncommon Ground: Rethinking the Human Place in Nature,* ed. Cronon (New York: Norton, 1995), 74.

33. Poe, "Morning," 865.

34. Crane, "Fairmount Park," 236.

35. Mary C. Robbins, "Park-Making as a National Act," *Atlantic Monthly,* January 1897, 94.

36. Poe, "Morning," 865.

37. Cronon, "Trouble with Wilderness," 79; Richard White, "Are You an Environmentalist or Do You Work for a Living?" in *Uncommon Ground,* ed. Cronon, 175, 185.

38. Poe, "Morning," 865–66.

39. Qtd. in Louis S. Warren, *The Hunter's Game: Poachers and Conservationists in Twentieth-Century America* (New Haven, Conn.: Yale University Press, 1997), 48, 67.

40. Ibid., 13; Theodore Roosevelt, *The Wilderness Hunter,* vol. 1 (New York: Putnam's, 1907), vii; Jan E. Dizard, *Going Wild: Hunting, Animal Rights, and the Contested Meaning of Nature* (Amherst: University of Massachusetts Press, 1999), 98; "Good Hunting Predicted in State," *New York Times,* August 24, 1919; Frye, *Deer Wars,* 5–7.

41. Thomas R. Dunlap, *Saving America's Wildlife* (Princeton, N.J.: Princeton University Press, 1988), 15; *Philadelphia Record,* February 10, 1914; *North American,* April 19, 1915; *Philadelphia Bulletin,* February 16, 1914.

42. *North American,* April 19, 1915.

43. *Philadelphia Inquirer,* April 1916.

44. Ibid.; *Philadelphia Inquirer,* May 1, 1916; *New York Sun,* May 7, 1916; *Philadelphia Record,* February 11, 1918.

45. Warren, *Hunter's Game,* 48–49.

46. Frye, *Deer Wars,* 10.

47. NRC report, 14–16; Andrew Isenberg, "The Moral Ecology of Wildlife," in *Representing Animals,* ed. Nigel Rothfels (Bloomington: Indiana University Press, 2002), 48.

48. Matt Cartmill, *A View to a Death in the Morning: Hunting and Nature through History* (Cambridge, Mass.: Harvard University Press, 1993), 55, 67, 159.

49. Ralph H. Lutts, "The Trouble with Bambi: Walt Disney's *Bambi* and the American Vision of Nature," *Forest and Conservation History* 36 (Oct. 1992): 160.

50. Jean M. Wallace, "Park Deer Not Getting a Fair Shot," *Philadelphia Daily News,* February 9, 1998; Lutts, "Trouble with Bambi," 160, 164, 165, 166; Cartmill, *View to a Death,* 90.

51. Chris Philo and Chris Wilbert, "An Introduction," in *Animal Spaces, Beastly Places: New Geographies of Human-Animal Relations,* ed. Chris Philo and Chris Wilbert (London: Routledge, 2000), 11; Edward Said, *Orientalism* (New York: Pantheon, 1978), 54; Stephen DeStefano, *The Coyote at the Kitchen Door: Living with Wildlife in the Suburbs* (Cambridge, Mass.: Harvard University Press, 2010), 58–59, 71; White, "Are You an Environmentalist?" 173.

52. "Girl, 17, Attacked While Jogging in Wissahickon Park," *Philadelphia Inquirer,* April 12, 2011, available at http://articles.philly.com/2011-04-12/news/29410182_1 _jogging-wissahickon-park-valley-green-inn (accessed May 19, 2011); "Crime Rates Philadelphia," available at http://westphillydata.library.upenn.edu/infoR _Crime&Safety_CrimeStats.htm#PH96-00 (accessed May 19, 2011).

53. "Suit Filed to Stop Deer Hunt at Valley Forge," *Philadelphia Inquirer,* November 12, 2009, available at http://www.philly.com/philly/blogs/pets/Suit_filed_to _stop_deer_hunting_at_Valley_Forge.html (accessed May 18, 2011). The *Inquirer* has carried a number of articles and letters about the Valley Forge deer situation; this one contains representative information and statements.

54. NRC report, 173; Frye, *Deer Wars,* xv; Nelson, *Heart and Blood,* 249, 310.

55. Aldo Leopold, "Thinking Like a Mountain," in *Sand County Almanac, with Essays on Conservation from Round River* (New York: Ballantine, 1977), 140.

56. Molly H. Mullin, "Mirrors and Windows: Sociocultural Studies of Human-Animal Relationships," *Annual Review of Anthropology* 28 (1999): 216.

Contributors

Carolyn Adams is a professor of geography and urban studies at Temple University, where she teaches courses in urban development, city problems, and policies. Her many articles and several books about Philadelphia include *Restructuring the Philadelphia Region: Metropolitan Divisions and Inequality* (2008). Along with several colleagues, Professor Adams established the Metropolitan Philadelphia Indicators Project in 2003 to track important trends in the quality of life in southeastern Pennsylvania by analyzing and mapping social, environmental, and economic data.

Thomas Apel is a graduate student at Georgetown University, where he studies the histories of science, medicine, and the environment.

Brian C. Black is a professor of history and environmental studies at Penn State–Altoona, where he currently serves as the head of the College of Arts and Humanities. His research emphasis is on the landscape and environmental history of North America, particularly in relation to the application and use of energy and technology. He is the author of several books, including the award-winning *Petrolia: The Landscape of America's First Oil Boom* (2003) and *Crude Reality: Petroleum in World History* (2012). He is also the editor of a number of books as well as a former editor of *Pennsylvania History.*

Michael J. Chiarappa received his PhD from the University of Pennsylvania and is an associate professor of history at Quinnipiac University. He is the coauthor of *Fish for All: An Oral History of Multiple Claims and Divided Sentiment on Lake Michigan* (2003) and the author of articles focusing on vernacular landscapes, regionalism, and the use of natural resources in maritime environments. Dr. Chiarappa's research and teaching focus on American environmental history, the history of America's built environments and landscapes, American maritime history, and local and regional history. He also specializes in public history and formerly codirected the Public History Program at Western Michigan University. A graduate of the Munson Institute of American Maritime Studies and a member of the Board of Directors of the Vernacular Architecture Forum, he has worked extensively with a variety of museums and government agencies, including the Smithsonian Institution and the National Park Service.

Ann Norton Greene is an assistant professor and associate director for undergraduate studies in the History and Sociology of Science Department at the University of Pennsylvania. She is the author of *Horses at Work: Harnessing Power in Industrial America* (2008) and has essays in *Healing the Herds: Disease, Livestock Economies and the Globalization of Veterinary Medicine,* edited by Karen Brown and Michael Gilfoyle (2010) and *Industrializing Organisms: Introducing Evolutionary History,* edited by Susan Schrepfer and Philip Scranton (2004).

Adam Levine, an independent environmental historian, has a special interest in the drainage systems and historical topography of urban areas. Since 1998 he has been a historical consultant to the Philadelphia Water Department, helping to develop watershed education programs and managing the department's extensive archive of historical material. He is also the author or coauthor of five books about gardening, including *A Guide to the Great Gardens of the Philadelphia Region,* and hundreds of articles on gardening for a wide variety of publications. His website is www.phillyh2o.org.

Robert J. Mason is a professor of geography and urban studies at Temple University. He is author of *Collaborative Land Use Management: The Quieter Revolution in Place-Based Planning* (2007), *Contested Lands: Conflict and Compromise in New Jersey's Pine Barrens* (1992), *Atlas of United States Environmental Issues* (1990), and various articles and book chapters on land-use planning, protected-areas management, metropolitan growth issues, and environmentalism in Japan.

Michal McMahon taught most recently at West Virginia University, where he is now an associate professor emeritus of history. He has published several other essays on early Philadelphia, including "Beyond Therapeutics: Technology, Disease, and the Question of Public Health in Late 18th-Century Philadelphia," a chapter in *"The Melancholy Scene of Devastation,"* edited by Billy G. Smith (1997); and "'Small Matters': Benjamin Franklin, Philadelphia, and the 'Progress of Cities'" in the *Pennsylvania Magazine of History and Biography.* He is now writing a series of historical essays on a city and river in southwest Louisiana.

Elizabeth Milroy is the Zoë and Dean Pappas Curator of Education for Public Programs at the Philadelphia Museum of Art. Her recent publications include "'For the like Uses, as the Moor-Fields': The Politics of Penn's Squares," in the *Pennsylvania Magazine of History and Biography* 130 (2006), and "Repairing the Myth and Reality of Philadelphia's Public Squares, 1800-1850" in *Change over Time* (2011). She is currently completing a major history of Philadelphia's cultural landscapes.

Donna J. Rilling is an associate professor of history at the State University of New York at Stony Brook. She is author of *Making Houses, Crafting Capitalism; Builders in Philadelphia, 1790-1850* (2001). Her current research investigates how diverse people understood and came to terms with pollution in the age of early American industrialization.

Diane Sicotte is an associate professor of sociology at Drexel University in Philadelphia. Her research focuses on urban inequality and the development of environmental inequality and injustice. She is the author of several articles in these areas.

Anne Whiston Spirn, a professor of landscape architecture and planning at MIT, is an award-winning author, scholar, teacher, and practitioner. Her books include *The Granite Garden: Urban Nature and Human Design*

(1984), *The Language of Landscape* (1998), *Daring to Look* (2008), and *The Eye Is a Door* (forthcoming). Since 1987 Spirn has directed the West Philadelphia Landscape Project, an action research program integrating research, teaching, and community service that has been recognized by many awards. For a gateway to her work and activities, see www.annewhistonspirn.com.

Domenic Vitiello is an assistant professor of city and regional planning and urban studies at the University of Pennsylvania. He was the founding president of the Philadelphia Orchard Project (www.phillyorchards.org) and has helped Philadelphia, Camden, and other cities develop food and agriculture policies. His research includes books and articles on planning history and community development, with a focus on industrialization, immigration, and food systems.

Craig Zabel, PhD, is an associate professor of art history at the Pennsylvania State University. He has taught at Penn State since 1985 and has been the head of the Department of Art History since 1996. His research and publications have focused on American architectural history.

Index